# L.A. EXPOSED

*Also by Paul Young*

**Buzzword: L.A. Fresh Speak**

# L.A. EXPOSED

## STRANGE MYTHS AND CURIOUS LEGENDS IN THE CITY OF ANGELS

by Paul Young

THOMAS DUNNE BOOKS

ST. MARTIN'S GRIFFIN ❧ NEW YORK

THOMAS DUNNE BOOKS

An imprint of St. Martin's Press

www.stmartins.com

Book design by pink design, inc. (www.pinkdesigninc.com)

ISBN 0-312-20646-1

First Edition: April 2002

10  9  8  7  6  5  4  3  2  1

*In the memory of*

*Lothar Hubert Spehn*

The great
enemy
of **truth**
is very often
not in the **lie** deliberate,
contrived, and dishonest,
but in the **myth** persistent,
persuasive,
and unrealistic.

-JOHN F. KENNEDY

# CONTENTS

# THE SECRET LIFE OF PLACES:
## THE LEGENDS AND LORE OF L.A. LANDMARKS 48

# 3

# THE MARCH OF VULGARIA
## L.A.'S ROCKIN' RUMORS 100

# A MOST UNLIKELY PARADISE:
## SOUTHERN CALIFORNIA'S UNNATURAL HISTORY

**4**

**140**

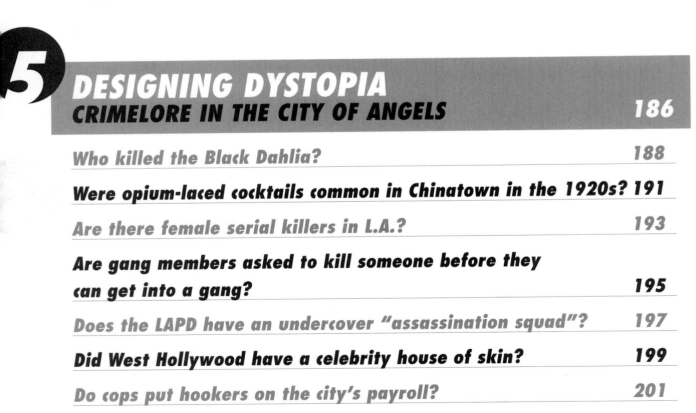

# 5

## DESIGNING DYSTOPIA
### CRIMELORE IN THE CITY OF ANGELS
186

# THE SHADOW OF DISCONTENT:
## CORRUPTION AND CONSPIRACY IN THE LAND OF SUNSHINE AND HEALTH

**228**

**6**

La La Land,

Lotus Land,

Libido Land,

Plastic Land,

The City of Angels,

The City of Fallen Angels,

The City of Dreams,

The City of Broken Dreams,

The City of Queens,

Tinseltown,

Tattletown,

Ho Town,

Hollyweird,

Babylon,

Flake Central,

Paradise with a Lobotomy...

# PREFACE

When I began this project in the mid-1990s, I wanted to bring together as many of the prevailing myths of Los Angeles as I could find and feature them in a single volume. It was an experiment of sorts, an attempt to bypass mainstream fare and tap into what Justin Bennett once described as the "noise, the disturbances, and the unidentified sounds on the edge of perception." In other words, instead of looking at the narratives of literature, cinema, television, and print media, I wanted to explore those narratives that are everywhere and nowhere at the same time; those narratives that guide us through the streets when we wander, spark everyday conversations, and fuel our imaginations, anxieties, and premonitions. These are, in my view, all those urgent, mischievous, little monsters that hide in the cracks of what is known and unknown, laying in wait for the least vigilant or most susceptible. Some call them rumors or hearsay, others call them urban legends or myths, and others still call them gossip or tall tales. They may be all of those things and more, since like memories, they resist easy explanations.

One could compare this project to the rumor clinics of the 1940s, initially set up by Robert H. Knapp in conjunction with the Massachusetts Committee on Public Safety. Under Knapp's direction, rumor clinics were originally designed to collect, examine, and debunk the cultural narrative found circulating in American culture at the time. Knapp was hardly impartial, however, since he and his staff were working under the auspices of the U.S. War Department and wanted to dispel malicious, "wedge-driving," anti-American, or anti-victory narratives, in an attempt to quell civic unrest.

My interest, on the other hand, was slightly less presumptuous. While I undoubtedly tried to uncover the roots of each story and tried to dispel falsehoods whenever possible, I resisted the temptation to examine cycles, performance techniques, folk context and/or morphologies—the essential analytical tools of folklore analysis—just as I resisted semiotic, memetic, and/or Marxist analysis as well. Not out of laziness or lack of interest, but out of a desire to present each story as I found it, and letting the reader determine its meaning on his or her own. (That said, I still tried to give a brief, if not unorthodox, psychological and/or ideological reading whenever appropriate, primarily because I believe that rumors satisfy certain psychological/ideological needs that are essential in their propagation.) What's more, I had to honor my own initial impulse, which was to enjoy the narratives for what they are—totally subjective, low-fidelity, abstract ideas that revel in the suspension of disbelief and notions of chaos.

Not surprisingly, the format proved to be frustratingly limiting, however, since it would have been impossible to include the smallest per-

cent of the rumors circulating in Los Angeles in the late 1990s; and that's to say nothing of its legendary tales of the past. As a result I had to choose the narratives that were either the most popular or misunderstood, or the most intrinsic to the city itself.

What's more, the limitations of fitting each story in such a tight format meant that I had to give cursory overviews that undoubtedly bastardized each tale. (I encourage each reader to seek out original sources for each story and pursue them on his or her own if interested.) That meant that I had to severely limit the number of versions in circulation, and focus on the most essential ones. The speculation over the Black Dahlia murder for example, could fill an entire chapter in itself.

Accuracy on the other hand, was always a priority, and I spent countless hours interviewing, reporting, and digesting as much information as possible. My conclusions should not be read as the final word, however—even when entries include headings such as "the truth" or "the bottom line"—since rumors after all, are by definition, totally sourceless, ambiguous, subjective texts that cannot be pigeonholed so easily. In fact, if you come away with anything from this book, it's that all utterances should be viewed with some suspicion—even from the most credible sources. For as you'll see on these very pages, truth is every bit as subjective, mal-leable, and elusive as a falsehood, and *nothing* should be taken as gospel. As Voltaire once said, "Doubt is an uncomfortable condition, but certainty is a ridiculous one."

In any case, I have an exhaustive list of authors, professors, historians, journalists, librarians, folklorists, and rumor aficionados that I need to thank in the realization of this book, yet I cannot include them all here. Nonetheless, there are a number of people that I owe a special debt:

**Chapter 1 (Hollywood):** The Academy of Motion Arts and Sciences, James Bacon, Eddie Brandt's Saturday Matinee, Janet Charlton, John Connolly, Hal Defoe, Larry Edmond's Books, Kirk Ellis, David Friedman, Steven Gains, Charles Higham, Jim Holiday, Ron Jeremy, Pete Lee, Bill "The Bear" Margold, Jerry Martinez, Maitland McDonagh, Ted McIvanna, Eddie Muller, Shake Books, Jim South, Pete Tombs, and David Walker.

**Chapter 3 (Rock 'n' roll):** Terry Allen, Ron Athey, Nicole Blackman, Phillip Blaine, Curtis Blow, Paul Bodi, Carrie Borzillo, Denny Bruce, Nancy Clark, Cheo Coker, Kent Crowley, Theo Davis, Pamela Des Barres, Boyd Elder, Randall Fuller, Ruben Guevara, Lily Haden, Bruce Haring, Barney Hoskyns, David Jove, Sabrina Kaleta, Bob Keane, Paul Krassner, Harvey

Kubernick, Greg Mack, Tequilla Mockingbird, Michael Ochs, Joe Nick Patowski, Cathy Scott, Joe Seehee, Bruce Spence, Laurel Stearns, Bryan Thomas, Ray Trakin, and Chris Wilder.

**Chapters 2 and 4 (Landmarks/Unnatural History):** Charles Abrahamson, Ron Adams, Dana Bass-Smith, Dr. Paul Beggs, Harvey Beigel, Robbie Benson, Frank Bogert, Jean Bruce Poole, Margaret Burke, Margaret Burton, California Film Commission, Center for Land Interpretation Use, Matt Coolidge, Mike Davis, Bob Engles, Paul Gregory, Bill Helmer, Charles Hillenger, Dan Hirsch, Hollywood Chamber of Commerce, The Hollywood Heritage Museum, Hal Horn, Sharon Howe, Lucy Jones, Jeanne Kazer, David Koenig, Art Kunkin, Milt Larson, L.A. Aboretum, L.A. Conservancy, L.A. Historical Society, L.A. History Museum, Barbara Lilly, Long Beach Historical Society, The Maritime Museum, James McGaugh, Jeff McNeill, Barbara Miller, Lisa Mosher, Chris Nichols, Warren Olney, Palm Springs Historical Society, Jonathan Parfrey, Domenic Piori, Sally Presley Rippingdale, San Diego Historical Society, Santa Monica Historical Society, Ariane Simard, Diana Simons, U.S. Coast Guard, Marc Wannamaker, The Simon Wiesenthal Center, John and Nancy Wilkmans, Robert Winter, and Zorthian.

**Chapters 5 and 6 (Crime/ Conspiracy):** Det. Richard Aldahl, Norma Jean Almadovar, Amok Books, Greg Bishop, Bob Black, Eric Bloom, Joe Bosco, Tom Bowden and the Conspiracy Museum, Scott Carrier, Sgt. Sean Collinsworth, Alex Constantine, Det. Louie Danoff, Red Elk, James Ellroy, Donald Freed, John Gilmore, Bert Grimm, Joe Gunn, Sgt. Robert Harms, Norio Hayakowa, Stephen Yangman, Richard Lasting, L.A. Police Historical Society, Dennis McDougal, Tony Mendoza, Leon Metz, Richard Metzger, Monte Nicholson, the Pleasure Chest, William Secrest, Cathy Scott, Sanyika Shakur, Jennifer Snyder, Robert Sterling, Jill Stewart, Dace Taube at the USC Regional History Center, Myra Thomas, Bill O'Neal, Det. Richard Valdemar, Det. Raymond Verdogo, Gary Webb, Louis Joylon West, and Robert Anton Wilson.

My sincerest gratitude goes to Jim Fitzgerald and Nina Wiener, who had the foresight to recognize the potential of this project in the first place; Tom Waits for providing the initial inspiration, and Albert Friedman, who gave me some key pointers in its early stages. I would also like to thank Pauline Ploquin for her exhaustive work in securing photographs, and most importantly, David Wooldridge and Barbara Young, who provided the most crucial support, love, and encouragement of all.

# INTRODUCTION

```
La La Land,
Lotus Land,
Libido Land,
Plastic Land,
The City of Angels,
The City of Fallen Angels,
The City of Dreams,
The City of Broken Dreams,
The City of Queens,
Tinseltown,
Tattletown,
Ho Town,
Hollyweird,
Babylon,
Flake Central,
Paradise with a Lobotomy...
```

What is it about Los Angeles that inspires such rancor? Is it envy over its natural beauty and perfect weather? Is it resentfulness over its wealth and power? Is it *schadenfreude* over its movie stars and carefree lifestyle? Or is it something else, something more intrinsic to the place itself? "It's an inconceivably shoddy place," wrote H. L. Mencken. "It's a city with a curse on it," railed Nathanael West. "It's deceitful and illusory," claimed Carey McWilliams. "It's both heaven and hell," scoffed Bertolt Brecht. "It's a sad flower in the sand," cried John Fante. "It has the personality of paper cup," sneered Raymond Chandler. "It's the plastic asshole of the world," screamed William Faulkner. "It's like a middle-aged, obese woman from the Midwest laying naked in the sun," laughed Myron Brinig. "It's like being nowhere and talking to nobody about nothing," taunted Michelangelo Antonioni.

There's no doubt that such mockery has been inspired by L.A.'s well known blemishes—its vulgar over development, embarrassing vapidity, dizzying decentralization, and absolute lack of identity—and that's to say nothing of Hollywood, that bastion of superficiality, egoism, and narrow-mindedness. But as a number of historians have noted, L.A. bashing goes back a lot further than most people seem to realize, long before Tinseltown appeared on the scene and long before the city was a sprawling, smog-infested metropolis. It was just as common, for example, for people to mockingly refer to the City of Angels as the City of *Diablos* back in the nineteenth century, and just as common to hear jokes about laziness, stupidity, boastfulness, and immoderation.

With that in mind, it seems quite obvious that the primary target for such antipathy has

generally been Angelenos themselves and their complete and total embrace of individualism, nonconformism, and self-indulgence. For early academics, especially those from the east, such traits were often seen as a curiosity at best, an abomination at worst. But for Harvard's Professor Josiah Royce, who investigated the root causes of such behavior in 1898, they may be unavoidable. After all, when you exist in a land defined by arid weather, extreme isolation, and such horrific natural phenomenon as apocalyptic fires, "Satanic" winds, and horrific earthquakes, you're bound to be a little more accepting of the extreme. "The influence of nature upon custom," he told his audience at the National Geographic Society, "which every civilization depicts, is precisely the kind of influence that, from moment to moment, expresses itself psychologically in the more typical emotions of sensitive souls."

In contrast, James J. Parsons argued that the real determining factor may be more cultural than environmental. In a study presented in 1955 at UC Berkeley, he suggested that since California was, and still is, considered "the last frontier," is has always been the preferred destination for immigrants—immigrants that tend to be courageous, opportunistic, restless, transient, idealistic, boastful, dreamy, and/or romantic by nature. (As Michelle Phillips once remarked, L.A. brings those with "holes in their souls.") And for Parsons, that can only have obvious cultural consequences. "The resultant fusion of ideas, cultures, and shills seems to have produced not only a buoyant optimism and self-confidence, but also a sort of hybrid vigor, unfettered by convention, which may account for many of the contradictions and paradoxes within the state."

In other words, Royce may have gotten it backwards: It's not that Angelenos reflect the extremism of the California landscape, but that the landscape reflects the extremism of the Angeleno character. Or to think of it another way, it's entirely possible that those drawn to L.A. may be responding to an inner psychological need that mirrors the land itself. Whether that's a penchant for radicalism or complete insipidness depends on the individual. For David Fine, author of *Imagining Los Angeles: A City in Fiction*, that need essentially defines the canon of L.A. literature, which in itself, has always been chock full of schemers, dreamers, and killers too desperate to accept reality head on. "The distanced perspective of the outsider marked by a sense of dislocation and estrangement," he writes, "is the central and essential feature of the fiction of Los Angeles… [and that fiction plays] at times obsessively, on themes of unreality, masquerade, and deception." (Upon closer inspection of course, the same could be said of nearly all intellectual work produced in Los Angeles—its art, architecture, interior design, entertainment, music, scientific theories, theme parks, spiritualism and more. They, too, traffic in themes of theatricality, self-indulgence, novelty, deviance, illusion, and/or fantasy.)

With that in mind, it shouldn't be surprising that L.A. has been such a fertile breeding ground of secrecy over the years. As Sissela Bok notes in *Secrets: On the Ethics of Concealment and Revelation*, secrets tend to thrive on egoism, selfishness, insecurity, and duplicity; and when you combine those traits—which are so ubiquitous in L.A.—with a desperate need to control and exploit, you often end up with rampant corruption. That certainly has been the case in L.A., where venality, police brutality, spectacular violence, widespread racism, and insidious cults

*"The resultant fusion of ideas, cultures, and skills seems to have produced not only a buoyant optimism and self-confidence, but also a sort of **hybrid vigor**, unfettered by convention, which may account for many of the contradictions and paradoxes within the state."*

have been the norm since the nineteenth century. (In fact, in keeping with its extremist tendencies, L.A. has been named the Murder Capital, the Serial Killer Capital, the Heroin Capital, the Porno Capital, the Counterfeit Capital, the Street Gang Capital, and the Black Magic Capital of the U.S. at various times in its sordid history.)

Likewise, an increase in secrecy will inevitably lead to an increase in rumor, hearsay, and gossip—especially in a place like Southern California where low communication and low critical sensibility flourish. And indeed, even the most cursory glance over the past two hundred years will prove that the City of Angels has been seducing Dame Rumor, that age-old whore of hearsay, since the first pioneers set foot on Angeleno soil. In fact, the city's very image—an image which includes such "indigenous" traits as Spanish architecture, "native" palm trees, and a "healthy" climate—turns out to be nothing more than a fabrication itself, embroidered, designed, and manufactured to capitalize on a woefully gullible L.A. public.

Rumors have their dark side, too, of course, and there's little doubt that they've had serious consequences over the years. This book collects as many of those as possible, including those too controversial for mainstream publication. (Unfortunately, many were removed at last minute thanks to jittery lawyers.) That means you'll read about extralegal cover-ups by the FBI, LAPD, and studio executives; outright treachery by movie stars, politicians, and the media; and dozens of hidden truths usually reserved for back rooms, private parlors, and secured office suites.

It's hardly a pretty picture, at least not by tourist bureau standards, but as social psychologists Gordon Allport and Leo Portman have pointed out, that's why we have rumors, hearsay, and gossip in the first place: to express the fears, anxieties, and wish-fulfillment fantasies of the masses. Besides, what do you expect from a place that brought you the cafeteria, Valley speak, Ronald Reagan, pornography, Michael Jackson, suburban chic, freeways, and Richard Nixon?

I don't give a shit about anything pertaining to the movies. All I want to know is who's a homosexual, who's a nymphomaniac, who's a lesbian, who has the biggest dick, and who is the woman who will fuck absolutely anybody—the driver, the car park, the boy who delivers the pizza. That's all.

—JAMES ELLROY

# SCANDAL

# XXX

# NEVER SLEEPS

## THE TALL TALES OF TINSELTOWN

# THE LEGEND:

The actress Virginia Rappe died after silent movie star Fatty Arbuckle raped her with a Coke bottle in 1921.

**Fatty Arbuckle**

## What People Are Saying:

While this rumor was rampant throughout the early part of the twentieth century, it wasn't until the release of Kenneth Anger's classic tome of Hollywood debauchery, *Hollywood Babylon*, that it found a place in the firmament of L.A. lore. Before that, opinion was sharply divided over Roscoe "Fatty" Arbuckle's complicity in the death of a young actress named Virginia Rappe. But since then perception has shifted slightly, with the majority of Angelenos leaning toward Anger's construction of the events. And according to Anger, the entire fiasco went down something like this:

On Labor Day weekend 1921, Arbuckle invited a select group of fellow actors to San Francisco to celebrate his new $3 million contract with Paramount Studios. After checking into the luxurious St.

Hartsook

**Virginia Rappe**

Francis Hotel and taking over three adjoining rooms, the 300-pound star began a three-day carouse that included illegal bootleg liquor, nude dancing, and nonstop orgies. As Anger put it:

Some shed their tops to do the shimmy; guests were trading pajama bottoms and the empty beer bottles were piling up. About a quarter after three (P.M.), Arbuckle, flapping around in pajamas and a bathrobe, grabbed Virginia and steered the tipsy model to the bedroom of suite 1221. He gave the revelers his famous leering wink, saying, "This is the chance I've waited for a long time," and locked the door. Bambina Maude Delmont (Virginia's close friend) later testified that the festivities were stilled when sharp screams rang out in the adjoining bedroom. Weird moans were heard through the door. After much pounding and kicking, a giggling Arbuckle sallied forth in ripped pajamas, Virginia's hat squashed on his head at a crazy angle, and quipped to the girls, "Go in and get her dressed and take her to the Palace (Hotel). She makes too much noise." When Virginia kept screaming, he yelled, "Shut up or I'll throw you out of the window." Bambina found the girl nearly nude on the disordered bed, writhing in pain, moaning, "I'm dying, I'm dying . . . He hurt me."

Virginia's pain was real enough. She died four days later at the age of twenty-five. According to the official coroner's report, she suffered from a ruptured bladder, which in turn led to a fatal case of peritonitis. Yet to this day no one really knows how the injury occurred. Some have suggested that Arbuckle jumped on top of her and literally "popped" her bladder during sex. Yet when physicians denounced that theory, arguing that bladders do not pop under that kind of weight, a handful of journalists and gossip hounds speculated that he must have used a device of some sort—an idea that Anger exploited in *Hollywood Babylon.* "Enraged at his drunken impotence," wrote Anger, "Arbuckle ravaged Virginia with a Coca-Cola bottle, *or* a champagne bottle, then repeated the act with a jagged piece of ice."

## What Really Happened:

According to the most credible accounts, Arbuckle never touched Rappe, much less had sex with her. Evidently, he found her on the floor of his bathroom drunkenly vomiting into the toilet. After wiping her mouth with a towel, he picked her up and carried her to the bed. But as soon as he set her down, she began crying out

*...she was in San Francisco getting an abortion— her sixth apparently— and just happened to run into a friend of Arbuckle's who extended her the invitation—despite Arbuckle's protests.*

and grabbing her stomach, complaining of severe pains. "It's too hot in here," she screamed, plucking at her blouse furiously. "I'm burning up!" Hearing the screams from the other room, Rappe's friend, Maude Delmont, came running in just as Arbuckle began applying some ice to her abdomen. Horrified, Delmont pushed Arbuckle out of the way and ordered him out of the room. Arbuckle then returned to the party and thought little of the episode. But when he returned thirty minutes later, after a physician appeared on the scene, he was shocked to hear Rappe drunkenly scream, "Get away from me! *You* did this to me!"

While it was hardly reported in the press at the time, Rappe was never actually invited to the party. In truth, she was in San Francisco getting an abortion—her sixth apparently— and just happened to run into a friend of Arbuckle's who extended her the invitation— despite Arbuckle's protests. In any case, there's a good chance that her injuries actually came from her abortion the day before. After all, her abortionist, Dr. Rumwell, was the same doctor that appeared at the hotel after Arbuckle supposedly ravished her, the same doctor that took care of her during her hospital stay, the same doctor that performed the autopsy after she died, and the same doctor that destroyed her bladder *before* the trial.

Yet even if Dr. Rumwell was responsible for Rappe's death, he wasn't responsible for shifting the blame onto Arbuckle. That was mostly due to the accusations made by Maude Delmont. In fact, Delmont, a notorious figure in her own right, with previous experience in extortion, prostitution, and theft, not only came up with the idea to extort money out of Arbuckle in the first place but convinced Rappe that she could make a fortune on the deal.

## What Could Have Happened:

Yet there is another theory, too, that's just as plausible and just as consistent with the facts. And it's a theory that Adolph Zukor, the then-president of Paramount Studios, orchestrated the entire sequence of events. Apparently Zukor had a long-standing feud with Arbuckle, one that had to do with previous misunderstandings and Arbuckle's continual disrespect of the producer. In Zukor's mind, Arbuckle "blackmailed" him into increasing his salary to $1 million per year—an outrageous sum at the time—and that's to say nothing of the actor's repeated snubs toward publicity. (In fact, Arbuckle was supposed to do some publicity on the weekend that he ran off to San Francisco, which apparently made Zukor "livid.")

That's why many believe that Zukor may have pulled some strings to make sure that there was illegal booze and known prostitutes at Arbuckle's party. Because if Arbuckle's party just happened to get raided by the police, and if Zukor could come rushing in to save the day, he could certainly "knock Fatty down a few pegs," as he once threatened. But Zukor failed to foresee Rappe's accidental death, or the extraordinary media frenzy that would ensue. So when he found himself in a scandal of dizzying proportions, he decided to not only lead the charge against Arbuckle's victimization, pushing Hollywood's moral czar, Will Hays, to have him blacklisted and removing his entire film catalog from distribution, but to work behind the scenes to push Arbuckle's trial toward conviction. That way he could draw attention away from himself and Hollywood in general.

During the research for her book *Frame Up!*, author Andy Edmonds found evidence that Zukor undoubtedly financed some of the overt bribes, perjured testimonies, and coverups that occurred during Arbuckle's trial. In fact she found a cancelled check for $10,000 made out to the prosecutor in the case, Matthew Brady, the San Francisco D.A.—a check that was endorsed by none other than Zukor himself.

## The Aftermath:

Arbuckle was eventually acquitted on April 12, 1922, after three previous scandal-plagued mistrials. And when the jury read the verdict they added: "Acquittal is not enough for Roscoe Arbuckle. We feel a great injustice has been done to him." Yet it was too late. The rumors had already eclipsed the facts, and continue do so to this day.

## What It All Means:

Symbolically speaking, Arbuckle, by no fault of his own, became the prodigal son, deeply despised for doing little more than "making silly faces" at a time when the country was reeling from financial woes, war inflation, foreign threats, and Bolshevik panics. In other words, Arbuckle had to be scapegoated to appease the mounting anxieties of the age. Yet it wasn't the public that placed him on the cross, but Hollywood itself, as represented by Zukor, who not only buckled under his own fear of anti-Semitism, but his own self-hatred and greed.

> *...if Arbuckle's party just happened to get raided by the police, and if Zukor could come rushing in to save the day, he could certainly "knock Fatty down a few pegs," as he once threatened.*

# THE LEGEND:

A group of Hollywood actors stole John Barrymore's corpse from a funeral parlor, set it up in a chair, and threw a party in his honor.

## A Little Background:

In his day John Barrymore (Drew's grandfather) was considered an actor's actor. His theatrical performances were—and still are—the stuff of legend. Unfortunately, Hollywood failed to offer him the kind of material worthy of his abilities, and he ended up squandering his talents on cheap roles and silly comedies. His secondary talent, meanwhile, blossomed amidst Hollywood's sybaritic set, and that was his talent for consuming liquor. According to some sources he could down just about anything, anything with a kick that is, including his wife's perfume, cleaning supplies, and high-octane fuel. W. C. Fields—who was arguably Hollywood's *second* greatest drinker—recalled that he once watched him siphon the alcohol out of his boat's cooling system and fix himself a "diesel martini" without so much as a flinch.

Barrymore's bad habits finally caught up with him, however. He passed away in a hospital room apparently while trying to make a pass at a nurse on May 29, 1942, at the age of sixty. His best friend, Gene Fowler, accompanied his body to the Pierce Funeral Home and claimed that he was the only one there, save for an old prostitute that showed up for a few minutes and left without saying a word.

### ...fix himself a "diesel martini" without so much as a flinch.

## What People Are Saying:

It all started as a prank, really, just a humorous joke between friends. Yet it has grown into one of the most talked-about anecdotes in Hollywood history. Apparently it went something like this: After Barrymore's funeral, his drinking buddies—known as the Bundy Boys—gathered at the Cock and Bull restaurant in Hollywood to reminisce about their friend's life of contumacy. Errol Flynn was particularly saddened by Barrymore's death, and took it badly. In fact, he left early to drown his sorrows in the arms of a seventeen-year-old model that he picked up earlier in the week. Raoul Walsh, the director of such classics as *High Sierra* and a notorious

7

prankster, also left early. But rather than return home, he went straight to the mortuary to see if he could convince the caretaker to lend him Barrymore's corpse. "John's sister is ill and can't leave the house," he explained to a mortician. "And she's terribly distraught over the fact that she can't pay her last respects to her dearly beloved. It would mean a great deal to her—and the entire, great, Barrymore family—if I could bring him to her so that she can say good-bye before he's laid to rest."

The caretaker refused, however, at least until Walsh produced a crisp $100 bill. "This is very unorthodox," exclaimed the now-sweating mortician. "You must have him back here in less than an hour, or it will mean a lot of trouble for the both of us." Walsh smiled, and assured him that he would.

Flynn returned home about an hour later, feeling a bit worse for wear when suddenly, out of the corner of his eye, he caught a glimpse of his old buddy sitting in his favorite chair with a fresh martini in his hand. "Can you imagine the shock I felt after being at Jack's wake to come home and find that son of a bitch sitting there?" he

later told columnist James Bacon. "I aged thirty years on the spot. It scared the living bejesus out of me, but you know what I did? I just sat down in the chair next to him and had a drink with him. . . . Then Raoul, that prick, came in and had a big laugh. And so did I. It was the crazy sort of thing that Jack would have appreciated. . . . And then we had more drinks."

## The Truth:

According to Bob Engles, a sixty-year veteran of the Pierce Funeral Home, nothing of the sort ever happened. "I saw Barrymore's body," he recalls. "And I can tell you it never left the building. If it did I would have known about it. And I can tell you this: There's no way on earth that anyone else would have let that body out of the mortuary without a signed authorization from the family—especially a big star like Barrymore. Imagine if something happened to it and it wasn't returned? I can assure you it never happened. That's just a bunch of Hollywood hokey."

# THE LEGEND:

Fidel Castro appeared in numerous Hollywood movies before his career as Cuba's communist dictator.

## The Context:

While the attraction between Hollywood and Washington may be a fairly recent phenomenon, there's some evidence that it goes back much further, almost to Hollywood's infancy. It's no secret, for instance, that scores of dignitaries made their way to Hollywood in the 1920s to seek fame and fortune on the silver screen. The Russian General Lodijenski, for

example, appeared in King Vidor's *His Hour* in 1924. The Archduke Leopold of Austria appeared in John Ford's *Four Sons* in 1928. Leon Trotsky, one of the architects of the Russian revolution of 1917, appeared in Emil Vester's World War I spy drama, *My Official Wife*, as an extra. And Pancho Villa, the lawless leader of Mexico's revolution of 1910, appeared in a number of pictures for Mutual.

The trend slowed down after World War II,

but still continues to this day. John Lindsay, for example, the former mayor of New York, took a role in 1975's *Rosebud* and was nearly laughed out of the theaters. Julian Bond, the Georgia State legislator, had a similar experience with his performance in *Greased Lightning* in 1977. And more recently, L.A.'s own mayor Richard Riordan has taken more than his share of stage time, including a part in a 1997 production of *Love Letters* at the Madrid Theater, and a role in P. G. Wodehouse's *The Inimitable Jeeves* in 1998.

## What People Are Saying:

Since the 1960s there has been a persistent rumor that Fidel Castro, Cuba's flamboyant dictator, appeared in at least one Hollywood movie in his early years. Columnist L. M. Boyd for example, of the *Herald Examiner*, once confirmed the rumor, by stating that Castro appeared in several movies—all with his Cuban compatriot, bandleader Xavier Cugat—including *You Were Never Lovelier* (1942), *The Heat's On* (1943), *Bathing Beauty* (1944), and *Holiday in Mexico* (1946).

## The Truth:

Yet according to the Academy of Motion Picture Arts and Sciences, no one has been able to find Castro's name in the credits of a Hollywood movie made between 1940 and 1960—not as an extra, bit player, or crew member. Meanwhile, historians have flatly denied that he ever came anywhere near the West Coast during that period, save for his four-year-stay in Mexico when he was preparing for his Cuban coup. (He visited Miami and New York in 1955, but failed to make it to L.A..)

## Where It Comes From:

According to the *Hollywood Reporter*, there were over twenty films being shot in Mexico in 1955, many near the ranch where Castro was holding combat exercises, including *Comanche*, *Serenade*,

Liborio Noval

**Fidel Castro**

*Seven Cities of Gold*, *The Treasure of Pancho Villa*, *The Last Frontier* and *The Come-On*. (None of which included Xavier Cugat, however.)

According to most historians, it's certainly possible that Castro could have poked his nose around one of those productions, but it doesn't seem very likely. As his biographer Robert E. Quirk points out, Castro was a strong disciplinarian with little tolerance for play. As one friend described him, "He is not a Cuban at all. He doesn't like music, he doesn't drink, and he works eighteen to twenty hours a day." (His associate, Ernesto "Che" Guevara, on the other hand, was known to be a true cinephile.)

## The Legacy:

In recent years Castro has warmed slightly to the idea of being in front of the camera. As the daily *Variety* reported in 1984 he invited the producers of the show *OceanQuest*—Jon Peters and Peter Guber—to produce a segment in his country. Apparently he was a fan of the short-lived series which followed the adventures of a team of researchers exploring the Caribbean on their ship, *Oz*. According to *Variety*, the producers accepted the offer, and were thrilled when Castro himself, an avid diver, donned some scuba gear and explored Havana's harbor at Peters's direction.

# THE RUMOR:

Tom Cruise is gay.

Paul Young

## What People Are Saying:

As the irreverent magazine, *Might*, wrote in 1996: "Is Tom Cruise gay? Puh-leeze, Tom Cruise is as gay as the night is long and everyone knows it. We heard it from a friend of ours at a party—who's gay—and he said that he knew some people that worked on *Top Gun* and it really was like Quentin Tarantino said in *Sleep with Me*. Also Tom lives in a *bungalow*, with his wife Nicole Kidman, who this same guy said just might be gay, too. Either way: Tom Cruise = Gay!"

While *Might* may have been poking fun at the rumor, it was typical for the 1990s, when rumors of Cruise's alleged homosexuality reached a near–fever pitch—much to Cruise's chagrin. "I think it's absolutely disgusting that someone would say [that my wife and I are gay]," he growled to *Premiere*. "It's ridiculous, it fucking pisses me off. Personally, I have nothing against [homosexuality] at all, but this is my relationship and I'm being called a liar about it. I've called lawyers. I say, 'You want to say that? Fine, go ahead, you fucking prove it.'"

## The Evidence:

And nobody *has* been able to prove it. While Cruise has been "caught" in a few heterosexual affairs—including a sexual romp in the back of a limo with Rebecca DeMornay—no one has been able to confirm his gay dalliances. Veteran gossip columnist Janet Charlton for example, who has been following Cruise's career since it began with *Endless Love* in 1981 and who has heard all the rumors about alleged affairs with male hustlers, has never found any evidence to support the rumor. "But that doesn't mean that he's necessarily straight," she admits. "It just means that he hasn't done anything that indiscreet to prove otherwise. But as far as the rumor goes, I personally don't believe it."

## Where It Comes From:

In 1990 Mimi Rogers, Cruise's ex-wife, may have unwittingly bolstered the Cruise-is-gay rumor when she gave an exclusive interview to *Playboy* magazine shortly after their divorce. "Tom was seriously thinking of becoming a monk," she reported with a hint of disdain. It looked as though the marriage wouldn't fit into his spiritual need. And he thought that he had to be celibate to maintain the purity of his instrument. Therefore it became obvious that we had to split."

Rogers's quotes prompted Cruise's new wife, Nicole Kidman, to make a few comments of her own. "Tom is anything but a monk," she fumed. "And he's a *very* sexual guy."

Nonetheless, Cruise's own comments came back to haunt him in 1996. That's when the German magazine *Brunte* asked him about his choice to adopt children, and he allegedly responded by saying that he was unable to father children because his sperm count was zero. When the article came out, Cruise nearly had a heart attack. He emphatically denied that he ever made such a statement and responded with a $60 million lawsuit against the publishers. "I'm sick of having to deny that I'm either celibate, sterile, or homosexual!" screamed Cruise. "Enough is enough!"

Still, it failed to turn the tide of public speculation. Because after Cruise filed for divorce from Kidman in February 2001, and Kidman miscarried their child, the grapevine exploded once again with even more specious gossip of their alleged transgressions. The French magazine *Actustar* for instance, claimed that gay porn star Kyle Bradford "confessed" about a homosexual relationship with Cruise, forcing the star to respond with yet another lawsuit, this time for $100 million. (Bradford later denied knowing Cruise or speaking to the magazine.)

## What It's All About:

As Cruise's biographer Robert Sellers noted in 1998, the rumor may be a function of Cruise's screen persona. Because if one looks carefully at his preferred choice of material it would seem that he favors subtle homosexual themes. *Top Gun* for example, was described by critic Pauline Kael as a "shiny homoerotic commercial," and several years later *The Independent* called *Interview with a Vampire* "the most can-

didly gay movie to come out of mainstream Hollywood in years." And since then Cruise, whose very name reflects the gay practice of "cruising," has continued to play men that have either been asexual or misogynistic. Even his much-ballyhooed appearance in Stanley Kubrick's final masterpiece *Eyes Wide Shut*—obviously chosen for its blatant *heterosexual* content—followed a similar pattern.

## The Bottom Line:

The incessant speculation over Cruise's sexuality is a complex subject, just as it is for any gay rumor. In some cases, such speculation may alleviate tension among straight men who not only feel uncomfortable with their female companion's attraction toward good-looking actors, but the unsettling homosexual themes in their films. On the other hand, such speculation also tends to center on those individuals who seem overprotective or controlling of their public images. Cruise in particular has worked tirelessly to perfect his public persona, a goal of most Scientoligists, and his bitter response to gay allegations has led many to believe that he's hiding something. In fact, the vehemence of Cruise's denial of homosexuality can be measured by the size of his libel suits. (If libel suits are designed to put a monetary value on damage incurred, Cruise seems to think that he stands to lose $100 million dollars for being considered a homosexual, despite the fact that he has been hounded by that same rumor for nearly fifteen years, yet continues to demand one of the highest salaries in the business.) Sociologists, meanwhile, have determined that celebrity scandals are really nothing more than an attempt by the public to uncover a star's true identity—an identity inextricably linked to his or her sexuality. As critic Richard de Cordova writes, "Scandal is the primal scene of all star discourse."

# THE RUMOR:

## A Little History:

While rumors of transsexuality are rare in the movie business, they're not unheard of. It was sometimes rumored that Marlene Dietrich, Greta Garbo, Mercedes De Acosta, and Mae West were packing more than a wicked wit underneath those sleek suits and riding pants,[1] a specious rumor that has also been leveled at singer Eartha Kitt, disco queen Grace Jones, and soap star Eileen Davidson of *The Young and the Restless*.[2] The rumor is absurd, of course, if not downright tasteless, and it seems to reveal a deep-seated misogyny that goes far beyond everyday homosexual rumors. Perhaps that's because it's not enough to call someone a lesbian, which is still considered a lesser "crime" than male homosexuality.

## What People Are Saying:

Jamie Lee Curtis, the great comedienne and star of such classics as *A Fish Called Wanda* and *True Lies*, seems to be the most recent victim of this rumor. Many have alleged that they "knew the doctor that performed the operation"; knew someone that "picked up her prescription for female hormone pills," or knew someone that saw "the scar on her ass where skin was taken for her vagina."

## Where It Comes From:

The only real "confirmation" of the rumor came in 1996 when William O. Beeman, an associate professor of anthropology at Brown University, published an article for the *Baltimore Morning Sun* titled, *What are you? Male, Merm, Herm, Ferm or Female?* That's where he not only tried to explain "intersexuality" in lay terms, but tried to use Jamie Lee Curtis as an example of what's called a "fermaphrodite."

## A Little Background:

To understand what's going on here, it should be pointed out that in a typical pregnancy, a woman's egg reacts to male sperm by creating an embryo. If the egg, which already contains an X chromosome receives another X chromosome, the embryo reacts to the effects of estrogen and begins to evolve into a female child. If it receives a Y, it reacts to androgens and forms a male child. But in some cases, perhaps one in 20,000 the XY embryo fails to fully react to the male hormone and the masculinization process is arrested. As a result, a male child develops the physical characteristics of a female, yet retains XY chromosomes and male traits. (A similar process works in the opposite direction when the embryo rejects the feminization process as well.) In more extreme cases, women with Androgen Insensitity Syndrome, or AIS, may fail to develop ovaries and show signs of male genitalia at birth. In such cases, the genitalia may be removed at birth—often without the parents' knowledge.

In any case, most women with AIS tend to be taller than most of their female counterparts, and are said to have good skin, large teeth, elongated limbs, large hands and feet, an exceptionally small vagina, large breasts, and juvenile nipples.

## The Evidence:

In any case, when Beeman needed to give an example of a typical "ferm," he cited a quote from a credible physician who tried to name Jamie Lee Curtis, the famous actress and author of the children's book, *Tell Me Again About the Night I Was Born*, as a "known" AIS patient. Quoting a medical source, Beeman states, "There are perhaps millions of XX males and XY females living in the United States today. These are cultural males with male genitalia who are genetically female, and cultural females with female genitalia who are genetically male. The film star Jamie Lee Curtis is one well-known individual who is genetically male, but phenotypically female."

## The Truth:

The editors of the *Baltimore Morning Sun* removed Curtis's name after Beeman admitted that he "couldn't authenticate [her] story to his satisfaction." Apparently that was because Beeman's source had obtained the information from members of the AIS community "who had heard about Jamie Lee Curtis from her plastic surgeons."

Since it is unlawful to discuss a patient's medical history without written permission, it's quite possible that Beeman's source chose Curtis—who has *not* been proven to be suffering from AIS—precisely because of the apparently specious rumor. In other words, the rumor that Curtis suffers from AIS has never been proven and is almost certainly false. It would have been much easier to pick someone like Joan of Arc, Queen Elizabeth, Eva Braun, or Elizabeth "Black Dahlia" Short, since they were known to be *genuine* AIS patients.

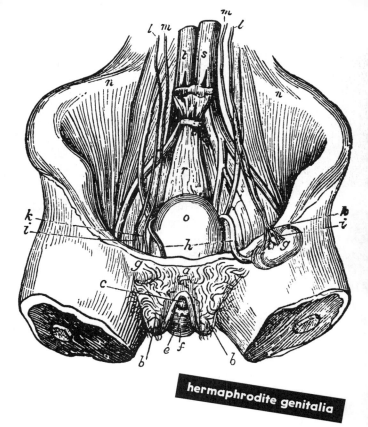

**hermaphrodite genitalia**

## The Context:

In truth, there have only been a handful of real sex changes in the entertainment biz. Wendy Carlos for example, the composer of *Switched on Bach* and *A Clockwork Orange*, was really *Walter* Carlos before he had a complete sex change in the early 1970s; and in 1978 director Doris Wishman made a movie called *Let Me Die a Woman* that featured actual footage of a sex change operation. (The star was not an actor, however, but a genuine patient.) More recently Jayne (Wayne) County, a well-known habitue of Warhol's factory and a punk-rock star in his/her own right, had a full boob job done before changing officially to Jayne. (S/he kept his male genitals intact, however.)

# THE RUMOR:

Harry Cohn, the head of Columbia Studios, hired a hit man to murder Sammy Davis, Jr. after he found out he was dating actress Kim Novak.

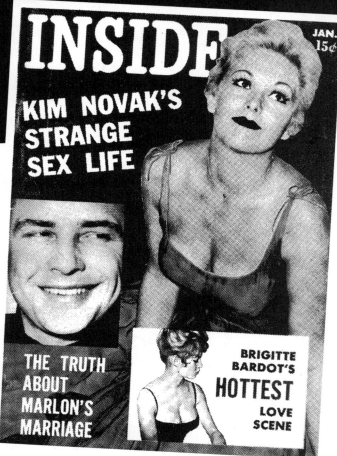

INSIDE

JAN. 15¢

KIM NOVAK'S STRANGE SEX LIFE

THE TRUTH ABOUT MARLON'S MARRIAGE

BRIGITTE BARDOT'S HOTTEST LOVE SCENE

## What Happened:

In 1957 Harry Cohn, the president of Columbia Studios, called his Mafia friends in Chicago to ask them for a favor. Cohn was introduced to the Chicago mob through Johnny Roselli, a member of Al Capone's gang in the 1920s, and it was Roselli that helped Cohn purchase a controlling interest in Columbia Studios—with mob money—in 1932.

In any case, Cohn's request was promptly passed to Frank Costello, the head of the New York family, and Costello in turn, called Mickey Cohen in L. A. and instructed him to "make a meet" with Mr. Harry Cohn to see "what the hell his problem is." Mickey, who always enjoyed rubbing elbows with the stars, promptly scheduled an appointment, and drove out the following day.

Harry Cohn put it to him bluntly. His top star, Kim Novak, was "banging a nigger" as he put it, and he didn't like it one bit. "She met this scumbag at Tony Curtis's house one night after a show," he continued working himself into a lather. "And after that he wouldn't leave her alone. He'd call her day and night, he'd send her flowers, he'd send her gifts, he'd send her tickets to Mexico and Hawaii—that cocksucker even rented a goddamned house in Malibu just so that they had a place to fuck in private. And then he goes to Aurora and asks her parents for permis-

sion to marry her. And when I heard that I figured I had to do something about this little prick. Because there's no way in hell that she's going to have a career if she's bangin' this guy. No way in hell. Do you understand what I'm saying? Her career is finished if this gets out. And I've already put a lot of goddamned money into that broad."

Cohn sat back in his chair for a moment, then leveled his eyes at Mickey. "His name is Sammy Davis, Jr. and I want that son of a bitch knocked in," he said flatly. "And I want it done yesterday, do you understand me? I don't give a damn what it costs."

By then Mickey had heard enough. As he

told reporter Peer Nugent years later, "It was as if he had told me that he wanted Benny Siegel knocked in. Sammy's my friend, Sammy's mother and father are my friends. I love little Sammy like I love anyone in my family. So I told this Cohn, I said, 'Lookit, you're way out of line here. Not only am I going to give ya a negative answer to this, but I'm going to give ya a negative answer that you better see that it doesn't happen. Because if it does happen, I'm going to kill *you*.'"

That wasn't the answer Cohn wanted to hear. Without saying a word, the rotund producer jumped out of his chair and marched off to his car. Minutes later he was on the line with Costello again, chewing his ear off. Costello then called Chicago and arranged for two thugs to fly out to L.A. the following day and pay Davis a visit. As Davis later told his biographer, a rental car pulled into his driveway and two no-nose thugs ordered him to jump in. Two hours later he found himself in the middle of the Mojave Desert with the business end of a .45 pressed into his face. "You already got one eye missing," growled the gangster. "Unless you want

to try for two you better stay away from that Kim Novak broad. And you better marry a colored girl as soon as possible. It don't matter who, just so she's black."

Weeks later, on January 10, 1958, Davis married Loray White, a very attractive, and very black twenty-three-year-old singer from Texas. The marriage only lasted six months, however, and White later revealed that she never once slept with Davis, not even on their wedding night. Still, she received $25,000 for her efforts.

## The Truth:

In retrospect, Davis's desire to marry Kim Novak was, in his own words, "a big *fuck you*" to the industry. As he told a reporter years later, he had received so much racial abuse as a black performer in a white entertainment world, that he wanted nothing more than to make them all green with envy. "*I had* to get the whitest, most famous chick in the world," he said. "And just *show 'em*."

# THE LEGEND:

Errol Flynn secretly worked for the Nazis during WWII, and was, perhaps, one of the most important spies of the century.

## What People Are Saying:

When author Charles Higham released his in-depth investigation into the many lives and loves of Errol Flynn, the much-beloved Hollywood sybarite best known for his swash-buckling turns in *The Adventures of Robin Hood*, and *Captain Blood*, he started a firestorm of controversy that continues to this day. That book, *Errol Flynn: The Untold Story*, first published in 1979, not only charged Flynn with being a rapist, pederast, and bisexual, but a gun runner, drug

dealer, murderer, and a virulent anti-Semite who not only spied for the Nazis during World War II, but secretly hoped that Hitler would wipe every Jew off the face of the planet.

Flynn's still-living wife was so shocked at Higham's claims that she swore her husband would have "flattened him" if he were still alive. Sir William Stephenson, the Canadian Director of Allied Wartime Intelligence, also discounted Higham's allegations, arguing that there was no proof of Flynn's covert activities and if there were, he would know about it. A short time later, author Tony Thomas got into the act with his 1990 book, *Errol Flynn: The Spy Who Never Was*, claiming that "it takes little examination of *The Untold Story* to reach the conclusion that the charges [against Flynn] are based on statements of people long dead or those who do not wish to be identified. Other conclusions on the part of Higham are reached by inference, supposition, innuendo, and strained deduction. But the basis for the charge of Nazism is Flynn's friendship with an Austrian doctor named Hermann Friedrich Erben. It is more than a basis; take away Erben and there is nothing left with which to tackle Flynn in regard to his supposed interest in Nazi Germany."

## The Truth:

The mysterious Dr. Erben is indeed the key to Flynn's Nazism. But according to Thomas, who looked at many of the same FBI files as Higham, the Austrian physician, often described as a "crackpot" by those that knew him, was never the "high-ranking" Nazi that Higham claimed. If anything, he was too inept, boisterous—and *Jewish*—to be a genuine Nazi spy.[3]

Still, as author Rudolf Stoiber claims in his well-researched book, *The Spy That Wanted to Be Hitler*, Erben was not someone to be discounted so easily. While he may have been reckless, he indeed conducted espionage conquests all over the world, sometimes with dire consequences. In 1937 for example, he used Flynn and his celebrity contacts to raise $1.5 million for the loyalists, the ragtag rebel army at war against Franco's Nazi-backed Spanish offensive, primarily as an excuse to get behind rebel lines. But when he arrived with Flynn in tow, the actor refused to hand over the money, leaving Erben to make up something about the missing funds. What's more, Erben also used Flynn's cover to sneak behind rebel lines and gather the names of German soldiers secretly fighting for rebel forces.

And once he returned to Paris, he passed those names over to Nazi officials, who later went after those same soldiers and their families.

Yet that was hardly an isolated case. Journalist Gerry Brown, an award-winning journalist in England, uncovered secret MI6 files documenting a meeting between Flynn and Sean Russell, the quartermaster general of the IRA, which clearly showed that Flynn was trying to help the IRA secure funding from the Third Reich to increase the chance of a Nazi takeover. And perhaps even more alarming is the report that Flynn may have taken photographs of Pearl Harbor in 1938 from his boat, the *Sirocco*, and passed them to Ulrich von der Osten, the notorious Nazi spy who helped the Japanese plan the surprise attack on Pearl Harbor in 1941. "Let's be frank here," says Higham in a recent interview. "And I say this after twenty years of much thought and consideration: Errol Flynn was a major Nazi agent. In fact, he may have been one of the most important German agents of WWII."

If so many people in Hollywood knew about Flynn's secret activities—which apparently they did—then why didn't they do anything about it? There's a great deal of evidence, for example, that Flynn's boss, Jack Warner, knew all about his affairs, and yet Warner was a virulent anti-Nazi. In fact, he not only produced such inflammatory anti-Nazi propaganda as *Confessions of a Nazi Spy*, but publicly announced that anyone suspected of fomenting sabotage or indicating disloyalty to the American flag on his lot would be "turned over to the authorities."

The only explanation for Flynn's freedom, it seems, had to do with the fact that it was easier to hide his activities than risk the consequences of revealing them to the public. "They simply had to pretend that it didn't exist," says Higham. "Because if they ever let this kind of information out, it was serious enough to bring the entire industry to its knees. Everyone would be implicated. And considering [Warner's] associations

> "...he may have been one of the most important German agents of WWII."

Flynn and friends

Courtesy of Red Herring

in Washington, the studios couldn't, under any circumstances, allow that to happen."

## The Bottom Line:

Aristotle calls the man without a society a game piece without a game, and Flynn, a lifelong runaway with no allegiances to any country, spent his life searching for a game—on and off the screen. So when he met Erben on a steamer headed for England in 1933, the budding twenty-four-year-old actor became immediately enchanted with the mad doctor. After all, Erben lived a life of genuine adventure and intrigue, one that took him around the world and into truly dangerous situations. For someone like Flynn, that kind of adventure was intoxicating. As Stoiber explains, "I think Flynn caught the spying bug from Erben, because as Erben told me, spying is like alcoholism: that you do one act of espionage and then another, and another, until

you're hooked and you cannot stop."

In other words, Flynn undoubtedly fraternized with Nazi spies in Mexico, Rio, and Buenos Aires; transported delicate information to enemy agents here and abroad; and adopted anti-Semitic views. (He once wrote a letter to Erben in 1933 in his own hand stating, "I wish we could bring Hitler over here to show these Isaacs a thing or two.") Nonetheless, there has never been any proof that he was officially sanctioned by the Nazis during World War II.[4] That may be a matter of semantics for some, but it certainly makes his title as "the greatest spy of WWII" somewhat doubtful.

ERROL

# THE LEGEND:

Clark Gable accidentally killed a pedestrian along Sunset Boulevard one night while driving drunk, and the studios successfully covered up the incident.

Bison Archives

"Hey, Clark, look where you're going!" Gable behind the wheel instead of behind bars

## A Brief History:

In the 1930s Clark Gable was one of MGM's most popular stars. He was making an average of three pictures a year including *It Happened One Night* and *Mutiny on the Bounty,* and many considered him to be MGM's greatest asset. Yet despite his success, he was deeply unhappy with his professional life. Not only was he trapped in a loveless marriage to Josephine Dillon, his first acting coach, but his income was far below that of his costars.

## What People Are Saying:

One night, while driving west on Sunset Boulevard after a bout of drinking with some friends, Gable failed to see a young woman crossing the road and slammed right into her, catching her with the front bumper of his Duesenberg and sending her flying twenty feet in the air. Shaken sober, Gable climbed out of his car and ran over to the woman, who was out cold and bleeding badly. He tried reviving her with mouth-to-mouth resuscitation, but the injuries were too severe. What's more, he realized that she was pregnant. Panicking, he ran to the nearest phone and called Howard Strickling, one of his closest friends and the head of publicity at MGM. Strickling sent Whitely Hendry to pick him up and bring him back to his house. Meanwhile, Strickling called Louis B. Mayer, the head of MGM, and told him what happened. "Keep Clark in your house," ordered Mayer. "And don't let him talk to anybody. Not until we get this thing straightened out." Mayer then called District Attorney Buron Fitts and explained the situation, adding, "I'm confident that we can find a way to work this out."

As soon as he got into his office the following morning, Mayer called Eddie Mannix, his usual cohort in such matters, and asked him to find a fall guy, someone that could claim he was driving Gable's car that night. Mannix in turn, suggested a young executive who had just joined the company and was eager to please. Without hesitation, Mayer called the upstart into his office and put it to him bluntly, "I'm going to make you a proposition. But before I do, you must swear that you will sign a piece of paper stating that you will never utter a word of this conversation to anyone for as long as you live. Will you do that for me?"

"Yes, sir," replied the young man nervously.

Then Mayer outlined the proposition: He would claim responsibility for the accident and serve a ten-month sentence in the lowest security prison available. In return he'd be rewarded a guaranteed income for the rest of his life and a permanent position at MGM.

The young man mulled it over for a few minutes and asked if he could sleep on it.

"No you can't sleep on it!" bellowed Mayer. "What's your answer?"

Frustrated, the young man sunk back into his chair and nervously agreed to take the fall. Seconds later, Mayer was on the phone with Fitts again, and the young man was hauled off to LAPD headquarters. Meanwhile, as Gable moved to Cedars-Sinai Medical Center to recuperate, Fitts brokered a deal between Mayer and the LAPD to purchase the police dockets for $1 million.

## Where It Comes From:

Not surprisingly, there has never been a credible validation of Gable's hit-and-run story. The only recorded episode in Gable's life that bears any resemblance occurred on June 20, 1933 when he drunkenly ran his Duesenberg into a tree. According to the *Los Angeles Examiner*, he was on his way to visit Strickling when he misjudged the driveway and piled right into a large eucalyptus. According to the *Examiner*, Strickling rushed Gable to Cedars-Sinai and told reporters that he had swerved to avoid a drunk driver traveling in the opposite direction, apparently to hide Gable's own intoxication. And just to make sure that the public felt sorry for him, Strickling forced him to stay in the hospital for an entire week.

## The Truth:

Gable's mysterious hospital stay in 1933 seems to be the real basis of the rumor. Yet, even that is of questionable origin. In fact, it's likely that Strickling made up the story about crashing into a tree to hide something else, something slightly more embarrassing. According to his biographer, Lyn Tornabene, the real reason for Gable's secretive hospital stay was to get cosmetic surgery done on his famously large ears and tobacco-stained teeth, and he didn't want anyone to know about it, including his studio bosses.

## The Bottom Line:

The *Examiner*'s story about the tree could have easily been a cover story for the manslaughter incident. And yet, the tree could have easily been a cover for the plastic surgery story as well. In any case, it provides a perfect model for all pre-Vietnam Hollywood rumors: offering "proof" that the studios protected their stars, even to the point of helping them get away with murder.

# THE RUMOR:

Richard Gere was once admitted to Cedars-Sinai where a live gerbil was removed from his ass.

THE SEXIEST MAN ALIVE 1999 Richard Gere

PLUS: 78 Pages of Men You'll Love!

Paul Young

## What People Are Saying:

Apparently this rumor began sometime in the late 1980s or early 1990s, and supposedly it went like this: One night, after being admitted into Cedars-Sinai's emergency room, a famous actor, supposedly Richard Gere, the star of *American Gigolo* and *An Officer and a Gentleman,* was found to have a live gerbil lodged deep within his rectal cavity. Apparently the actor believed that the wiggling motions of the rodent, which had been shaved, declawed, and sheathed in a large condom, would bring him extraordinary sexual pleasure once inserted.

After the operation, Gere supposedly paid off the entire medical team for their silence and asked them to sign confidentiality contracts as insurance. But unbeknownst to him, a technician at the nearby radiology center accidentally came upon a copy of his X ray and alerted the ASPCA. In response, the ASPCA sent out hundreds of faxes deriding Gere, Hollywood, and the homosexual community for engaging in a practice known to be cruel to animals.

## The Truth:

Despite the utter absurdity of the story, thousands of people have claimed that they were at the hospital on the night that Gere was supposedly there—or at least knew someone that was. Nonetheless, no one has ever been able to prove the validity of the story. Mike Walker, a reporter for the *National Enquirer* spent months trying to

track down the attending physician that supposedly performed the procedure and found no evidence that Gere was even in the hospital. "I've never worked harder on a story in my life," he told the *Palm Beach Post.* "I'm convinced that it's nothing more than an urban legend."

Meanwhile, other reporters scanned the records of Cedars-Sinai's patient list for the entire year, spoke with every doctor on duty that night, and came to the same conclusion: Gere wasn't even there. And to make the story even more incredible, gerbils are considered a menace to native agriculture and are illegal to sell or purchase anywhere in the state of California. (What's more, does anyone really believe that Gere would even know how to declaw a rodent?)

## The Context:

As the rumor swept through the country in the early 1990s, Drs. David B. Busch and James R. Starling began conducting their own survey of hospitals to see if they could find another case of gerbil abuse. Yet after months of searching, they failed to find a single one. They found other examples of Rectal Foreign Objects (RFOs), however, including cases of apples, vegetables, candles, perfume bottles, spatulas, flashlights, curling irons, baseballs, pool cues, light bulbs, axe handles, ice picks, peanut butter jars, six-inch stones, frozen pig's tails, and in one case a *live* World War II artillery shell.[5]

## Where It Comes From:

Like most urban legends, the story has a number of interesting precedents. Some folktales from the eighteenth century for example, describe a mouse crawling into a woman's vagina and giving her pleasure by its movements. A couple hundred years later, during the Vietnam War, it was rumored that draft dodgers often inserted rats up their backsides to either prove that they were too crazy or too gay to go into military service.

The rumor took a new spin in the 1970s and eighties however. Jan Harold Brunvand, one of America's leading folklorists specializing in urban legends, reported that he heard similar narrative in 1984, from places as scattered as Pennsylvania, Colorado, New York, and California. Meanwhile, a supervisor for the Society for the Prevention of Cruelty to Animals told writer Catherine Seipp of *The Advocate* that she heard the story attributed to at least ten different celebrities between the years 1967 and 1990.

Yet it is the case of Rick Segal, a TV weatherman in Wichita Falls, that seems to have the greatest significance. Apparently, in 1989—not long before the Gere story hit—someone claimed that Segal had spent the night at the local hospital getting his own gerbilectomy. As a result, the rumor—which was completely false and led to Segal's dismissal—spread like wildfire through the entire southwest. Meanwhile, at the same time, the grapevine was abuzz over Richard Gere's alleged homosexuality. The French tabloid *Voici* even went so far as to claim that he was planning to divorce his then-wife, supermodel Cindy Crawford, because he was planning to "come out of the closet," an allegation Gere felt compelled to deny in a full-page *London Times* advertisement. Finally, as the news of Segal's alleged sexual practice made it out west, it naturally dovetailed with Gere's rumored homosexuality until it ultimately morphed into a story about Richard Gere using a gerbil.

## The Bottom Line:

As much as people really want to believe that Richard Gere attempted such an act, it's almost certainly false that he did. If anything, it's a prime example of the moralizing subtext of urban legends, a subtext that condemns as much as it entertains. What's more, the rumor itself is deeply homophobic, sexist, and malicious.

*They found other examples of Rectal Foreign Objects (RFOs), including cases of apples, vegetables, candles, perfume bottles, spatulas, flashlights, curling irons, baseballs, pool cues, light bulbs, axe handles, ice picks, peanut butter jars, six-inch stones, frozen pig's tails, and in one case a live World War II artillery shell.*

# THE RUMOR:

After unsuccessfully trying to initiate sex with an artificial penis on his wife Jean Harlow, Paul Bern committed suicide.

## The Back Story:

On September 5, 1932, Paul Bern, producer Irving Thalberg's top assistant, was found nude in Jean Harlow's bedroom with a bullet in his head. As shocking as it was, detectives quickly ruled the case a suicide, pointing to two key pieces of evidence: the gun in his hand and a suicide note found nearby—a note which read:

```
Unfortunately this is the only
way to make good the frightful
wrong I have done you and wipe
out my abject humiliation. I
love you. Paul. P.S. You under-
stand that last night was only
a comedy.
```

Bern's note was checked with handwriting experts and proven to be authentic. Yet those words: "abject humiliation," "frightful wrong," and "comedy" would vex journalists, biographers, and fans alike for years to come. In fact, Bern's alleged suicide has gone down in the history books as one of the most mysterious, sordid, and perplexing affairs in Hollywood history.

## Where It Comes From:

Fans and friends alike were baffled by the Bern/Harlow marriage, which in turn led to numerous rumors and jokes. Bern, after all, was a full twenty-six years older than Harlow and the complete opposite of the macho type that she generally pursued. What's more, Harlow was at the peak of sexual attractiveness, a legendary sexual dynamo, while Bern was a quiet, mild-mannered "schoolteacher-type" as some

described him. (That led many to believe that she must have had a father fixation stemming from her own father's near-pathological control of her.) Yet according to Irving Shulman, the author of 1964's *Harlow*, Bern was a lot darker than he led on. In fact, he claims that Bern was an outright monster, beating his wife viciously on occasion, almost to the point of hospitalization. And to make matter's even weirder, Shulman also claims that Bern had the genitals of a "six-year-old-boy" and was completely impotent.

While those charges still remain unresolved, there seems to be some evidence that Harlow called her agent, Arthur Landau, on the day after their wedding night, demanding that he start divorce proceedings immediately. (Shulman claims that it was because she laughed at his inadequacies when he tried to consummate the marriage, and he responded by beating her savagely.) Instead Landau called MGM's Irving Thalberg, who in turn called Louis B. Mayer. That led to an emergency meeting where it was quickly decided that Bern would move out of his house and into a nearby apartment, yet "pretend" to be Harlow's husband for at least a year.

According to Shulman, everything went according to plan, save for the fact that Harlow began having casual sex with just about anybody that came along, including studio messengers, cab drivers, and limo drivers. Bern refused to give up, however, and began seeing a sex therapist in private, secretly hoping that he might satisfy his wife one day. Apparently that day came on September 5. As Shulman describes it:

```
Paul untied the belt of the
robe and stepped out of it. He
was nude. And Jean stood in
amazement, her mouth slack
```

open, because strapped around
Paul's middle, just above his
true parts, were a large artificial penis and testicles.
This formidable apparatus, har-
nessed around Paul's hips with
a series of straps, appeared to
be made of a soft suedelike
leather dyed the color of natural flesh, except that the
enormous head was bright red.
The testicles were huge, too,
and from the sack extended a
little bulb to squirt warm
water.

Apparently Harlow found the contraption absurd and laughed so hard that she cried. But rather than get angry, Bern sheepishly retired to the dressing room where he found one of his guns and blew his brains out.

## What Probably Happened:

Shulman's account has been widely dismissed by historians and critics alike. The *New York Times*, for example, claimed that he "would have been better off calling it fiction." Screenwriter Samuel Marx, on the other hand, who had known Harlow and Bern personally, was so infuriated by the book that he began investigating the story on his own. Using police records and new research, he and his coauthor, Joyce Vanderveen, reconstructed the events of Bern's final night, and came to the conclusion that he was murdered.

According to their book, *Deadly Illusions*, the scenario went down like this: A mysterious woman by the name of Dorothy Millette arrived at Bern's house at around two in the morning, specifically to meet with Bern in private. (Harlow was conveniently away that night, staying at her parents' house.) Bern answered the door in a bathing suit and offered her a glass of champagne. Soft music was playing on the turntable and he had candles placed all around the pool, casting a lambent, romantic mood. Yet seduction wasn't on Bern's mind. If anything, he simply wanted to keep Millette calm. After all, he knew that she was prone to schizophrenic fits

Paul Bern

*Apparently Harlow found the contraption absurd and laughed so hard that she cried.*

and irrational thinking; he knew that because he used to live with her, back when they were both struggling actors in New York. They even had a binding, common-law marriage by New York standards, one that required Bern to pay for her monthly psychiatric bills.

Millette was, in other words, a highly volatile woman, and Bern knew that she had come to L.A. to reclaim him for herself.

Within minutes of arriving, Millette launched into Bern with a storm of vindictive remarks. "You're still my husband!" she screamed. "How could you do this to me?" Bern reacted by smashing a champagne glass on a table which left him with a small cut on his hand. (A neighbor later testified that he heard Bern scream, "Get out of my life," around 2:30 in the morning.)

Bern then went inside to dress his wound and get out of his wet suit; and apparently as he did, Millette appeared in his dressing room without a stitch of clothing on, pressing herself up against his nude body from behind. Bern recoiled slightly, and when he did, Millette produced one of Bern's handguns that she found in the other room. Both froze for a moment until Millette broke the ice with a laugh and a mock threat. But before he could react, she pulled the trigger, sending a bullet whizzing through his skull.

No one knows if Millette really meant to kill him or not, and there's a good chance that she was just playing around, thinking that the gun was empty. In any case, no one will ever know for sure. Millette disappeared shortly after that, only to wind up drowning in a river near Sacramento—probably by her own hand.

## What Really Happened:

Marx and Vanderveen offer some compelling evidence to back up their theory, yet none of it actually proves that Dorothy Millette killed Paul Bern.[6] David Stenn offers a much more balanced account in his book, *Bombshell: The Life and Death of Jean Harlow,* and according to him, Bern's suicide had already been a foregone conclusion. He was, in fact, a genuinely compassion-

ate soul who rarely, if ever, raised his voice. Nonetheless, he was a deeply troubled man. His mother had killed herself years earlier—supposedly after she found out that he was "living in sin" with Dorothy Millette—and the event scarred him for life. (It also led to Millette's breakdown and subsequent mental illness.) In fact, Bern had already tried to kill himself once before after actress Barbara La Marr rejected his request for marriage a couple years earlier.

On the night of September 5, he invited Millette over to the house because he wanted to introduce her to Harlow so that they could discuss what could be done in a civilized manner. But when Harlow, who later died, surprisingly, at age twenty-six, grabbed her coat and hissed, "Call me when you figure out who you're married to," before storming out the door, he crumbled. His love for Harlow was profound, and at that moment he realized that he had crossed the line and that there was no turning back. He tried to go for a swim to relax, but Millette's recriminations only made him feel worse. So when he went to change his clothes and found one of his guns on the dresser, he picked it up, put it to his temple and pulled the trigger.

## The Aftermath:

If the rumor has continued through the years, it's primarily because of the skillful cover-up performed by Harlow's studio, MGM. As Stenn reports, L. B. Mayer was so terrified at the potential scandal that he did everything that he could to ensure that everyone—including the police— would agree that it was a suicide. He not only came up with Bern's "impotency idea," but moved Bern's body in front of the mirror and placed a note in his hand—a note that Bern had written weeks earlier.

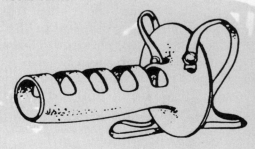

# THE LEGEND:

While on his private yacht, William Randolph Hearst killed producer Thomas Ince and successfully covered up the murder by buying everybody off.

## What People Are Saying:

On Friday, November 16, 1924, William Randolph Hearst, the wealthy newspaper tycoon, boarded his 280-foot yacht, the *Oneida*, and took off for a weekend rendezvous with thirty of his nearest and dearest friends. What happened after that has never been fully documented, but many people seem to believe that Hearst walked in on his mistress, actress Marion Davies, in bed with another man—possibly Charlie Chaplin—and tried to kill him. Exactly how he delivered the fatal blow, or even if it was Chaplin at all, has been debated for years. Most, however, seem to agree that producer Thomas Ince died at Hearst's hands, either by a stray bullet meant for Chaplin or from a bullet meant for him after he caught him diddling Davies.

Fearing a scandal, Hearst then dumped the body overboard and then forced everybody to sign confidentiality contracts, while promising them all hefty bribes for their silence. (Famed gossip columnist Louella Parsons, who was nothing more than a struggling writer at the time, supposedly refused to sign unless Hearst put her in charge of all the gossip columns in his newspapers around the country—an ultimatum that Hearst was forced to accept.) Meanwhile, Hearst allegedly gave Ince's widow, Mrs. Elinor Ince, the newly built $2.5 million, one hundred-room luxury mansion called the Chateau Elysee, now the Church of Scientology's celebrity center in Hollywood, as well as a multimillion dollar trust fund that would take care of her for the rest of her life.

## What Really Happened:

While no one will ever know if Hearst was capable of murder, there's no doubt that he was a duplicitous character. He may have had friendship in mind when he invited Ince to join them in the first place, yet in truth, he was more concerned with getting him to sign a contract that would bring Ince's highly successful Triangle Pictures under the umbrella of Hearst enterprises—a contract that Ince had no intention of signing.

In any case, Ince still managed to have a good time, indulging himself on salted almonds

Hearst and wife

and rich desserts despite his doctor's warnings. And sure enough, he started complaining of severe chest pains a short time later. Dr. Daniel Carson Goodman, who was on board at the time, came to his aid and gave him some medication, saying that he needed to rest. But when Dr. Goodman went to check on him the following morning, he found that his condition had worsened. So he loaded him onto a dinghy and escorted him ashore to the nearest train station.

Within minutes into the trip back to L.A., Ince suffered a minor heart attack, and was forced to disembark at Del Mar. There, a team of doctors, including Dr. Truman Parker and Dr. Horace Lazelle of San Diego, met him at the station and took him to a nearby hospital. His doctors suggested that he stay in Del Mar and get some rest, but when Dr. Parker returned to check on him the following morning he was gone. Apparently his wife and son picked him up in the middle of the night and took him back to L.A. on a private line.

Sadly, Ince passed away the following morning (Wednesday, November 21, 1924) in his Benedict Canyon home. The coroner claimed that his death was due to heart failure. Yet rather than allow an autopsy to be performed, Mrs. Ince had his body cremated and interned days later as per her husband's request. (She had no reason to disagree with the coroner's ruling since she knew all about her husband's heart problems and no one, including the chief medical examiner, found evidence of poison or bullet holes.)

## Where It Came From:

How or why people came up with the idea that Hearst tried to murder Charlie Chaplin and mistakenly shot Ince is still unclear. It could be that people placed Chaplin on board simply because everyone knew that Hearst was insanely jealous over Marion Davies's affections for him. In fact, the New York *Daily News* printed a gossip item on November 16, 1924—the same day as the infamous voyage—suggesting that they were having a full-blown affair.[7]

## The Truth:

Yet Chaplin wasn't within a hundred miles of San Diego that day. He was actually mad at work on his epic, *The Gold Rush*, while dealing with a messy scandal of his own involving a sixteen-year-old actress named Lita Grey who claimed that she was pregnant with his baby.[8] Meanwhile Louella Parsons was in New York tending to a nasty cold, and she didn't move out to Hollywood until May 1925, a full year *after* the alleged incident. (Furthermore, she didn't force Hearst into giving her the job at his newspaper. As her biographer has pointed out, the only reason that he gave her the position was because he knew that she'd never print anything negative about Davies, at least not while he was paying her.) And lastly, Hearst couldn't have given the Chateau Elysee to Elinor Ince either, simply because he never had anything to do with the building. According to public records, Mrs. Ince built the chateau on her own accord, mostly with the money that she received from her husband's estate.

## What It All Means:

If the rumor has remained popular over the years it's simply because people *want* to believe that Hearst was capable of such egregious behavior. In fact, even D. W. Griffith, the great director, went on record saying, "All you had to do to make Hearst turn white as a ghost is mention Ince's name. There's plenty wrong there, but Hearst is too big to touch." Hearst, after all, was a miserable human being; wealthy beyond anyone's dreams, yet miserly, selfish, insecure, chauvinistic, and treacherous. If anyone was going to pull such a stunt, it was he. Yet in truth, he may have unwittingly fostered the tale by refusing to confront it in public. As he once told Davies, "Never sue a paper. That only enlarges the thing, keeps it going, and makes it worse."

# THE RUMOR:

Alfred Hitchcock used to spy on Grace Kelly with a telescope, but only after she agreed to take her clothes off before a large, picture-frame window.

Hitch enjoying his work
Courtesy of Red Herring

## What People Are Saying:

In 1984 Kenneth Anger wrote about Hitch's scopophilia in *Hollywood Babylon II*, claiming that the beautiful Grace Kelly, the star of Hitchcock's *Rear Window*, consented to going home and doing a sensual striptease before a large picture window. According to Anger, Hitchcock had a house across the canyon and would masturbate while watching Kelly through a telescope. As he put it:

> "Slowly, thoughtfully, as if returning from a night on the town, Kelly disrobed. Her hat came first, then the gloves. The straps of her evening gown slipped down from her white shoulders, allowing the sensuous crepe de chine to glide to the floor. The last to fall were her French lace panties. Across the shadowed canyon, 'Cocky' rose to the occasion."

## The Truth:

It's not hard to figure out how such a rumor could evolve. Hitchcock was notorious for his fetishistic behavior toward his leading ladies. In 1963 for example, he was so harsh on Tippi Hedren during the making of *The Birds* that she had to be institutionalized. (And as if that wasn't sadistic enough, he also sent her five-year-old daughter, Melanie Griffith, an exact replica of her mother—in a casket.)

Yet according to most biographers, Hitch never treated Kelly in the same way. In fact, of all his leading ladies, she received the greatest respect. "He was in love with her to be sure," writes James Spada in *Grace: The Secret Lives of a Princess*. "But he never made any overt attempts to woo her."

In any case, even if she performed in her living room, as Anger claims, it's not likely that Hitch could have seen it. Kelly lived in an apartment with two other girls at 6329 Hollywood Boulevard at the time, a full *eight miles* from Hitch's house at 10957 Bellagio Road in Bel Air. Yet, on the other hand, she was also known to be having an affair with Ray Milland during the making of *Dial M for Murder* and Milland owned a house less than a mile away from Hitchcock at 10664 Bellagio. (In fact the affair led to a legal separation, after which Kelly apparently moved in with Milland for a short period.) Nonetheless, Milland later claimed that he never brought Kelly to his house during the affair, and even if he had, there's no way that Hitch could have spied on them from his house either, because if you visit the two houses today you'll see that they are completely obscured from each other.

## Where It Came From:

In all probability, Kenneth Anger picked up on a little incident that occurred during the making of *Dial M*. Apparently during the production, Hitch became frustrated over what should have been an easy scene to shoot. The script called for Kelly to climb out of bed in the middle of the night to answer the telephone in another room. The studios wanted her to get up and put on a robe first, but that slowed the scene down considerably. So after numerous takes, Kelly came forward with a suggestion. "If I were home alone," she argued, "and I had to get up and answer the telephone in the middle of the night, I would simply get up and answer it no matter what I had on." Naturally Hitch loved the idea and shot the scene just as Kelly proposed, with her rolling out of bed in what was considered to be quite revealing lingerie for the 1950s. What's more, Hitch then proceeded to direct her in how she should "saunter" across the room and up to a window, where she was supposed to answer the phone. In all likelihood, *that* was the infamous striptease for Alfred Hitchcock.

# THE RUMOR:

Actor Dennis Hopper was abducted by aliens while on vacation in Mexico.

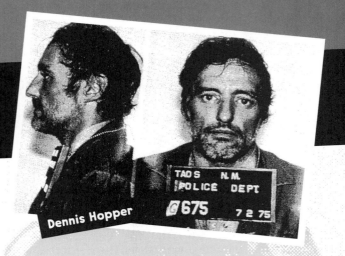

Dennis Hopper

TAOS N.M. POLICE DEPT C675 7 2 75

## A Little Background:

Dennis Hopper is perhaps Hollywood's greatest libertine. Since his early years as an artist in Southern California's nascent art scene, he has pursued a life as an impassioned sensualist with a genuine dedication to personal freedom and the expression of his artistic impulses. That, of course, has led him into areas that most of us can only dream of, including trying to jump out of an airplane without a parachute, blowing himself up with dynamite, and making love to a quadriplegic that he picked up on Western Avenue.[9] "You can't make discoveries by sitting around waiting for something to happen," he once said. "You've got to get out there. And sometimes that means exploring all kinds of stimuli. Not only drugs and alcohol, but sex, anger, hate, love, passion, everything."

## Where It Comes From:

Apparently the alien-abduction rumor can be traced back to a little incident that occurred during the making of *Jungle Fever* in Mexico. As his biographer Elena Rodriguez points out in *Dennis Hopper: A Madness to His Method*, Hopper was suffering from severe exhaustion during the production, a condition aggravated by years of chronic drug and alcohol use, extreme stress, and neurotic symptoms. And at some point, while locked in his hotel room with a bottle of tequila, he began hearing voices and hallucinating. "I thought that there were people in the bowels of [the hotel] who were being tortured and cremated," he explained to Rodriguez. "These people had come to save me and they were being killed and tortured and it was my fault."

Apparently that was only the beginning, however, because then he started seeing "bugs and snakes" crawling underneath his skin. All at once, he let out a bloodcurdling scream, ripped off every stitch of clothing, and ran outside into a thicket of trees where, as he later put it, "two unseen armies were in the midst of a spectacular battle." The nightmare ultimately took a turn for the better when he spotted a flying saucer overhead that "guided him" to safety.

Those hallucinations, while better than some of his movies, were nothing to laugh at. As his doctor later claimed, he was so close to the edge that he could have easily slipped over into a condition that was irreversible, leaving him with a permanent case of schizophrenia.

Not surprisingly, he's been clean ever since.

## The Context:

Evidently Hopper is not the first—or last—celebrity to see a UFO. Actress Lillian Roth (*Animal Crackers*), Ed Asner (*The Mary Tyler Moore Show*), Olivia Newton-John (*Grease*), Cliff Robertson (*Charly*), Eddie Bracken (*National Lampoon's Vacation*), William Shatner (Captain Kirk on *Star Trek*), Gloria Swanson (*Sunset Boulevard*), DeForest Kelley (Dr. McCoy on *Star Trek*), Kaye Ballard (*The Girl Most Likely*), Lisa Hart (*Another Time, Another Place*) and Shirley MacLaine (*The Apartment*) have all claimed that they've seen flying saucers now and then.

Yet that's nothing compared to the stars that have claimed to have extraterrestrial ancestry. Elvis Presley, for example, once confided to a close friend that he had come from another planet

# Little man in flying saucer reported near San Diego

SAN DIEGO, March 31.-(UP)-An unidentified woman today telephoned local newspapers that a flying saucer landed on Highway 80 near Jacumba and "a little man jumped out and ran down the highway in the direction of Imperial valley."

"He ran faster than Jesse Owens," the woman told reporters.

Sheriff's deputies at Jacumba, 75 miles east of here, could find no trace of the reported saucer or the "little man." The woman who telephoned could not be located and Jacumba residents said they had seen no saucer.

Meanwhile, at San Diego State college today a plywood "flying saucer," about three feet in diameter, was found on the campus lawn.

On one side was inscribed the printed words: "Lamba Chi Alpha" and on another: "To our earth chapter from Mars."

Tiny footprints led from the circular cockpit in the center of the "saucer," down the side and along the sidewalk until they disappeared at the highway.

## 14 IOWANS JOIN 'FLYING SAUCER CLUB'

SIOUX CITY, Ia., March 31.-(UP)-Fourteen Iowans, including five National Guardsmen and a weather observer, today joined the swelling ranks of the I've-Seen-a Flying-Saucer club.

Leo Jeske, employe of the U.S. Weather Bureau, said he saw a strange object yesterday and at first thought it merely was a weather balloon.

"Then I decided it wasn't," he

# Little man, disc again

(Continued from Page 2)

to 12,000 feet for a while, then flashed out of sight.

The National Guardsmen at the Sioux City air base said they saw a white, round "something" apparently following an airplane.

Leroy Wagner said "the disc seemed to hover about 300 feet above the plane," but air base officials were unable to contact the plane by radio to find out if the pilot saw the object.

U. S. Air Force officials repeatedly have denied any knowledge of the saucers and have reported that thorough investigations have failed to turn up any proof that they exist.

## NAVY DOUBTS PLANE MISTAKEN FOR SAUCER

WASHINGTON, March 31.-(UP)-The Navy today discounted a California report that perhaps its twin-engine Chance - Vought XF-5U fighter plane had been mistaken for a flying saucer.

The plane was nicknamed the "flying flounder" for it broad, flat appearance.

But the Navy said it bought only one of this type of aircraft and that was two years ago. The plane was not successful, the Navy said and the project was dropped.

A Naval aviation headquarters spokesman said he did not know the plane ever had been flown. H said it probably is now stored some Naval aviation hangar.

—a "blue-star planet with several moons" to be exact—and that he used to vacation on "many planets in our solar system including the ninth moon of Jupiter."

On the other hand, there are also celebrities that are allegedly *related* to aliens. As Dr. Patricia Rochelle Diegel, a specialist in past-life regression therapy, told authors Brad and Sherry Steiger, Steven Spielberg, Tom Hanks, Martin Sheen, Donald Sutherland, Sir Laurence Olivier, Alan Alda, and Robin Williams are all descendants of little green men from Mars, or Jupiter, or some other galactic universe. How or why they all ended up in Hollywood is another story.

# THE LEGEND:

Jayne Mansfield died because of a curse put on her by Anton LaVey, the high priest of the Church of Satan.

Bison Archives

Jayne Mansfield

"Jayne was never cool. As much as anyone, she represented the moral and sexual dishonesty of the 1950s. She stood for titillation rather than honest sexual expression. She was completely artificial: bleach, makeup, tight clothes, fake voice . . . (But) artifice had no place in the evolution of the decade. For the radicals, dishonesty had given us the war in Indochina, racism, and poverty."

While she may have weathered the derision of the hippie generation, Mansfield—who once claimed to have an IQ of 163—never shied away from trends, including Satanism, which enjoyed a brief stint of popularity in the ultraprogressive era of the 1960s. So when she and her boyfriend-attorney, Sam Brody, were decapitated in a horrific car crash on Highway 90 in 1967, many assumed that she had been the unfortunate victim of a black-magic curse.[10]

## A Little Background:

From her debut in 1956's *Female Jungle*, to her peak in 1957's *Will Success Spoil Rock Hunter?*, Jayne Mansfield was the ideal star for postwar America. Cute, nonthreatening, and magnificently stacked, she made no bones of her desire to "get men all stirred up." Yet despite her blatant exhibitionism, she was ultimately a traditionalist. She considered herself a dedicated Republican, and took anyone to task that disrespected her country. That didn't square so well with the progressive atmosphere of the 1960s, however. As author Martha Saxton argues in *Jayne Mansfield and the American Fifties,*

## What People Are Saying:

Anton Szandor LaVey, the self-appointed high priest of the Church of Satan, has done little to dispel the curse rumor. He describes the entire event in his authorized biography by Blanche Barton, *The Secret Life of a Satanist,* claiming that he met Mansfield at a film festival in 1966, tutored her in occult practices for several months, and ended up having a sexual affair with her. He also claims that Brody "disrespected" him every chance that he could, mishandled some of his most cherished Satanic artifacts during photo sessions at his church, and mocked him publicly with derisive jokes. And when he found out that he was seducing his bombshell girlfriend, he apparently went ballistic, forbidding her from ever seeing him again.

What happened next was right out of a B-grade Roger Corman picture: LaVey, with his shaved head and pet lion, was sitting in his church in San Francisco when he got a call from a very hysterical Mansfield late one night in 1966. According to the black priest, she was lying on the floor of her bathroom in her Bel Air mansion, bruised and beaten, and scared out of her mind. After catching her breath, she allegedly recounted all the horrors that Brody had subjected her to, including the time he supposedly drugged her and took photographs of her in bed with another man so that he could blackmail her into staying with him. "I can't stand it anymore," she cried. "Please help me get away him, Anton!" That's when LaVey claims that he went directly into his black chapel and conducted one of the most powerful and dangerous rituals known to occultists, an arcane pagan ritual summoning the deepest, darkest forces of nature. And when he finally emerged five hours later, he immediately called Mansfield and warned her to stay away from Brody. "Because," he said ominously, "he will be dead in a year."

Unfortunately, she didn't stay away from him. And the very next day, as she and Brody were speeding home from La Scala restaurant in their new sports car, they were broadsided by another car and nearly killed. A month later, Mansfield's five-year-old son, Zoltan—whose name was the same as LaVey's pet lion—was attacked by a lioness at Jungleland in Thousand Oaks and nearly mauled to death. Then came a virtual tidal wave of bad luck: They were then robbed in Japan, physically attacked in Rio de Janeiro, charged by the Venezuelan government for tax evasion, sued by Mansfield's daughter Jayne Marie for child abuse, and involved in yet another car wreck that left Brody hospitalized with a broken leg.

## The Truth:

While there's something tantalizing about the idea of a sexy starlet like Mansfield becoming the victim of black magic, the rumor is pure fiction. LaVey's daughter, Zeena, has debunked her father's claims in a number of articles, saying that she only knew of *one* instance where Mansfield visited her father's church, and even that was for publicity photos and nothing else.[11] Moreover, much of the misfortune that LaVey supposedly caused—the robberies, the accidents, etc.—occurred long *before* LaVey met Mansfield in 1966.

## The Bottom Line:

Both Mansfield and LaVey were bent on manufacturing images for themselves, and used the media to their own advantages. Mansfield in particular was nothing if not a genius at manipulating the press. There are innumerable accounts of her "accidentally" losing her bra strap at press junkets, or "accidentally" forgetting to wear underwear at public appearances. She also went to great lengths to stage fictitious fights, breakups, and reunions simply to get her name in the papers; and she even orchestrated an elaborate boating accident once just to get noticed by reporters. "Everything had to be thrilling," writes Martha Saxton. "She couldn't stand it when things began to slow down."

*What happened next was right out of a B-grade Roger Corman picture.*

# THE RUMOR:

The FBI and members of the Hollywood establishment helped set up Robert Mitchum's famous marijuana arrest in the 1940s.

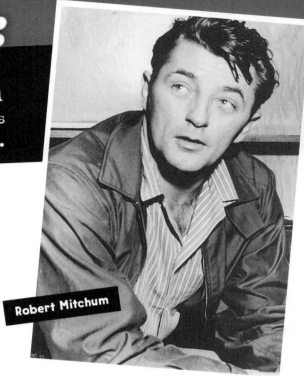

Robert Mitchum

## A Little Background:

It's not always easy to separate fact from fiction when it comes to Robert Mitchum. While he was one of the most popular actors of his generation, he was also a consummate storyteller with a knack for exaggeration. As a close friend told his biographer, George Eells, "If he tells a story and it works, the next time the story is going to get better . . . Minor details don't bother him."

He used to boast about the time that he went to visit David Selzenick in his hotel room, but couldn't wait long enough to use the bathroom. Spying an ashtray near the elevators, he decided to unzip and unleash—just as the elevator doors opened to reveal a carload of passengers. And then there was the one about his evening in the White House where he chanced upon Eleanor Roosevelt's pink nightgown and tried it on for size. "I looked pretty good if I do say so myself," he recounted. "So good that Noël Coward tried to kiss me."

Perhaps his greatest story, however—at least the one that he relished telling in mixed company the most—was the one where he and his brother found a beached shark on a Mexican shoreline one afternoon. As he liked to tell it, he felt sorry for the poor thing and thought that it looked terribly lonely—so he had sex with it. "It wasn't a serious affair," he told Jack Lemmon. "I mean, I didn't kiss it or anything."

Not surprisingly, Mitchum has been the subject of a few whoppers himself. In the 1950s for example, *Confidential* magazine claimed that he once showed up to a party in the Hollywood Hills without a stitch of clothing on. And when no one laughed, he allegedly took out a bottle of catsup, poured it on his head and said, "This is a masquerade party, isn't it? Well, I'm a hamburger!"[12] Apparently Mitchum was furious about the accusation, however, and tried to sue the paper after it wrongly suggested that he was at the party with another woman. "I might joke around," he fumed, "but I don't *fool* around."

## What Happened:

The infamous marijuana bust occurred on September 1, 1948. Apparently two LAPD cops, A. M. Barr and J. B. McKinnin, had stationed themselves outside of actress Lila Leeds's house at 8334 Ridpath Drive in Laurel Canyon. They had information that there was going to be a "reefer party" there and to their surprise "Battling Bob" Mitchum showed up with a local fringe character named Robin "Danny" Ford at around midnight. Approximately twenty minutes later, the two officers burst in the door and found Mitchum, still wearing dark sunglasses, sharing a joint with Leeds. "Yes, boys, I was smoking a marijuana cigarette," he admitted proudly. "I knew I'd get caught sooner or later."

## The Truth:

Unlike most of his peers in the 1940s, Mitchum was shockingly brazen with his marijuana use.[13] "Never before had they seen a prominent star make himself such a high-visibility risk," writes George Eells, in *Robert Mitchum*. "Strutting around as he did in a straw Stetson and cowboy boots, with a reefer tucked behind each ear or carrying a package of cigarettes in which the regular ones were alternated

Lila Leeds

> "Yes, boys, I was smoking a marijuana cigarette," he admitted proudly. "I knew I'd get caught sooner or later."

with hand-rolled joints."

Nonetheless, detectives refused to admit that they wanted to make an example of Mitchum, using his celebrity status to put a famous face on a very insidious problem. If anything, they argued, they were acting on a tip and had "no idea" who'd be at the party. Yet after the scandal died down, some reporters discovered that the LAPD had in fact targeted Leeds's house by planting bugs and informants inside. That means they knew perfectly well that the actor would be there. Still, even after that information was disclosed, the LAPD justified their actions by saying that they were only interested in breaking a major drug-dealing ring known to operate in Hollywood, a ring that the FBI had been tracking for months, and not gunning for Mitchum at all.

In any case, there is some evidence that Betty Doss, a friend of Leeds's and a guest at the party, had been "squealing" to the LAPD in the weeks preceding the event, apparently to alleviate the criminal charges against her, and she repeatedly asked Leeds to invite Mitchum over that night—so much so that Leeds thought that it was "weird." What's more, Robin Ford, the man that drove the actor to the scene, seemed to be dealing with his own problems with the LAPD, and may have been forced to deliver Mitchum in return for leniency.

## The Other Truth:

Yet according to Fred Otash, a former cop under Chief William Parker and a well-known Hollywood private detective, the bust wasn't entirely the FBI's doing. As he argues, Howard Hughes may have orchestrated the entire scenario from start to finish. After all, Hughes, the then-president of RKO Pictures and a

when Hughes allegedly contacted the FBI and helped them arrest his own star on drug charges to solidify his image as a bad boy once and for all.

## The Bottom Line:

While Otash's theory sounds plausible when one considers Hughes's legendary obsession with covert activities, most historians have dismissed the idea that he set up Mitchum's bust. George Eells, for example, points out that Hughes was sitting on three Mitchum movies at the time of the arrest—at a combined cost of over $5 million—and there was every chance that his arrest would have hurt the potential box office for each. Furthermore, Mitchum's attorney, Jerry Geisler, claims in his book, *The Jerry Geisler Story,* that Hughes was furious over his decision to throw Mitchum on the mercy of the court. In fact he pleaded with Geisler to take the case to trial so that they could "expose" the FBI's obvious "frame-up."

If the rumor has any validity at all, it may have to do with the fact that Hughes spent a lot of money to help reduce Mitchum's prison stay from two years to sixty days; and just to make sure that he was comfortable, he also kept him stocked with a continual supply of expensive wine and gourmet food. Perhaps that's why Mitchum later claimed that, "Jail is like Palm Springs without the riffraff. A great place to get in shape, only you meet a better class of people."

consummate manipulator, had a history of unethical publicity practices. In 1949, for example, he deliberately leaked word about actress Ingrid Bergman's illegitimate pregnancy with director Robert Rossellini to the press, which in turn ignited a firestorm of scandal. The reason he did it, he later confessed, was to drum up interest in what he considered an "unsellable" Bergman/Rossellini picture called *Stromboli,* a project that he produced yet despised. (He released the news days before the picture opened.) He never considered the fact that the scandal would literally destroy Bergman's career—which it did—and force her to leave the country in shame.

Otash believes that a similar scenario played itself out five years earlier, shortly after Hughes took over Mitchum's contract from David Selznick. As he argues, Hughes understood that Mitchum's appeal was his notoriety, and that's why he immediately signed the actor up for a string of tough-guy pictures. Yet Mitchum was moving in another direction at the time and supposedly threatened to walk off any set where he had to play yet another "dumb GI, cop, or criminal." That's

**"Jail is like Palm Springs without the riffraff. A great place to get in shape, only you meet a better class of people."**

# THE RUMOR:

The Mexican Mafia has put a contract on the life of actor Edward James Olmos for exposing gang secrets to Hollywood.

Olmos street graffiti in East L.A.

¡MUERTE!

Paul Young

## A Little Background:

In 1993 the attorney general filed a federal racketeering case against reputed members of the so-called Mexican Mafia, or EME, for thirty-three counts of extortion, blackmail, and wholesale murder. According to court records, the gangsters—who were known to control much of the drug trade in the California prison system—believed that Olmos betrayed the EME during the production of his 1991 Latino gang movie, *American Me*, perhaps the best movie ever made about Latino prison life.

The irony, of course, is that Olmos went to great lengths to ensure the accuracy of the production. Yet it was that same perfectionism that nearly cost him his life. Because according to some insiders, his screenplay not only disrespected the EME, but gave away a number of essential gang secrets.

## What Really Went Down:

In 1993 gang member, Ernest "Chuco" Castro agreed to turn state's evidence against the EME in exchange for his freedom. The following year Castro donned a wire and went into a meeting with some of the top lieutenants of the EME, ostensibly to talk about problems within the ranks, and turned the discussion toward the subject of Edward James Olmos. Many claimed that they felt betrayed by the actor, and were furious over the fact that he based his screenplay on Joe "Pegleg" Morgan, the original godfather of the

EME, without getting permission. That wasn't enough for Castro, however, who was obviously leading the discussion toward criminal activity to satisfy his FBI listeners; so he asked what people thought of the prison scene where Morgan gets raped by fellow inmates. Many argued that Olmos should "pay" for that since it was pure fiction, prompting one member to stand up and declare Olmos "fair game."

What happened after that has never fully been documented, but according to some sources, Olmos may have sat down with some of the leaders of the EME and worked out a deal. (Court transcripts show that he offered Morgan's wife $5,000 shortly after the film was released, yet no one has been able to prove that it was tribute money.)

## The Context:

Olmos is not the first or last actor to receive death threats by organized crime members. During the 1920s for example, Al "Scarface" Capone, the then-head of the Chicago mob, sent some goons to Hollywood to intimidate screenwriter Ben Hecht who had been hired to write a screenplay based on the godfather's life.

Fortunately Hecht, a hard-drinking, tough-talking, Chicago newspaperman, convinced Capone's hired guns that his version of the story wasn't based on Capone at all, but his rival, Deanie O'Banion. "Why youse callin' it *Scarface*, den?" sneered one of the thugs. "'Cause it'll help sell the picture," argued Hecht. "Stay here long enough and you'll find out that Hollywood is just like any other racket."

That's all they needed to hear apparently, because the thugs returned to Chicago a short time later and the movie went on to great success. In fact, according to some reports, Capone liked it so much that he sent director Howard Hawks his own submachine gun as a token of his appreciation.

A similar situation occurred approximately twenty-five years later when Desi Arnaz, Sr. of *I Love Lucy* fame produced a television show based on the book, *The Untouchables*, the hugely popular, yet highly biased account of the FBI's attack on Capone's gang in the 1920s. Mae Capone, Scarface's widow, understood the potential racist implications of the series, and pleaded with Arnaz to refrain from putting it on the air. Nonetheless, Arnaz went ahead with the production as planned, and a few days later, the new leaders of the Chicago family, Sam Giancana, Joe Batters, and Paul Ricca, decided to put a contract on his life. But according to mafioso Jimmy Fratianno, the plans were scotched two weeks later. "He never knew how close he came to getting clipped," he told Ovid Demaris in *The Last Mafioso*.

A similar scene played out with James Caan in the early 1990s. Best known for his performance in *The Godfather*, Caan claimed that he had "permission" to do a screenplay based on the life of Meyer Lansky, the legendary mafioso "mastermind." What Caan didn't realize, however, was that Martin Bacow, a former associate of Detroit's Purple Gang, and a producer in his own right, had already sold a screenplay based on Lansky's life to MCA's Eugene Giaquinto—allegedly the subject of an FBI racketeering probe. And when Giaquinto heard that Caan was himself trying to muscle in on *his* idea, he had John Gotti, the infamous New York mobster, send out a small army of wiseguys to convince him to back off. Meanwhile, Caan contacted members of the L.A. family, and some of his buddies in the Genovese family, and built up a small army of his own.

Luckily no one was hurt in the dispute—save for the thousands of HBO viewers that tried to sit through David Mamet's painfully maudlin version of *Lansky* in 1999. Hollywood has continued its fascination with mobsters. As Hank Messick's *Beauties and the Beasts: The Mob in Show Business* points out, gangsters helped move Hollywood away from aesthetics in the 1920s, toward a strategy of fast-buck productions designed to appeal to the largest common denominator—a policy that continues to this day. "As always," writes Messick, "when the gangster goes into business, art takes a second billing to the fast buck."

**Jean Seberg**

*Courtesy of Red Herring*

## Where It Comes From:

On September 8, 1979, the lovely actress Jean Seberg, star of *A Bout de Souffle*, *Saint Joan*, and *Lilith*, was found dead of an apparent overdose in Paris, France. She was alone, save for an empty bottle of barbiturates and a suicide note addressed to her son. By all accounts, it was a tragic ending to an incandescent, deeply misunderstood, star.

Two days later, Seberg's former husband, Romain Gary, shocked the world by claiming that his wife had been "destroyed by the FBI." At a press conference held in Paris a short time later, he produced a number of official documents detailing the FBI's smear campaign against his late wife, which in turn led to her suicide. In response, the FBI denied the charges but admitted that they had put her under surveillance after they discovered her association with black militant groups in Los Angeles.

## What Really Happened:

Evidently the smear campaign was the handiwork of Richard Wallace Held, the head of the FBI's COINTEL program in L.A. Held had a particular dislike for "Hollywood leftists" and went to great lengths to subvert their reputations. Jane Fonda was one of his favorite targets, as were a number of stars sympathetic to militant causes including Marlon Brando, Warren Beatty, Shirley MacLaine, Harry Belafonte, and Paul Newman.

Yet Seberg undoubtedly suffered the worst fate of all. In fact, she became Held's personal *bête noire* once she began associating with Panther leader Raymond "Masai" Hewitt and providing him with "funds, weapons, and refuge." Agent M.

Wesley Swearingen, a newcomer to the L.A. office, commented on Held's obsession with Seberg in an interoffice memo stating:

> "The giving of her white body to a black man was an unbearable thought for many of the white agents [in the L.A. bureau]. An agent (probably Held) was overheard saying a few days after I arrived from New York, 'I wonder how she'd like to gobble my dick while I shoved my .38 up that black bastard's ass?'"

In 1970, Held was informed that Seberg was pregnant with her second child. On May 27, 1970, Held asked J. Edgar Hoover permission to plant a story with some Hollywood gossip columnists suggesting that Seberg had been impregnated, not by her husband Romain Gary, but by a Black Panther. Hoover granted permission, but with the caveat that Held wait a couple of months until her pregnancy was "more visible."

On June 19, 1970, Joyce Haber of the *Los Angeles Times* printed the first mention of the FBI planted story. Not surprisingly, it spread like wildfire with subsequent stories in *Newsweek*, the *New York Times*, and the *Washington Post*.

The news devastated Seberg however, and she emphatically denied the accusations, saying, "If you just wait a while longer, you'll see for yourself!"

Two months later, on August 23, 1970, she

> *Still suffering from the indignity of the false rumors, Seberg placed her dead infant in an open casket and brought her to a press conference the following day. "Now you can see for yourself," she exclaimed. "My baby was not black!"*

gave birth prematurely to a baby girl which she named Nina. According to those closest to her, the event gave her a new lease on life. Her infant had severe troubles breathing, however, and went in and out of consciousness until finally, after all attempts to save her failed, she passed away a mere two days later.

Still suffering from the indignity of the false rumors, Seberg placed her dead infant in an open casket and brought her to a press conference the following day. "Now you can see for yourself," she exclaimed. "My baby was *not* black!"

From that day on, Seberg tried to commit suicide each and every year on the eve of Nina's death.

## A Little History:

Seberg made some startling revelations in the days shortly before she was found dead in her car. Namely that it wasn't Nina's death that drove her to make seven attempts on her life, but the failure of her career. Since the debacle of *Saint Joan* in 1956, where she was literally tortured by

director Otto Preminger and humiliated by critics, she never managed to receive the recognition that she deserved. She turned in a brilliant performance in *Lilith* in 1964 opposite Warren Beatty, yet Hollywood failed to take notice. She fared better in Europe, however, where she was praised for her work in Godard's classic, *A Bout de Souffle*. And things definitely took a turn for the better when she met Gary and became pregnant with his child. Yet even that turned sour when he began using her name to secure financing for his own ridiculously exploitive pictures, and placing her in scenes where she was either raped, institutionalized, and/or murdered.

## The Bottom Line:

The other startling revelation that Seberg made shortly before she died was that Nina's real father *was* a revolutionary with whom she had an affair. He wasn't black as the FBI claimed, however, but Mexican. According to her, she met him while shooting a movie in Durango, Mexico in 1969.

# THE RUMOR:

## Where It Comes From:

While there has been volumes written on the sometimes bizarre sex practices of Hollywood players—the free sex scene of the 1960s, the live-in sex therapists of the 1970s, the S&M dungeons of the 1980s—there has been relatively little written about Hollywood's alleged "anti-sex" practice of the 1990s. But in 1993, journalist Mary Gwynn wrote a piece for *Buzz* claiming that the practice of "semen retention" had gained considerable popularity within the movie colony. At the time, the guru of self-restraint was Drew Francis, a doctor of Chinese medicine, herbalism, and acupuncture at the Golden Cabinet in West Los Angeles. Francis apparently believed that there was a direct corollary between one's love juices and creative energy. Ejaculation, he argues, depletes a man of his essential energy, or "vital force," while semen retention makes him "smarter, more creative, and more powerful."

Francis wasn't necessarily teaching abstinence. His program still promoted sex, *lots* of sex in fact, only practitioners had to learn a host of retention techniques that would in his words, "enhance rather than frustrate." By applying just the right amount of pressure to the "Million-Dollar Point," for example, a zone located just below the scrotum, a man could apparently orgasm without ejaculating; which means that his "essence" remains intact. And according to Gwynn, a number of big-name Hollywood types subscribed to the practice, and apparently it gave them more testosterone than they knew what to do with. "I like to build up for my week," said one executive. "All that testosterone gives me an edge. It makes me nasty and more aggressive."

## The Legacy:

Not surprisingly, most of the Hollywood crowd returned to their dirty old tricks by the end of the decade. In fact, *Details* magazine questioned over 2,000 movie-industry professionals for their 1999 *Mondo Hollywood* issue, and discovered that nearly half of Tinseltown engaged in some form of S&M, prostitution, voyeurism, and multiple-partner sex. Around the same time, the always irreverent newspaper, *The New Times*, discovered a host of sex "consultants" working in Hollywood as well. There was, for instance, Irene Kassorla who taught industry insiders how to "strengthen" their vaginal muscles, how to have as many as 101 orgasms in a single night, and how to get in touch with their "magical push muscles."[14] Then there was Lou Paget, a former Fox employee, who spent much of her time teaching Hollywood players the "art of the blow job." (Over wine and cheese and dildoes, she detailed the specifics of such moves as the "Pearly Gates," the "Italian Method," "Tea Bagging," and "Ode to Bryan.")

If there's anything to glean from all of this, it's that Hollywood takes its sex *a little too seriously!*

> *"I like to build up for my week," said one executive. "All that testosterone gives me an edge. It makes me nasty and more aggressive."*

# THE RUMOR:

Barbra Streisand used to perform in pornographic movies before she became famous.

Paul Young

## Where It Comes From:

"Nose size usually doesn't figure in the popularity of an adult film," wrote the *Buffalo News* on May 9, 1993. "But recently a passel of porn connoisseurs have been freezing the frames of one crudely made videotape to determine if the skin starlet with an unusually large proboscis is a prefame Streisand."

That same movie has haunted actress-producer Barbra Streisand for most of her career, yet no one has been able to determine if she really appeared in the film or not. Author William Poundstone looked at the movie for his book, *Bigger Secrets* and claimed that it was virtually impossible to tell by simply viewing that material. There are no closeups of her face, the grain is too pronounced, and the soundtrack is dubbed. What's more, the entire affair seems suspect by the sheer audacity of its presentation. "The filmmakers clearly want you to think that it's Streisand," writes Poundstone. "The tape cuts several times between a publicity photo of Streisand and the porn footage . . . it's conceivable that someone produced the film as a hoax, hiring a Streisand look-alike and intentionally making the tape amateurish and grainy to simulate authenticity."

## The Truth:

Considering the fact that the girl in the porno is approximately eighteen-years-old, it's not very likely that it could have been Streisand. After all, Babs was twenty-seven when she did *Funny Girl* in 1968, and that means that she would have been in her mid-thirties when the alleged loop was made.

## The Context:

Streisand, who later went on to initiate the Streisand Professorship in Intimacy and Sexuality at USC, was not the first or last star to indulge in alleged pornographic activity—not by a long shot. Joan Crawford, for example, the vampish star of the 1930s and a well-known exhibitionist in her own right, allegedly appeared in a soft-core skin flick called the *Casting Couch* in 1923. Like Streisand's salacious fare, no one has ever been able to prove the validity of that performance either, since it was quite common for early sexploitation directors to use celebrity look-alikes whenever possible. (Apparently there was a young woman—a dead ringer for Crawford—working in porn at the time.)

*Streisand, who later went on to initiate the Streisand Professorship in Intimacy and Sexuality at USC, was not the first or last star to indulge in alleged pornographic activity.*

In any case, as the flesh trade picked up steam in the fifties and early sixties, so did the rumor mill. Just about every top star was alleged to have appeared in at least one stag film during their careers, including Marilyn Monroe, Hedy Lamarr, Diana Dors, Vickie Dugan, Yvonne de Carlo, Mickey Hargitay, Jayne Mansfield, Mamie Van Doren, Barbara Nichols, Marlon Brando, Sharon Tate, Dennis Hopper, and Barbara Payton.[15]

But if there was a golden age for celebrity porn it would have to be the 1970s. That's when Sylvester Stallone appeared in a cheap XXX sex romp called *Party at Kitty and Stud's*; Spalding Gray supposedly appeared in a porn flick called *Farmers' Daughters*; Chuck Conners, the star of TV's *The Rifleman*, allegedly did a gay scene; and Damu King, famous for such blacksploitation classics as the *Black Godfather*, supposedly did some black porn. And that's not counting the endless array of home movies that were made around the same time. As Ted McIlvenna of the Institute for Advanced Study of Human Sexuality remembers, "There were a lot of homemade movies being done back then—either as instructional tools or as erotic play toys. Most, I would say, were probably recorded at parties, though, where people generally felt a little less inhibited."[16]

The practice continued to grow throughout the eighties and nineties, yet most of the actors who are said to have crossed over into professional porn were B-level at best, including Dana Plato, Sonny Landham, Stephen Geoffreys, Jack Baker, Simon Rex, Angelique Pettyjohn, and Edie Williams. Even executives working behind the scenes felt compelled to get in on the action including Craig Baumgarten, an executive producer at Columbia, and Neil Bogart, the CEO of Casablanca.[17]

## The Bottom Line:

No one has ever been able to determine *exactly* how many stars have gone all the way on camera. The only person on record that has actually made an attempt to come up with a verifiable number was the late Jack Spund, a popular sex therapist in L.A. and a professor at UCLA. In the 1970s, Spund made celebrity skin his passion, and through his insider contacts, put together a reel consisting of every celebrity porn scene ever made. In the early 1980s he claimed that he had 200 "big name" movie stars doing the nasty in a variety of situations. Yet no one has been able to fully verify his findings to date.

# THE LEGEND:

Actress Thelma Todd was murdered by hit men working for gangster Lucky Luciano because she wouldn't help him set up a secret casino in her popular café.

## A Little Background:

On Monday afternoon, December 16, 1935, the sheriff's department got a call from the proprietors of Thelma Todd's Roadside Café on Pacific Coast Highway near Santa Monica, claiming that someone had just found Thelma Todd, the comely thirty-year-old star of such comedy classics as *Horse Feathers* and *Monkey Business*, slumped over the wheel of her car, dead. When officers arrived, they found the car, a new convertible Lincoln Phaeton, parked inside of a garage near the back of the property with the door closed. Todd was still wearing the dress that

Delmar Watson Photography

she had worn the previous Saturday night: a sexy silver evening gown, mink coat, and $20,000 worth of jewels, and there were no visible marks, cuts, or injuries to her body—at least none that were reported. The cause of death, it was later determined, was due to carbon monoxide poisoning which led detectives to the conclusion that she had locked herself in the garage with the engine running on purpose. "It was a clear case of suicide," said one of the investigators. "There's no mystery here."

## Where It Comes From:

Journalists, reporters, and armchair detectives have been trying to solve Thelma Todd's murder for the better part of the last century, partly because the LAPD's ruling failed to answer some vexing inconsistencies. After all, if Todd killed herself by inhaling car fumes, then why did she have two cracked ribs and bruises around her neck? Why were her shoes perfectly clean after drunkenly navigating the 270 steps from the apartment to the garage? And what about the numerous death threats that she received in the weeks preceding her death?

More importantly, why were there so many eyewitness accounts of Todd driving around Hollywood on Sunday—the day *after* she allegedly died—with a "dark stranger" in the passenger seat? As one of her friends testified under oath, she spoke with the actress at around four P.M. and invited her to a party later that night. "But she couldn't make it," she recounted, "because she was with someone that had other plans."

According to Andy Edmonds's *Hot Toddy: The True Story of Hollywood's Most Shocking Crime*, the "dark-looking" man was none other than Charlie "Lucky" Luciano, the legendary head of the New York crime family. (They had met years earlier through Todd's former husband, Pat DiCicco.) According to Edmonds, Luciano was interested in establishing a stranglehold on extortion, vice, and drug trafficking in Los Angeles, and he saw Todd's new restaurant as a premier place to open a gambling operation. Todd, however, was against the idea, and refused to have anything to do with the gangster. Nonetheless, Luciano kept after her, pressuring her to change her mind, until finally, after receiving too many threats, she went to the police. The following day, someone called Luciano, someone possibly inside the LAPD, and informed him that Todd was "ratting him out."

Edmonds interviewed a friend of Luciano's in 1980 who claimed that the gangster brought Todd over to his house Sunday night for a leisurely visit. Little did the actress know, however, that Luciano had arranged for a Mafia thug—apparently a member of Detroit's Purple Gang—to get into position outside of her apartment at the same time. Hours later, as the clock approached three A.M., he drove her home and said good-bye for the very last time. What happened next has never been documented, but Edmonds believes that the killer knocked her unconscious as she walked toward her door, carried her to the garage, placed her in her car, started the engine, shut the door, and waited for her to die.

## What Probably Happened:

While many Angelenos would like to believe that Thelma Todd was murdered by one of the most ruthless Mafia leaders in history, the theory still remains frustratingly inconclusive. Marvin Wolf and Katherine Mader on the other hand, have come up with a theory that seems to be slightly more plausible. As they suggest in their book, *Fallen Angels*, there's a good chance that Roland West may have had something to do with it. West was the director of such twisted classics as *The Bat Whispers*, and was a brilliant, if not darkly beguiling, character who caught Todd's eye one afternoon on a cruise ship to Catalina. Apparently they hit it off, and together they hatched a number of ideas, not the least of which was the roadhouse

café on Pacific Coast Highway. Problems began to surface almost immediately, however, as West did little to hide his burning infatuation for the star. That in turn led to a strained relationship between the two, since Todd had no intention of getting romantically involved with him. Still, the restaurant became a resounding success, despite West's aggressive, almost pathological control over her. In fact, witnesses testified that he "screamed at her" on Saturday night—the last night that she was seen alive—because she wanted to go to a party at the Trocadero in Hollywood. "It's the busiest night of the year!" he shrieked. "You can't leave now."

Apparently she did leave, and as she did, West who shared an adjoining apartment with her above the restaurant, ran after her screaming, "Fine! Go ahead and go! But if you're not home by two, you'll be locked out."

According to Wolf and Mader, West eventually confessed to killing Todd, but it was, according to him, more accidental than homicidal. As he later told a reporter in the 1980s, shortly before he passed away, he simply hated the fact that Todd disrespected him the way she did. So when she sauntered in around 3:30 in the morning, well past her curfew, he immediately assumed that she did it just to spite him. That led to a bitter fight until Todd, who had about all she could take from him, grabbed her coat and her car keys, and walked out the door.

That made West even angrier, and at least one neighbor later testified that he heard him screaming at her out back, apparently as they

## "It's the busiest night of the year!" he shrieked. "You can't leave now."

walked toward the garage. According to West, he never intended to kill her however, he just wanted to stop her from going anywhere. So when she climbed into her car and started the engine, he simply slammed the garage door and locked her in. He didn't realize, however, just how fast the fumes would fill her lungs.

It's a plausible theory, and perhaps makes the most sense, and yet West may be even more culpable than he ever admitted to. After all, there were enough marks around her neck to suggest that she was strangled before she got into her car, and some have even speculated that he forced her to perform oral sex on him—which may explain the bruises found *inside* her throat.

# THE RUMOR:

John Travolta is gay.

## What People Are Saying:

"John Travolta," wrote film critic Pauline Kael in 1983, "is in danger of turning into a laughing-stock if he doesn't put some clothes on and stop posing for magazine covers as though it were Hiawatha Night at the OK Corral." Kael was responding to the flood of media surrounding the film *Staying Alive,* which, despite its success at the box office, received unanimous opprobrium by movie critics everywhere. Kael was also referring to the shots of Travolta in a 1983 issue of *Rolling Stone* where he appeared nude while denying his alleged homosexuality. "They say that about everybody," he explained. "That's a notorious rumor. They say that about me, Marlon Brando, every male, especially the first year that you become a star."

Unfortunately for Travolta they didn't stop saying it about him. While gossip columns buzzed over his affairs with the likes of Diana Hyland, Olivia Newton-John, Marilu Henner, and Debra Winger, there were also stories of alleged homosexual flings, romances, and affairs. In fact, *Time* magazine, which is hardly known for its gossip pages, may have added fuel to the fire when it suggested that members of the Church of Scientology were the only ones that knew the "true nature" of his homosexuality. As

the piece stated, "High-level officials [in the church] claim that Travolta has long feared that if he defected from Scientology details of his sexual life would be made public . . . [As a former director for Scientology stated] 'There were no outright threats made but it was implicit: If you leave, they immediately start digging up everything.' "

Travolta never denied that the church "knew something" about his sexuality, but he has been quite vociferous against those attacking his religion. As he told *Los Angeles* magazine a short time later, "I've seen many media reports on Scientology, and they've never gotten it right. It stands for integrity and honesty. And all the Scientologists that I know are living fulfilling lives—without drugs or other vices."

## The Evidence:

In 1990 the *National Enquirer* dropped a bomb when they uncovered a secret tryst between Travolta and a nude model/porn star named Paul Barresi. In a sensational story, Barresi claimed that Travolta approached him while working out in a L.A. health club and asked if he could "get to know him better." The affair supposedly lasted for two years, (1983 to 1985), and it included dates at private hotels, long phone-sex sessions, and quickie trysts in the middle of the night. "He wanted to know how much I made for starring in porno movies," said the Sicilian-born Barresi. "I told him four hundred dollars a day. He said, 'Then that's what I'll pay you to be with me.' "

According to Nigel Andrews, author of *Travolta: The Life,* Travolta never took any legal action against Barresi.[18] He merely denied the story in the press and announced his plans to marry Kelly Preston—who was two months pregnant with his child at the time. Meanwhile, his fans suggested that the entire Barresi affair was little more than "character research" for his upcoming role in *Eyes of an Angel* where he played a man on the run from mobsters. And by the end of the decade it became obvious that his love for Preston was genuine. His career soared to new heights with *Pulp Fiction* and he seemed to be happier than ever . . . Then that pesky rumored surfaced again.

In 1998 an issue of *The Cult Observer* reported that a Beverly Hills artist named Michael Pattinson mounted a multimillon dollar lawsuit against the Church of Scientology and John Travolta claiming that when he joined the church twenty-five years earlier, it was because church officials promised that they were going to "cure" him of his homosexuality. According to Pattinson, they used Travolta as "proof" that they could do it. Yet after $500,000 and twenty-five years of Scientology, Pattinson still had an urge for sexual congress with men.

Travolta refused to comment on the case, however. Yet he remains happily married and resolute in his defense of the church. "Scientology is only fifty years old," he stated. "I'm sure Christianity had some problems, too, in its first fifty years."

Everybody loves John

Paul Young

## What It All Means:

Whether Travolta is gay or not is less important than the fact that people seem to believe that he's hiding his true sexuality. After all, the image of homosexuality—at least in the symbolic and/or psychological sense—may represent a manifestation of the arrested ego and the overt domination of the male or female subconscious. It is generally known, for example, that children forced to live in terror of a parent of the opposite sex, may react by shutting his or her ego development down and allowing the converse side of his or her subconscious to take over. (If the mother is the source of the terror for example, a son may react by embracing the anima side of his subconscious.) That in turn may lead to a widespread fascination with tales of homosexuality—even within straight fans.

# TRAVOLTA

# STAR GAMES

It is often said that jokes, disguises, and slips of the tongue reveal certain aspects of the personality that lie in the subconscious. And if that's true, then movie stars may be showing more of themselves than they realize when they assume aliases at restaurants, hotels, and airports. Consider the following:

★ Fatty Arbuckle used Will B. Good.
★ Richard Belzer signs in as Don Corleone.
★ Marlon Brando often checked in as Lord Greystroke.
★ George Burns preferred Willie Delight or Buddy Links.
★ Cher has been known to use Bonnie Jo Mason.
★ Kevin Costner will answer to Tom Feral.
★ Wes Craven occasionally goes by Abe Snake.
★ Johnny Depp likes Santa Del Vecchio, Oprah Noodlemantra, Mr. Stench, and Mr. Donkey Penis.
★ Shannen Doherty prefers Doobie Love.
★ W. C. Fields had a virtual library of aliases including John Barleycorn, Figley E. Whitesides, Elmer Mergatroid-Haines, Aristotle Hoop, Sneed Hearn, Senior Guillermo McKinley, Mahatma Kane Jeeves, and Otis Criblecoblis.
★ Greta Garbo pretended to be Miss Brown.
★ Melanie Griffith gets a kick out of being Miss Hoover.
★ Jean Harlow went by Mrs. Webb.
★ W. R. Hearst sometimes went by Mr. Miami or Carl Fischer.
★ Virginia Hill went by Norma Hall, Onie D'Algy, and Virginia Gonzales.
★ Elizabeth Hurley loves Rebecca de Winter.
★ Elton John occasionally goes by Sir Horace Pussy, Sir Tarquin Bugerigan, Bobo Latrine, or Blinky Poodle Clip.
★ Madonna pretends to be Sugar Kane.
★ Courtney Love occasionally checks in as Neely O'Hara.
★ David Lynch goes by Judas Booth.
★ River Phoenix was fond of Earl Grey.
★ Frank Sinatra went by Robert Blakeley.
★ Ed Wood occasionally used Akdo V. Telmig. (Read it backward.)

Paul Young

# HUNG JURY

"There isn't another place in the world that seems to care more about the size of a man's cock than Hollywood," wrote columnist James Bacon in *Hollywood Is a Four Letter Town*. "People in Hollywood love to gossip about who's the biggest, the longest, or the hardest."

Actor Forrest Tucker (TV's *F-Troop*) and comedian Milton Berle (*The Milton Berle Show*) were known as the twin pillars of wonderment in Hollywood's golden age, and as such, received the greatest respect from their peers. They also found themselves the subject of some clever—if not perverse—ploys to reveal themselves. There was a regular occurrence at the Lakeside Golf Course in the early 1960s, for example, where Tucker was known to play golf on a weekly basis. According to Bacon, the actor would conclude his day with a cocktail in the bar and a rubdown in the club's spa. And after succumbing to the soothing music and gentle kneading, he'd inevitably fall asleep on the table—and that's when the fun began. Because once he was out, a signal would be given, and the club's patrons would line up at the door hoping to get a chance to peek under Tucker's towel. "There were a lot of oohs and ahhs," writes Bacon. "And Forrest never had any idea what was going on."

## In any case, the following are said to have the *loins of legend*:

THE ACTORS

★ Marcus Allen*
★ Scott Bakula
★ Billy Baldwin
★ Ed Begley Jr.
★ Milton Berle*
★ Humphrey Bogart*
★ David Carradine
★ Jim Carrey
★ Dick Cavett
★ Wilt Chamberlain*
★ Charlie Chaplin
★ Gary Cooper
★ Kevin Costner
★ Willem Dafoe
★ Gerard Depardieu
★ David Duchovny

★ Errol Flynn
★ Jeff Goldblum
★ Arsenio Hall
★ Woody Harrelson
★ Don Johnson
★ Tommy Lee Jones
★ Eric Lutes
★ Michael Madsen
★ Chico Marx*
★ Roddy McDowall
★ Harry Morgan
★ Eddie Murphy
★ Jim Nabors
★ Liam Neeson*
★ Jason Patric
★ Sean Penn

★ Anthony Perkins
★ Aldo Ray
★ Christopher Reeve
★ Dennis Rodman
★ John Schneider
★ Frank Sinatra
★ Jimmy Smits
★ John Stamos
★ Patrick Stewart
★ Donald Sutherland
★ David Thewlis
★ Forrest Tucker*
★ Carl Weathers
★ Freddy "OK Freddy" Wolfman*
★ James Woods

*Biggest of the big

THE SEC
LIFE OF

# 'RET PLACES

California is
a hard state
to lie about;
no matter what
you tell, it
might be true.

— WILL ROGERS

## THE LEGENDS AND LORE OF L.A. LANDMARKS

# THE RUMOR:

Angelenos have a one-in-three chance of moving into an apartment or house formerly occupied by a `celebrity`.

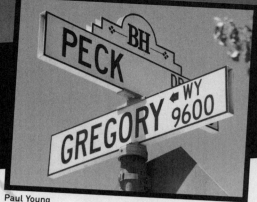

Paul Young

## What People Are Saying:

As any realtor will tell you, the best-selling houses in L.A. are, without a doubt, those formerly owned by movie stars—at least big movie stars. "That fact that a James Dean or Marilyn Monroe lived in a house definitely adds cachet," explains one celebrity-house dealer. "It has nothing to do with real value, or the actual appraisal of the house. But it definitely makes it more desirable."

On the other hand, there are also thousands of living quarters scattered all over Los Angeles that may have an equal, albeit lesser known, celebrity value as well. These are the apartments, guest houses, and garages that provided shelter for stars in their leaner years. Yet since few of those have ever been documented, it's impossible to really know just how many of those there are. As a result, when you consider the sheer volume of actors, writers, producers, photographers, singers, musicians, models, personalities, criminals, etc., that have lived in the city over the last hundred years, it seems plausible that there's a pretty good chance of moving into a home formerly occupied by a star. In fact, many seem to believe that it's as high as one in three.

## The Truth:

Unfortunately, no one has ever attempted to map the migratory patterns of the rich and famous. Realtors have celebrity home listings, but they're hardly comprehensive or historical. Besides, the definition of a "star" is so ambiguous that it would be virtually impossible to do with any precision. Is that guy that played the desk sergeant on *Barney Miller* a star? How about the guy that recorded "How High the Moon"? Or how about the kid that gets a birthday cake in *The Happy Hooker Goes to Hollywood*? It's impossible to say. Nonetheless, it is possible to look at directories such as *The International Motion Picture Almanac's* "Who's Who" listings and *Christensen's Ultimate Celebrity Address Directory* for a clue. Because if you add all the names listed from 1920–1997, subtract all nonresidents, and "noncelebrities," and figure in a career factor of twenty years to eliminate overlap, you get a grand total of 63,575 names. That's all the stars that have lived in L.A. from the silent era to today, including well-known directors, producers, writers, and musicians.

Figuring the number of residences is a little easier. Adding all the addresses in the celebrity-heavy cities of West Hollywood, Beverly Hills, Santa Monica, and Malibu to the number of residences in Los Angeles amounts to 1,597,000 homes and apartments. That means that your chances of moving into a home formerly occupied by a star are one in twenty-five.

But one should also consider that stars, like most people, move around fairly often, especially in the early stages of their careers. Raymond Chandler, for example, supposedly lived in as many as sixty different apartments in L.A. alone. Taking a slightly more realistic figure of, say, seven moves and factoring that into the equation, one gets, believe it or not, a ratio of *one in three*!

Yet it should also be noted that famous people often buy houses formerly owned by *other* stars. So if you divide the number of houses by half to compensate, you end up with a figure of one in six. But who's counting?

# THE LEGEND:

After Louise Aileen Barnsdall, the legendary oil heiress best known for Barnsdall Park, passed away in her home, her dogs were forced to sustain themselves on her corpse for several days.

**Louise Aileen Barnsdall**

Photo Collection/Los Angeles Public Library

## Where It Comes From:

Aileen Barnsdall passed away in her home at the top of Olive Hill on December 18, 1946. As the *Hollywood Citizen News* reported: "An autopsy held today on Miss Barnsdall disclosed that her death was due to coronary thrombosis. She is believed to have been in her sixties. The autopsy was ordered because no one apparently was present when she died, save for her numerous dogs." Somehow that line—the one about her numerous dogs—eventually led to the ugly rumor of her becoming puppy chow. And that's unfortunate, because she was undoubtedly one of L.A.'s most extraordinary cultural leaders, a true maverick who could have made L.A. a better place to live if she had her way. On the other hand, the rumor is also symbolic of Barnsdall's forty-year fight with the hounds of L.A. government, a fight that she ultimately lost.

## A Little History:

As the daughter of a wealthy industrialist, Barnsdall was sensitive to issues of inequality, and found herself in revolt against the Victorian mores of the day. But after meeting the Russian anarchist Emma Goldman at Chicago's Fine Arts Building in 1914, she began to understand the influence of art upon the masses and dedicated her life to bringing artistic expression to the mainstream.

While she could have opened a theater anywhere in the world, she chose Los Angeles , only because it was, in her words, "the city of the future." A short time later, in 1916, she opened a small theater at Ninth and Figuroa downtown, where she put on a number of experimental and avant-garde productions. Around the same time, Barnsdall secured a thirty-six-acre plot called Olive Hill at Vermont and Prospect Avenue (now Hollywood Boulevard), and began building her dream: an enormous theater-arts complex with state-of-the-art theaters, lecture halls, dance facilities, art galleries, a children's center, dorm rooms, and much more.

Frank Lloyd Wright, whom she had a brief affair with earlier, provided the initial designs for the project, but lost interest early on, preferring to spend his time designing other, "more important," projects instead. Nonetheless, he still managed to produce what is now considered one of L.A.'s great architectural achievements although when Barnsdall finally moved into the main residential unit years later, she found it so unlivable that she was forced to move out and buy a house elsewhere.

Finally, after years of bickering with Wright, her contractors, and the city itself, she decided to donate the grounds to the public and let the city transform the main house into a public library. But after weighing costs and property values, civic leaders passed on the offer, saying that they "couldn't afford it." Ten years later, after Rudolf Schindler and John Lautner completed construction on two guest units, she offered the buildings once again, only this time with rights to the entire hill. Again the city declined at first, until finally, after months of negotiations, they declared it a public park in 1927.

Unfortunately, that was only the beginning of Barnsdall's problems. Not long after the contracts were signed, a clever attorney found a loophole in the agreement which basically rendered it null and void. As a result, the city refused to put any money into the facility whatsoever, and the buildings fell into disrepair. (In fact, the city even had plans to have them demolished.) Frustrated, Barnsdall sued the city in 1932 seeking the return of the property, which in turn led to what has become known as the "Battle of Barnsdall."

## What Happened:

The first incident involving Barnsdall's dogs occurred in March 1945. By then she had moved back onto the property and transformed Residence B into her home. In 1945, shortly before the close of World War II, she erected some fences to protect children—and her dogs—from running into the street. Members of the City Parks and Recreation Department considered the fences a hazard, however, and immediately ordered her to take them down. She refused, naturally, until March 7, 1945, when a

squad of police officers arrived to take them down themselves. And that's when they saw her twenty-two cocker spaniels running around the property without supervision. Consequently, Barnsdall was arrested for failing to have her dogs on a leash.

Meanwhile, as her fight with the city became more pronounced, her iconoclasm became even more audacious. As soon as she moved back into Residence B, she erected a number of billboards along the edge of the property that promoted everything from the release of alleged communists like Tom Mooney to advertisements for ultra-left-wing books such as Emery Reves's *Anatomy of Peace*. Needless to say, that made her even less popular in civic circles, and the subject of increased FBI scrutiny.

Nonetheless, despite the hardships, Barnsdall never gave up on her dream. As she told a reporter, "No country can be great until the least of its citizens has been touched by beauty, truth and freedom. Unless all three radiate from this hill, it is as nothing."

# "That made her even less popular in civic circles, and the subject of increased FBI scrutiny."

# THE LEGEND:

Barney's Beanery on Santa Monica Boulevard in West Hollywood used to display a sign that read FAGGOTS STAY OUT.

## The Truth:

It's true. Barney's—the popular eatery renowned for its rustic interior, pool tables, and extensive beer menu—really did have a sign that read FAGGOTS STAY OUT. It was painted in block letters on a 4 x 21-inch piece of wood and placed directly at eye level over the bar.[1] It wasn't very popular with the local community, however. After all, Barney's is situated in the heart of the most heavily populated gay community in Los Angeles: West Hollywood. Yet despite numerous complaints, Barney Anthony, the original owner, refused to take it down. "It's just a funny sign, that's all," he told a reporter. "It doesn't really mean anything. It's just a sign. Look around, there are signs all over. I collect old signs. But that doesn't mean that I'm going to kick someone out because they're a homosexual. Besides, how can you tell who's a homosexual anyway? You tell me."

## A Little History:

The irony, of course, is that Anthony has always been more inclusive than most of his peers. During the 1920s, for example, when it was common for restaurants, hotels, and bars to display signs that read NO DOGS OR ACTORS ALLOWED, Barney's made it a policy to embrace members of the "creative community." And during the 1930s, forties, and fifties, when segregation was

Edward Kienholz, "Barney's Beanery," 1965. Courtesy of L.A. Louver Gallery, Venice, California

Edward Kienholz's Barney's Beanery, 1965

still enforced in Hollywood, Barney's was also one of the few venues in the area to allow African-Americans in to dine.

That may have changed in the early sixties, however. According to some sources, there were so many homosexual customers patronizing his restaurant, that they were, according to Anthony, "scaring away" some of his regulars. But according to Morris Knight, a gay activist who commented on the controversy in a 1985 issue of the *Los Angeles Times*, it wasn't Anthony who decided to curb the homosexual patronage, but the State Alcoholic Beverage Commission. Apparently, "They pressured him to keep the gay clientele to a minimum."

In any case, the sign caused such a furor that it led to a small-scale war. Regulars argued that the sign was so famous that it brought tourists from all over the world.[2] Others argued that the sign was originally from England where a "fag" is a common term for a cigarette. And others still argued that it should be kept for no other reason than its historical value. But when militant gays

began commandeering tables to nurse a single cup of coffee for hours on end, the situation turned ugly in short order. Skirmishes and shouting matches became commonplace, and some gay activists tried to initiate a full-scale boycott of the restaurant.

## The Legacy:

The battle eventually died down in the late 1970s as more openly gay venues opened their doors nearby. Still, the sign remained controversial throughout the early 1980s, at least until November 29, 1984, when the newly incorporated city of West Hollywood passed an ordinance banning discrimination against homosexuals. That meant that Irwin Held, the new owner, could have been liable for penalties worth $500 a day if he kept the sign up. Needless to say, he took it down a short time later.

# THE RUMOR:

There is a nuclear waste dump buried under the Barrington Recreational Center in Brentwood.

Paul Young

## What People Are Saying:

The first to do any kind of investigation into this rumor was Dan Hirsch, head of an antinuclear coalition called the Committee to Bridge the Gap. In the late 1970s, while teaching at UCLA, he heard through one of his students that VA doctors were dumping nuclear waste at the Veteran's Administration, located between Wil-

shire and Sunset in West L.A., and had been doing so for decades. "I didn't believe it at first," explains Hirsch. "But then one of my students went over to the VA and sat down with the person who was, at that point, the radiation safety officer and asked if it was true. The officer reluctantly admitted that they had been disposing of

What's buried below?

Paul Young

radioactive waste on the north side of Barrington Avenue, for a long time, possibly more than twenty years."

## The Story:

Coincidentally, there was another group that had its eyes on the VA's land, and that was a group of homeowners who wanted to build a public soccer/baseball field for their kids. Few were aware of the so-called "waste dump rumor," and those that were considered it an urban legend at best. So with the help of councilman Marvin Braude, they worked to get the area rezoned for public use, an act that required months of intensive lobbying, letter writing, and meetings.

Meanwhile, Hirsch and his students uncovered a partial log from the VA that proved unequivocally that radioactive waste—either from UCLA's radiation therapy program, nuclear reactor, or "secret" human radiation experiments—had been buried in the area, often in little more than plastic garbage bags. "The main concern here is that the radiation could have gotten into the soil, which in turn would have been absorbed into the vegetation," says Hirsch. "Remember, this is stuff that sticks around for hundreds of years."

> "Remember, this is stuff that sticks around for hundreds of years."

Finally, just as Councilman Braude succeeded in getting a green light for public use of the property, Hirsch and his students made their findings public. The reaction, however, was less than they expected. "If you've ever read Ibsen's play, *An Enemy of the People,* you'll understand what happened," recalls Hirsch. "Suddenly they were furious that we brought this to light. We were the enemy of progress. Here were all these people getting up before the committee and saying that they had worked for years on this park and that their kids absolutely *had* to have this soccer field. And they could care less about our findings."

What followed was a series of curious coincidences. The Nuclear Regulatory Commission, arguably the most biased regulatory agency in the federal government, agreed to do an investigation of the area. But rather than take soil samples, a procedure that would certainly have been more conclusive, they simply waltzed through with a Geiger counter. The following day, they announced their findings, which not surprisingly claimed that there was no hazard to speak of.

Meanwhile, Hirsch learned that infrared film would reveal "hot spots" in the vegetation, and possibly suggest how dangerous the park really was. But he needed a helicopter to get the proper angle. So after weeks of pleading his case to Councilman Braude, the LAPD finally agreed to take him up with a photographer. But when he showed up at the prearranged time, he was greeted with a shocking sight. "When I got there I suddenly realized that there was a tractor plowing the field," explains Hirsch. "Someone was tearing up all the vegetation—and you need vegetation to make an infrared photograph. I was told later that it was merely a coincidence, that the fire department had planned to plow the area for fire control for some time. And who knows, maybe it was a coincidence, I don't know. They're known to do that once in a while. But in any case, it scared the hell out of me because it made me realize that maybe it *wasn't* a coincidence."

## The Legacy:

To this day a portion of the park remains open to the public. But is it dangerous? "I don't know," admits Hirsch. "And I'm not alleging that it is. We were never allowed to do the proper testing to determine that. What we do know is this: that radioactive material was buried there, the VA failed to let people know about it, and the park was built without any adequate testing. That's all."

Braude, on the other hand, believes that the amount of waste buried was hardly anything to be concerned about. "My understanding was that there may have been some contaminated items buried there, syringes, whatever," he admits. "But the contamination was very, very minor. The VA was very conscientious in its investigation in the matter and the results were negligible. These people that were making these claims were very inexperienced [in these matters], and were doing it just to make some big announcement of some kind. But no one took it very seriously."

# THE RUMOR:

Asian gangs control the famous Bel Gardens casino, the Bicycle Club.

## A Little History:

Few areas of urban life incite quite as many rumors, superstitions, and tall tales as a gambling casino. As any inveterate gambler will tell you, the gods of chance may be seduced in innumerable ways, from picking cards that flow in the direction of the bathtub, to tying a bat's heart to one's sleeve. But when Benjamin Barry Kramer took a chance on the Bicycle Club in Bel Gardens, the largest card club in Southern California, his luck definitely took a turn for the worse.

Before he came to L.A., Kramer was one of the most successful speedboat racers in the country. But in 1990, shortly after investing $12 million in the club and taking a controlling interest, the U.S. Justice Department discovered that his investment had come from illegal drug sales. Days later, the FBI stormed the offices of the Bicycle Club and seized control of the venue under asset forfeiture laws. That in turn led to a complete overhaul of the club's staff, its operations, and its income—which was reportedly $10 million annually.

Paul Young

That should have been the end of any rumors about the club having ties to organized crime. Yet it wasn't. In fact it was only the beginning. In 1996, Attorney General Dan Lungren alleged that a number of employees were "knowingly allowing scams, kickbacks, loan sharking, illegal games, and cheating" at the club, often in collusion with alleged gangsters.

## What People Are Saying:

Lungren was referring to Hollman Cheung, who was hired to run the Asian game room two years earlier. In 1996 one of Cheung's associates, Tony Wang, was arrested for threatening to kill a gambler who had borrowed some money from Cheung months earlier. During his testimony, Wang alleged that Cheung—who reportedly made $6 million per year—had extensive ties to Asian gang members, especially the notorious Wah Ching family, and that he hired him on occasion as his collection agency.

In any case, none of it fared well for the feds. So in 1996, after much hemming and hawing, they finally washed their hands of the entire affair and sold their controlling interest in the club for $25.3 million to Ladbrokes International, a British company that had betting parlors, racetracks, and hotels around the world.

## The Legacy:

The incident at the Bicycle Club was hardly unusual for Southern California. After all, Asian gangs have been infiltrating and controlling nightclub and gambling operations throughout Los Angeles for the better part of the last 150 years. In 1994, for example, the *Los Angeles Times* reported that law enforcement agencies were predicting that Asian organized crime was going to be "the single biggest concern for law enforcement in the future."

Such hysteria undoubtedly set the stage for the Bicycle Club's alleged ties to Asian mobsters, however apocryphal. "This is a classy place," says a representative of the club. "There's nothing like that going on here at all. I don't see why you can't just say that this is the best club of its kind instead of trying to spread rumors."

*"I don't see why you can't just say that this is the best club of its kind instead of trying to spread rumors."*

Coincidentally, when a group of investors announced plans to expand a small bridge and rummy operation on La Brea Avenue to include Pan and Pai Gow under Proposition D in June 1993, fears of Asian gang infestation surfaced once again. And within a few days, there was a flyer being posted at every business along La Brea featuring the image of a gun-toting Asian gangster and the question, "How will West Hollywood control Asian gang members?" Not surprisingly, many denounced the flyers as being racist and sensational. Yet they were effective enough to keep Proposition D from being passed. That, of course, made the staff at the Bicycle Club very happy. After all, *they* were allegedly the sponsors of the flyer in the first place!

# THE LEGEND:

Caioti restaurant has a special salad that can help induce labor in pregnant women.

It's the cheese

Paul Young

## The Context:

There's something about pregnancy that brings out the superstitious in women. Even the most practical sort will find themselves refraining from stepping on cracks or avoiding graveyards. Others still may brush their newborn with a rabbit's foot as soon as it's born, or carry it to the top of the building to ensure success and happiness.

## The Story:

Ed Ladou found himself besieged by superstitious women in the mid-1990s, shortly after a rumor started going around concerning his restaurant, Caioti, a quaint little Italian place on Laurel Canyon. Apparently the rumor started in 1992 after two women—who had been overdue by weeks—discovered that they had both eaten at Caioti the day before they went into labor.

What's more, they both had the *exact* same romaine and watercress salad.

Ladou's business picked up significantly after that, although he was a little uncomfortable with the fact that most of his new clients were too big to fit in their chairs. Nonetheless, testimonials continued to pour in, and by the end of the year it was said that ten women had successfully given birth shortly after eating Ladou's salad—sometimes within hours.

## ...most of his new clients were too big to fit in their chairs...

## The Truth:

Apparently there is evidence that balsamic vinegar can produce contractions of the uterus, but according to a number of obstetricians, there was *nothing* in Caioti's salad that couldn't be found at the local supermarket. Save for the power of suggestion. The rumor, meanwhile, provides an excellent model for examining the social psychology of pipe dreams, or wishes, as defined by Robert Knapp and Gordon Allport of the Boston Rumor Clinic. "The pipe dream is just one type of rumor," they write, "which tends to be rooted in a deep-seated need to decrease anxiety over an ambiguous situation."

# THE LEGEND:

Earl Carroll's infamous signature plates were stolen and destroyed by a rival promoter.

## A Little History:

Everything that Earl Carroll did was larger than life. As a promoter in the 1920s, he was famous for producing Broadway shows that rivaled only Florenz Ziegfeld in sheer audacity and sensationalism. And when he grew tired of that, he then turned his sights on Hollywood, with equal, if not greater bravado. But after a few failed attempts at producing a series of cinematic musicals featuring his "World Famous Carroll Girls," he purchased a plot of land at 6230 Sunset Boulevard and promised to build "the most spectacular theater that Hollywood had ever seen." And in many respects, he did. As some critics suggested, it was the "most modern theater in America," featuring double revolving stages, a floating stage for montage effects, and an auditorium large enough for 1,000 sit-down guests.

Carroll naturally carried on his tradition for outlandish shows. With an endless parade of comedians, vaudeville skits, and elaborate dance routines, he anticipated the type of show that would later define Las Vegas. He rarely, if ever, had celebrity entertainers, however. As columnist Hedda Hopper once remarked, "Carroll didn't need celebrities in his shows—he had his girls. They were the real stars of his theater."

Girls were also Carroll's passion off stage. In fact, some claim that he was the father of the casting couch. As Ken Murray writes in *The Body Merchant*, "It was more than just rumor that he liked to sit in the front row of his theater and watch an endless supply of naked hopefuls parading past him on the fully lighted stage."

Lost forever? Earl Carroll's masterpiece

Bison Archives

## What Happened:

In 1938, shortly after the theater was completed, Carroll decided to capitalize on the number of celebrities passing through his door by having each sign a piece of paper as they left. That in turn was transferred to a 2 x 2½–foot block of cement which was later hung outside the building by the main entrance. Less than three years later, his wall of fame, which had over a hundred names, became one of L.A.'s great pop architectural gems, the first stop on every tourist's itinerary, and a popular backdrop for premieres and events.

Unfortunately, Carroll's career came to a sudden and tragic end in 1948 when his plane crashed on the way to New York for a publicity tour. And without Carroll, the club failed miserably, at least until some promoters bought it in the 1950s and had a modicum of success with the Moulin Rouge, a similar Vegas-style revue. After that it changed hands nearly a dozen times, becoming the temporary home of the TV studio for *Queen for a Day*, the rock and roll club Hullabaloo, and the sixties theater spectacular, *Hair*. (Today it's the home of Nickelodeon Television network.)

Apparently the famous signatures remained intact throughout its many facelifts, but at some point during the 1980s they suddenly disappeared. While some wondered if they had been stolen or destroyed, Milt Larson, the owner of the Magic Castle, eventually found them buried in the basement of the theater. After getting permission from the new owners, he piled them into a truck and moved them across town to his newly formed Society for the Preservation of Variety Arts (SPVA) downtown. What Larson didn't realize, however, was that Gene Autry had already purchased the signatures and had plans to move them into his own museum. "After Autry called and said that he wanted them back, we decided to reproduce as many of them as we could," recalls Larson. "And we managed to get quite a few of them done. And most of those eventually went to Debbie Reynolds, who now has them in her place in Vegas. But as far as I know Autry has all of the originals."[3]

## The Bottom Line:

To date there is a tentative plan to move the collection to the new Motion Picture Museum at the former Pacific Theater on Hollywood Boulevard. Unfortunately, a lot of the original plates are still missing, and several have been ruined beyond repair. Nevertheless, the legend lives on.

# THE LEGEND:

There are secret tunnels under Chinatown.

## The Context:

Just about every city in the world has its tunnel lore and Los Angeles is no exception. Hopi Indians, for example, claim that a race of pre-Columbians called the Lizard People built an underground empire under what is now downtown Los Angeles in the year 3000 B.C.[4] Meanwhile the Paiute Indians claim that a similar group of indigenous people built Shin-au-av, another underground city said to be underneath the Death Valley National Monument. Others still claim that a race of "Reptilioids," the last of the pre-Scandinavians, constructed a vast labyrinth under the Panamint Mountains.

Modern Los Angeles has its share of tunnel lore, too. It has been rumored, for example, that there are underground tunnels beneath the Ambassador Hotel, the Biltmore Hotel, the Capitol Records building, Columbia studios, Disneyland, the Getty Center, the *Herald-Examiner* building, the *Los Angeles Times* build-ing, the old Hughes aircraft headquarters in Hollywood, Paramount studios, Sony studios, Universal Studios, UCLA, and all the federal buildings downtown (which are said to be interconnected).

Apparently many of those rumors are true surprisingly enough, although none of the aforementioned are the kind of nefarious inner sanctums that we'd like to believe. Disneyland, for instance, has a number of passageways running beneath the park, but they were only designed for retailer access. "Most of them lead to restaurants within the park," says David Koenig, author of several books on Disneyland. "Because it would be virtually impossible to deliver a hundred pounds of hamburger buns through a crowd of 100,000 people on a summer day."

Considering that power is often associated with covert or "underground" activities, it should be no surprise that the most interesting tunnel tales tend to revolve around military organizations and/or criminal hideouts. The alleged tunnels under the Tejon Ranch, for example, are some of the most notorious on record. Located just north of Santa Barbara, these tunnels are said to connect various branches of a secret military base known to exist on the property; a base primarily used to conduct top-secret experiments in radar and stealth technologies for Northrop Grumman and Bechtel. (According to lore, the complex descends twenty stories below the surface.[5] Yet little can be seen from the air, save for a small group of buildings and an extremely short runway.)

Meanwhile, there are also said to be tunnels underneath some of L.A.'s most notorious criminal and cult hideouts. In his book *We Only Kill Each Other*, for example, Dean Jennings describes Bugsy Siegel's house at 250 Delfern in Holmby Hills as having "sliding panels activated by concealed buttons, bookshelves on hinges, and three hidden trapdoors just in case he needed to leave in a hurry." At the same time the owners of Two Bunch Palms resort near Palm Springs maintain that Al Capone built some tunnels under their property in the 1930s, primarily as an escape route; and there's some compelling evidence to support the idea that cults such as the

Manson family, the Brotherhood of the Sun, and the Fountain of the World WKFL built their own, secret hideaways in places like Chatsworth, Death Valley, and Santa Barbara.

Many have also claimed that there are tunnels under certain private residences throughout L.A. as well, mostly of unknown origin. It has been said, for example, that there are hidden passageways under Harold Lloyd's famous Greenacres estate in Beverly Hills, Elinor Ince's Chateau Elysée in Hollywood, William Workman's adobe house in La Puente, Houdini's alleged mansion in Laurel Canyon, Johnny Carson's mansion in Malibu, the Chateau Marmont on the Sunset Strip, and the apartment building once occupied by Rudolf Valentino, now on the Paramount lot. Nonetheless, there seems to be little evidence to support those claims. "A lot of these places have underground passageways that are only to provide access to the sewer system or underground utilities," says historian Marc Wanamaker. "But they are not secret tunnels by any means."

On the other hand, there *are* secret tunnels connecting some of the homes in Beachwood Canyon near Holly Mount Drive which have

Chinatown, L.A., 1936

never been satisfactorily explained. Laurie Jacobson discovered them after she heard reports of higher than normal paranormal activity in the area. As she reveals in her book *Hollywood Haunted*, many of the residents believe that they were either built to provide access to a monastery that used to be at the top of the hill, or they were designed to store bootleg liquor in the 1920s. In any case, like all the tunnels in L.A.—real or imagined—they continue to inspire countless rumors.

## What People Are Saying:

Yet the rumor of the Chinatown tunnels remains the most ubiquitous of all. According to lore, the tunnels were supposedly built in response to the bloody riot of 1871 when nearly two dozen Chinese men and women were lynched for unknown crimes. And there seems to be some evidence that there were tunnels underneath the old plaza, in particular below the Garnier Building, and they may have extended into Chinatown and Calle de Los Negros. Yet to this day no one has been able to determine just how extensive they were. After all, the original Chinatown was razed in 1933 and moved several blocks away to make room for the new train station. Still, many believe that they amounted to an entire labyrinth of passageways stretching all the way to the Los Angeles River. Historians on the other hand, argue that the rumor is greatly exaggerated. "There is no catacomb, or any series of interlocking tunnels," says Jean Bruce Poole, the lead historian for El Pueblo de Los Angeles. "They are simply pedestrian tunnels that lead from various buildings to the street, that's all. The one under Sanchez Street, for example, which was built in 1968 and still exists today, was to provide access for the delivery of goods to the Pico House. None of them were built for protection or to provide escape routes. That rumor is completely unfounded."[6]

## What It All Means:

Yet the truth of the Chinatown tunnels is actually less important than the subtext. Because once you understand that the tunnels are more symbolic than real—a projection of the "dark unknown" for example—then you begin to realize that the rumors belie a racist undertone, one that suggests that the Chinese were only interested in committing illegal acts outside the white man's view. The *Los Angeles Star*, for example, reflected that mistrust best when it printed a typical editorial on July 19, 1871, a few days before the riot: "We venture the assertion that many a dark and horrible deed has been perpetrated by these heathens in their secret dens, which will never come to the knowledge of the Christians whose places they are usurping."

> "We venture the assertion that many a dark and horrible deed has been perpetrated by these heathens in their secret dens, which will never come to the knowledge of the Christians whose places they are usurping."

# THE RUMOR:

The basement of the Mann's Chinese Theater is full of footprints of actors and actresses deemed "not worthy enough" to be in front of the theater.

**The ultimate Hollywood club: The forecourt at the Chinese**

Paul Young

## The Truth:

"I've been hearing that rumor for years," says Laval How, the current manager of the legendary theater on Hollywood Boulevard. "Sometimes we even get calls from people who are planning to fly to L.A. for a vacation and they want to know if they can get a tour to see the *other* footprints. But we don't have a basement. There's a boiler room down there, but no basement. And I can assure you, it doesn't have any leftover footprints in it."

## The Background:

Since Norma Talmadge put her footprints in wet cement in front of the world-famous Grauman's Chinese Theater on May 18, 1927, the forecourt of the theater has immortalized the signatures of nearly 200 stars. But for some reason people have assumed that the theater has an equally large collection of "less worthy" prints "hidden" somewhere else.

## Where It Comes From:

The most likely source for the rumor has to do with the fact that the theater makes numerous prints throughout the year, often with obscure celebrities such as Bob Denver, Tony the Tiger, and the Power Rangers. Yet for some reason, *those* prints never seem to make it to the forecourt. "We do a lot of promotional events," says a representative of the Mann's theater chain. "But those are usually sold or donated to various organizations. People probably see somebody like Jackie Chan doing a footprint in front of the building on TV, but when they get here it seems to be missing. So they assume that it's in storage somewhere."

## The Legacy:

So who does get their prints immortalized in the forecourt? According to the theater's corporate office, it sometimes has more to do with politics than a star's popularity. "Years ago when the theater was owned by Twentieth Century Fox [most] of the celebrities that received prints were under contract with Fox," says the Mann's official. "When Warner Bros. took it over, you suddenly had a lot of Warner's stars. Then Paramount did the same thing. Today the prints are there by invitation only by the theater's owners: West Star Cinemas. They have the last say."

# THE RUMOR:

Culver City tried to "steal" the Hollywood name.

## What People Are Saying:

It's true. Culver City thought about changings its name to Hollywood back in the 1930s, although no one really knows who came up with the idea. Apparently it occurred around the same time that MGM, which was based in Culver City, began adding a title card which read, MADE IN HOLLYWOOD, USA, at the end of its movies. That in turn may have inspired Culver City's Chamber of Commerce to realize that the name "Hollywood" was free to use since the *real* Hollywood had been absorbed into the city of L.A. in 1910.

While the name change may have brought more tourism to Culver City, the idea didn't go over so well with the public. Many sent angry letters and denounced the idea in editorials. That in turn, prompted MGM to change its credit to MADE IN CULVER CITY, which in turn convinced Culver City's Chamber of Commerce to announce that it wouldn't pursue the idea any further.

## The Truth:

"I don't think it was ever a very serious idea," explains Hal Horn of the Culver City Historical Society. "It was never seriously considered by the municipal governmental entity of the city. It was just an idea that some public officials and citizens played around with. They even held a ceremony in front of the Chinese Theater in 1937 where they literally buried a hatchet and shook hands. Ironically, the ceremony was before the premiere of David O. Selznick's *The Prisoner of Zenda* which of course was made in Culver City."

Los Angeles Examiner/USC Special Collections

Dueling chambers: A mock battle between Hollywood and Culver City fighting for the Hollywood name

# THE RUMOR:

W. C. Fields used a fake name on his tombstone at Forest Lawn.

W. C. Fields

## A Little History:

When screenwriter Ben Hecht went to pay W. C. Fields a visit in Palm Springs toward the end of his life, he found the famously cantankerous comedian sitting poolside, poring over a Bible. Surprised at his choice of reading material, Hecht asked him, "Uncle Claude, why the Holy Book?" Fields looked up, took another sip of scotch, and said, "I'm looking for loopholes."

## What People Are Saying:

Fields finally passed away on Christmas Day, 1946, and was supposedly buried at Forest Lawn. Fans had difficulty finding his gravesite, however, and Forest Lawn employees were curiously circumspect about revealing his whereabouts. Meanwhile the *Los Angeles Times* reported that the comedian had left dozens of bank accounts all over the world under assumed names including Elmer Mergatroid-Haines, Aristotle Hoop, Figley E. Whitesides, and Sneed Hearn. (In fact, Fields left $2,000 to a bank clerk he hardly knew because he enjoyed her name so much, a woman called Mabel Clapsaddle.) Not surprisingly, that led to a rumor suggesting that he had himself buried under an alias.

## The Truth:

Today Fields lies in niche number 20805 of the Columbarium of Nativity, and according to Margaret Burton, who runs the Forest Lawn Museum, his name is inscribed just as any other.

"It says W. C. Fields," she explains. "There's no alias or anything like that. It's marked just like any other inscription."

If the rumor has any validity at all, it may have to do with the fact that Fields went without a grave or tombstone for years—apparently because he had so many relatives, girlfriends, and ex-wives fighting over his estate that no one really knew what to do with his remains. As a result he wasn't buried until 1951, a full four-and-a-half years after his death on Christmas Day 1946. That, of course, could be where the rumor came from.

W. C.

# THE LEGEND:

The Errol Flynn estate contained two-way mirrors to view sexual orgies.

## A Little History:

When it comes to swashbuckling lady-killers, few stars past or present can compete with Errol Flynn. He once calculated that he had over 12,000 sexual conquests in his lifetime, many of which were in his adopted home of Hollywood. "He was a sexual athlete from the beginning," wrote Charles Higham in *Errol Flynn: The Untold Story*. "He had extraordinary staying power and a deep understanding of women's bodies."

So when he finally decided to build an estate for himself in the Hollywood Hills, you can be sure it was full of bacchanalian amusements. Located at 3100 Torryson Place, Flynn's "House of Pleasure" had subtle, and not so subtle, sexual innuendos throughout. "There were phallic suggestions everywhere," says Higham. "To open a liquor cabinet in the bar you had to squeeze a pair of bull testicles; there were images of bulls and cocks everywhere, and some of the chairs were rigged to surprise guests between their legs."

## Where It Comes From:

There seems to be some truth to the rumor of Flynn's infamous two-way mirror—at least according to Higham. Apparently it ran the length of his "orgy room," a second living room dedicated to sexual exploits; and during parties, he would encourage his friends to use the room while he watched from a side room hidden behind a two-way mirror. According to Higham, the view wasn't always to his liking, however, so with the help of his buddy, Jim Fleming, he installed a two-way mirror in the ceiling directly

Errol Flynn's sin bin

Bison Archives

**"And I remember that it had, for example, a large fish tank running the length of the room, on the back of which were paintings of fish with oversized genitals."**

over the bed. Then he transformed the attic into a plush "viewing room" that had all of the comforts of a brothel, including a private bar and an oversized, fluffy couch. "He continued the sexual innuendos throughout that room, too," explained Higham in a recent interview. "I was able to visit the house some years ago and I saw the room for myself. And I remember that it had, for example, a large fish tank running the length of the room, on the back of which were paintings of fish with oversized genitals."

The legendary madam Lee Francis saw the room as well. According to her autobiography, Flynn called her shortly after its completion and asked for four of her finest girls. They weren't for himself, however, but for a sex contest that he wanted to have with four of his best friends, a contest that would prove once and for all who had the longest staying power among his mates.[7] As Francis described it, "For a several-hundred-dollar purse they tried to determine who could have the most conquests in a single night," she writes in *Ladies on Call*. "Spectators, intimate cronies of the men, kept tabs and the competition lasted until dawn when the exhausted foursome quit. I've forgotten what the score was, but [Flynn] dropped out of circulation for several weeks following this experience. I had to give the girls a night off, too."

# THE RUMOR:

F. Scott Fitzgerald died at the infamous hotel the Garden of Allah.

## A Short History:

Alla Nazimova originally moved to her new home at 8152 Sunset Boulevard in 1918, when Adolph Zukor was paying her $1,400,000 per year, plus fifty percent of the profits from her films. That's where she built her dream house, a large, handsome estate fashioned in the architectural style of her native Romania—complete with *pom de cracium* trees, gothic turrets, and a 65 x 45–foot black-bottom swimming pool fashioned after the Black Sea.

The 1920s weren't very kind to Nazimova, however, and her career slowed considerably. Eventually her manager, Mrs. Adams, suggested that she turn her home into a hotel to ensure a regular income. Nazimova apparently liked the

Bison Archives

The Garden of Allah, 1930

# Farewell, Garden of Allah
# End of Fantastic Playground

AUG 16 1959

*Hollywood's legendary hotel, the Garden of Allah, since 1927 a playground for the more volatile celebrities of the show world rather than a place of rest and quiet, will be razed next month to make way for an office building and business center.*

*Here is the first of a series of articles depicting life in the picturesque cluster of Spanish-type villas built by early-day Actresss Alla Nazimova and named for her.*

### By JEAN BOSQUET

One by one, Hollywood's storied landmarks are disintegrating in the jet-blast of changing times.

Castle Rock, on the beach near Santa Monica, where Mack Sennett's bathing beauties ushered in the cheesecake era . . .

The Trocadero, first social stronghold of the stars and starlets thumbing rides on the movie rocket, where everybody who was anybody in Hollywood dined, danced and drank . . .

The old Hollywood Hotel, gathering place for the carriage trade of show business on both coasts . . .

### WRECKERS IN WINGS

And now the Garden of Allah, fabulous Baghdad-on-the-Sunset-Strip which for a quarter century was the abode and playpen of mercurial movie madcaps.

Next month the white stucco villas of the legend-laden Garden and the big swimming pool shaped like the Black Sea will crumble under the wreckers' sledges clearing the two and one-half acre site for a $5,000,000 commercial and business center.

Lytton Savings and Loan Association, which purchased the acres at the beginning of the Sunset Strip, will develop the property.

The ghost of Alla Nazimova, tempestuous dramatic star who built the hostelry in 1926, named it for herself and had its pool fashioned after the shape of the sea near her native Yalta, will stir uneasily as the hammers ring.

### MOOD WAS SET

The party given by Nazimova at the opening of the hotel in January, 1927, set the mood for the hijinks that were to follow during the lush years of the Garden's existence.

The bash began in the big manor house which had originally been Alla's home and spread to all of the 25 villas built by her as units of

**ALLA NAZIMOVA**
*Built fabulous "playpen."*

Errol Flynn, Fanny Brice, Alice Brady, Ronald Colman and many other stars of their stamp.

### FAMED WRITERS

Such writers as F. Scott Fitzgerald, Thomas Wolfe, Ernest Hemingway, Lucius Beebe, Alexander Woollcott, Budd Schulberg and Playwright Arthur Kober also tarried at the Garden and actually managed to get work done there despite the frolicking that continued on almost a 24-hour basis.

Describing the place later, Beebe said, "Nothing interrupted the continual tumult that was life at the Garden of Allah. Now and then the men in white came with a van and took somebody away, or bankruptcy, divorce or even jail claimed a participant in its strictly unstately sarabands. Nobody paid any mind."

The Man with the Bag from the Internal Revenue

boulevards, creating the impression of being movie stars; some of them heightened the conceit by carrying a director's megaphone, for the benefit of visiting yokels.

### CENSORS ALARMED

The prefect of Bergamo, Italy, climaxed a reform campaign with an order banning publications featuring pictures of lightly draped Hollywood starlets, and censors around our own country viewed with alarm the possible harmful effects of gangster epics and bedroom scenes on the screen.

But this, too, was paid no mind at the Garden, where a sparkling roulette wheel of songs, dances and funny sayings was kept spinning day and night.

Science has long known that a dazzling, spinning object produces hypnotic sleep in a person who stares at it, but it had little or no effect on these children of Allah.

### CEASELESS SPLASHES

The jingle-jangle and razzmatazz went on, the celebrities came and went, and the drunks kept falling into the Garden's pool in a monotonous succession of splashes.

"I used to wait for them to leave a party and fall in," Arthur Kober recalled in later years. "It was like waiting for a shoe to drop. I'd hear the splash and then I'd go to sleep."

*NEXT: Benchley, Barrymore, Fitzgerald and Butterworth team up in a frantic fight against boredom. Don't miss an article of this penetrating series. Phone RIchmond 8-1212 for prompt home delivery.*

*"No doctor,"*
*crowed*
*Fitzgerald*
*thinking his*
*number had*
*come up.*
*"Just get me*
*somewhere*
*that I can die*
*in peace."*

idea and built twenty-five individual villas around the circumference of the property at a cost then of $1.5 million. The construction was completed on January 9, 1927, whereupon she called 200 of her nearest and dearest friends and hosted a party that lasted for three days. From that moment on, the Garden of Allah was off and running.

If Nazimova's hotel appealed to artists, it was because it was more like a village than a hotel. As bandleader Artie Shaw described it:

```
"It was like your own home. The
bungalows were all around the
pool, so you felt like you were
in your own place. And it was
always a little run down. You
almost expected the rats to
come. No one was polishing the
tops of the palm trees. It was
one of the few places that was
so absurd that people could be
themselves. And there were
never any producers—the common
enemy—hanging around, just hip
actors and good writers. It was
a colony of expatriates in the
middle of Hollywood."
```

While actors such as Greta Garbo, Errol Flynn, Humphrey Bogart, Marlene Dietrich, and Frank Sinatra were often in attendance, it was really the writers who made the Garden what it was. Robert Benchley, in particular, was the hotel's most conspicuous guest, often spinning mad tales poolside, organizing lavish parties, or pulling some of the most outrageous pranks in the hotel's history. Other writers such as Ernest Hemingway, Dorothy Parker, Thomas Wolfe, Ben Hecht, and Orson Welles also made use of the communal setting, and often took advantage of the in-house secretary on call twenty-four hours a day.[8]

## Where It Comes From:

While F. Scott Fitzgerald was another one of the great writers who lived at the Garden, he didn't die there, as some have suggested. When he passed away on December 21, 1940, he was staying at 1403 Laurel Avenue, an apartment build-ing a mere stone's throw from the Garden, with a young journalist and sometimes-mistress named Sheila Graham. There was, however, a small incident at the hotel that may have initiated the rumor. Apparently one night in 1938, after a typical drinking binge, Fitzgerald apparently crawled out of his villa on his hands and knees and slithered all the way to the front desk a good hundred yards away. An astonished receptionist ran to his aid and asked him if he needed a doctor. "No doctor," crowed Fitzgerald thinking his number had come up. "Just get me somewhere that I can die in peace."

## The Legacy:

Curiously, Fitzgerald's real death seemed to parallel the demise of the Garden itself. By the end of the 1940s the stars had checked out, and the rats, as Artie Shaw predicted, had checked in. "There wasn't a week that went by that there wasn't another robbery, mugging, con game, or even a murder," recalls one old-timer. "It had become a cold, ugly place. But the saddest part of all was that nobody could really care less."

After being sold to two different investors, the wrecking ball finally moved in 1959 to make room for a strip mall based around the Litton Savings and Loan. According to newspaper reports, a public auction was held the day before the hotel was razed and the only relic that returned any money was—not surprisingly—Errol Flynn's favorite mattress.

# THE RUMOR:

Griffith Park is the site for an `annual` `nude` `marathon`.

Paul Young

## A Little History:

If all the public venues in L.A. got together and held a popularity contest for those interested in public sex, Griffith Park would undoubtedly be the odds-on favorite, even over such obvious, sex-obsessed places as Santa Monica Boulevard or Topanga Canyon. After all, lusty Angelenos have been using its hidden coves and ample foliage for decades. In the 1940s and fifties, for example, it was *the* spot for necking parties after football games and dances. Ten years later, those parties turned into full-blown "love-ins" with accompanying riots and police sweeps. Then, in the 1980s, the practice took a slightly different turn. As the *Los Angeles Times* reported, the park was then the most popular trysting spot for gay couples in the city. That didn't please some of the school teachers that used the park for field trips, however. In a sensational plea for "decency," the L.A. Unified School District initiated a firestorm of charges against the Department of Parks and Recreation, claiming that it was their responsibility to clean up the blatant acts of homosexuality among the park's flora and fauna.

That in turn led to massive sweeps through the park by the LAPD. (The gay community vociferously denounced the action, claiming that they were being harassed.)

## Where It Comes From:

If the rumor of a nude marathon persists, it's because there seems to be an element of truth to it. As Mike Eberts writes in *Griffith Park, A Centennial History:* "Beginning in 1979 Griffith Park became the site of the Tetrick Trail, an event promoters called America's only X-rated eight-miler. Ceremoniously started by firing an arrow into the air, the eccentric run on the park's trails and fire roads became a Griffith Park legend. The semisecret event was known mostly for its human mile markers, who were, well, *buck naked.* By 1988, the run was drawing about 800 participants, many toting cameras."

## The Legacy:

Griffith Park has lost some of its sex appeal since the more sexually adventurous days of the past. According to a 1998 poll conducted by *Details* magazine, the park dropped to second place for preferred trysting spots while Mulholland Drive in the Santa Monica Mountains took first. Other top contenders included underneath the Hollywood sign, inside Mann's Chinese Theater, on the roof of the Beverly Center, in a tomb at the Hollywood Forever Cemetary, poolside at the Argyle, Mondrian, or Chateau, and for those truly daring enough, inside the *Psycho* house on the Universal Studios lot.

# THE RUMOR:

Harry Houdini once owned a house on Laurel Canyon Boulevard.

## What People Are Saying:

Despite the fact that Harry Houdini—the world's greatest magician of the early 1900s—only made it out to L.A. a few times in his life, there are a number of Angelenos who genuinely believe that he owned the estate at 2398 Laurel Canyon Boulevard. In fact, tour buses, real estate agents, fans, and scores of occultists have made pilgrimages to the site for years, either to look in awe at the mysterious remains, or to hold private occult ceremonies in an attempt to invoke his ghost.

Nonetheless, opinions vary on whether Houdini actually lived there or not. Many believe that Houdini's good friend, R. J. Walker, whose name shows up on the property deeds, bequeathed the property to the great magician in 1925, shortly before he died. Others say that Houdini merely visited Walker's house on occasion, usually when he was in town making a movie or performing one of his spectacular shows. Others still seem to believe that he lived in Walker's guest house across the street, which was allegedly connected to the main house through a subterranean tunnel.

## The Truth:

Nonetheless, there doesn't seem to be much truth to the tale. When Houdini came to L.A. to perform his act, he inevitably stayed at the Alexandria Hotel. And years later, when he returned in 1919 to perform in *The Grim Game* for

Houdini levitated here

Paul Young

73

Famous Players-Lasky-Paramount, the studio rented him a small, craftsman-style bungalow in the heart of Hollywood apparently within blocks of the studio. Then, the following year when he came out to make *Terror Island* for the same company, he lived on Catalina Island—where the movie was shot—for the duration of his stay.

Nonetheless, it's certainly possible that Houdini could have met R. J. Walker during the production of either movie. Yet according to most historians, Houdini rarely socialized during the making of his movies, and no one has been able find a credible link between the two. What's more, Houdini's name fails to appear on any of the property deeds, transfer of title forms, or invoices for Walker's estate.

## Where It Comes From:

It's possible that the rumor has something to do with Houdini's wife, Beatrice. Apparently Beatrice moved into Laurel Canyon in the 1930s, and took a small house around the corner from the Walker estate.[9] Throughout her stay, she conducted an annual séance on the eve of her husband's death in an attempt to summon his spirit. And according to newspaper reports, these events were a hot ticket amongst L.A.'s glitterati, many of which hoped to feel the "presence" of the great master himself.

In any case, a massive fire roared through Laurel Canyon in 1959 and destroyed most of the homes in the area, including the Beatrice residence and the Walker estate. Soon visitors began whispering about the devastation done to the "Houdini House." Yet for some unknown reason, people automatically assumed that the Walker estate was the "Houdini estate." (After all, the Walker estate—with its indoor swimming pool, theatrical stage, and acres of lush passage ways and ponds—was certainly *spookier* than any of the other houses in the area). As historian Marc Wanamaker says, "The rumor about Harry Houdini living in Laurel Canyon really didn't start until the 1960s. And I think it's because after the fires, the Walker house remained empty for several years. And for some reason people just assumed that it was Houdini's. Either because it was so exotic looking or because they confused it for his wife's. I don't really know why the rumor started, but what I do know is that Houdini *never* lived there."

# THE RUMOR:

L.A.'s Hyperion Waste Treatment Plant finds an average of 300 fetuses a month in the L.A. sewer system.

## The Context:

In the early 1960s, there was a specious tale going around New York claiming that the sewers were teaming with giant albino alligators that survived off sewage, rats, and the occasional homeless person. Not surprisingly, the rumor has been debunked by authorities and folklorists alike. Although Jan Harold Brunvand has suggested that the story has some interesting factual precedents. During the 1980s it was common to hear that a number of "miniature" alligators, allegedly imported from Brazil, had been flushed down into the sewer system and forgotten about. And, after years of living on sewage, those very same gators supposedly spawned a race of "albino" alligators large enough to kill humans. While few really believe the rumor, folklorist Jan Harold Brunvand traced it back to a newspaper report from the 1930s describing an actual alligator found in a storm drain at 123rd Street. That in turn led to an investigation by commissioner Teddy May, who eventually found several small, two-foot alligators living in the sewers. May never offered an explanation for the strange find, yet announced a city-wide campaign to eradicate the "sewer-gators." That, of course, led to the rumor which continues to this day.

## What People Are Saying:

In 1996 Ralph Rugoff reported that some Angelenos believed that as many as 300 human fetuses were being flushed into L.A.'s sewer system each month, primarily through illegal abortions. Many end up as meals for coyotes, rats, and other vermin, while the rest end up at the Hyperion treatment facilities in El Segundo.

## The Truth:

Like New York's infamous alligator-in-the-sewer rumor, the fetus myth may be based on an actual incident. In the mid-1990s a female sanitation worker allegedly came across a human fetus on one of the bar screens at the plant. It was in fact the *only* time that a fetus had been discovered at the plant—at least in the previous three decades—and it caused a minor sensation in the press. "I've been here for seventeen years," says a plant representative, "and I've heard stories of that kind of stuff happening, but I've never witnessed one myself."[10]

## What It All Means:

If the rumor continues to be popular with urban audiences, it's simply because city folks are subconsciously fascinated with what's *really* floating around in the sewers, i.e., excrement and contamination. And they're not alone either. There seems to be an equal, albeit more accepted, fascination among indigenous cultures as well, a

Mining the muck

HYPERION TREATMENT PLANT 7650 IMPERIAL HWY. GATE A

Paul Young

fascination that informs both art and daily life. California Indians, for example, were known to use human feces during certain ceremonies, smearing it on themselves in absurdist routines, or eating it in spiritual incantations. Such acts, as sociologists have remarked, are rife with spiritual and symbolic import having to do with excrement's association with riches or gold.

## The Other Truth:

While fetuses may be rare at Hyperion, staff members admit that they've found other, equally curious items, including bags of money, a finger, a mattress, various sex toys, a full set of kitchen cabinets, a complete motorcycle, a five-foot grease ball, and a *fully intact, adult male horse*.

# THE RUMOR:

The ☐Lamb☐ ☐Funeral☐ ☐Home☐ secretly sells the eyeballs of every corpse that it puts to rest.

## Where It Comes From:

In late 1986, a neighbor of the Oscar Ceramics Company in Hesperia, a small town just north of San Bernardino, called the sheriff's department to complain about something "very sinister" going on at the Oscar warehouse. He claimed that he saw trucks unloading what looked like corpses to the warehouse on a daily basis. And judging from the noxious plume of black smoke that spat from its smokestack, it was fairly obvious that they weren't putting them underground. "Don't tell me that they're not burning bodies," he told the officer. "I was at Auschwitz. I know what that smells like."

Surprisingly, the charges turned out to be true. The employees at the ceramic company were in fact burning bodies—loads of bodies—from ten on a slow day to sixty on a weekend.

The revelation was shocking to say the least, especially to the residents of Hesperia who failed to see how a ceramic company could be involved with cremation. But as investigators later found

Rest in pieces

out, the warehouse was really a front for the Lamb Funeral Home in Pasadena, a prestigious company with a sixty-seven-year history. David Sconce, a former football coach who inherited the business from his wife, Laurieanne Lamb, had purchased the warehouse months earlier, and used it to triple his cremation business—although he rarely, if ever, played by standard funerary rules. When investigators descended upon the Oscar Ceramics shop on January 20, 1987, they not only found a massive, apartment-sized oven, but crates of human bones, teeth, and skulls, and several large petrol drums filled with human oil. (Investigators also found boxes of bones hidden under Sconce's house at 1103 Comstock Avenue in Glendora.)

Yet that's not all they found. As investigators looked further into the case, they discovered that each corpse had been thoroughly plundered: Gold and silver fillings were ripped out and melted down for cash; organs—including brains, lungs, and hearts—were removed and sold to biological companies; false teeth were yanked out and sold to dental supply companies; eyeballs were popped out and sold to eye research companies, and hair was cut off and sold to wigmakers.

What's more, Sconce hired thugs and hit men to go after those who threatened to expose his operation. Timothy Waters, for example, perhaps Sconce's most vociferous rival, received beatings and death threats on at least two occasions, as did some of his associates, until he finally swallowed some poison and "accidentally" died. What's more, it was also alleged that Sconce even went so far as to hire killers to knock off his own grandparents, who were cooperating with the investigation. "He wouldn't stop at killing anybody," said one witness, "if they deterred him from making a living or hurt his family."

## ...they not only found a massive, apartment-sized oven, but crates of human bones, teeth, and skulls, and several large, petrol drums filled with human oil.

### The Aftermath:

Finally, in 1992, relatives of over 5,000 deceased loved ones brought a class-action suit against the mortuary for commingling remains and forging signatures to sell organs without permission. The suit ended with a $15.4 million judgment against the funeral home in 1995. Two years later, Sconce pleaded guilty to conspiracy charges and received life probation.

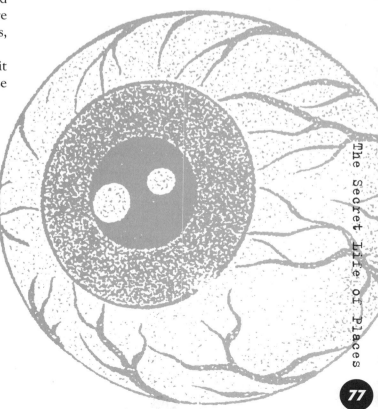

# THE RUMOR:

There's a top-secret movie studio somewhere in the Hollywood Hills, owned and operated by the U.S. government, that is used for the production of propaganda.

## A Little History:

Few would contest the idea that the entertainment industry is one of the most influential media known to man. But few may realize the extent to which politicians, big business, and ideologues may go to harness that power. During the first world war, for example, Washington's Committee on Public Information (CPI), worked closely with Hollywood to produce popular movies that would mobilize the American public. The idea, of course, was to get Americans behind the European war effort, and that yielded a rich crop of anti-Axis themes, negative stereotypes, and racist paranoia. Propaganda works both ways, however, and it wasn't long before the public began to question Hollywood's true motives. It was often said, for example, that William Randolph Hearst worked secretly with German investors to counteract Washington's not-so-secret agenda.[11] Twenty years later, shortly after World War II, the FBI initiated a "Mass Media Program" specifically to "influence public opinion." As a 1946 memo by J. Edgar Hoover states, the program was designed to release "educational material [i.e., pro-American propaganda] through available news channels." Available channels, of course, meant Hollywood, the news media, and popular magazines.

It must also be noted, however, that when Hollywood producers engage in propaganda, they tend to do so of their own free will. Even at the height of World War II, when the Office of War Information stepped in once again to "instruct" Hollywood on how to sell the war to the American public, producers were never required to adhere to its guidelines. When Jack Warner, for example, made the openly political *Mission to Moscow*, in 1943, at the personal request of FDR, he did it primarily to increase his stature in Washington—which at the time was more important than money.

Apparently Hollywood still works with Washington in much the same way, although the rewards have changed slightly. In January 2000, it was disclosed that all of the top major television networks were working with President Clinton's drug czar, General Barry McCaffrey, to foist propaganda on the American audience without their knowledge. The deal basically put millions of dollars in the pockets of producers who quite readily included antidrug themes in their prime-time movies, shows, and sitcoms—but only after the scripts were approved by McCaffrey's office.[12]

## What People Are Saying:

Since the 1960s, there has been a persistent rumor that the CIA has its own "secret" movie studio right in the heart of Hollywood. The CIA has continually denied such claims, however, saying that when it engages in propaganda—meaning biased pamphlets, fake documentaries, and forged autobiographies—it does so specifically to undermine Communist advances in foreign territories such as Southeast Asia, the Middle East, and Latin America.[13] Domestic propaganda, on the other hand, is another issue entirely, and rarely, if ever, admitted to by the agency—despite evidence to the contrary.[14]

## The Truth:

Apparently the military *did* have its own studio in Hollywood once. As recent declassified files show, it sat at the top of Laurel Canyon for nearly fifty years, and it contained a fully operational movie studio with over 100,000 square feet of soundstages, screening rooms, independent film-processing labs (color and black-and-white), an animation department, editing facilities, and film vaults. In fact, it was an amazingly self-sufficient operation that could rival many of Hollywood's independent production companies.

According to Peter Kuran, who discovered the facility known as the Lookout Mountain Laboratory while doing research for his award-winning 1995 documentary, *Trinity and Beyond,* the studio produced 19,000 classified movies between the years 1947 and 1997. That's around 500 more than Hollywood produced during the same period, and did everything to ensure that they remained top secret.

## The Bottom Line:

While it would be easy to assume that the film-makers were involved in some sort of nefarious propaganda production for the CIA, the Air Force has stressed that the facility was used solely for the Atomic Energy Commission. Apparently the cameramen, who referred to themselves as the "atomic" cinematographers, were hired to shoot footage of the atomic bomb tests in Nevada, Utah, New Mexico, and the South Pacific, and those were the only movies made at the studio.

Nonetheless, there is evidence that the studio also conducted R & D experiments for Hollywood as well, developing such new techniques as 3-D and Vista Vision long before anyone else. What's more Walt Disney, John Ford, Jimmy Stewart, Howard Hawks, Bing Crosby, Susan Hayward, Marilyn Monroe, Ronald Reagan, Hedda Hopper, and more were given special clearance to use the facilities on occasion, apparently for undisclosed projects. Were they working for the CIA as well? If they were, no one's telling.

The American Film Institute

Hollywood's secret studio in the 1950s

# THE LEGEND:

Burbank has a group of houses that were designed and inhabited by Munchkins.

## What People Are Saying:

Of all the legends of L.A. landmarks, none have captured the imagination of Angelenos quite as much as the alleged "Munchkinville" has. Depending on whom you talk to, the miniature housing tract—supposedly built by the midgets from *The Wizard of Oz*—was constructed in Los Feliz, Burbank, Culver City, Sierra Madre, or La Jolla.[15]

## The Truth:

Author Gwyn Headley spent over a year trying to track down the alleged neighborhood for her book, *Architectural Follies in America*; and when she discovered a group of houses near La Jolla that some locals called "Munchkinville," she thought she hit gold. They, too, were said to be built in half-scale, with miniature doors, windows, and chimneys, and according to lore, they were indeed built by midgets in the 1930s. Not *Wizard of Oz* midgets, however, but mean, dangerous little monsters who trafficked in white slavery and cannibalism. Yet according to Headley, the houses weren't built by little people, however, since they're actually of normal size. As she writes,

"They're perched on struts on the side of Mount Soledad looking over Torrey Pines Beach. They are perfectly normal bungalows, unobtrusive as you drive up the narrow winding hill, but when you drive back down the reason for the legend becomes clearer. When seen from above the ordinary houses are transformed into picturesque medleys of broad and low-pitched, red-pantiled roofs, with deep eaves providing shelter from the hot summer sun. The size of the roofs gives the illusion that the walls are lower than they should be."

## Where It Comes From:

According to the *San Diego Reader*, the idea may have come from an article written in the *La Jolla Light* in the 1950s. As a Halloween joke, the paper printed a filler piece describing how the "Happy Munchkins that lived in the hills in La Jolla" were going to celebrate the holiday with the community. Though in fun dozens of people flocked to the area looking for the alleged "Munchkin houses" which in turn led to a widespread belief that there was a Munchkinville at the top of Mount Soledad.

In any case, while the *Reader*'s account may or may not be the foundation for the rumor, it doesn't necessarily account for the rumor's presence in Los Angeles. An item in the *Los Angeles Examiner* in 1936, however, may have been responsible. The story concerned a new policy at the Biltmore Hotel, which the *Examiner* claimed was going to "revolutionize" the pageboy business. Apparently the hotel had been using children as pages—as per tradition—since the hotel opened in 1923. But after years of being disappointed by unruly ten-to-fourteen-year-olds, the hotel finally decided to use midgets instead. "The idea came with the midget village at the California Pacific International Exposition," states the article. "Two midgets from the Expo dropped by the Biltmore just about the time their pages had come to grief, one being discharged and the other among the missing. They got the job."

The "midget village" may in fact be the original source for the infamous Munchkinville. After all, it was located blocks from Disneyland and consisted of a "complete neighborhood" including houses, stores, and a church built to scale.

## What It All Means:

Every country has its own folkloric history of dwarves, midgets, elves, and wizards, and in general, they tend to represent, in psychoanalytical terms, the "half-formed" impulses lodged in the unconscious. And if that's true, that may be why little people are often portrayed as mischievous or nefarious characters, since half-formed impulses tend to sneak up on us and take "revenge" on the psyche when ignored.

# "The Happy Munchkins that lived in the hills of La Jolla were going to celebrate with the community."

Paul Young

One of the miniature homes in La Jolla

# THE LEGEND:

The Nazi Party has a top-secret headquarters in Rustic Canyon.

## What People Are Saying:

High up in the Santa Monica Mountains, lodged deep in one of the remote canyons, is one of the most mysterious ranches ever built in Southern California. Said to exist in the 1930s and 1940s, it was rumored to be the training headquarters for hundreds of blond-haired, blue-eyed Nazis bent on conducting a fifth-column assault on the West Coast.

## A Little History:

According to records, the ranch was originally built by a widow named Jessie M. Murphy in 1933. Using the money from her late husband, she initially planned to transform the property into a functioning plantation, complete with a 395,000-gallon water tank fed by a natural spring, a 20,000-gallon diesel fuel tank, and a power station with double generators large enough to light a small city. She also had plans to build a twenty-two-bedroom house with a full-scale gymnasium and an Olympic-size swimming pool. Yet in 1938, after she had completed most of the utilities and some temporary living quarters, a fire raged through the property and destroyed nearly everything that she owned. Heartbroken, she packed all that she could salvage and put the property up for sale.

Three years later, Mrs. Winnona Stephens, the daughter of a wealthy industrialist, and her husband, Norman Stephens, an engineer with silver mine interests, purchased the property through a realtor and set out to build their own dream

Paul Young

Rustic's secret Nazi training field

house. They were impressed with Murphy's original vision, however, and realized that it would be easier to restore what was already there. So after securing the original blueprints, they hired a contractor and built the entire twenty-two-bedroom complex, complete with gymnasium and swimming pool. Meanwhile, the electric generators were repaired, the water spring mended, and several amenities were added, including a working livestock farm, butchering facilities, a walk-in refrigerated locker, and dairy facilities.

## Where It Comes From:

Shortly after the ranch was completed in 1942, a workman told an associate that he had seen "troops dressed in paramilitary outfits" on the property, and they were apparently being trained by an "overbearing German named Herr Schmidt." This was shortly after Pearl Harbor, and any suggestion of terrorism was taken seriously, especially by federal authorities.

## The Truth:

As Betty Lou Young reveals in *Rustic Canyon and the Story of the Uplifters,* there was in fact a Nazi sympathizer living at the Murphy ranch, and his name was indeed Herr Schmidt. Evidently Mrs. Stephens had fallen under his spell in the early 1930s, and came to believe that World War II was going to escalate to the point of total annihilation. The only salvation, she believed, was to make sure that she and her family had the resources to survive the onslaught on their own, and Schmidt helped her organize self-defense classes, sharp-shooting exercises, and physical training classes.

Apparently this went on for several months until the OSS intercepted some secret communiqués between Schmidt and Nazi officers in Mexico, South America, and Europe. Days later Schmidt was arrested and imprisoned for being a Nazi spy, while Winnona and Norman Stephens, who knew nothing of his secret communiqués, were taken into custody and later cleared.

## The Context:

The Murphy Ranch was never the Nazi headquarters that some have suggested. But there were other secret Nazi meeting places not that far away that were very real and very dangerous. "There are 300 sworn Nazis in and around Los Angeles," stated a 1941 article in the *Los Angeles Examiner.* "Their center of activity is the Deutscher Haus on West 15th street [in downtown]. That is where boys and girls are inoculated with the Nazi philosophy. In back rooms they hold target practice using enlarged photographs of leaders of the Jewish community. In the front room, members of the group draw up plans to blow up water works, munitions plants, and docks. Meanwhile, some of their associate groups, the Silver Shirt Legion of America, the Christian Mobilizers, the American Rangers, the Knights of the White Camellia, and the Ku Klux Klan, work in collusion to aid them in their mission."

> *...there were other secret Nazi meeting places not that far away that were very real and very dangerous...*

# THE RUMOR:

There are dozens of illegal gambling operations throughout Palm Springs.

Palm Springs Historical Society

The Wertheimers at work

## A Short History:

If there was a golden era for the gambler in Southern California, it was the late 1920s and early 1930s. That's when Tony Cornero had his floating casino, the Rex, sailing off the coast of Santa Monica, Chinese dealers had their back-room gambling parlors in Chinatown, and racketeers had their secret games in just about every nightclub and bar in town.

Yet it was perhaps Al, Lou, and Mert Wertheimer, three brothers from Detroit, who raised the stakes for illicit gambling in the City of Angels. They came to L.A. in the early 1920s with an impressive Mafia pedigree, and quickly set up shop on the Sunset Strip, which at the time was still a sleepy residential area with dirt sidewalks and few businesses to speak of. Their first clubs were the ultra-exclusive Clover Club,

and the luxurious Colony Club which became hugely popular with the glamour crowd, especially movie producers.

Meanwhile the brothers continued to expand with their own individual operations. In 1945, for example, Lou set up a full-scale gambling casino inside producer Joseph Schenck's house in Bel Air complete with crap tables, roulette wheels, and slot machines, which ran for two years before the sheriff's department moved in and shut it down. "We used a living room on the first floor toward the back of the house," Wertheimer later testified before a grand jury. "And we kept the front of the house dark so that it wouldn't attract attention. But we eventually had to knock down a wall to make more room."

## Where It Comes From:

In 1936 Al Wertheimer built the Dunes Casino in Cathedral City, a small town just outside of Palm Springs. "It was a gorgeous place," recalls the former mayor of Palm Springs, Frank Bogert. "It had a beautiful gaming room with dozens of tables, chandeliers, red carpets, the whole bit. And there was always a top-notch orchestra featured on weekends for dancing. It was a real class act. And the restaurant served the best damned steaks that you ever saw."

Because of the success of the Dunes, a number of rival casinos opened up, including Frank Portnoy's Cove Club and Earl Sausser's 139 Club. And before long, Cathedral City became a swinging place for gamblers. "It was a hell of a deal back then," says Bogert. "There was gambling every night, beautiful women, and more money than you could shake a stick at. And the best thing was that there was never any trouble. Everything ran like clockwork. There were no shootouts or any of that crap that you see in movies."

There was one tragedy that changed the face of Cathedral City almost overnight however. On March 25, 1941, Al Wertheimer was speeding home from his club at about three A.M. when a tow truck came "from nowhere," as he later testified, and forced him to swerve out of the way. That's when his wheel then caught some sand and his vehicle to flipped end over end for 400 yards. Somehow Wertheimer managed to survive

the accident—but just barely. He suffered severe internal injuries and needed extensive surgery. And that was just the beginning of his troubles. In his passenger seat was Mrs. Bernice Mannix, a friend and colleague who died at the scene. While Wertheimer claimed that he was merely driving her home, he appeared to be taking her back to his house for a little nightcap; and to make matters worse, there were also rumors that he pocketed her jewelry which mysteriously disappeared before officers arrived. Bernie was the wife of Eddie Mannix, the MGM executive who was generally believed to be "connected" to New Jersey's crime family, and Eddie was said to be furious over the event. (Mannix was later suspected of ordering the murder of George Reeves, a.k.a. Superman, in 1959.)

Yet it wasn't Mannix who sunk the Dunes, but law enforcement. 1941 was also the year that Carl Rayburn won the office of Riverside County Sheriff, mostly on the promise to clean up racketeering, gambling, and corruption in the county. His first order of business was to indict Al Wertheimer on the newly established Riverside antigambling ordinance even while Wertheimer was still in the hospital. (Portnoy and Sausser were also indicted.)

At the same time, Wertheimer's brothers, Lou and Mert, ran into a little trouble of their own. Shortly after opening the Riverside Country Club in Reno, Mert was kidnapped by Fred "Killer" Burke, the prime suspect in Chicago's St. Valentine's Day massacre, and held for a $50,000 ransom. As legend has it, Lou stood up to the man that the FBI called "the most dangerous man alive" and managed to secure Mert without having to pay a cent.

## The Legacy:

In any case, the legacy that the Wertheimers left behind can now be seen in the growth of a small town about 200 miles to the east called Las Vegas.

# THE LEGEND:

A consortium of conservative politicians and the LAPD conspired to shut down Pandora's Box, the top rock and roll club of the 1960s.

## A Little History:

While rock and roll riots are legion in the City of Angels, perhaps none have been quite as spectacular as the one that centered around the Pandora's Box nightclub in September 1966. On that day hundreds of kids—and a handful of celebrities including Peter Fonda, Sal Mineo, Dennis Hopper, and Sonny and Cher—went head to head with police officers in a three-hour melee that resulted in buses being overturned, windows being shattered, and fires started. It has since become the inspiration for a number of classic rock songs—most notably "For What It's Worth (Stop, Hey, What's That Sound)" by Stephen Stills—and a movie, 1967's *Riot on Sunset Strip* starring Tim Rooney and Mimsey Farmer.

## Where It Comes From:

According to most reports, the nexus of the riot was the club itself, a small, unassuming place situated at the corner of Sunset Boulevard and Crescent Heights. Designed to look like a coffeehouse on Paris' Left Bank, the former private residence featured small wooden tables, mismatched chairs, and a slightly elevated stage. In the 1950s, the club became the locus of the beatnik movement, where hipsters clad in black turtlenecks and French berets gathered to sip espressos and hear artists such as Preston Epps playing bongos. (The club also featured such off-the-menu items as hashish and marijuana.)

But as rock and roll became the new avant garde thanks to four Brits named the Beatles, the club transformed almost overnight into a rock-and-roll venue. Preston Epps soon gave way to rock regulars such as the Standells, the Chocolate Watchband, Love, and Buffalo Springfield, and by 1965, the Sunset Strip had morphed into a mecca for long-haired hippies who often arrived by bus and stayed for weeks in homemade tents pitched on the side of the road. (Other popular venues included The Scene, The Trip, the Sea Witch, the Fifth Estate, and the Telephone Booth.)

Needless to say, most of the business owners in the area complained bitterly about the situation, leading to regular sweeps by the LAPD. Finally, in early 1966, the owners of Pandora's Box announced that they were being forced out of business. That in turn led to a widespread rumor that the club had been targeted by "squares" bent on "stopping rock and roll from spreading."

## The Truth:

Considering the animosity between long-hairs and erstwhile martini mavens, it's hardly surprising that most people came to see Pandora's as a symbol of police oppression. But if anyone looked at the practical aspects of the situation, they may have understood the need for removing the club. After all, the building was situated on a traffic triangle in the middle of one of the busiest intersections in town; and when the club was overbooked, as it usually was, kids often spilled into the thoroughfare and caused serious traffic hazards. Consequently, the city purchased the property and tore it down, primarily to widen the road. If perchance, that meant that long-haired rock and rollers would have to go somewhere else to enjoy their music, so much the better.

**Pandora's Box announced that they were being forced out of business. That in turn led to a widespread rumor that the club had been targeted by "squares" bent on "stopping rock and roll from spreading."**

# THE LEGEND:

During World War II, the `Japanese Imperial Navy` had a secret air base in California from which they launched a major strike against the West Coast.

## The Truth:

Apparently this rumor is partially true. There really was an enemy attack on Los Angeles in the early stages of World War II. It took place at approximately seven P.M. on February 23, 1942, when a lone Japanese submarine opened fire at the Barnsdall Oil Company's main absorption plant at Elwood field in Goleta. The barrage lasted for a half an hour with sixteen twenty-five-inch shells being launched. Then, on February 26, four days later, the 4th Interceptor Command announced "enemy aircraft" flying over the same area. That led to a mandatory blackout for all residents in Southern California. No bombs were dropped, luckily enough, but American anti-aircraft guns peppered the darkened skies for approximately fifty-six minutes.

Nonetheless, it would be an overstatement to say that the Japanese actually conducted an assault on Los Angeles. In fact, the attack on Elwood was insignificant at best. Few buildings were hit, and the field suffered a mere $500 worth of damage. As one eyewitness told the *Los Angeles Times*, "Their marksmanship was rotten. Maybe one shell out of sixteen hit something." (Nonetheless, the Japanese Imperial headquarters claimed that the raid was a "great military success" while the President of the United States called it "political warfare".)

Furthermore, despite reports that the 4th Interceptor Command saw an entire squadron of Japanese bombers flying overhead, there seems to be little evidence that they saw anything at all. "There never were any enemy aircraft," says author Harvey Biegel, who has written extensively on submarine warfare in the Pacific. "One of the Water and Power transformers blew up accidentally in San Pedro and someone thought it was an attack and returned fire. That caused the sirens to go off. But there wasn't a Japanese squadron flying overhead."

## The Aftermath:

Already shaken by the surprise attack on Pearl Harbor in 1941, Los Angeles had plenty of reason to believe it could be next. After all, Southern California was highly vulnerable to terrorist attacks since it was home to more army bases, naval ports, and air strips than any other coastal city on the West Coast. That meant that *all* Japanese citizens were considered suspect in the eyes of most Axis-hating jingoists. In fact, District Attorney Percy Heckendorf came forward to say that there was "convincing proof" that "signals" were flashed to the sub just before the shelling—signals flashed by a Japanese family that lived on shore—while the *Los Angeles Times* reported that the Japanese had set up a number of secret air strips throughout Southern California in their preparation for an all-out assault.[16]

That in turn inspired Mayor Bowron to call Washington and demand that they send out the FBI to round up every Japanese resident in the area and ship them off to concentration camps. Bowron's request found support on the floor of the House of Representatives when A. J. Elliott

ALL THE NEWS ALL THE TIME
LARGEST HOME-DELIVERED CIRCULATION
LARGEST ADVERTISING VOLUME
MAdison 2345
The Times Telephone Number

EQUAL RIGHTS

# Los Angeles Times

LIBERTY UNDER THE LAW — TRUE INDUSTRIAL FREEDOM

IN THREE PARTS — 36 PAGES
Part I — GENERAL NEWS — 18 Pages
TIMES OFFICE
202 West First Street

VOL. LXI | CC | TUESDAY MORNING, FEBRUARY 24, 1942. | DAILY, FIVE CENTS

# SUBMARINE SHELLS SOUTHLAND OIL FIELD

## Noble Pleads Jap Case at Hearing Here

### Attack on Pearl Harbor Justified, He Says at Un-American Acts Inquiry

Inured to shocking testimony by months of hearings on un-American activities, the Assembly investigating committee at its hearing in the State Building yesterday was all but floored when they heard from the lips of Robert Noble, founder and leader of the Friends of Progress, a declaration that he thought that in their attack on Pearl Harbor "the Japanese did the proper thing under the exigencies of the time."

Prior to that the committee had wrung from Noble the admission that he had received a dishonorable discharge from the United States Navy after he ran away and had been arrested for desertion.

**DESERTION EXPLAINED**

He shrugged it off, however, with an explanation that he then was only 19, was ill and, anyway, he did not want to fight against the Germans in the first World War. He was really a pacifist then, he said.

Another statement credited to Noble by an earlier witness was that Gen. MacArthur and his men were "not heroes but fools."

**PRESIDENT 'TRIED'**

Noble later denied a statement credited to him in which he urged people not to buy Defense Bonds or Stamps. He said it would have been foolish for him to have done so because it would not have done any good. Asked if he had purchased any himself, he said he had not.

Ellis O. Jones, a codirector with Noble in the Friends of Progress meetings, held weekly in a downtown hotel auditorium, admitted that the organization had conducted a mock trial of President Roosevelt on charges of being "traitorous to the American people and had gotten them into war." Jones acted as "chief justice" and at the conclusion of

Turn to Page 13, Column 3

## President Pledges to Take Offensive

### Roosevelt Assures Nation Pacific Fleet Intact and Engaging Foe; Promises Destruction of Jap Militarism

BY KYLE PALMER
Times Staff Representative

WASHINGTON, Feb. 23.—On a rugged note of confidence, with a certain promise that the nation's enemies soon will be on the defensive, in a pledge to victory that held no proviso or reservation, President Roosevelt tonight gave his answer to critics of his administration and told the American people what they must face in the way of sacrifice and service before the war is won.

Speaking from the White House to a radio audience that listened throughout the world and encompassed the vast spread of oceans and continents which he discussed, the President analyzed the war strategy of friend and foe, told of the mighty prep-

Turn to Page 6, Part I, for full text of President Roosevelt's talk.

arations that are being made for victory, and spiked many of the false rumors which are being circulated about our war efforts and losses.

**LOSSES SUFFERED**

Reiterating a pledge he made to the people on Dec. 9, in which he said the government would keep the public informed of events, good or bad, Mr. Roosevelt said on their part the people must have confidence that the government will keep nothing from them which can be published without aiding the enemy.

We have suffered and will continue to suffer losses in the Atlantic and in the Pacific, Mr. Roosevelt said, but, he added:

"Speaking for the United States of America, let me say once and for all to the people of the world: We Americans have been compelled to yield ground, but we will regain it. We and the other United Nations are committed to the destruction of the militarism of Japan and Germany.

**STRENGTH INCREASING**

"We are daily increasing our strength. Soon we, and not our enemies, will have the offensive; we, not they, will win the final battles, and we, not they, will make the final peace."

Germany, Italy and Japan, he pointed out, "are very close to their maximum output of planes, guns, tanks and ships," while "the United Nations are not—es-

Turn to Page 5, Column 1

## Desperate Stand Taken in Burma

### Last Line of Defense Before Rangoon Pounded With Terrific Intensity

LONDON, Feb. 23. (U.P.)—Burma's defenders are making a desperate stand east of the Sittang River, last defense barrier before Rangoon, but the Japanese are pressing their attacks with "utmost intensity" and are aided by reinforcements fresh from the conquest of Singapore, Far East advices said today.

**CLAIM NEW LANDINGS**

(Vichy and Rome radio reports said that Japanese reinforcements had landed on the west coast of the Gulf of Martaban, south of Rangoon. If true, the troops could have come by sea from Singapore through Malacca Strait and Martaban Gulf and would be in position to flank Rangoon by driving up one or more mouths of the Irrawaddy River.)

(Chungking advices said Saturday that a large Japanese convoy had been observed steaming up the gulf.)

(An American Volunteer Group officer told United Press Correspondent Karl Eskelund at A.V.G. headquarters in Southwest China that telegraphic communication with Rangoon had been cut and that fall of the city was a matter of days.)

**R.A.F. REPORT**

The All-India Radio heard an R.A.F. communique broadcast from Rangoon today saying that the military situation was unchanged but that violent fighting continued between the Bilin and

Turn to Page 3, Column 7

## Japs on Bali Shut Off From Fleet

### Enemy Ships Smashed by Bomber Assaults; Drive Deeper Into Burma

Times Pacific War Summary

Three Japanese columns, reinforced by divisions released by the fall of Singapore, were driving deeper into British Burma yesterday but in the Netherlands Indies the Nipponese appeared to have been stopped, for the moment at least, on their partly won bases off the eastern and western ends of Java.

Batavia said that planes and warships of the United Nations had smashed a Japanese invasion fleet which landed troops on Bali, off the tip of Eastern Java, and Washington reinforced this by announcing that the United States Army Air Force in the Netherlands Indies since Jan. 1 has sunk at least 9 enemy vessels and damaged 24 others. The Bali invaders were cut off by the Jap fleet losses.

It was admitted, however, that the Japanese hold the important Denpasar Airdrome and other strategic points on Bali and that their conquest of Southeastern Sumatra is virtually complete.

The situation in the Far East yesterday as summarized from United Press and Associated Press dispatches was:

**EAST INDIES**—It seemed certain that the Japanese invasion fleet suffered heavily. Estimates ranged from 5 to 15 Jap ships were sunk, most of them victims of airplanes. The Japanese apparently captured the Denpasar Airdrome in good condition since the communique said that American planes bombed it yesterday, damaging the runways and field.

**BURMA** — London admitted the prospects in Burma were gloomy but it was asserted that combined forces of Indian, British and American-volunteer fighter planes had established air superiority over the battle front, which apparently was along the Sittang River, just west of the vital Rangoon-Lashio Railway.

**PHILIPPINES**—There was little change in the situation on the Bataan Peninsula where Gen. Douglas MacArthur's durable Filipino and American troops again had fought the Japanese to a standstill.

## Japs Control Bali Airport

BANDOENG (Dutch East Indies) Feb. 23. (AP)—The Japanese enemy has overrun part of Bali and controls the airport at Denpasar, on the southeast of the island near its only good harbor, but his entire invading fleet has been destroyed, damaged or dispersed and his landing troops are isolated, the Dutch announced tonight.

Thus was summed up the first phase of the invader's thrust at the near approaches to the Java keystone in the Allied arch—a thrust in which Japanese sea power suffered, under co-ordinated American-Dutch bomber and warship fire, its gravest wounds

Turn to Page 3, Column 3

## Japanese Make Direct Hit North of Santa Barbara

### No Lives Lost and Little Damage Inflicted by First Enemy Assault on Soil of United States Since War Started in December; Witnesses Declare Submersible Fired 16 Shots From Mile Offshore

In the first attack upon United States soil since this war began, an enemy submarine rose out of the sea off the rich oil fields at Ellwood, 12 miles north of Santa Barbara, shortly after 7 p.m. yesterday and pumped 16 shells into the tidewater fields, but caused only superficial damage.

A single oil well derrick was reported by eyewitnesses to have been hit, but there were no casualties in human life.

Choosing the dramatic instant of the halfway mark in President Roosevelt's fireside chat, the commander of the presumably Japanese submarine opened fire from his deck guns at 7:15 p.m.

Three of the shells dug up the sands off the Bankline Oil Co. refinery. The only damage in the raid was the destruction of rigging and pumping equipment of a well about a quarter of a mile from the beach. Loss was estimated at several thousand dollars.

**NAVY BEGINS HUNT FOR SUB**

One of the shells whistled three miles inland to the Tecolote ranch where it exploded. Another missile gouged out a five-foot-wide crater on the Staniff ranch near by. The other salvos fell short of their marks, it was asserted, and dropped into the sea.

Navy planes roared over the channel a short time later and counteroperations were begun.

Four Japanese and one Italian were taken into custody

Illustrated on Page B

by Ventura County Sheriff's authorities last night shortly after the attack. Two Japs were said to have been riding around the city during the blackout in a station wagon, armed with guns. For more than two hours after the raid, brilliant yellow flares burst over darkened Ventura. Authorities said it was clearly an effort to signal the enemy.

**RAIDER LAST SEEN HEADED SOUTH**

When last reported, about 8:30 p.m. by a minister at Montecito, the submarine was slipping out of the Santa Barbara Channel in the direction of Los Angeles. The clergyman, Rev. Arthur Basham of Pomona, who was visiting there, said he observed the "pigboat" flashing signal lights, apparently to someone on shore.

The Ventura County Sheriff's office received reports that flares had been sighted lighting the skies at several points along the coast in Ventura County near Hueneme.

At 7:58 p.m. upon orders of the Fourth Interceptor Command all radio stations in Southern California abruptly left the air. A few minutes later the coast line was completely blacked out from Carpinteria to Goleta. The blackout area covered a distance of about 25 miles. The yellow alert flashed simultaneously in police headquarters in Los Angeles.

The "all-clear" signal light was flashed in Los Angeles at 12:11 a.m., four hours and 13 minutes later.

**SANTA BARBARA BLACKED OUT**

Air-raid sirens screamed in Santa Barbara and within a few moments the entire city was dark.

At 12:20 a.m. today the all clear was sounded.

First report of the submarine reached the Sheriff's office from Mrs. George Heaney on San Marcos Pass, northwest of Santa Barbara. She informed authorities that she heard the first gun report shortly after 7 p.m. With field glasses, she said she sighted the submarine. It was lying about a mile offshore.

The next report came from Bob Miller of the Bankline Oil Co., who gave a similar report. By this time, the guns of the submarine were speaking repeatedly and shells shrieking overhead.

F. W. Borden, superintendent of the Bankline plant, gave this eyewitness account of the raid to the 11th Naval District.

"At 7:10 P.W.T., one large submarine came to the surface

Turn to Page A, Column 3

## Shelling of Oil Field Described by Eyewitness

### Restaurant Man First Believed Explosions Caused by Army Conducting Target Practice

"Their marksmanship was rotten!"

Thus did Lawrence Wheeler, proprietor of a roadside inn situated in the heart of the Ellwood oil fields, describe the shelling of the fields by enemy submarine deck guns last night.

"It started about 7:15 p.m.," he said. "I know it was about that time because we were serving dinners to customers and listening to the President's speech, and he was about halfway through.

**HEARD LOUD REPORT**

"Suddenly we heard a loud report, followed in a few moments by another. Some soldiers who were in my place said it was probably just target practice.

"We heard a bit later that the oil fields were being shelled. I went outside and ran over to a point whence I could see the ocean. It looked like a submarine, about a mile offshore, cruising slowly down the coast and firing at regular intervals.

"I could see the flashes as the gun went off.

**AIMED AT PLANT**

"The submarine seemed to be aiming at the Barnsdall Oil Co.'s main absorption plant, located almost on the beach.

"They missed with all their shots at this plant, though some of the shells landed fairly close, throwing up geysers of dirt and sand near the building.

"One shell hit a well and blew the pumping plant and derrick to bits.

"That was the only real damage they did.

"There must have been 20 or 25 men working in the field at the time. Nobody was injured.

**NOTIFIED SHERIFF**

"One of their shots whistled over my inn, which is a good mile from the shore line, and burst up the canyon on the Hollister estate across the highway.

"We notified the Sheriff's office and they said planes would be here in 10 minutes.

"It seemed to me as if the enemy vessel was firing a 5 or 6-inch gun. Their shooting wasn't very good, because that absorption plant was a beautiful target and they didn't hit it."

**CUSTOMRRS CALM**

Mrs. Wheeler added this account:

"I saw the explosions. At first they were very faint. I thought it was the Army practicing but then I heard a shell fly overhead and strike in a canyon inshore from our place."

Wheeler said there was no panic among his customers.

"We immediately blacked out the place," he said. "One shell landed about a quarter of a mile from here and the concussion shook the building but nobody was scared much."

## Suspicious Lights Flashed Here After Submarine Attack

Flashlights in the hands of suspicious persons, possibly signalers, were reported to police last night shortly after a Japanese submarine dropped shells near Santa Barbara.

Six calls were received by the police complaint board, telling of the blinking flashlights in various parts of the city. One witness said he saw one or two persons at the end of the Venice pier with flashlights.

Policemen were dispatched to the locations given, but in all instances the suspicious persons were gone.

During the radio blackout coincident with the shelling, hundreds of phone calls were received by the board inquiring whether residence lights should be doused. Callers were reminded that one of the rules during an alert was not to use the telephone.

## IN THE 'TIMES' TODAY

TUESDAY
FEBRUARY 24, 1942

stated, "Don't kid yourselves and don't let someone tell you [that] there are good Japs. Perhaps one out of a thousand."

President Roosevelt eventually succumbed to political pressure and signed Executive Order 9066. (German-Americans, meanwhile, went untouched.) As a result, approximately 120,000 Japanese were rounded up and sent away to internment camps in central California. More than sixty percent were American citizens and/or born in the U.S. The action was not only racist, but illegal.

President Gerald Ford ordered a full investigation of the internment camps in 1976, but it wasn't until 1980 that the Commission on Wartime Relocation called the action a "grave injustice." Finally, in 1988, nearly fifty years later, the U.S. government contacted the remaining survivors and cut each one a check for $20,000.

# THE LEGEND:

The Silent Movie Theater was shut down after owner Larry Austin was murdered in a robbery attempt run afoul.

Silence is golden

Paul Young

## Where It Comes From:

On January 19, 1997, at approximately eight P.M., Christian Rodriguez, a nineteen-year-old Mexican-American gangbanger decorated with tattoos, walked up to the Silent Movie Theater in the heart of the Fairfax district and bought a ticket to see F. W. Murnau's *Sunrise*. The theater was, and still is, one of the lesser known jewels in the area: a fifty-year-old, homespun operation featuring hard-to-see cinematic fare, hand-printed notes, personal appearances by legendary stars, and live musical accompaniment. But by the time Rodriguez took his seat in the back of the theater, the lights had already dimmed and the first Felix the Cat cartoon was well into its classic mayhem.

A few minutes later, as a Larry Semon short began, Rodriguez climbed out of his seat and made his way into the lobby. There he found nineteen-year-old Mary Gilles in the ticket booth counting receipts. Rodriguez approached her cautiously, looking around nervously with his hand inside his coat pocket. "I need to buy some tickets in advance," he asked. "For next week."

Gilles called out to Larry Austin, the seventy-four-year-old owner, who was in the other room, and asked him to take care of the transaction, since only he dealt with such affairs. But as soon as Austin appeared Rodriguez produced a thirteen-inch, .357 Magnum and ordered him to empty the register. Austin obeyed without saying a word. Then, without provocation, Rodriguez raised the gun and shot Austin at near point-blank range causing Gilles to scream at the top of her lungs. Staying cool, Rodriguez then turned the gun on Gilles and shot her, too, then spun back around and pumped several more rounds into Austin's already limp body. Some members in the audience, meanwhile, crawled under their seats after hearing Gilles's screams, and many were horrified to see Rodriguez run back into the theater and dart out a rear exit.

## What Really Happened:

When police arrived at the scene they assumed that it was just another robbery gone horribly wrong. But after several weeks of inquiry, they came upon an ex-con by the name of Paul Moreland who gave them some surprising information. Supposedly James Van Sickle, a thirty-four-year-old ex-bodybuilder who worked as the theater's projectionist, had offered him $20,000 to kill Austin, who he claimed was "his uncle." Moreland backed out of the deal however, when Van Sickle failed to give him half the money up front. That forced Van Sickle to find someone else.

As detectives looked into Moreland's claims, they discovered that Van Sickle—who had been charged with attempted murder in 1988 and felony drug trafficking in 1989—wasn't Austin's nephew at all. If anything, he was his gay lover. According to the *Los Angeles Times*, Van Sickle met Austin in 1990 when he answered an ad for a painter, and within months they were living together in the small apartment above the theater.

Yet as some reporters have since revealed, Austin was hardly an angel himself. In 1983 he was convicted on one count of grand theft as the result of an embezzlement case, and served twenty-two months in state prison. What's more, there's also evidence that he illegally "coerced" the previous owner of the Silent Movie Theater, Dorothy Hampton, into signing over the rights to the property and all her holdings while she was in a convalescent home suffering from Alzheimer's.

According to court testimony, Van Sickle began thinking about bumping off his lover as early as 1994 when he learned that Austin's holdings were worth over $1 million. And as soon as he convinced Austin to make out a will naming Van Sickle as the sole benefactor, he found Moreland—and then Rodriguez—to assassinate him.

## The Legacy:

Rodriguez was found guilty of murder on January 21, 1999, and five days later Van Sickle was found guilty of the same charge. At the time of this writing, he's serving a life sentence without the possibility of parole. Meanwhile the theater has been reopened by Charles Lustman, a local songwriter, and revamped with an orchestra pit, patio dining, and a cappuccino bar.

# THE LEGEND:

The Spanish Kitchen, the infamous restaurant on Beverly Boulevard, was closed after one of the owners was murdered.

## What People Are Saying:

Like the Silent Movie Theater, the Spanish Kitchen has its own murder story, and it has fueled people's imaginations for decades. Author Erika Taylor based her novel *The Sun Maiden,* on it and the producers of *Lou Grant* used it for an episode in the 1970s. Yet to this day no one really knows what actually happened at the restaurant. Some say it was a murder, others say it was a gang war, and others still say that it was an accident.

## A Little History:

In the 1930s and forties, the Spanish Kitchen Original was considered one of L.A.'s best-kept secrets. Its first incarnation was located on the outskirts of downtown, and was known to draw a heavy celebrity crowd, including the likes of Mary Pickford, Errol Flynn, Buster Keaton, W. C. Fields, and John Barrymore. Eventually the owners, John and Pearl Caretto, outgrew their space, and opened a sister restaurant on the West Side. After securing a venue at 7373 Beverly Boulevard near Martel Avenue, just down the street from the popular El Coyote Café, they soon found that their celebrity clientele virtually doubled. As the *Los Angeles Examiner* put it, "The Carettos' choice has proven to be an auspicious one. It may even be more successful than the *original* Spanish Kitchen Original."

## Where It Comes From:

At some point, at the height of the restaurant's popularity, Pearl Caretto's husband died under "mysterious" circumstances and Pearl closed the front door, hung a CLOSED sign in the window, and walked away forever. From that day on, the restaurant sat with its chairs on the tables, dishes in the sink, and menus in their holders for *twenty years*.

Throughout the 1960s, it was common to hear that something "terrible" happened at the restaurant, something so horrible that Pearl had to "disappear." Meanwhile, Pearl refused to talk to reporters about any aspect of the restaurant, and even made her daughter swear that she'd keep her mouth shut, too (an oath that the daughter continues to live by to this day). That, of course, led to all kinds of wild theories, mostly having to do with John's untimely demise. A popular version appeared in the 1970s, for example, detailing how a group of mobsters walked into the restaurant and opened fire Al Capone–style, killing John and at least one other person. (Apparently John wasn't the intended victim, but rather a private detective living upstairs in the tiny apartment above the restaurant.) Another theory was that John had gotten involved with some vengeful gamblers who killed him for failing to pay back his debts. And another still had it that two corrupt cops got into a shootout in the back of the restaurant and accidentally caught John in the cross fire, which in turn led to a cover-up.

## What Really Happened:

In truth, the restaurant didn't open its doors until 1955, long after L.A.'s gangster glory days, and according to public records there has *never* been a shooting at the location. If the rumor has

John Caretto's Waterloo

James Fee

## Throughout the 1960s, it was common to hear that something "terrible" happened at the restaurant, something so horrible that Pearl had to "disappear."

any basis in fact at all, it may have something to do with some of the other shady clubs in the area. The Bar of Music, for instance, which was located right next door (now a Hebrew academy), was known to cater to all kinds of questionable characters, including mafiosi.

According to the best reconstruction of the facts, John Caretto began suffering from Parkinson's disease in the late 1950s and by the end of the decade his condition had become so severe that he needed to be hospitalized. Pearl tried to keep the restaurant going during that time, but had difficulty on her own. Finally after John passed away in his hospital bed in 1960, Pearl was so devastated that she refused to step foot inside the restaurant ever again. After all, the restaurant had become a symbol of their love, and to go on without him would be meaningless, or worse, ruinous to the beauty of what they once had. So she simply walked away and never looked back.

## The Legacy:

Ron Mavaddat purchased the building in 1997 with the sole intention or restoring it to its original glory. He spent a fortune hunting down original fixtures, renovating materials, and tracking down early photographs from the Caretto family. It was a difficult process, but Mavaddat remained optimistic. "I heard all the stories the the the place was haunted and jinxed," says Movaddat, "and I talked to the family. I learned the history and discovered that none of it was true." What he didn't count on, however, was that the largely Jewish neighborhood would back a team of "professional protestors and encourage them to thwart Mavaddat's plans. That led to a three-year battle with the protestors thwarting Mavaddat's attempts to get building permits and a liquor license, and Mavaddat doing his best to stay true to Pearl's vision. Finally, after years of headaches, harassment, and threats, he gave up and leased the building to the French couple, Laurent and Fabienne Dufourg, in 2000. Since then, it has been transformed into a hair salon, Prive, and an upscale day spa, Ona.

# THE LEGEND:

Obscene messages are embedded in the tiki gods adorning Trader Vic's.

## A Little Background:

Thanks to World War I, President Theodore Roosevelt's legendary adventures in Africa, and the prevalence of new, handheld movie cameras, the greatest fashion trend of the 1920s was the exotic. Even famous architects such as Welton Becket and Meyer and Holler began incorporating Third World designs in their buildings. In fact, the exotic has since become the very essence of L.A.'s most "indigenous" architectural styles including L.A. Craftsman, L.A. Modernism, and Mediterranean revival.

According to Bruce Henstell's *Sunshine and Wealth*, Baron Long, a former fight promoter with numerous underworld contacts, was the first to open a Hawaiian-themed restaurant in the city, and that soon led to a host of imitators.[17] Perhaps the most famous was Don the Beachcomber's, a lush tropical affair located at 1727 McCadden Place in Hollywood. Don the Beachcomber's was so successful in fact that Victor Jules Bergeron, also known as Trader Vic, borrowed a similar Polynesian flair for his eponymous eatery in Oakland, which opened a short time later.

## What People Are Saying:

Bergeron's restaurant at the Beverly Hilton Hotel in Beverly Hills remains one of the greatest testaments to the Hawaiian-chic genre ever produced. Begun in 1955, under the leadership of Eddie Carlson, the restaurant was meant to be a truly high-class affair, several notches above Don the Beachcomber's, with nothing but the most authentic Polynesian fabrics, designs, and knick-knacks used for decor. To that end, Bergeron scoured the South Pacific for the best artifacts that he could find, and he eventually came across a magnificent, eight-foot statue of a tiki god in Fiji. Believing that it would be perfect for the front of the restaurant, he gave the vendor

**OUCH!**

Paul Young

*A hush fell over the crowd as the statue was revealed to be a fertility god rather than a tiki god—and it had a three-foot hard-on.*

explicit instructions on how to send it to Beverly Hills, and paid the shipping fees in advance.[18]

Meanwhile construction on the restaurant continued at its usual pace. But as the completion date neared, there still was no sign of Bergeron's tiki god. Finally, on the last day of construction—twenty-four hours before opening day—the statue arrived. Workers quickly moved it into place and set it into cement. Then, the following day, dozens of investors, designers, and planners showed up to have a look before opening night. Someone noticed that the tiki god was still wrapped in plastic, however, and asked to have it removed. Acting quickly, two workers climbed up the side of the statue and pulled off the plastic. A hush fell over the crowd as the statue was revealed to be a fertility god rather than a tiki god—*and it had a three-foot hard-on.*

The president of the hotel immediately demanded that the statue be removed at once. But by then the cement had hardened and if anyone tried to remove it, it would undoubtedly take half the building with it. As the workers continued to bicker over the dilemma, a voice perked up from the back of the crowd. "Excuse me," said a carpenter, making his way forward. "But I think I can fix it."

"Then go to it!" ordered the contractor.

Moments later, the carpenter hoisted himself up along the side of the statue, stood over the figure's appendage, and whacked it off with a single strike of his hammer. All at once came a chorus of "Ouch!" from the crowd of workers below.

## The Legacy:

The castrated fertility god still stands in front of the restaurant to this day. In fact, according to legend, any male patron who fails to pay his respects to the god on the way in will suffer the humiliation of failing in the art of love that night.

# THE RUMOR:

The notorious gangster `Al Capone` built his desert hideaway in Two Bunch Palms.

## Capone and Pal Persuaded to Leave L.A. Area

## A Little Background:

In an area originally discovered by military surveyors in the nineteenth century, the Two Bunch Palms Resort and Spa is considered one of the most beautiful resorts in all of Southern California. The fifty-acre, forty-four-room hotel boasts natural artesian mineral springs, mud baths, saunas, indoor and outdoor massage rooms, watsu pools, and more. Perhaps its greatest allure, however, at least for Angelenos, is that it once belonged to Al Capone. In fact, the owners have labeled one room the "Al Capone suite" and claimed that the alleged bullet hole in the dresser, came from one of his guns.

## Where It Comes From:

According to Dana Bass Smith, the current manager of the resort, the rumor may have been started after some visitors from Chicago checked into the hotel in the 1970s and claimed that they were related to Thomas H. Lipps, the man who allegedly oversaw the construction of the building. "They said that Lipps was Capone's lawyer in Chicago in the 1920s," explains Bass Smith. "And that he was sent to California in the early 1930s to build a house, or a hideaway, for Capone when he needed to get out of Chicago. And that's when he built Two Bunch Palms."

## The Evidence:

At first glance the original building—supposedly Al's living quarters—appears to have a "hideout"

quality to it. There's a small room situated on top of the house that resembles a lookout tower. There's a trapdoor near the back that leads to a large tunnel—large enough to drive a car through—that may have served as an escape route. And the walls themselves—consistent with architecture of the early 1930s—are decidedly thicker than usual, possibly designed to withstand a fusillade of firepower.

## A Little History:

Nonetheless, no one has ever been able to find any evidence that Capone ever set foot in the building. In fact, the only time that Capone ever came to Southern California was on December 12, 1927, when he came to visit some associates in San Diego. After that he took in a bullfight in nearby Tijuana and then entrained to Los Angeles the following day, where he checked into the Biltmore Hotel under the name Al Brown. According to most historians, he only spent twenty-four hours in the City of Angels, however, much of it visiting movie studios and Pickfair, the legendary home of Douglas Fairbanks and Mary Pickford. Yet when he returned to the Biltmore he found himself face to face with Detective "Roughhouse" Brown. "We have no room for any visiting gangsters," threatened Brown. "Whether they're here on pleasure tours or not."

Apparently Capone complied with the LAPD's ultimatum, and boarded the next train to Florida. But he wasn't happy about it. "Why

> # "He always had the same bathroom complete with a double showerhead and special Nile tile with lavender trim imported from Europe. It was almost his signature."

should everybody in this town pick on me?" he complained. "I wasn't going to do anything here. Besides, I thought you guys liked tourists."

Nonetheless, Capone was smitten with L.A. and hoped to return. As he told a reporter a short time later, "When I get a little business done in Chicago I'm going to spend a lot of money out here and have a real estate man buy me a large house right in Beverly Hills." Unfortunately, 1929 proved to be a fatal year for the gangster. After his monumental blunder, the St. Valentine's Day Massacre, he was arrested on income tax evasion and locked up for eleven years. Five years later, in 1934, he was transferred to Alcatraz Island, where he began suffering from severe bouts of dementia thanks to an old, untreated case of syphilis.

Meanwhile, as his release date loomed, Capone's successors—Tony Accardo, Charles Fishetti, Paul Ricca, and Frank Nitti—built him a number of high-security homes around the country. According to Chicago historian Bill

Heller, one was built in Wisconsin and another one was built in Florida off Route 41 on the way to Miami. Both had lookout towers and subterranean tunnels large enough to park cars in. "Each one had a special trademark," explains Heller. "He always had the same bathroom complete with a double showerhead and special Nile tile with lavender trim imported from Europe. It was almost his signature."

## The Bottom Line:

It's not a stretch to believe that Two Bunch Palms could have been one of those hideouts. A number of Capone's lieutenants made it to Palm Springs in the 1930s, including Frank Nitti, Paul Ricca, Capone's brother Ralph, his wife, Mae, and his son, Sonny. Yet no one has been able to find any connection between them and the resort. What's more, despite claims by the Lipps family, Thomas H. Lipps was from New York rather than Chicago,

Al Capone slept here

at least according to a 1924 *Who's Who in California,* and had little, if any association with members of the Chicago Mafia.[19] In fact, the best explanation for the underground tunnels, thick walls, and covert watchtowers may have to do with the fact that Lipps had planned to build a full-scale gambling casino much like the Dunes in nearby Cathedral City. But after the crackdown on gambling in Riverside County he decided to let his wife, a former dancer named Billie, transform the grounds into a health spa instead.

## Where It Really Comes From:

It's possible that Lipps has been confused for another lawyer in Palm Springs who *did* have connections to Al Capone—Abraham Teitelbaum. According to a number of mob experts, Teitelbaum was one of Capone's top "fixers" in Chicago, and he moved to Palm Springs in the late 1920s. Yet there are no records proving that *he* had anything to do with Two Bunch Palms Inn, Thomas Lipps, or anyone else at the spa either.[20] "There's no chance in hell that anyone involved with Two Bunch had anything to do with Al Capone," says Frank Bogert, the former mayor of Palm Springs. "I knew Lipps real well, and I know that he never had any dealings with Capone or any of his gang. As far as I'm concerned, that's all bullshit. *I* was the one that took Lipps to that area in the first place. He needed to bury a dog so I took him out there. When he started digging he discovered water. And that's how the spa was born. That's all there is to it. If any gangsters showed up there, they were there to get a rubdown and that's about it. Don't believe any of that horseshit about Capone. They're just saying all that to sell more rooms over there."

Jesus lived here

# THERE GOES THE NEIGHBORHOOD

While celebrity maps have always been popular with tourists, most fail to list the addresses of the most famous figure of all: Jesus Christ. As phone records show, the Son of God has lived in a number of homes around L.A., including the following:

| DATE | LISTING | ADDRESS | PHONE |
|------|---------|---------|-------|
| ★ 1928 | J. Christ | 1133 E. 42nd St., L.A. | HU-1397 |
| ★ 1938 | J. Christ | 2286 Vasanta Way, L.A. | HI-5789 |
| ★ 1949 | J. H. Christ | 626 E. Elmwood, Burbank | CH8-2637 |
| ★ 1952 | J. H. Christ | 1244 Otsego Dr., N. Hollywood | SU3-1433 |
| ★ 1955 | J. Christ | 1345 W. 22nd St., L.A. | RI7-9234 |
| ★ 1962 | J. Christ | 8134 Calhoun St., Panorama City | ST2-5306 |
| ★ 1976 | Jesus Christ | 15216 Florewood Ave., Lawndale | 644-0687 |
| ★ 1982 | J. Christ | 4211 Jackson Ave., Culver City | 838-3550 |
| ★ 1987 | J. H. Christ | 950 2nd Ave., Santa Monica | 394-4657 |
| ★ 1995 | Jesus Christ | 1809 N. Bronson Ave., L.A. | 467-2571 |
| ★ 1998 | Jesus Christ | 1322 Euclid Ave., Santa Monica | Unlisted |

Notice a pattern? It seems that Mr. Christ has renounced the godforsaken lands of the inner city and moved to the Westside—complete with an unlisted number!

In a sense, we're living the myth of the Dying God. It's the Icarus myth, the Elvis Presley myth, and the Sid Vicious myth. Society wants it and craves it.

—STING

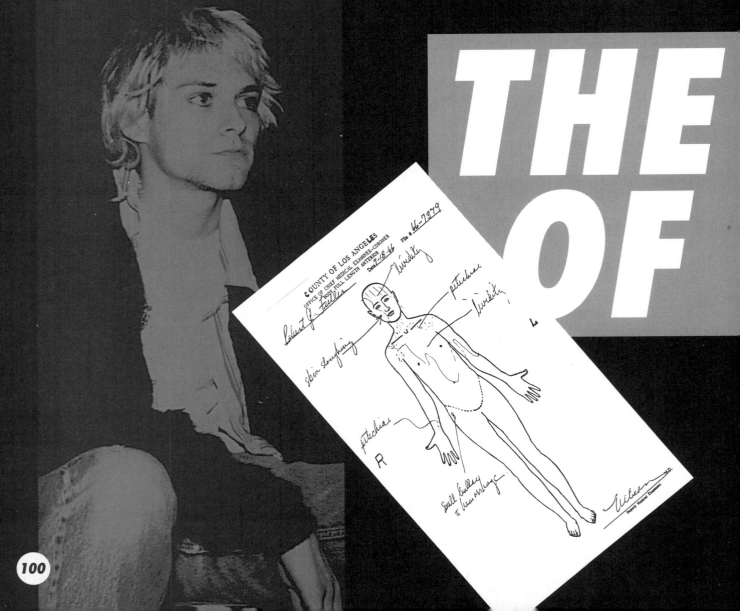

THE OF

# MARCH
# VULGARIA

## L.A.'S ROCKIN' RUMORS

# THE LEGEND:

One night, while high on drugs, singer Sam Cooke tried to rape a young girl at a cheap motel in South Central only to be shot to death by the hotel manager.

## A Little Background:

While there have been dozens of tragic deaths in L.A.'s long and sordid rock history, the untimely death of Sam Cooke remains one of the most puzzling. Cooke, the elegant soul crooner responsible for such classics as "You Send Me" and "Little Red Rooster," was found dead in the lobby of the Hacienda, a small motel along Figueroa on the night of December 11, 1964. The motel's manager admitted to shooting him, yet to this day there has never been a satisfactory explanation of what *really* happened that night. That, of course, has led to a few interesting theories.

## What People Are Saying:

Apparently Cooke's evening began at Martoni's in Hollywood, one of his favorite restaurants. It was there that he spotted Elisa Boyer, a sexy young model with musical aspirations. After a drink, and a few minutes of small talk, he eventually asked her to accompany him to PJs, a popular music venue nearby. She smiled but declined, stating that she was tired and wanted to go home. Being the gentleman that he was, he then offered to give her a lift to her house instead.

To this day no one really knows what happened after that, but many have speculated that a few minutes after getting into Cooke's car, the two started getting intimate with each other. Whether it was Cooke or Boyer that decided to then continue the activities at a nearby motel may never be known, but the two ended up at the Hacienda a short time later. Things took a turn for the worse, however, when Boyer refused to sleep with the crooner on the first date. That infuriated Cooke, who was not only wildly drunk at that point, but nearly nude. He then jumped on top of her, trying to force himself on her, until she started fighting back. That's when Boyer thought that if she ran out the door with his clothes, he probably wouldn't follow since he was already quite aroused by then. So that's exactly what she did, grabbing his trousers and making a beeline for the manager's office. But when Cooke realized that she had accidentally run off with his wallet, he quickly donned a topcoat and stumbled up to the manager's door—only to find it locked. "Open the goddamn door!" he screamed. "I want my goddamn money!"

The manager, Bertha Franklin, a woman in her sixties, later claimed that she thought Cooke was a thief. "He kept shouting, I want money, I want money," she later testified. "I thought he wanted to steal my money." Moments later, Cooke kicked in the door and stormed inside. That's when she grabbed a gun from under the counter and unleashed three rounds into his chest, knocking him to the floor. And as if that wasn't enough, she then picked up a club and struck him repeatedly.

## To The Contrary:

The second version of the story is similar to the first, yet it shifts the blame slightly. According to the biographers, Cooke was suffering from a crippling depression at the time of the incident, primarily due to his marital problems and the accidental drowning of his eighteen-month-old son, Vincent, a couple of months earlier. And according to the LAPD, Boyer may not have been quite as innocent as some have made her out to be either. Apparently, she had had a history of prostitution,[3] and there's a good chance that *she* took *him* to the motel rather than vice versa. In fact some have suggested that Franklin received money for protecting her.

In other words the scenario went something like this: Boyer saw Cooke at Martoni's, made a pass at him, and proceeded to ply him with drinks until he was intoxicated. Then she took him to the Hacienda where she screwed his brains out and waited for him to fall asleep. Once out, she grabbed his pants and wallet, and trotted off to the manager's office where she gave Franklin her cut and disappeared out a side door.

## The Paranoid View:

Another theory, which is perhaps the most cynical of all, is that Cooke may have been assassinated. The basis for the rumor has to do with the fact that Cooke had begun courting black militant groups around the time of the tragedy, which apparently took many by surprise. After all,

# There's a good chance that she took him to the motel rather than vice versa.

Cooke had built his career on entertaining white, rather than black, audiences, and few in the black community—at least in the politicized 1960s—considered him a true brother. But by 1964, he began fraternizing and supporting the Black Panthers and Malcolm X quite openly, giving them an unprecedented amount of free publicity, support, and financing. The theory then—as absurd as it sounds—is that the FBI simply had to put an end to his career—permanently.

## The Bottom Line:

None of the three theories are out of the question—yet in all likelihood the scene went down like this: Cooke hired a hooker, she stole his wallet, and the manager shot him out of fear. Case closed.

Paul Young

Cooke's murder site, as it stands today

# THE RUMOR:

Cooley
D.A. Calls It 'Murder by Torture'

Los Angeles Examiner/USC Special Collections

Love Hurts: Spade and Ella in happier times

6645

## A Little Background:

Like a number of early country artists, Donnell Clyde "Spade" Cooley was no stranger to the dark side of life. Aside from severe bouts of depression and alcoholism, he was known to have a hot temper, and was once charged with attempted rape. Nonetheless, his public image remained untarnished throughout the 1940s and fifties. His weekly shows at the Redondo Beach pier attracted as many as 10,000 fans a night, and his popularity eventually brought him his own television show, *The Spade Cooley Hour*.

Popular music changed dramatically in the 1960s, however, and it wasn't long before Cooley began to realize that his days were numbered. Consequently, he lashed out at nearly everyone that he came into contact with. His second wife Ella Mae, a twenty-one-year-old fiddle player in his band, was too young and ill-equipped to handle such mood swings, however, and that led to numerous fights.

## The Legend:

Sadly, the Cooleys failed to realize the trauma that they were inflicting on their daughter, Melody, who later told a reporter that she "hated" weekends because they always ended in "drunken orgies, fistfights, and screaming matches." Yet no one could have predicted the horror that Melody would have to witness a short time later, a horror that would haunt her for the rest of her life.

Apparently it all started when Cooley overheard his wife flirting with someone else over the phone. He had come home unexpectedly and found her locked in her room chatting away to another man. Yet rather than storm in and confront her, he retired to the living room, took a seat on the couch, lit a cigarette, and waited for her to come out. Apparently, he remained there for an hour until she finally came out, and when she did, he simply gave her a hard stare, put on his best poker face and said, "I had the phone line tapped, Ella Mae. I've been listening to every word that you said."

To his surprise, she responded with a defiant tone. "Yeah?" she said with a sneer. "Well then now you know, don't you? So what?"

That's when it all came out: Ella Mae had been spending time with two men, Bud Davenport and Luther Jackson, two part-time employees at UCLA's medical laboratories. Cooley wanted further proof, however, so he paid both men a visit the following day, making sure to keep a handgun conspicuously displayed in his belt. Davenport emphatically denied any romantic involvement with his wife, although he admitted that he once spent time with her and Jackson at a beachside motel. That sent Cooley into a rage and he attacked both men, nearly beating Davenport senseless. "And if I ever find out that you're messing with my mentally ill wife again I'll come back here and kill both of you!" he screamed.

On April 3, 1961, Cooley stormed into his house and confronted Ella Mae about her infidelities, and that's when she promised to tell him "everything," but only if he'd promise not to kill her. After a few moments, Cooley sat down in a chair, lit another cigarette, and said, "Fine. I'm all ears."

"Spade, there's something that I've been meaning to tell you for some time," she confessed. "And if you go get Melody, I'll tell you both something."

Frustrated, Cooley climbed back out of his chair, strutted into his daughter's room, grabbed the fourteen-year-old by the arm, and dragged her back into the room and forced her to sit down. "All right, let's have it," he said, sitting back down.

Trying to collect herself, Ella Mae claimed that Davenport and Jackson had "initiated" her into a new "free love" cult based near Ventura, and that she had made the decision to give up everything to become a member—including her family. "Spade," she said, "my first meeting with Bud alone would make you never want me in this house ever again. But that is in the past. Now I can only look to the future. I know this is something that you will have trouble understanding, but I have to do this. They're buying land near the ocean. And it's going to be a very private club of only a hundred members of both sexes."

Cooley later testified that his brain suddenly "caught on fire." He jumped up and punched her in the face, knocking her across the room. Melody screamed, and ran back to her bedroom as Ella Mae tried to pull herself up. "What can I do to prove to you that I still love you?" she cried. "What can I do to prove how much this means to me?" Then she stood up almost defiantly, walked over to Cooley, grabbed the cigarette out of his hand and said "You want to know how much I love you, Spade? Well, I'll show you how much." Then she ripped open her blouse and pressed the burning embers into her breast several times, screaming, "This is how much I love you, Spade!"[1]

The act did nothing to mollify Cooley's anger, however. Because all he wanted to know was whether or not she had sex with Davenport and Jackson. So he asked her again, and this time she admitted that she had, claiming that it was part of the "initiation into their cult."

Cooley lost all comprehension of what happened next. "Rockets were going off in my head," he later testified. "I couldn't tell right from wrong anymore."

Melody later told a grand jury that she ran back into the room when she heard her mother's screams, and saw her father with his hands around her neck. "That's when he let go of her," she testified. "And came over and picked me up, put me on the couch, and said, 'Now you're going to watch me kill this whore.'"

Melody later testified that her father "stomped on her mother until she stopped moving." And when he finally finished, he casually stepped back, lit another cigarette, and asked his daughter, "Do you think she's really dead? Well, let's see if she is." Then he bent down over her limp body and began poking the burning cigarette into her flesh again.

## The Result:

During his trial Cooley's defense team tried to prove that Davenport and Jackson were thieves by producing a letter purportedly written by Ella Mae which claimed that she gave them $580 to invest in a new business venture. (In fact she gave them the money to start a "nest egg" once she divorced from Cooley.) The defense also produced a tape recording that contained a conversation between Ella Mae and a private detective (hired by Cooley) which clearly proved that she was having "intimate relationships" with Davenport and Jackson. Yet none of it helped Cooley's case. Thanks to Melody's testimony, he was found guilty of first-degree murder and sentenced to twenty years imprisonment at Vacaville Prison.

Eight years later, he was paroled for good behavior and immediately scheduled a comeback performance in Oakland, California. The concert was a tremendous success. He received a standing ovation after the first set. As he walked backstage he told a friend, "Tonight was the happiest day of my life." He then turned around and walked back to his dressing room where he suffered a massive heart attack and died on the spot.

*...he bent down over her limp body and began poking the burning cigarette into her flesh again...*

# THE RUMOR:

Peter Criss

Steve Granitz/Retna Ltd. USA

## Where It Came From:

This rumor was rampant in the late 1980s after someone allegedly saw Criss panhandling along the Venice boardwalk in tattered clothes. One of the tabloids, *Star*, picked up on the story and sent out a reporter to investigate. *Star* later reported that the sighting was accurate, and that Criss was in fact homeless. "He was devastated by the break of the band," said *Star*. "And he spent every penny he had on cocaine and alcohol."

The news was sensational and many of his fans, including celebrities such as Tom Arnold, went looking for him, hoping to offer him money or a place to stay. An ex-girlfriend, who was living in Boston at the time, heard the story and told a reporter that she had purchased an airline ticket in his name and promised to put him up at her place until he got back on his feet.

Apparently, that's all Criss needed to hear. A week later he appeared at his girlfriend's door eagerly anticipating their reunion. Yet one can only imagine the look on her face when she saw him. Because it wasn't Criss at all, but an impostor.

"Sweetheart!" he cried. "It's so good to see you again."

She called the police.

## The Truth:

It was well known that Criss had announced his departure from Kiss in 1980, stating that he was unhappy with the direction that the band was headed. It was also well known that his solo album, *Out of Control*, bombed miserably the following year. In fact, when he tried to perform in support of the album in 1981, there were so few venues interested that the best he could get was a gig at a high school in Stamford, Connecticut. (And even that was canceled due to poor ticket

PETER CRISS

sales.) As Dale Sherman writes in *Black Diamond,* "He went from playing stadiums to high school auditoriums and the news crushed him."

All of which provided ample background for the rumor. Yet in truth, Criss was quite happy, living comfortably with his wife and kids in Redondo Beach at the time that the rumor broke. Furthermore, he had been getting regular session work around Los Angeles and his solo albums were actually selling a lot better than most Kiss fans have suggested. So when *Star* reported the story, Criss merely passed it off as an unfortunate misunderstanding.

## The Context:

Of course Criss has not been the only star that has been forced into a life of destitution—real or imagined. Rock lore is full of similar cases. As Mike Mills of R.E.M. once pointed out, "There are guys that have had top ten hits that are fry

cooks right now. They're in prison, or they're digging ditches, or they're living with their mom somewhere. It happens. You don't ever want to get overly confident in this business."

Arthur Lee of the 1960s rock group Love is a prime example. In his day he was considered on equal footing with Jim Morrison and Brian Wilson, but after years of heavy drug use, mismanagement, and bad business choices, he fell into a tragic downward spiral. Like Criss's look-alike, many claimed that they saw him cadging change from pedestrians, too. In fact, one of his longtime music associates, Bruce Botnick, told the *New York Times* in 1999: "I was going to the Whiskey in the eighties and this bum stopped me and it scared the hell out of me. He said, 'Hey man, do you have any money?' He was obviously strung out. [Then after I went inside] I realized that it was Arthur and he didn't even recognize me. It made me feel terrible." (Regrettably, Lee is still incarcerated at the time of this writing.)

# THE RUMOR:

Singer Mama Cass Elliot of the sixties pop group, the Mamas and the Papas, ate herself to death.

## What People Are Saying:

There seems to be a deep-seated desire on the part of the public to see overweight people as sad, lonely, and miserable. That may be because overweight people personify a "weakness" or "failure" of the ego to control unconscious urges, or they signify the "monstrous" danger of indulgence. In any case, Mama Cass Elliot, the former front woman of the popular sixties pop group, the Mamas and the Papas, has earned a similar

reputation ever since she was found dead in Harry Nilsson's London flat on July 29, 1974. For many, the tragedy was the result of Elliot's depression due to the untimely breakup of her former band and the failure of her solo career.

## The Truth:

According to those closest to her, Elliot was anything but miserable in her latter days. In fact, at the time of her death she was receiving rave

Baron Wolman, Retna Ltd. USA

Mama Cass Elliot

reviews for her single, "Don't Call Me Mama," and audiences at London's Palladium gave her an astounding fifteen-minute standing ovation after a sellout show there. And as far as choking on a ham sandwich—which was widely reported in the press at the time of her death—the pathologist that performed the autopsy, Dr. Keith Simpson, claimed unequivocally that there was *never* any evidence of food in her throat. (Nor was there any evidence of heroin or any other drugs as some have suggested.) In fact, there was never any evidence that she suffocated. "The rumors were cruel and ludicrous," writes her former partner, John Phillips, in his autobiography, *Papa John*. "According to the pathologist, some of the muscle tissue in her heart had turned to fat and weakened it. Her heart had just given out after thirty-three years. And that was some big heart."

## Where It Comes From:

Elliot, of course, struggled with her weight throughout her career. In 1968, shortly after the breakup of her band, she went from 285 pounds to 110 pounds in a matter of months after embarking on a strict regiment of crash dieting, medication, and exercise. Her plan was to shed her hippie, earth mother image for her Las Vegas debut, but the transformation took its toll. Within days of opening night, she contracted mononucleosis, tonsillitis, and hepatitis and had to cancel the rest of the run. She continued seeing doctors after that, as her weight continued to fluctuate wildly. And by 1974 she was tipping the scales at well over 225 pounds—twice the weight for a woman of her age and height.

## What May Have Happened:

No one really knows exactly what happened on the night of July 29, 1974. But there is some evidence to support the theory that something far more sinister occurred. Elliot, after all, had been hanging out with some fairly unsavory types at the time of her death. As Phillips claims, "She was always around losers and cruel users. . . . They were sometimes drugged out, belligerent dealers in leather with weapons, chains, and cycles."

One of the dealers turned out to be Pic Dawson, a shady character wanted by the FBI for

# "She probably choked on a sandwich or something."

Paul Young

international drug smuggling. Another was Voytek Frykowski, one of Elliot's boyfriends in the late 1960s, who may have been trafficking as well. In fact, when Elliot was arrested at a London hotel, ostensibly for stealing towels, the FBI tried to persuade her to turn against Frykowski and testify against him before a grand jury. (Frykowski was murdered by members of Charlie Manson's clan at the Tate residence the following year.)

In his autobiography Phillips, who passed away of natural causes in March 2001, claims that when he went to visit Elliot in Las Vegas shortly before her death, he found her in the company of a dealer named Billy, a close associate of Frykowski's. "Billy had brought an immense block of Iranian hash," writes Phillips, "with the words 'Gift of God' stamped on the side in Farsi." And to complicate matters, some have also speculated that she may have gotten involved with organized crime members, perhaps even assassins. In 1972, two years before her death, she apparently blew the whistle on New Jersey's Dunhill Records for selling "cut-outs" of her music illegally and refusing to report the income. An investigation ultimately proved that Elliot was correct, that Dunhill had in fact stolen millions from both Elliot and Phillips, and they were prosecuted as a result. Elliot failed to realize, however, that Dunhill had extensive Mafia connections to New Jersey's top crime family. Thus it may not have been a coincidence that Bill Mentzer, the East Coast mobster who eventually went to prison for the murder of producer Roy Radin in the infamous "Cotton Club" murder case, just happened to befriend Elliot a short time before she died.

Did the mob get revenge? Did she squeal on the wrong guys? Did a drug dealer have her killed? Or was she another victim of the FBI's COINTELPRO or CHAOS?

## The Bottom Line:

The jury is still out. What is known however is that she *didn't* choke to death on a ham sandwich. That rumor began after a paramedic took one look at her body and quipped, "She probably choked on a sandwich or something." (Evidently there were leftovers on the nightstand, and the paramedic made the assumption without examining her body first.) Then a short time later, the coroner made the same remark *before* conducting an autopsy. Naturally the press picked up on the quote and printed it everywhere.

# THE LEGEND:

Bobby Fuller, the lead singer of the Bobby Fuller Four and the composer of such hits as "I Fought the Law," was murdered by the Mob.

## A Little Background:

If L.A.'s rock lore has a quintessential murder mystery, it would be this one. In the late fifties and early sixties Bobby Fuller was a brilliant newcomer to the Hollywood rock scene. Tall, handsome, and earthy, he introduced a new sound to the West Coast: a hybrid style of Tex-Mex, surf, and rockabilly. And thanks to some killer singles such as "Wolfman," "Those Memories of You," and the classic "I Fought The Law (and the Law Won)," that sound eventually found a wide audience with Angelenos.

But at approximately five P.M. on July 18, 1966, his mother found his body slumped over the front seat of his car. At first she thought that he was sleeping because he still had his pajamas on and he didn't look injured, at least not at first glance. But there was gasoline all over the interior of the car—on the seat, the rug, his clothes, his hair, even *in his throat*—and there was a partially opened book of matches sitting on the seat next to him and an open container of gas.[2] As strange as it appeared, the LAPD concluded that Fuller had climbed into the car into the middle of the night, doused himself with gasoline, and tried to commit suicide by lighting himself on fire. If he failed it was only because he was asthmatic and he asphyxiated on the fumes before he could light a match.

## What People Are Saying:

Bobby Fuller's family and friends were completely baffled over the LAPD's "suicide" ruling. They knew that he had been disappointed with the

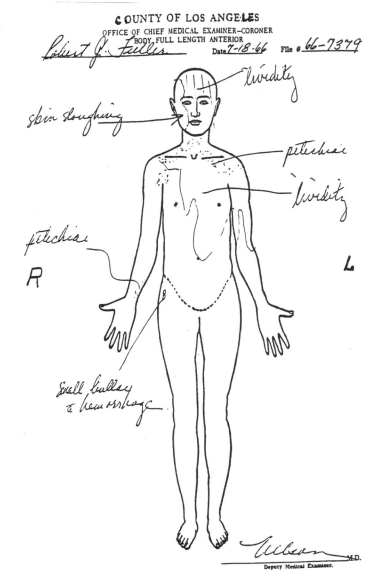

COUNTY OF LOS ANGELES
OFFICE OF CHIEF MEDICAL EXAMINER–CORONER
BODY, FULL LENGTH ANTERIOR
*Robert G. Fuller*   Date 7-18-66   File # 66-7379

lividity

skin sloughing

petechiae

lividity

petechiae

R

L

small bullous & hemorrhage

M.D.
Deputy Medical Examiner.

results of Bob Keane's recent production of "Magic Touch," and that he was prone to black moods, but few believed that he could take his own life. Moreover, the ruling failed to account for the fact that there were small cuts and bruises on his chest, face, and shoulders; a hairline fracture in his right hand; and dried blood around his chin and mouth. The ruling also failed to take into account the coroner's proof that the gasoline had been poured on his body and down his throat *after* he had died. (Apparently there were no signs of internal skin irritation.)

Perhaps the most important clue in the case is a mysterious phone call that Fuller supposedly received at around two or three A.M., shortly before he was last seen. While no one has ever been able to trace the call's source, there's little doubt that it lured him out of the house. "I think it was a setup," says Fuller's younger brother, Randall. "Because after all this time, no one has ever come forward to claim that they made that call. Which is not surprising because that call was the key to the whole thing. Someone asked him to be somewhere, and he left right after that. No one knows where he went or why, but it was the last time that he was seen alive."

Many people believe that the caller was Melody, a part-time hooker and full-time waitress at PJ's nightclub, where Fuller often played. Melody was known to drive Fuller to and from the club on the nights that he was performing, and she was also known to provide him with sexual favors now and then. (Although she's denied it in the press, Bobby spent the previous night at her place—just as he had done many nights before.) The theory is that someone became very jealous over Bobby's affair with Melody and sent over a couple of goons to rough him up. And if that's true, then perhaps they roughed him up a little *too well* and tried to hide his body by setting it on fire. But before they could, a cop car appeared in the distance, turning off of Franklin, and they decided to make a run for it instead.

## To The Contrary:

There are other interesting theories, too, including the idea that Bob Keane, the owner of Del-Fi Records, and one of his mobster associates, had something to do with it. Many, in fact, have claimed that Keane, who was supposedly furious over Fuller's decision to break up the band, held a $1 million life insurance policy on his top star, and collected a short time later. And if that's true, the theory that Keane was in bed with mobsters may make more sense. Because if Keane owed the mob money for starting Del-Fi Records as some have argued, and the mob found out about Keane's insurance policy on Fuller, they

Fuller's death site: What's that smell?

Paul Young

# "...I distinctly remember joking about the fact that Bobby was worth a million bucks and the rest of us were worth a lot less."

may have committed the murder just to force Keane to pay off his debts. "I'm positive that we signed a life insurance policy," says Randy Fuller. "I know that Bob has said that there wasn't one, but I distinctly remember joking about the fact that Bobby was worth a million bucks and the rest of us were worth a lot less."

## The Truth:

The Mafia boyfriend idea seems to make sense when you consider that Melody worked at PJ's, which was co-owned by Dominic Lucci and Eddie Nash (Adel Nasrallah). The former has been linked to East Coast Mafia families, while the latter has been called nothing less than L.A.'s top crime boss.[3] To date, he has escaped three consecutive convictions—allegedly through bribery and intimidation—for running arson-for-hire rings, drug trafficking, and wholesale murder. In 1981 for example, Nash, an émigré from Lebanon and an alleged associate of Russian Armenian mobsters, was charged with the assassination of four people who apparently stole $1 million worth of cocaine and jewelry from his house. "He's an extremely jealous man," testified his wife Jeanna after he threatened to throw acid in her face. "With an extremely volatile temper."

But according to Melody, the idea that Nash or her boyfriend (who was also said to be a mafioso) would have Fuller killed over jealousy is "crazy." "That stuff only happens in the movies," she said in a recent interview. "There was nothing going on between me and Bobby. We were just friends—that's all."

Moreover, the theory that Bob Keane had anything to do with the Mafia or Fuller's death seems equally fallacious. Apparently his main investors were Greek rather than Italian, and they had no discernible criminal ties.[4] "He may be a snake," says a former Del-Fi artist, "but he's not a murderer. I'll say that much for him."

## The Bottom Line:

The jury is still out thanks to the successful cover-up by the LAPD. In any case, even if Bobby Fuller did commit suicide as the LAPD claimed, there are still a few people that seem to know more than they're telling—including Bob Keane. Then again, the reason for Keane's discretion should be fairly obvious: The more mysterious his death remains, the more interest there will be in Fuller's music.

# THE RUMOR:

Music mogul David Geffen married actor Keanu Reeves in a secret ceremony on a beach.

**Everybody loves David**

Paul Young

## What People Are Saying:

This rumor started making the rounds in the late 1990s after somebody reportedly saw Keanu Reeves charging $12,000 worth of clothing on David Geffen's credit card at a posh Beverly Hills clothing store. England's *Daily Mirror* was the first to print the item saying that the two were spotted shopping together and "giggling like schoolboys as they tried on mounds of $500 shirts." France's *Voice* followed suit, adding that the clothes were for their wedding, which supposedly took place on a private beach somewhere, with Steven Spielberg, Claudia Schiffer, and Elizabeth Taylor in attendance. "The jovial pair were married by a rabbi," said *Voice*, "making them Hollywood's first openly gay marriage in the history of show business."

Then the *Hollywood Reporter*, the *Boston Herald* and the *Toronto Star* printed their own versions of the event, and pretty soon there were eyewitness testimonials popping up everywhere, including a hairdresser who claimed that he styled the wedding party, and a caterer who said that he prepared the food.

## The Truth:

Reeves was the first to come forward to dispel the rumor, yet he failed to convince anyone that it was erroneous. For *Out* magazine for example, he joked, "Supposedly I got a bunch of great clothes out of it . . . I guess that means I have to give 'em back." A couple of months later he told *Interview*

magazine that the rumor was "nothing but gossip . . . but ya never know." Then he told *Vanity Fair*, "There's nothing wrong with being gay. So to deny it is to make a judgment. And why make a big deal of it?"

Reeves wasn't the real target of the rumor, however. For all intents and purposes it was designed to make fun of Geffen. After all, despite his charitable donations to AIDS research and his philanthropic efforts in Los Angeles, he has made more than his share of enemies over the years. Walter Yetnicoff for example, the feisty president of CBS Records, supposedly disliked him so much that he ridiculed him constantly behind his back, allegedly once asking Geffen's secretary if she could get him to teach his girlfriend "the art of giving head." On another occasion, Brian Rohan, a well-liked industry insider, allegedly throttled Geffen before a crowd of fellow executives at the Beverly Hills Hotel and received a stack of congratulatory telegrams the following morning.

## The Evidence:

An even nastier turn occurred during the making of *Personal Best*, the directorial debut of Robert Towne, the Academy award–winning writer of *Chinatown*. According to Fred Goodman's book, *Mansion on the Hill*, Geffen—who was described as being "vain, arrogant, and an incorrigible gossip"—was so meddlesome during the production of that movie that Towne came close to abandoning the project entirely. But when Towne began resisting—or rather, fighting—Geffen's manipulations, Geffen threatened that he would have him "destroyed."

Eventually Towne slapped him with a $155 million lawsuit alleging in no uncertain terms that, "This is not an isolated instance of Geffen using libel, slander, and other vindictive and coercive tactics to punish and coerce those with whom he deals and has disputes."

As the *Los Angeles Times* reported in 1990, Towne eventually settled out of court with Geffen, but not before the record mogul made sure to paint him as a "highly unstable" character in his then-pending divorce case. In fact, Geffen swore that he saw Towne using illegal drugs during the production of *Personal Best,* and stopped at nothing to paint him as someone "prone to violent outbursts." Needless to say, Towne was taken to the cleaners in the divorce case and his reputation compromised.

According to some industry insiders, there are even more salacious and disturbing tales floating around Hollywood, but few ever make it to the public, thanks to Geffen's ability to control the press. Apparently he has stopped the publications of at least three tell-alls: one by John Medelssohn, which supposedly portrayed him as a "tantrum-throwing control freak" who liked to practice "scorched-earth business tactics;" another by Gavin Geoffrey Dillard called *In the Flesh* (Dutton/Penguin) which supposedly detailed his homosexual exploits in embarrassing detail; and a third by author Steven Gaines called *Obsession* (G. P. Putnam) which, despite

being about his best friend, Calvin Klein, was said to be equally scathing.

Moreover, he has also used the same practice to stop unflattering songs from hitting the airwaves. In 1995 Mojo Nixon, the always irreverent blues-billy-rocker known for such rabble-rousing classics as "Debbie Gibson Is Pregnant with My Two-Headed Love Child," wrote a song called "Bring Me the Head of David Geffen." But thanks to some legal pressure levied against Nixon's handlers, the singer was forced to cut the track from his then-pending album, *Whereabouts Unknown.*[5]

## Where It Comes From:

This is not the first time that Geffen has been the subject of such a rumor. In 1990 Geffen tried to stop Frederic Dannen from including a passage in his book, *Hit Men,* which reportedly "exposed" Geffen's alleged gay marriage to one of his young lovers years earlier. (Dannen also claimed that Irving Azoff, another one of Geffen's detractors, used to refer to him as "Mrs. Geffen.") Moreover, Tom King reports in his biography, *The Operator,* that Geffen was also known as a flagrant philanderer in the gay community in the 1980s and nineties, picking up young guys at parties, industry events, and weddings with wild abandon. That in turn led many to believe that he had become the stereotypical epitome of a sexist, arrogant Hollywood mogul indulging in "bimbos." (It may not have been a coincidence that Reeves just happened to appear on the cover of *Buzz* magazine to illustrate a story on "male bimbos" [or *himbos*] days before the rumor's genesis. In other words, the entire episode was rife with latent homophobia, jealousy, envy, and plain old malice.)

> *"There's nothing wrong with being gay. So to deny it is to make a judgment. And why make a big deal of it?"*

GEFFEN

Peter Ivers, the host of TV's *New Wave Theater*, was murdered by a consortium of television executives.

## A Little Background:

The relevance of the early 1980s cable access TV show, *New Wave Theater* has been sorely overlooked in the history of L.A.'s rock scene. Not only was it a significant forerunner to MTV, but it provided numerous local acts with the chance to play to a national audience of 20 million. Yet even more importantly, it provided the rest of the country with a glimpse into the sardonic, low-tech, darkly humorous world of L.A. punk and all its nihilistic attitude. It was a scrappy, cheaply made variety show complete with parodies, fake commercials, and interviews that bordered on the ridiculous. As reporter Theo Davis once described it, it was "a multilayered and fast-paced, cryptic assault on the average television viewer's cathode-addled brain."

The show's focal point was its inimitable host, Peter Ivers, a diminutive man-child with deceptively conventional looks. When he first arrived in L.A. in 1971 from his native New York, he had dreams of making it as a solo artist, yet failed to find much big label interest. The fates threw him a bone in 1976, however, when he met a young filmmaker named David Lynch at the American Film Institute. Lynch was working on his masterpiece, *Eraserhead*, at the time, and Ivers went on to score the soundtrack, which included the classic, "In Heaven (Lady in the Radiator Song)."

Around the same time, David Jove came up with the idea for *New Wave Theater* while poking around the burgeoning punk-rock nightclub scene. Jove, an erstwhile artist-cum-filmmaker, had high hopes for the program. In fact, he saw it as nothing less than an "enlightenment program" for the "clueless" masses. Yet it was Ivers

that made the show palatable for middle America. With his outrageous costumes and almost laughable in-your-face attitude, he brought a kind of Brechtian flippancy to Jove's dark, anarchistic diatribes. The combination ultimately proved to be inspired, and the show began drawing large numbers of fans and detractors alike.

Then on March 3, 1983, Peter Ivers was murdered.

His friend, Jim Tucker, was the first to find the body. He had gone over to Ivers's loft the following day and found Ivers in his bed—fully clothed and *under* the covers—covered in blood. At first he believed that someone had used a shotgun because the top of his head was virtually missing. Yet when he looked closer, he realized that the killer had literally beaten his skull in with a blunt object, perhaps a baseball bat.[6]

## What People Are Saying:

When detectives began to investigate Ivers's murder, they soon discovered that he had lost his wallet a couple of days earlier. That eventually led to the theory that someone had found the wallet, discovered several hundred dollars inside, and went back for more. It was hardly a perfect theory, however, since it didn't account for the fact that the killers failed to take his expensive video equipment, Fostex eight-track recorder, or watch. Nor did it explain how the killer got inside his loft, since there weren't any signs of a break-in or struggle.

That may be why so many people have theorized that the assassin was a friend of Ivers, or someone that he knew well enough to let in the

Peter Ivers

**New Wave Theater was overtly antigovernment and full of nihilistic remarks, violent provocations, and not-so-subtle attacks on corporations— including some of television's biggest sponsors.**

door. As some have suggested, it could even have been some-one like his *New Wave Theater* partner David Jove who was said to have an explosive temper.

On the other hand, there are those that believe that he may have been the victim of something far more sinister. After all, *New Wave Theater* was overtly antigovernment and full of nihilistic remarks, violent provocations, and not-so-subtle attacks on corporations—including some of television's biggest sponsors. For that reason, there's some speculation that he may have been silenced for political reasons.

## The Truth:

According to the LAPD, Jove was never a suspect in the case. Family members and friends have claimed that he was terribly upset about Ivers's death. In fact, he held a memorial service for him three days after the murder, showing true signs of grief. Moreover, he helped to initiate a personal investigation into his death, and assisted Ivers's bereaved girlfriend Lucy Fisher, now a top executive at Warner Bros., in establishing a $50,000 reward for information leading to the suspect's arrest.

The conspiracy theory, however, may not be as bizarre as it sounds. There was an unprecedented level of systematic suppression of journalists, broadcasters, and DJs in the 1980s. In fact, according to Angus MacKenzie's award-winning investigation during 1992, *Secrets: The CIA's War at Home*, the 1980s witnessed the "first true instance of peacetime censorship in U.S. history." Programs such as the CIA's MHCHAOS (a.k.a. CHAOS) were designed to "silence" radical, dissenting views of the Reagan Administration's foreign policy—thus clearing the way for such affairs as the Iran/Contra scandal. That in turn led to suppression of *all* radical thought in the media.

Former KPFK DJ Michael Taylor, for example, who was instrumental in setting up the underground station, L.A. Liberation Radio in the mid-1990s, was mysteriously kidnapped and murdered execution-style in an abandoned lot in South Central on April 22, 1996. While no one has been able to prove that the CIA organized that murder, it was no secret that he was considered a threat to politicos. After all, L.A. Liberation Radio was highly critical of U.S. policies and often encouraged African Americans to mobilize against the powers that be. That, of course, may have made someone a little nervous.[7]

## The Bottom Line:

As of this writing, no one knows the truth behind Ivers's death. So, in the words of Ivers, we'll just have to "embrace the ambiguity, man."

# THE RUMOR:

Etta James is the illegitimate daughter of Alan Hale, Jr., best known as the Skipper on the TV show *Gilligan's Island*.

## Where It Comes From:

This rumor started going around in the 1960s just after *Gilligan's Island* hit the airwaves. Somebody—and no one really knows who—noticed that the Skipper, played by Alan Hale, Jr. bore a striking resemblance to Etta James, the superhot, soul singer from South Central. At the time James was just beginning to gain national attention for her brand of saucy R & B, and she often admitted in interviews that she had never known her father. "The question was there when I was born and it's still there," she told her biographer David Ritz. "The question haunts me, worries me, troubles my sleep. You wouldn't

think it would matter after all this time, but it does."

But could she be the Skipper's love child?

## What People Are Saying:

Jamesetta "Etta" James was born in Watts, California in 1938. Her mother, Dorothy Hawkins, was only fourteen years old when she delivered the baby and because of her age, she had to give her up to a foster home. Years later, Etta tracked her mother down and moved back in with her in Oakland, California. But whenever the subject of her father came up, her mother

"Your daddy's a white boy,"
she'd say,
"a real famous white boy."

Alan Hale, Jr.

Sandra Johnson/Retna Ltd. USA

Etta James

remained curiously circumspect. "Your daddy's a white boy," she'd say, "a real famous white boy." Sometimes she'd refer to him as Theodore, and then other days later she'd refer to him as *Al*.

Alan Hale, Jr. was born in 1918; that means that he would have been twenty years old when James was born. Until his first acting role in 1942, he spent much of his youth visiting his father on movie sets. (His father, Alan Hale, Sr., was one of Errol Flynn's cohorts in the 1930s.) Meanwhile Dorothy Hawkins, who was still living in Watts at the time, was dreaming of becoming an actress. "She always wanted to be in the movies," James wrote in her autobiography. "And when she wasn't at the movies she was hanging out in jazz clubs. She was Miss Hip Jazz Chick. That was Dorothy. A ravishingly beautiful young girl."

According to James, Dorothy pressured one of her best friends, Willie Best, the well-known goggle-eyes character actor, to let her visit him on the set once in a while. And there's certainly a chance that she crossed paths with Hale during one of her visits. But did she?

## The Real Story:

According to her autobiography, *Rage to Survive*, James eventually found a copy of her birth certificate which listed Al Anderson as her father. But according to her mother's sister, Aunt Cozetta, Al Anderson was merely a family friend that took her mother to the hospital on the day that she went into labor. "He wasn't your father," said Aunt Cozetta. "Because your father was a white boy, and Anderson was most definitely black."

ETTA

Finally, after years of wondering, James concluded that her father was none other than Minnesota Fats, the legendary pool hustler. Her mother eventually told her as much while they were watching television one evening and Fats appeared on the screen. "You keep bugging me about your daddy," she said. "Well, there he is."

## The Bottom Line:

No one will probably ever know if Hale is James's father, and in all likelihood, he isn't. (James refused to comment for this book.) But if he is, it certainly makes those old episodes of *Gilligan's Island* a little bit more interesting.

# THE LEGEND:

Singer Inger Lorre of the Nymphs once climbed onto Tom Zutaut's desk at Geffen Records, and urinated all over him.

## Little Background:

Mick Jagger once claimed: "You spend all your time trying to get into trouble, then once you're in trouble, you're *always* in trouble." Singer/songwriter Inger Lorre may know that maxim better than most. She burst on the L.A. rock scene in the mid-1980s, and burned an indelible trail from Santa Monica to Silverlake without once looking back.

## Where It Comes From:

As Jory Farr points out in his book, *Moguls and Madmen*, Tom Zutaut was one of Geffen Record's golden boys of the 1980s. Seven of the bands that he signed to the label went on to earn platinum and multiplatinum records, including Guns N' Roses and Mötley

Lynn McAfee/Rema Ltd. USA

Catch a rising star: Lorre and Rodney Bingenheimer

INGER

Crüe. So when he met Inger Lorre in December 1989 at a Chrysalis Records party he knew that he could do something with her. And it wasn't long before he was taking her to five-star restaurants, buying her clothes, and flying her off to lavish hotels in Hawaii and New York.

What happened next is still a matter of controversy, but according to Lorre, Zutaut used his munificence to hang his most perverse fantasies on, forcing her to do his bidding while abusing her sexually in private. Meanwhile, Zutaut, who categorically denied Lorre's charges, claims that she was on a virtual fire pole of self-destruction, missing rehearsals, picking fights, and doing everything that she could to destroy her professional career. (During one infamous show at Anaheim's Marques Theater for example, she crawled over to her boyfriend, Rodney Eastman, during the middle of a song, unzipped his pants and gave him a blow job before a crowd of 300 screaming fans.)

Apparently things only got worse after that, with Zutaut putting greater restrictions on Lorre, and Lorre fighting back. Finally, after numerous ultimatums, pleadings, and innuendoes, Lorre checked into a rehab center in Minnesota. (Zutaut claims her parents talked her into going, while Lorre claims that Zutaut threatened her into going.) In any case, she walked out of the hospital less than a week later and returned to Los Angeles. And that's when she came up with the idea for the ultimate revenge. As she told a reporter for the *LA Weekly* years later, "One day I got really, really drunk and said to Jeff, our guitar player, 'You know, [Zutaut] is such a fucker. I should just walk in there and piss on his desk.' Jeff laughed and said, 'If you do that you'll be my hero.'" And apparently that's all she needed to hear. Armed with a bouquet of freshly cut flowers and a belly of beer, she stormed into Zutaut's office and attacked him vociferously. Zutaut tried to calm her down, but before he could get a word in edgewise, she was standing astride his desk with her panties around her ankles. Suddenly a stream of urine rained across his phone, Rolodex, and desk.

"This is for Jeff," she said picking a flower and throwing it at him. "And this is for Alex," she said throwing another flower. As she named every member of her band, she was still whizzing away. "And this is for me!" she hissed, throwing the rest of the bouquet in his face. "And don't ever piss on my fucking band again!"

## The Legacy:

The news of the incident spread like wildfire through the industry, occasioning numerous jabs at Zutaut's expense. ("Golden boy gets golden shower," wrote one of the dailies.) Yet the news drove Lorre into a deeper depression and ultimately forced her to give up music for a while and move to New York. To her surprise, however, she found herself the envy of artists everywhere. "Suddenly people treated me like the patron saint of fucked-over musicians," she told the *Weekly*. "[They'd come up to me and say], 'You did that for every musician that had ever been screwed over!'"

Lorre eventually made a comeback in 1999 with a well-received solo effort called *Transcendental Medication*. Needless to say, she refused to record it for a major label. Yet the legend of her pissy fit—with its inherent fetishistic symbolism—will undoubtedly die hard.

*"Suddenly people treated me like the patron saint of fucked-over musicians."*

LORRE

Courtney Love had her husband, Kurt Cobain, murdered.

## What People Are Saying:

None of Courtney Love's outrageous antics, lies, and boastings, have plagued her quite like the rumor of her alleged involvement in Kurt Cobain's death, not even the rumors of stabbing a kid in grade school, getting golden showers in Taiwan, setting houses on fire in Portland, and harassing journalists with physical violence in Seattle and L.A. (All of which are supposedly true.) After all, there are a lot of people that genuinely believe that she latched on to Cobain's rising star in the early 1990s, then had him murdered in 1994 merely to satisfy her own obsessive greed. But did she?

Not according to the Seattle Police Department. When officers arrived at her Lake Washington home on April 8, 1994, they found Cobain's lifeless body lying on the floor of what was called the "greenhouse," a small workroom over the garage. His head had been almost blown off by a single shotgun blast from inside his mouth, and nearby was a Remington 20-gauge Model 11 rifle with a freshly spent round in the chamber. A stool had been placed in front of the door, and there was a suicide note on a nearby table apologizing to his fans for his act, and wishing his wife and newborn baby strength. It was, for all intents and purposes, a suicide.

*...the note that he clutched in his hand, a note which allegedly read, "It's obvious that you don't love me . . . I'd rather die than get a divorce."*

## A Little History:

In her book, *Courtney Love: Queen of Noise,* Melissa Rossi suggests that Cobain and Love couldn't have been more diametrically opposed. He was devoted to artistic integrity and she was devoted to money and fame. And that difference—exasperated by frequent drug use—led to innumerable, knockdown, drag-out fights. What's more, Cobain had reason to believe that Love was unfaithful to him, and suspected that she was seeing Billy Corgan of the Smashing Pumpkins on the side. Supposedly, Cobain confronted his wife with the charge in April 1994 while he was on tour with Nirvana in Italy. Yet when she failed to give him the answer he wanted to hear, he fell into such despair that he went into another room, quietly penned a suicide note, and downed a handful of Rohypnol.

Love didn't find him until the following morning, after he had already slipped into a coma. She then called an ambulance and rushed him to the hospital. Allegedly, during the trip, she managed to hide the note that he clutched in his hand, a note which allegedly read, "It's obvious that you don't love me . . . I'd rather die than get a divorce."

Tensions settled slightly after Cobain returned to the West Coast, but only briefly. Thanks to too much money, too much success, and too much pressure, he began taking his heroin use to new levels—and so

Courtney Love

Kurt Cobain

Steve Pyke/Retna Ltd. USA

did his wife. But when Cobain refused a reported $9.5 million to go on the Lollapalooza tour, Love was allegedly so furious that she threatened to leave him and take custody of their child. That in turn, prompted Cobain to initiate divorce papers and remove Love from his will, thereby cutting her out of an estate allegedly worth $40 million. Love then called her attorney, Rosemary Carroll, and ordered her to get "the meanest, most vicious divorce lawyer" that she could find.

By April the tension was so thick in the Cobain household that nursemaids were quitting on a daily basis. Finally, Love checked herself into the luxurious Peninsula Hotel in Beverly Hills and hired a private physician to help her kick her drug habit. Cobain on the other hand, checked into the Exodus Recovery Center in Marina Del Rey, and then disappeared a few days later, sneaking out of his bed in the middle of the night. He was never seen or heard from again.

After several days of not knowing where he was, Love hired Tom Grant to track him down.

Grant, a private detective that advertised in the yellow pages, eventually discovered that Cobain had moved into his country house in Northern California. But he wasn't alone. According to Grant he was there with another woman that he met years earlier, a folksinger by the name of Mary Lou Lord. Cobain was found dead a short time later.

## The Evidence:

There were a number of curious questions left unanswered by the police department's ruling that may, in fact, point to foul play in the case. Why, for example, were the last two lines on the suicide note ("Please keep going, Courtney, for Frances") written in a different handwriting style? Why did the Seattle Police Department tamper and withhold delicate information about the case? Why was the gun wiped clean of fingerprints *before* the police arrived? And most important, how could Cobain inject 1.52 milligrams of heroin—enough to kill *three* people—into *both* arms, then roll his shirtsleeves down, button each, put away all his drug paraphernalia, load a shotgun with three shells and pull the trigger? As some criminologists have pointed out, there has *never* been another case of someone doing that much heroin and being able to do *anything* afterward—much less all that. If anything, the drug would have rendered him incapacitated within seconds.

## What May Have Happened:

Tom Grant has come to his own conclusions about Cobain's death. He believes that Cobain actually called Love while she was staying at the Peninsula Hotel and bragged about his affair with Lord as a way of getting even with her for her affair with Corgan. He also believes that Love was so furious—not only over his infidelities, but over the possibility of losing an estate worth $40 million—that she went out and hired someone to kill him. And in fact, one of L.A.'s most infamous rockers, El Duce, claimed that Love offered him the job. As he told filmmaker Nick Blumfield, Love called him in March 1994 and offered him $50,000 to kill her husband. And according to Blumfield, El Duce may have been telling the truth. Days after his revelation he was given a lie detector test by one of the foremost polygraph experts in the country, Dr. Edward Gelb, and passed with flying colors.

Yet he was never able to say much more on the subject. El Duce was killed in a freak car accident in Riverside, California just eight days later.

Grant has found a number of allies in his theory about Love's orchestration of Cobain's death, including Love's own father, Hank Harrison. "I hope I don't get killed for saying this," he told investigative reporter Ian Halperin, "but I'm now convinced that Courtney had something to do with Kurt's death or at least knows who did it."

## The Bottom Line:

While the evidence paints a very bleak picture of Love, it doesn't prove that she had anything to do with Cobain's death. (Other than *driving* him to commit suicide as many have suggested.) Neither Grant nor Harrison are very credible sources, and both of them stood to gain financially by making such outrageous accusations. Moreover, Cobain's tolerance for heroin was so high that there's a chance that he could have pulled the trigger after all. In other words, the rumor itself may be nothing more than the public's wish to paint Courtney Love as a Black Widow, if only because she bulldozed her way into Cobain's life and greedily indulged her own sulfurous whims rather than play the sweet, all-American housewife role. But does that mean she would resort to killing the father of her child? The evidence is interesting yet inconclusive.

*...Love was so furious—not only over his infidelities, but over the possibility of losing an estate worth $40 million—that she went out and hired someone to kill him.*

Marilyn Manson had one of his eyeballs removed and offered it to the devil in an elaborate Satanic ritual.

Ross Halfin/Retna Ltd. USA

Manson: Am I scaring you yet?

## The Context:

As author Robert Pattison argues in his book *The Triumph of Vulgarity*, rock and roll's psychological function—whether it's latent or pronounced—has *always* been to provide kids with something that they can call their own; a new sound that provides a voice for their feelings, fears, sexual frustrations, and identity problems. But, as Pattison argues, that has resulted in an impossible endgame of radical novelty that cannot sustain itself from generation to generation.

(Compare Screamin' Jay Hawkins's "voodoo antics" in the 1950s for example, to the live sex acts, scatological displays, pornography, and bloodletting by the likes of Throbbing Gristle, the Plasmatics, the Butthole Surfers, and G. G. Allin of the 1980s.)

## What People Are Saying:

Marilyn Manson is nothing more than the latest in a long line of shock rockers. If you believe everything that has been said about him, he has trafficked in an extraordinary array of filth including:

★ Mutilating animals on stage (chickens, puppies, and kittens).
★ Having sex with dogs and/or sheep on stage.
★ Masturbating and performing oral and anal sex on stage.
★ Having his last two ribs removed so that he could perform oral sex on himself more easily.
★ Having an eye removed and setting it on fire as an offering to the devil.

The list goes on and on. In fact one could argue that Manson (né Brian Warner) has been the subject of more outrageous rumors than just about any other rock star in history. Yet if Manson has achieved such infamy it is purely by his own design. As his adopted name suggests, his aesthetic is a self-conscious bricolage of appropriated symbols from pop culture—in particular, fringe culture—including esoteric religious groups, hatemongers, and pornographers. The effect of course, is a potpourri of "scary" signifiers (read: gimmick). Meanwhile, he has gone to extraordinary lengths to manipulate the media by spreading specious stories about himself—including many of the above—in an effort to bolster his ersatz Satanic image (read: profit).

In other words, Manson's image is totally contrived, designed specifically to cause controversy. That, of course, has made him a magnet for every rumor imaginable. And it should be no surprise that many of the tales attributed to him have been borrowed from previous rockers, including the rumor that he ordered his audience to kill some puppies thrown from the stage—a rumor previously associated with Ozzy Osbourne.

## The Bottom Line:

Nonetheless, Manson's image is not *all* artifice. In the name of creating an evil persona he has had to do a few things that could be construed as being truly transgressive. They include the following:

★ Cutting his chest open on stage with a broken beer bottle.
★ Giving a male guitar player oral sex on stage.
★ Sexually humiliating dozens of women backstage with an S&M apparatus.
★ Sodomizing a male fan backstage with his fist.
★ Smothering a nude female fan in raw meat at a recording session and forcing her to play a "dick harmonica"—his own penis ducttaped to Twiggy Ramirez's—and then urinating on her face while she took a shower.

MARILYN

# THE LEGEND:

Jim Morrison was gay and once gave Jimi Hendrix a blow job on stage.

## A Little Background:

In April 1969, before a crowd of thousands at the Dinner Key Civic Auditorium in Miami, Jim Morrison began taunting his fans with, "You didn't come here only for *music*, did you? You came here for something else, didn't you? What is it? You want to see my cock, don't you? Do you want to see my cock?" As Morrison continued to tease his audience, toying with his zipper and rubbing himself, the band launched into a furious rendition of "Light My Fire." Moments later, after crawling across the stage screaming, "There are no rules, there are no limits!" and simulating oral sex on guitarist Robby Krieger, he dove into the crowd and began rubbing his crotch while screaming, "You wanna see my cock?" Suddenly, without warning, the entire concert hall went black and the promoters announced that the show was over.

To this day no one really knows how far Morrison really went in exposing himself that night. His subsequent arrest on obscenity charges caused a sensation in the press with conservatives and liberals alike weighing in on the subject. In any case, nobody in L.A. batted an eye at the news. After all, Morrison had been pulling the same stunt at clubs along the Sunset Strip for so long that it was downright boring. "The Whiskey was like his living room," explains one veteran scenester. "He'd jump in with anybody that was playing, start screaming something, rub his crotch, put the microphone

**Jim Morrison**

Chris Walter/Retna Ltd. USA

in his pants, pull his pants down, whatever. That was his act. It was always about his cock."

His penile publicity wasn't only reserved for the stage, however. He was also known to urinate in public, such as the time he allegedly pissed on some books inside UCLA's library before a crowd of astonished students, and the time that he apparently took a leak in a friend's living room during a party for his twenty-sixth birthday. In fact, his obsession with his rod was so pronounced that many people believed that he was a homosexual. His former girlfriend, Pamela Courson thought as much after numerous nights of being tied up and forced into anal sex, and she even sent so far as to write FAGGOT across the back of his favorite jacket in indelible ink.[8] Meanwhile, Morrison's former booking agent, Todd Schifman, claimed that he saw Morrison around town "with a certain male celebrity" in what looked like "a full-blown relationship." As Schifman says, "In fact, I *know* that Jim was into being gay."

## What People Are Saying:

A number of people have pointed to a little incident that went down in a New York club in 1968 as proof of Morrison's homosexuality. There are numerous versions of the story, but the most common is that the event took place at a club in the Village where Jimi Hendrix was playing. Morrison apparently went with Janis Joplin, and during the set Joplin boasted about the size of Hendrix's cock. In a drunken stupor, Morrison climbed onto the stage and began undoing Jimi's pants, shouting, "I want to see your cock!" What happened after that is still unclear, but supposedly, Morrison kept screaming, "I wanna suck your cock!" while tugging away at his belt. Hendrix meanwhile, apparently stoned himself and somewhat amused at the audience's delight of the situation, just kept churning out his trademark pyrotechnics on guitar. Finally, as Morrison fished out Jimi's organ and put it in his mouth to a roar of audience applause, Joplin jumped on stage, grabbed him by the hair and threw him off stage.

## The Truth:

According to Morrison's good friend and associate, Paul Ferrara, Morrison never came close to getting into Jimi's pants, and it wasn't Joplin that yanked him off stage but Ferrara himself. What's more, Morrison wasn't trying to give Jimi head. If anything, he was just trying to join him on stage in his own inimitable way. You can actually hear some of the event on a bootleg tape that occasionally makes the rounds called "Morrison's Lament." And if you listen carefully, you can hear a *very* drunk Morrison slurring such poetic sweet nothings as, "Fuck her in the ass! Fuck my baby in the asshole. Fuck my little woman in her little pussy. Fuck the little cunt in her asshole . . . Fuck you in the asshole . . . Little sweet asshole . . ."

You won't hear "I wanna suck your cock," however, unless you use your imagination.

*In a drunken stupor, Morrison climbed onto the stage and began undoing Jimi's pants, shouting, "I want to see your cock!"*

# "It should be noted that I didn't have a hard-on, which should relieve me of any accusations of being gay."

## The Legacy:

Performing oral sex on stage has become something of a requirement for outré rockers since then. Aside from the aforementioned incident with Inger Lorre, many punks remember the time that an amorous fan gave punk Stiv Bators a blow job on stage during a Dead Boys set. Another fan supposedly did the same to Iggy Pop while performing at Bimbos in San Francisco during a rendition of "Wet My Bed." (The fan turned out to be a drag queen.) And a female fan did the same to Marilyn Manson at a gig in the mid-1990s. (Manson returned the favor a few years later, when he took his guitar player's cock out of his pants during a song, and gave him a blow job before a crowd of screaming fans. "But not really long enough to constitute it being a real blow job," he later clarified. "It should be noted that I didn't have a hard-on, which should relieve me of any accusations of being gay.") L.A. glam rockers Sexy Xrist meanwhile began including blow jobs in their act, too. As the *LA Weekly* reported in March 2000, Bassist Triple XXX, a former porn star and stripper at Jumbo's Clown Room, occasionally dropped singer Stevie's drawers in midset and massaged her vocal chords with his maleness.

And that's to say nothing of those that have had actual intercourse on stage. During one of Joplin's early performances at Pepperland in San Rafael for example, when 2,300 Hells Angels and Death's Head bikers showed up, there was a moment when two audience members climbed on stage, shed their clothes, and went at it for several minutes before getting yanked off. And more recently, during an infamous show at Danceteria in 1986, Gibby Haynes of the Butthole Surfers supposedly sodomized a female audience member for several minutes, apparently after she jumped on stage and removed her panties.

None of the above seem to have the philosophical underpinnings of Morrison's behavior, however. Because if Morrison had an agenda, it was to turn the world on its head. As he told a reporter in 1969, "I'm interested in anything about revolt, disorder, chaos—especially any activity that appears to have no meaning whatsoever. It seems to me the road toward freedom."

# THE LEGEND:

## The Context:

Next to stories of sexual indulgence and extravagant drug use, no other rumor in rock and roll is as common as that of animal sacrifice. Consider the following:

★ Alice Cooper is said to have slaughtered a number of animals on stage, including the time he supposedly bit the head off a chicken and drank its blood in Toronto, slaughtered a cow in Texas, and stomped on baby chicks in New York.[9]

★ ZZ Top, who were also fond of bringing wild beasts on stage, including wolves, buffaloes and long horn steer, were said to have killed a vulture on stage in the 1970s, allegedly in Texas.

★ Bryan Gregory of the Cramps supposedly conducted voodoo ceremonies before taking the stage in the late 1970s, ceremonies which included chicken sacrifices.

★ The Plasmatics, who filled their shows with chickens and dogs during their Dance of the Apocalypse tour of the late 1970s, were said to have killed chickens in every city that they performed.

★ John Cale, cofounder of the Velvet Underground, is said to have decapitated a chicken with a meat clever during a performance in London in 1977.

★ Glen Meadmore allegedly stuffed a chicken head up his ass at the Anti-Club in Hollywood in the early 1980s.

★ The band KLF supposedly slaughtered a sheep on stage in the early 1990s, apparently in reference to the infamous Viennese Action Group of the 1970s.

★ Marilyn Manson has, according to rock lore, killed chickens, sodomized cows, and fucked dogs on stage.

Not surprisingly, *none* of the above are true. (With the exception of Meadmore and Cale who *purchased* their already-dead props at the local butcher before their respective shows.) In fact, according to the ASPCA—who takes this stuff very seriously—no rock star in history has ever killed an animal on stage—at least that they know of.

## Where It Comes From:

Yet of all the stars that have supposedly trafficked in animal sacrifice, the impish leader of Black Sabbath, Ozzy Osborne, has been the most notorious. The rumor that he once bit the head off a live bat can be traced to an incident that occurred at a meeting at Epic Records in L.A. in 1981. The meeting was to discuss the marketing campaign of Ozzy's first solo effort, *Blizzard of*

*Ozz*, but when it came time to do a photo session for the album's press kit, Osborne struck a pose, placed a white dove in his mouth and chomped down on its neck.

By the time the story reached his fans, however, people were claiming that he bit the head off a live bat rather than a white dove. (Much more apropos of a man obsessed with the occult as Ozzy was said to be.) So when someone threw a *real* bat on stage during his *Diary of a Madman* tour the following year, Osborne naturally picked it up and tried to bite its head off just as he had done with the dove. "I saw this thing bounce across the stage," he later told a reporter. "And when I looked it wasn't moving. So I just assumed it was a rubber doll."

## What It All Means:

If such stories of animal sacrifice continue to run rampant through rock, it may be because the two share many similarities. As author Rene Girard points out in *Violence and the Sacred*, sacrifice provides an important, controlled release of pent-up aggressions. "When unappeased, violence seeks and always finds a surrogate victim," he writes. "The role of sacrifice is to stem this rising tide of indiscriminate substitution and redirect violence into proper channels." Rock, of course, has been doing the same thing for the better part of the last fifty years.

"I saw this thing bounce across the stage," he later told a reporter. "And when I looked it wasn't moving. So I just assumed it was a rubber doll."

Courtesy of Red Herring

# THE LEGEND:

Tupac Shakur was taken out by hit men hired by Puffy Combs's New York Bad Boy Entertainment as a way of shutting down his rival: Suge Knight's Death Row Records. In retaliation, Suge Knight ordered the murder of Bad Boy's number one rapper, Notorious B.I.G. as a payback.

## What People Are Saying:

It has been said that Tupac Shakur's murder is to the music industry what the JFK assassination is to the political arena. It has generated more conspiracy theories, rumors, and urban legends than just about any other single event in recent musical history.

According to most accounts, Shakur's downfall began the night of November 14, 1993, when he went to a nightclub in New York City with some friends. Over the course of the evening the twenty-two-year-old budding rap star was introduced to Ayanna Jackson, a gorgeous nineteen-year-old, who had previously gone out with director Allen Hughes. Within minutes of their introduction, Jackson was allegedly on her knees giving Shakur a blow job in the middle of the dance floor. Afterward, Shakur and his three friends—including Jacques Agnant, the one that introduced them in the first place—took her back to his hotel room and had sex with her. The following day, Jackson filed rape charges against all four, naming Shakur as the ringleader.

Two weeks later, while awaiting trial, Agnant introduced Shakur to a guy named Booker, an up-and-coming rap artist. Apparently Booker called Shakur the following day and asked him if he could come down to a friend's studio later that night, a studio owned by Biggie Smalls. Shakur declined at first, but Booker was persistent, offering him a quick $7,000 for some guest vocals. "All right," said Shakur reluctantly. "See you at around midnight."

Shakur never made that recording, however, because within minutes of showing up with a couple of friends he found himself face to face with a pair of gunmen. They claimed to be robbing the place, and forced everyone to the floor. Minutes later, one of the gunmen walked up to Shakur and shot him five times at near point-blank range. (One bullet went through his thigh and up into his balls, another went through his arm, and three more went into his chest, neck, and head.) No one else was injured in the incident, and Shakur hadn't done anything to provoke the attack.

Miraculously Shakur survived the ambush, although he didn't waste any time in pointing his finger at Biggie Smalls, whom he claimed was behind the hit. But before he could do anything about it, his lawyer called to tell him that the jury had reconvened on his rape charge. Still heavily bandaged, Shakur appeared in court the following morning to hear the jury read their verdict: guilty on three out of nine counts. He received a 1½ to 4½-year prison sentence, and was sent to the Clinton Correctional Center.

Shakur was allowed to post a $1.4 million bond for his parole, but he didn't have access to that kind of money. Marion "Suge" Knight, on the other hand, did. As the CEO of Death Row Records, Knight was considered the most successful—and feared—producer in the biz. Word on the street was that he built his company on drug money, MOB Piru Blood gang affiliations, and sheer intimidation.[10]

In October 1995, after Shakur had served eight months of his sentence, Shakur flew to New

A Tupac memorial in New York City

York to post bail. In return, Shakur signed a contract with Knight's Death Row records to produce at least five albums. From that point on, say his fans, the rivalry between Death Row and Bad Boy Records, the so-called East Coast–West Coast rivalry had officially begun. Yet it was Shakur that launched the first salvo. On his debut album for Death Row, *All Eyez on Me,* he included a line saying that he has sex with Smalls's wife and Smalls was said to be furious about it.

On September 7, 1996 Shakur attended the Tyson–Sheldon fight in Las Vegas with Knight and other Death Row employees. Around 8:45, they were strolling through the lobby of the MGM Grand on the way to the ring, when Travon "Tray Dee" Lane, a member of Death Row's group, spotted a known Southside Crip gang member named Orlando Anderson. Tray Dee remembered that Anderson and some fellow

Crips had ambushed him outisde a mall in Lakewood a few days earlier and had stolen his Death Row pendant. Before Anderson could run, however, Shakur, Knight, and the rest of their group jumped him and pummeled him into the ground.

At around 11:15 P.M., Tupac was riding in the passenger seat of Suge Knight's black 750 BMW, when a late-model white Cadillac pulled alongside him at the intersection of Flamingo and Koval. Someone sitting in the rear seat produced a high-powered, semiautomatic Glock .40-caliber handgun and began firing. Thirteen rounds were unleashed. Three went into Shakur. None went into Knight. (Although he was grazed with a piece of shrapnel.) Shakur was immediately taken into intensive care but died six days later.

TUPAC

## The Evidence:

Knight was said to be seething with rage over the death of his friend and believed that Smalls had something to do with it. In fact, word on the street was that Orlando Anderson or members of his gang, the Southside Crips, pulled the trigger and received a hefty sum of money from an undisclosed East Coast source shortly after the shooting.[11] But before Knight could retaliate with his own brand of MOB Piru Blood justice, he was arrested on assault charges stemming from the MGM pummeling and found to be in violation of his parole. He was quickly arraigned and sentenced to nine years in prison.

Then on March 9, 1997, Biggie Smalls was shot to death while sitting in the passenger seat of a friend's car only minutes after attending the 11th Annual Soul Train Awards in Los Angeles. As the LAPD claimed, it was an obvious copycat killing. Apparently the assassin ran up to Smalls's window as his car came to a stop at an intersection, and shot him at point-blank range with seven rounds of a high-powered handgun, then disappeared.

## The Bottom Line:

Did Suge Knight order the hit in retaliation for Shakur's murder? While the *Los Angeles Times* reported erroneously that Smalls's assassin may have been a member of Smalls's security team, investigators strongly believed that Knight planned the murder-for-hire plot from behind bars. Meanwhile Sean "Puffy" Combs, Smalls's partner in Bad Boy, went on to dominate the hip hop market, enjoy a well-publicized affair with actress Jennifer Lopez, deal with a nasty gun-possession charge, and become one of rap's wealthiest moguls. (See Chapter Six, *The Shadow of Discontent* for other theories on Shakur's death.)

# THE LEGEND:

Rod Stewart had his stomach pumped after an all night party with a group of footballers in London in the 1970s. What came out was a pint of sperm.

## The Truth:

Let's deconstruct this little scenario, shall we? First of all, sperm is nontoxic. So even if someone did manage to swallow a pint of it, it wouldn't require hospitalization. Secondly, it takes an average man at least four minutes to orgasm, which means it would have taken at least *eight hours* of consecutive cumming to manufacture a pint-o-sperm. And lastly, the average man ejaculates about nine cubic centimeters of baby gravy, which means that it would have taken slightly over 11,111 ejaculations—or footballers—to do the job.

Nonetheless, thousands of people still believe that Rod the Mod slobbed that many knobs. In fact it still resurfaces now and again at parties or industry events, generally as if it were a known fact.[12]

## Where It Comes From:

To this day no one really knows how or why the rumor started. Stewart remembers being on a honeymoon with his then wife Alana in Italy in 1979 and hearing the story on the radio. "That was really amazing!" he recalled years later.

"They said that I had been rushed off to the hospital and they pumped out twelve pints or something. Can you imagine that?"

So where did it come from? More than likely, it started in some pub somewhere in the 1970s, with a bunch of hardcore footballers bemoaning Stewart's sudden interest in the game. After all, Stewart was a glam rocker at the time, and glam rockers—*all* glam rockers—were essentially gay in the eyes of Britain's working class, no matter how much they claimed that they were just being "sexually ambiguous." Stewart, of course, was perhaps the proudest peacock of them all. In fact, writer Paul Nelson went so far as to compare him to Jayne Mansfield, claiming that he had a "movie-starlet image" that was downright embarrassing. "He was really trashy," wrote Nelson. "Sort of a male tart" who was prone to donning "feather boas, black eyeliner, and sheer, open-to-the waist blouses."

So when Rod's girlfriend, Deirdre "Dee" Harrington told reporters that he liked to wear her underwear on occasion—a claim repeated by Britt Ekland years later—it only solidified his image as a poof. In fact, his own father called him as much after he read one of his son's interviews where he claimed to like "dirty pictures."

So when Stewart began showing up to football games, often with the very-out-of-the-closet Elton John in tow, you can bet that the rest of the working-class crowd had a lot of fun at his expense. In fact, when Stewart announced that he was going to record a duet of "Angel" with soccer star Denis Law, there were more jokes about their alleged tryst than just about anything else in the news at the time. That may have laid the foundation for the cum-in-the-tummy story, but it wasn't the catalyst. That came a short time later when Stewart announced that he had to cancel a tour because of his "throat problems" due to LA smog. For many people that meant only one thing: that Rod must have had more in his mouth than foul air.

## The Bottom Line:

The truth is Stewart has had more heterosexual relations with beautiful women than just about

Dave Hogan/Retna Ltd. USA

any other rock star on record. As his biographer Geoffrey Giuliano points out in *Rod Stewart: Vagabond Heart,* even before he was dating the likes of Kathy Simmonds, Pauline Store, Mai Britt, Debbie Doranche, and Rachel Hunter, he was already legendary for his Polaroid collection—said to number in the thousands—of his nude female conquests. (And when he wasn't shooting stills according to Giuliano, he was also making home pornos.) "He was definitely oversexed," said Dee Harrington. "He wanted it all the time. He was just insatiable in that department."

The rumor, it seems, provides macho guys with the satisfaction of knowing that Stewart wasn't really sleeping with all those beautiful women. After all, macho guys like to think they're good, but no one's *that* good. If all those women like him, they argue, it must be because he's gay. Still, there may be a single source for the rumor. As Stewart once told *Q* magazine, "I think it was spread by a spiteful person who once worked for me. But I can't say who."

# THE LEGEND:

The Turtles, one of L.A.'s most cherished rock groups, were the first to do drugs in the White House.

## A Little History:

In 1996 members of the band Mudhoney tried to smoke pot in the White House—or at least they *thought* about smoking pot in the White House. Like most rock bands, they laughed when they received an invitation to the nation's capital and immediately began fantasizing about kicking back in the Oval Office and puffing on a fat doob. But as *High Times* magazine reported in 1999, they chickened out at the last minute. "The weed was smoked in the hotel before we went to the White House," explains lead singer Mark Arm. "I think Matt [Lukin] ate a joint in the van on the way when he realized the potential consequences of getting busted there."

Still, even if they succeeded, they wouldn't have been the first to light up in the executive mansion, not by a long shot. Evidently there have been drugs in the White House for a lot longer than most people realize. In 1978 for example, it was discovered that Dr. Peter Bourne, President Jimmy Carter's drug policy advisor, had written a prescription for a White House aide, authorizing the purchase of fifteen Quaaludes. When confronted with the accusation, Bourne admitted that he was supplying staff members with pharmaceuticals but that there was also a "high incidence" of marijuana and cocaine use going on in the White House already. Around the same time it was also believed that Phil Walden, the president of Capricorn Records, was spending an inordinate amount of time in some White House bathrooms. In 1977 *The New Times* published a story about Walden's friendship with President Carter, a friendship that began in 1975 when he helped raise $600,000 for Carter's presidential campaign through rock and roll concerts. The illustration depicted Walden with one arm around a smiling Jimmy Carter and the other around his top star, Gregg Allman. And as if that wasn't enough to make every Republican shake in his loafers, Allman had a spoonful of coke up his nose.

Country singer Willie Nelson on the other hand, has been quite candid in his admission of doing illicit drugs in the White House. In his book, *Willie: An Autobiography*, he describes a scene where, while visiting the White House in 1978, when he was there to perform for Jimmy and his wife Rosalynn, someone took him to the roof for a beer and a few puffs on a Nelson-rolled "Austin Torpedo."[13] "Nobody from the Secret Service was watching us," he writes. "Or if they were, it was with the intention of keeping us out of trouble instead of getting us into it."

The Secret Service was curiously absent for Crosby, Stills and Nash, too, when they played a concert for Carter the previous year, in 1977. Supposedly they, too,

*Country singer Willie Nelson on the other hand, has been quite candid in his admission of doing illicit drugs in the White House.*

The Turtles circa 1965

King Collection/Retna Ltd. USA

indulged in a little recreational smoke before getting on stage. That wasn't the case for Grace Slick of the Jefferson Airplane, however. When she received an invitation from President Richard Nixon's daughter, Patricia, to attend a Finch College reunion party on the White House lawn in 1970, she showed up in the smallest miniskirt that she could find, and "enough powdered acid to get a lot of people very high." The drug wasn't so much for her own pleasure as it was for the president himself. "The plan," she wrote, "was for me to reach my overly long pinky fingernail, grown especially for easy cocaine snorting, into my pocket, fill it with six hundred mics of pure powdered LSD, and with a large entertainer's gesture, drop the acid into Tricky Dick's teacup."

Not surprisingly, the FBI understood the threat that she and her coconspirator Abbie Hoffman posed, and refused to let them into the party. Slick, however, was able to talk her way in later, but Hoffman was forced to wait outside. Nonetheless, she failed to see the president, much less get him high.

## The Story:

The Turtles allegedly did drugs in the White House, too, and it was a full year before Slick tried her stunt. According to White House records, Chuck Portz, Howard Kaylan, Al Nichol, and Mark Volman appeared at the

# That's not all, however, some members boasted about doing a line of coke, too, apparently on a table formerly owned by Abraham Lincoln.

nation's capital on May 1, 1969, the same year that they released their classic, *The Turtles Present the Battle of the Bands*, their most psychedelic, drug-induced Beatlesesque album to date. They were there, along with the Temptations, to perform at a masked ball for the Nixon clan, and at some point "someone"—and it's always "someone"—apparently broke out a joint and passed it around. That's not all, however; some members boasted about doing a line of coke, too, apparently on a table formerly owned by Abraham Lincoln.

## The Bottom Line:

Did they or didn't they? Unfortunately, the band has failed to corroborate the story. In fact they've been downright presidential about it. As Kaylan once told a reporter in the 1980s, "Listen, maybe we did do those things, you know, or maybe we didn't. I really don't know. That was years ago."

## The Context:

In any case, the Turtles weren't the first to do illegal drugs in the nation's capital. Comedian Morey Amsterdam once admitted that he shared a joint with President John F. Kennedy on the grounds of the White House in 1963. And there seems to be some evidence that Mary Pinchot Meyer, a prominent Washington socialite, also shared a few joints with JFK on occasion, as well as dropping acid. As authors Martin A. Lee and Bruce Shlain point out in *Acid Dreams: The Complete Social History of LSD*:

```
[Meyer] struck up a cordial
friendship with Dr. Timothy
Leary during her occasional
visits to Cambridge in the
early 1960s. She asked him to
teach her how to guide an LSD
session so she could introduce
the drug to her circles in
Washington. "I have this friend
who's a very important man,"
she confided to Leary. "He's
very impressed with what I've
told him about my own LSD expe-
rience and what other people
have told him. He wants to try
it himself."
```

Leary had no way of knowing that "the very important man" was JFK, or that Meyer was one of his mistresses. In any case, no one will ever know for sure. Meyer was murdered less than a year after Kennedy was assassinated and "someone" stole her diary a short time later.

Was JFK the first? Not according to most presidential historians. Apparently Thomas Jefferson, the third president of the United States, was an avid pot smoker. In fact he even cultivated his own private pot farm with seeds smuggled in from Europe!

# HUNG JURY:
## THE MUSICAL

While fans may obsess on the size of their favorite actor, rock fans have been known to go to even more extraordinary lengths to uncover their idol's private dimensions. Groupies, after all, are the self-appointed gatekeepers of such information, and rock lore, perhaps even more than movie lore, thrives on such tales. In any case, here's a brief, albeit incomplete, look at rock's pantheon of schlong:

- ★ Jeff Beck
- ★ Chuck Berry
- ★ David Cassidy
- ★ Julian Cope
- ★ DJ Spooky
- ★ Eminem
- ★ Everlast
- ★ Perry Farrell
- ★ Levon Helm
- ★ Jimi Hendrix*
- ★ Lux Interior
- ★ Chris Isaak
- ★ Mick Jagger
- ★ Jim Kerr
- ★ Tommy Lee*
- ★ Huey Lewis*
- ★ Lyle Lovett
- ★ Robert Plant*
- ★ Iggy Pop
- ★ Rikki Rockett
- ★ Todd Rundgren
- ★ Snoop Doggy Dogg
- ★ Sly Stone
- ★ Peter Tork
- ★ Jimmy Witherspoon
- ★ Paul Young
  (that's the *other* Paul Young)
- ★ Billy Zoom

*Biggest of the big

Paul Young

The ghosts in the Los Angeles area are meaner than anywhere else. . . . There may be some kind of dimensional opening in the area.

—FRANK R. NOCERINO, DIRECTOR OF THE INSTITUTE OF PSYCHIC AND HYPNOTIC SCIENCES

# SOUTHERN CALIFORNIA'S

# A MOST UNLIKELY PARADISE

## UNNATURAL HISTORY

A monstrous beast called the Billiwhack Monster lives in an abandoned dairy near Aliso Canyon.

## A Little History:

Situated in a quiet, almost Arcadian valley in the San Rafael Mountains, the Billiwhack Dairy thrived in the early part of the twentieth century, thanks to the efforts of August Rubel, its owner. But Rubel struggled through the depression of the 1930s, and eventually had to file for bankruptcy in 1943. No one really knows what happened to him after that, although some have claimed that he went off on a mission for the OSS in World War II and never returned. In any case, the dairy remained empty for years, providing shelter for wayward animals, runaways, and curious kids alike.

## Where It Comes From:

In the late 1950s, a nine-year-old Aliso Canyon boy returned home late one evening with deep scratches across his arms and back claiming that he had been attacked by a "weird animal" at the Billiwhack. He had snuck on to the property with some friends and found a way into the building itself. But at some point this beast jumped out from nowhere and started chasing them; a beast that was over seven feet tall with long arms and gigantic claws like a bear. He also said that it was covered in shaggy hair, and had two horns growing out the top of its head that curled around its ears like a goat.

While the authorities never took the boy's claim very seriously, the news of the "Billiwhack Beast" eventually spread throughout the valley, prompting even more kids to make pilgrimages to the dairy. In 1964 the local sheriffs department caught nearly a dozen children armed with homemade swords as they were climbing the

Paul Young

**The Beast of Billiwhack**

fence. One claimed that he was going to slay the beast in the manner of St. Michael, while another professed that he was going to cut its head off and take it to the president of the United States.

## The Context:

The Billiwhack Beast is not the only sighting of a monster in Southern California. Several residents in Ojai, for example, a small town a mere fifteen miles to the west of the Billiwhack dairy, claimed that they saw a weird creature running through their yards in the 1930s. Mrs. Catherine Loughboro, for example, described it as a "half-monkey-half-man," and claimed that it had stolen two hens from her henhouse. Weeks later, in June 1939, Mrs. Tom Richards saw a similar beast sitting in her corn patch chewing on an ear of corn. She described it as being the size of a twelve-year-old boy, with long, black fur and long, gangly arms.

An even more curious beast appeared on November 8, 1958, near the Santa Ana River bridge in Riverside. According to the official police report, twenty-four-year-old Charles Wetzel was driving home one night when something jumped out in front of his car. Wetzel later claimed that it stood six feet tall, had legs growing out of its sides, arms that nearly touched the ground, and scaly, leaf-like skin. "It had a round, scarecrowish head," he explained. "With a kind of muzzle for a mouth."

Apparently the "black monster," as it was later dubbed, made a screeching noise and bolted straight for his car. Terrified, Wetzel began frantically searching for the .22 revolver that he kept under his seat as the beast climbed onto the roof and began pounding and scratching the windshield. Seconds later, he put the car in gear and gunned the engine, throwing the beast off the rear end.

Officers later agreed that there were scratch marks on Wetzel's car, and that was enough to warrant a sweep through the area with blood-

*...it was covered in shaggy hair, and had two horns growing out the top of its head that curled around its ears like a goat.*

hounds. Yet after days of searching they gave up the hunt.

Then there was the monster that appeared in the urban center of Watts in 1961. According to police reports, at approximately 3:15 P.M. a creature with the "body of a dog and the face of a woman" ran through the vicinity of 103rd and Grape. "At first I thought it was a crank call," Lieutenant L.D. Rottier told the *Los Angeles Examiner*. "But for the next three hours similar calls kept coming in from that general area. I guess a lot of people saw this thing and they all described it as running on all fours and covered in hair . . . But it wasn't a dog, or any other known animal, at least according to the reports."

## What It All Means:

In mythology, such animals are said to be the result of an unnatural coupling of a human female with a supernatural being. Psychologists explain such sightings as psychic manifestations, reflecting the storyteller's subconscious fears and/or neurotic projections. (Which is one reason why such sightings—and horror movies for that matter—are so common during times of turmoil or oppression.) Geneticists like to point out that such monsters are really physical aberrations, and that giants, dwarves, and people with horns are relatively common within certain groups. Crytozoologists on the other hand, argue that such species may be the result of a common species being forced to adapt to a radically different environment, such as the pink river dolphin. Meanwhile paranormalists maintain that such creatures are from other dimensions, passing back and forth between our world and theirs. Each theory has its merits, and each may or may not explain aspects of the phenomenon. As Robert H. Knapp of the seminal Boston Rumor Clinic suggests, rumors of monsters serve the dual purpose of channeling the anxieties of the teller while providing entertainment for the listener.

# THE MYTH:

There's a mysterious `batlike` `creature` living around Elizabeth Lake.

Paul Young

Where evil lurks: Elizabeth Lake

## A Short History:

Located about fifteen miles west of Lancaster, Elizabeth Lake has a long history of strange phenomena. Despite its natural beauty, Indians once claimed that it offered a passageway to the underworld, a passageway designed by the devil himself. And since then there have been scores of unnatural visions and sounds reported in the area. In the mid-1850s for example, a group of farmers tried to homestead the property, only to hightail it out of there two months later. They too heard the screams and wails and decided that the lake was haunted. The same happened to Don Pedro Carrillo of the great Carrillo family, who moved out of the area six months after moving in, claiming that the unnatural noises, screams, and visions made him "prematurely old." Perhaps Don Guillermo, a fourth generation Californian, described it best when he said, "By all accounts, Elizabeth Lake is a horrible, haunted body of water. It is the mouth of hell. Frightful and unearthly noises have emanated from its depths. Screams, shrieks and groans as though hell itself and its congregation of the damned might lie directly beneath it."

## Where It Comes From:

According to historian Horace Bell, Chico Vasquez, brother of Tiburcio Vasquez, the notorious bandit, moved to Elizabeth Lake in

*"It let out a shriek a hundred times louder than a screech owl."*

the 1870s. He, too, felt uneasy about the place until finally, one afternoon, he saw a horrific vision: there, in among the shallow margins of the lake, was a great beast large enough to outweigh a small whale, stuck in the mud. According to Vasquez, it let out a shriek a "hundred times louder than a screech owl," and looked as though it was trying to free itself from its earthly binds, thrashing about wildly with enormous, batlike wings. Terrified, he rode back to his ranch to get some help. Yet when he returned a short while later with a couple of friends, the beast had disappeared. "Best stay off the liquor," joked his friends. Frustrated, Vasquez turned around just as a great whistling, hissing, and screaming was heard from a growth of tules near the water's edge. Seconds later, a nauseating, fetid, smell filled the air, as a huge beast described as a cross between a bat and a "flying alligator," lifted itself out of the mud. The group staggered back as they watched it rise up into the air, caterwauling like a banshee and flapping its wings madly.

Unable to calm their horses the men returned home for the night. But when they returned the following morning with rifles, the creature had vanished. "Whether it had flown away or sunk beneath the mud, we could not determine," said Vasquez. "But the foul odor continued for a long time after that."

Since then, the Elizabeth Lake monster has made a handful of notable appearances. In 1886 a Los Angeles newspaper reported that a number of pigs and cattle were either mutilated or abducted from the area, and no one knew what to make of it. A short time later, a giant "python" was seen devouring an entire bronco steer near the water's edge. According to Don Felipe Rivera, who made the discovery, the beast was forty-four feet long, with six legs, a "bulldog" face, and large, leathery, batlike wings pulled close to its back. Rivera claimed that he emptied a .44 caliber Colt into its side, but the bullets bounced off "as if they were striking a great iron kettle." Then he ran like hell to get as far away as he possibly could.

According to Bell, the monster was last seen in 1886 by a character named El Basquo Grande, who saw it emerge from the lake one morning and fly east. And since then, the number of eyewitness accounts have all but disappeared, although many have reported *other* mysterious phenomena in the area.

## The Context:

Flying beasts of unknown origins are not entirely uncommon for Southern California. Some local Indian tribes, for example, have told stories of the Makalay, a terrifying winged-creature that was said to have a single horn growing out of its forehead, the body of a kangaroo and large batlike wings.[1]

More recently, a "kangaroo-bat" appeared

# A HOLY TERROR.

## The Fiery Dragon of Elizabeth Lake.

### A MODEST STORY FROM VENTURA.

#### The Hideous "Thing" with Dinner-Plate Scales, Headlight Eyes and a Harpoon Tail Now Paralyzing the Natives.

near Pacoima in the San Fernando Valley in July 1996. Three people reportedly saw the beast "bounding" through a field in broad daylight, and they described it as being between four or five feet tall and weighing anywhere from seventy to one hundred fifty pounds. One witness claimed that it looked like a cross between a "rat and a kangaroo" with leathery batlike wings. Another claimed that it had "red eyes, a brightly colored spine, spiky fur, and long, thin arms." And when a number of rabbit and goat carcasses turned up—completely drained of blood—there were rumors that it was none other than the legendary Chupacabra, or "goatsucker" that terrorized Puerto Rico between 1987 and 1996.

## What It All Means:

Bats are particularly potent symbols throughout the world. Their tendency to sleep upside down during the day, and carry out their activities at night has led many to believe that they are the incarnation of evil, or the inversion of mortal life. In fact, many tribes throughout the world believe that bats embody the souls of the dead, and as such can bring *good* luck if treated with respect. Psychologists on the other hand, seem to believe that such symbols represent "neglected" complexes in the subconscious and the desire to have them recognized by the psyche.

# THE RUMOR:

A popular form of entertainment in the nineteenth century was a fight between a **bull** and a **grizzly bear**.

## Where It Comes From:

You can always expect some pretty outrageous forms of entertainment when you put a bunch of cowboys together for a long period of time. That's just what happened during California's gold rush period of the 1850s for example, when miners cooked up a number of outrageous betting games, including bare-knuckle fistfights, coyote hunts, badger fights, dogfights, cockfights, shooting contests, and drinking contests.

Perhaps the most audacious of all however, was the fight to the death between a California grizzly and a thousand pound bull. According to historian Richard Erdoes, such contests eventually became so popular that they were featured in rodeos and bullfighting rings all over California. In fact by 1850, over one hundred men were making a living on trapping bears exclusively for such events.

## What Happened:

The conditions of each contest depended on the size of the bear and the availability of a foe. If the grizzly was extraordinarily large for instance, the promoters often used a series of bulls, one after the other, in an effort to wear it down. (Apparently a stronger grizzly could snap a bull's neck by grabbing its horns and twisting with all its might. But after several bulls in a row it would eventually tire and become vulnerable.) If the bear was undersized however, promoters would have to find more suitable adversaries. There are records for example of bears being pitted against donkeys—which were surprisingly tough competitors—and even dogs. As a typical poster of 1857 announced, "For a mere three dollars, a HE bear will be baited by relays of five dogs every thirty minutes while a SHE bear will be barbecued for dinner."

Clash of the titans

"The Powerful Exchange" (bronze), Produced by Millennium Fine Arts

Not all fights were successful however—especially when promoters tried to use a black or brown bear. "The bears *had* to be grizzlies," writes Erdoes. "If they tried to use anything else, the results were often deplorable." The reason of course, may have to do with the fact that bears and bulls are not natural enemies, so rather than fight, they'd usually walk around looking for a way out of the arena—or else they'd go after people in the audience instead—which always made for great entertainment. Wranglers eventually solved that problem by tying the bear to a stake, which of course, gave the bull an obvious, unfair advantage. And there are also reports of cowboys beating bears with two-by-fours embedded with nails or getting bulls riled by waving red flags.

## The Legacy:

Historian Horace Bell notes in his book, *On the Old West*, the state legislature eventually banned bear-and-bull fights in 1860 after a public outcry of inhumanity to animals. Nonetheless, the fights continued for several years after that. W. A. Chalfant mentions going to a fiesta in Bakersfield in September 1874, for example, where they "brought out a bull and a bear" for a "clash of the titans." And there were other, slightly less known matches that continued for decades. One promoter for example, was famous for pitting wildcats against bull terriers—although the cats rarely, if ever, had a chance—and another was known to throw as many as fifty rats into a pit and place bets on the number that his dog could rip to shreds.

## The Bottom Line:

Animal cruelty was almost a way of life in the nineteenth century, and hardly the politically incorrect thing that it is today. As Mike Davis points out in *Ecology of Fear*, the period of 1865 to 1890 in particular saw the largest deliberate destruction of local wildlife in California history. Fish and Game officials calculated that sportsmen killed off anywhere from 50 to 95 percent of California's game in a single generation.

# THE MYTH:

There are Bigfoot monsters in the Borrego Badlands.

## Where It Comes From:

While Northern California rightfully deserves the title as the Bigfoot capital of the world, Southern California has had enough sightings to claim a close second. On April 22, 1973, for example, at about ten P.M. on a clear night, William Roemermann, Brian Goldojarb and Richard Engles, three teenagers from the San Fernando Valley, were riding in the back of their friend's pickup near Big Rock Canyon, not far from Elizabeth Lake. All of a sudden, an eleven-foot, bearlike beast jumped out of the bushes and started chasing the truck at full stride. But when the driver heard his passengers scream, he became confused and slammed on his brakes. "No!" they shrieked. "Go! Go! Go!" Before they knew it, the beast was within inches of the tailgate, close enough for the boys to see his "glowing red eyes," and smell his "stinky" breath. Finally, just as it was about to leap into the back, the driver shifted into gear and sped off once again.

# 1st BIGFOOT CAPTURED!

The local sheriff had to bite his tongue as he listened to the boy's story. But when he went to the site the following morning and found several hundred three-toed footprints, approximately fourteen inches in length, he began to change his mind. Using plaster of Paris to make copies, he brought the prints to a local zoologist for validation, but the zoologist merely dismissed the notion out of hand saying, "There were no such things as Bigfoot monsters."

## The Context:

The incident was not the first sighting of a Bigfoot in the area. In the seventeenth century, Indians living nearby used to talk about a large hairy giant that lived in the upper part of the mountain; and in 1876 some hunters reported seeing an apelike beast in one of the foothills. Since then, the sightings have multiplied. In fact, Big Rock has been dubbed the home base of Southern California sasquatches. On January 28, 1936, for example, the *Los Angeles Examiner* reported that a "giant ape man" jumped out of a tree and grabbed a twenty-year-old woman, Birdie Bennett, and carried her several yards before dropping her and running off. Years later, in May 1973, a nineteen-year-old woman spotted something that was "seven-feet-tall and covered in hair" prowling around the back of her house. A short time later, a Marine saw a similar creature casually walking through a nearby residential area, occasionally hopping fences, and digging through garbage. (According to his

account, it "sneezed like a man.")[2]

There are also strange monsters living around the Borrego Sink, just outside of Borrego Springs near San Diego. Unlike northern Bigfoots however, these creatures are considerably smaller, standing five feet tall at the most, and have a coat of *white* hair. One of the first sightings took place in March 1888 when a group of hunters went into Dark Canyon to explore a cave allegedly filled with human remains. During the expedition, a creature "covered in white fur" tried to attack the men. One kept it at bay with a rifle until the group could escape, then ran for his life.

Harold Lancaster, a well-respected desert navigator, reported a similar beast in the same area a few years later. He was setting up camp around Borrego Palm Canyon, when he saw an "apeman" approaching him cautiously in the middle of the night. It was approximately five feet tall by his estimation and covered in long hair. It didn't stick around long however, at least not after Lancaster fired off a warning shot with his shotgun. Because when he did, the beast jumped three feet in the air and ran back into the hills.

Some of the residents of Deadman's Hole, a small town near Warner Hot Springs, have supposedly seen a similar beast there, too. According to reports in the *San Diego Union,* it was approximately five feet tall, with huge, broad shoulders, a small head, and a mane of jet black hair covering its entire body. Many of the residents believe that the beast was responsible for the scores of mysterious, unexplained murders that occurred in the late 1870s and 1880s. But after a young Indian girl named Belita was found slaughtered in a nearby cave, two hunters, John Weeks and Frank Cox, decided to track down the so-called "Wild Man of Deadman's Hole."

Two weeks later, after numerous false starts, the two hunters came across an immense animal hiding among some rocks. At first they thought it was a bear or a gorilla, but when it stood up on its hind legs and let out a horrific roar, they realized that it was something else entirely. As Weeks later described it, "It was at least six feet tall and it must have weighed eight hundred pounds. It looked more like a man than an animal though. It had a smooth face like an Indian, with only a few whiskers."

Before the beast could make a move, Weeks and Cox unleashed a roar of gunfire, causing the beast to fall to the ground in a bloody mess. It didn't die however, at least not at first. As the two men moved closer, it began to wail uncontrollably, sounding like a cross between a stuck pig and an ape. Then the two men reloaded their weapons and literally blew its head off just to make sure that it was "good 'n' dead."

According to Weeks, they eventually found what looked like a dugout filled with bones in the nearby foothills. "We also saw a partially eaten goat near the entrance," Cox told the *San Diego Union*, "and five human skulls hanging on a wall."

The *Union*'s report caused a great panic with the residents of Warner Springs, although few seemed to look very carefully at the date that it was printed. After all, it was published on *April Fools Day*.[3]

# THE LEGEND:

Giant Rock in Landers has a certain physical property that attracts UFOs.

## What People Are Saying:

Another strange geological site in Southern California is Giant Rock, a 100,000-ton, seven-story high, 100-million-year-old boulder located a short distance from Goat Mountain in Landers. Many of the locals claim that the rock—and Goat Mountain itself—"attracts" UFOs from outer space. In the 1950s Norman Paulsen, a founding member of the Self Realization Fellowship in 29 Palms, claimed that he witnessed at least a dozen unidentified flying objects in the area, many of which seemed to be hovering over Giant Rock; and since then there have been an untold number of sightings, including one by the deputy sheriff of Riverside County who allegedly took a photograph clearly documenting a glistening ship in mid-flight. Yet it was George Van Tassel, the former aircraft inspector from Hughes Aircraft, who made Giant Rock world famous for UFOlogy. While he later claimed that he was "directed" to the rock by intergalactic divination, Van Tassel originally hoped to build a dude ranch there so that he'd have a place to retire at the ripe old age

of 35. That all changed on August 24, 1953, however, when an "alien being" appeared at the foot of his bed and signaled for him to follow. As Van Tassel described the experience later, "I got up all right and followed the guy into the desert. After walking a short distance I saw this small, spherical, dome-shaped, space ship hovering about six feet above the sage brush. The ship was about sixty feet in diameter and consisting of a material such as I have never seen before."

## A Little History:

Van Tassel eventually acquired three sections of land around Giant Rock on a lease-option from the federal government, and devoted his life to transforming the small town into UFO-central. And for the next twenty-three years he hosted annual UFO conventions at the base of the rock, (featuring fellow abductees and saucer fanatics, including the truly deranged, George Adamski), conducted regular Friday night channelings, (where he conjured space beings such as Ashtar), published a UFO magazine called *Proceedings*,

Paul Young

wrote numerous books, including 1952's *I Rode a Flying Saucer,* and forged his own cult called the College of Universal Wisdom.

All of this brought Van Tassel a wealth of popularity in his later years, so much so that he was considered Giant Rock's unofficial mayor. In fact, he became so popular that he ran for president of the United States in 1959, apparently at the request of "the space people."[4]

## The Legacy:

Van Tassel's greatest invention still stands near Giant Rock. Based in part on the instructions given to him by his alien friends, and in part on the work of George Lakhovsky, he built an entire building that was supposed to "facilitate life extension." He called it the "Integratron," and it looks a bit like an oversized lighthouse, with portholes and ship features. Its main feature however, is a set of metallic rods that were designed to work in conjunction with a magnetic wave oscillator inside the building.

Once engaged, these mechanisms were designed to create an electrically charged force field that could replenish the human cell with new energy. "The human cell," he once wrote, "operates a lot like a car battery. If left alone it loses its energy and that leads to aging. The Integratron is designed to restore that energy to the human cell and prolong its life indefinitely."

If the process worked, it didn't work very well. Van Tassel died of a heart attack before he reached seventy.

In any case, he was no stranger to curious architecture. During one of his first visits to Giant Rock he met a German scientist and fellow UFO fanatic named Frank Critzer who lived *inside* the rock itself. Critzer was a part-time scientist, miner, and ham radio operator who came to the area to explore mining interests. But once he saw the wealth of strange phenomena in the area, he realized that he had stumbled upon something truly magnificent. That's when he placed a few sticks of dynamite around the edge of the boulder and created his own studio apartment inside.

He wasn't there long however. After the U.S. entered World War II, Air Force officials intercepted some of his radio signals—signals that were meant for intergalactic ears only—and they immediately charged him with being a spy. Critzer didn't deny the charges, although he refused to be taken into custody. So when a squad of deputies showed up at his front door he barricaded himself inside and refused to budge. That led to a four-hour standoff until finally, at around three in the afternoon, one of the deputies shot a tear gas canister through a small opening and it landed in a box of dynamite in Critzer's kitchen. The subsequent blast blew Critzer to smithereens. In fact, when Van Tassel moved his family into the rock a short time later, he claimed that he could still see bloodstains on the walls.

# THE RUMOR:

At the far end of the Mojave Desert, in an area called the Devil's Playground, there are a group of sand dunes that "sing."

The Kelso dune
Paula Ploquin

## What People Are Saying:

There's a rare phenomenon that occurs with sand dunes. Every so often, when the conditions are just right, they seem to sing. Charles Hillinger investigated the occurrence for his column in the *Los Angeles Times* and found a mining engineer named Jack Hereford who claimed firsthand experience of the phenomenon. As Hereford explained, he first heard the sound in 1964 while prospecting for magnetite in the Mojave. And after climbing to the top of a five-hundred-foot dune in the Devil's Playground area of San Bernadino County, he heard an eerie booming sound that resembled a tubalike "umpah." A few seconds later, as the booming continued, a slow chorus began to follow that sounded like "barking seals." According to Hereford, the entire concert lasted around four minutes.

## The Context:

Similar sounds have been reported in the deserts of Egypt, Chile, and the Middle East. Marco Polo wrote about singing dunes in his journal and members of Charles Darwin's party mentioned the phenomenon while traveling through South America in 1835. Closer to home, some of the Native American Indian tribes in the area have reportedly dubbed the sounds the "Devil's Refrain."

## What It All Means:

There's a natural propensity to attribute human, or lifelike, attributes to inanimate objects, especially among the uninformed. After all, folklore is full of talking trees, breathing skies, and sleeping mountains. As author Tom Chetwynd has pointed out, such beliefs may be due to the general notion that nature is the personification of the life force. Yet modern man has distanced himself from nature to such a degree that his sub-conscious continues to see a similar life force in everything, including inanimate objects.

## The Truth:

Studies of the phenomenon have proved to be frustratingly inconclusive. Some believe that the sound may be the result of the wind moving across the surface of the dune. Others believe that it may have to do with large planes of sand shifting all at once. Then again, people such as Hereford believe that the sound actually comes from *inside* the dune itself, without any relation to atmospheric conditions at all.

In any case, if you're interested in hearing the phenomenon for yourself be forewarned that it takes a pretty high dune to make such a noise. The Kelso dune, fifty miles southeast of Baker, is probably the best singing dune in the Mojave. It rises up about seven-hundred feet above the desert floor and it takes a good two hours in blistering heat to get to the top. Then again, being delirious may enhance the effect.

# THE RUMOR:

Southern California has earthquake weather, a subtle atmospheric condition that precedes a quake.

## What People Are Saying:

There's a condition in Southern California that can be defined as a certain "heaviness" in the air, a kind of pregnant pause that is conspicuously devoid of movement; a time when the birds stop singing, the wind stops blowing, and everything seems to come to a complete standstill. Others say that the light is different: it's a little warmer and "crisper" giving the environment a kind of ethereal, dreamlike appearance. Others still suggest that the condition occurs between extreme changes in the weather: when the days are extraordinarily hot and the nights extraordinarily cold.

## Where It Comes From:

Geologists have flatly denied that earthquake weather exists. "It's absolutely impossible," says Dr. Lucile Jones, scientist-in-charge at the California Institute of Technology in Pasadena, California (Caltech), the acknowledged epicen-

EXTRA

LATE
NEWS

Los Angeles Times

9 A.M.
FINAL

VOL. LXXI          IN FOUR PARTS          ★          MONDAY MORNING, JULY 21, 1952          60 PAGES          DAILY, 10¢

# BIG QUAKE ROCKS L.A.

ter for earthquake information. "For the simple fact that earthquakes happen ten to thirty miles below the earth's surface. It's as simple as that."

## The Context:

Still, there are a lot of people that believe otherwise.[5] Jack Coles, for instance, believes that he can "hear" earthquakes before they occur. That's how he supposedly predicted the Loma Prieta quake in 1989, the Upland quake in 1990, and the Sierra Madre quake in 1991. His theory basically suggests that earthquakes are the release of tension along fault lines, an idea most people seem to agree with. But he also believes that the mounting tension causes an escalating vibration deep within the plates, much like a pencil before it snaps. That vibration, he argues, causes quartz crystals to emit a long-wave, low frequency radio signal that can be registered on a radio receiver days, even weeks, before an earthquake hits.

Jim Berkland on the other hand, believes that quakes occur most often when the earth is situated between the sun and the moon—a peri-od that he calls the "seismic window." That's when gravitational forces are strong enough to create an eighteen-inch bulge on both sides of the planet—a bulge that he believes can shift plates along a fault line. With that in mind, Berkland carefully monitors tide movements, gravitational forces, and the axis of the Earth to make his predictions. And according to those in the prediction biz, he's so dead-on that he's known as the "Babe Ruth of Shakers."

Then there are the bio-sensitives, people that can detect atmospheric and geological changes in their very own bodies. Jerry Hurley, for example, who claims to have predicted over a dozen quakes, claims that he suffers from bad headaches, ringing ears, and irregular heartbeats just before a significant quake. And once those symptoms arise, symptoms that supposedly feel like "being punched in the stomach several times," he rotates his body like an antenna until the sensations peak. Then, and only then, can he determine the direction and the size of the quake.

Another bio-sensitive is Charlotte King of Oregon. Like Hurley, she makes her predictions

A Most Unlikely Paradise

**153**

through physical pain, too, only instead of rotating her body and waiting for a general sensation, she reacts to specific sensations in specific body parts. A bad headache for example, means that San Francisco may be due for a shaker, heart pain means activity in Landers or Big Bear, and diarrhea, not surprisingly, means trouble for L.A.[6]

## The Evidence:

Perhaps the most convincing case for earthquake weather is the commonly held belief that animals can detect tremblers long before they occur. Jim Berkland for example, claims that in addition to watching the Earth's gravitational pull, he watches the number of lost pet listings in the newspaper. And there seems to be some compelling evidence that the Chinese predicted a massive 7.3 rocker on February 4, 1975, a full twenty-four hours before it hit the Liaoning Province, and they did it, they claim, by monitoring animal behavior in the area.

## The Bottom Line:

Dr. Jones has an equally skeptical response to animal prediction, however. In fact, she has solid evidence that the Chinese *faked* their animal experiments at Liaoning just to appease government officials. "You have to understand that earthquakes have two distinct waves," she explains. "There's the primary wave, or the P wave, and the secondary, or S wave. The P waves are sound waves and they move much more quickly. The S wave, on the other hand, moves more slowly and causes more damage. It's a little like thunder and lightning. You can actually tell how far from the epicenter that you are by the difference between the two. But humans are not always as sensitive to the low frequency of the P wave as animals are. So what happens is that someone's pet will hear the rumble ten, twenty seconds before you, and run and hide. That's why people think that they can predict quakes. But they're only reacting to the sound—which humans generally can't hear. But if they ran and hid *ten hours* before—which they don't—that would be something else entirely."

# THE RUMOR:

There are the remains of an ancient Egyptian civilization buried under some sand dunes on the Central Coast.

## What People Are Saying:

They say these remains are buried somewhere near Santa Barbara: an entire Egyptian city complete with mummies, crypts, hieroglyphics, and giant statues, which are perhaps thousands, of years old. And they say that on certain days, when the winds are just right, the tip of a statue may appear briefly, only to be covered up again days later.[7]

This is the granddaddy of all buried treasure stories in Southern California. No other can compare. Not even the stories of ancient fossils said to be buried underneath downtown L.A., the stone effigies said to exist along the coast of Malibu, the 1,700-year-old Chinese anchors said to rest off Palos Verdes, or the gargantuan dinosaur tracks said to be in the Vallecito Mountains.

## Where It Comes From:

While this rumor sounds similar to the legend of Ubar, the fabled city said to be buried somewhere under the Sahara, archeologists *have* in fact found Egyptian relics buried near Santa Barbara—but they're *faux* relics. As befitting for Hollywood, they were designed for the production of *The Ten Commandments* in 1923 and left to rot in the desert sun shortly after the production was completed.

## A Little History:

In the early 1920s, Cecil B. DeMille, the original Hollywood megalomaniac, placed an ad in the *Los Angeles Times* offering $1,000 for the best movie idea. Apparently a handful of contestants suggested the Ten Commandments, and DeMille immediately commissioned a screenplay and hired the French production designer Paul Iribe to design "an authentic, full-scale Egyptian city." The site chosen was an eighteen-mile stretch of rolling sand dunes called the Nipomo Dunes, 170 miles north of L.A., near the town of Guadalupe.

After setting up a home base near the southern portion of the site, he brought in his own, fully staffed hospital, a restaurant capable of serving 7,500 meals per day, a dance hall complete with a jazz band, a housing tract for 2,500 extras, and a ranch that could shelter the production's 4,500 animals. Iribe meanwhile, built an entire eight-hundred-foot wide, Phoenician city with 110-foot steel gates, four thirty-five-foot statues of the Pharaoh, and an "avenue" of sphinxes—each weighing five tons each. The operating costs, not surprisingly, reached $40,000 per day (in 1923 dollars). After filming was completed, the landholder, Union Sugar, demanded that DeMille remove the set, as per their contract. Yet rather than pay for the cost of shipping, DeMille simply ordered his prop men to dig a hole and bulldoze it in. The temple itself was blown to pieces with dynamite first.

## The Legacy:

While no one really knows *exactly* where the remains are, a number of amateur archeologists have uncovered a few pieces here and there. Peter Brosnan and John Parker, two professional archeologists, have been struggling for years to find financing for a complete excavation, yet have been unable to secure any help from the major studios. To make matters more frustrating,

Bison Archives

DeMille's monument to megalomania

155

they're also up against time. Apparently the dunes are moving at a rate of three feet per year, threatening to crush the underground statues and/or expose sections to the elements. "All I want to do is to save a couple pieces and install them in a museum," says Brosnan. "I think it would give people an idea of the enormity of some of these early productions."

# THE LEGEND:

Mysterious explosions occur under the City of Commerce with no known geological explanation.

Paul Young

## Where It Comes From:

In the late 1980s the City of Commerce was home to one of the strangest natural phenomena in all of Los Angeles County. Between the hours of three and four A.M. residents living between East Gage Avenue and Zindell heard a series of deafening explosions that were violent enough to knock items off shelves. Apparently, these concussions occurred randomly, once every ten to twenty minutes, without any discernable pattern. At the time there was speculation that they were sonic booms caused by military aircraft flying overhead. Others likened them to the sensation of something hitting the floor with a sharp concussion, something heavy and solid. "It felt like an earthquake" claimed one resident, "or underground shock waves or something." Nonetheless, no one has been able to come up with an adequate explanation for the phenomenon. The Air Force denied any military activity in the area, seismologists failed to find any evidence of earthquake activity, and the city's engineers repudiated the notion of underground pipe work or digging. In fact, to this day nobody has any idea what caused the "Commerce Booms." They remain one of L.A.'s greatest natural mysteries.

## The Context:

The phenomenon is not unique to Southern California. Charles Fort has documented similar cases all over the world, and nearly all of them have occurred near large bodies of water. A similar phenomenon, for example, occurs near the mouth of the Ganges River in India, where the locals call them "Barisal Guns." The Belgians have a similar set of mysterious explosions called "fog pistols." The Italians have their *brontidis*, and the Japanese have their *uminaris*. While no one has come up with a definitive answer for this phenomenon, some have claimed quite convincingly, that they may be the result of heavy waves slapping into caverns or coves.

## The Bottom Line:

No one really knows what caused the Commerce booms for sure. Fort believes that they could be the result of "meteoric explosions" occurring high in the stratosphere. Some seismologists on the other hand, have likened them to "rock bursts," or a rare occurance of subterranean strata exploding under pressure. Yet Ray Ramirez, the assistant director of community development in the City of Commerce, may have a better explanation. As he explains, "When oil companies are going back in and redrilling on existing oil wells to look for oil that may still exist, they set up long cords. These cords are connected to a device that creates a shock wave that shoots through the well. These cords record the shock wave. And apparently they're pretty loud, loud enough to rattle a few homes. This may be the source of the legendary Commerce Booms."

# THE LEGEND:

A feral woman lives on San Nicholas Island.

## What People Are Saying:

In 1853 a fishing party led by George Nidever landed on San Nicholas Island, the most remote island of the Channel Island chain, and made a most unusual discovery: There, living amid the rock shoreline, was an Indian woman that he mistakenly believed to be forty or fifty years old, wearing little more than a few weeks of San Nicholas soil. At first he thought she was a Nicoleno Indian, a tribe known to inhabit the Channel Islands. But after setting up camp and watching her from afar, he concluded that she was very much alone on the island, and seemed ignorant of any known Indian custom. Still, she was surprisingly adept at survival, making her own hut out of whalebones and mud, fishing lines out of kelp and sea shells, and traps out of sharpened branches.

Nidever spent weeks watching her, until he finally managed to gain her trust, at least enough to share a meal with her, and that's when he realized that he had misjudged her age by nearly three decades. Rather than fifty, she was actually twenty, with "pleasant features and a nice, unwrinkled face." He had difficulty in communicating with her, however, since she had lost her power of speech entirely.

The captain eventually convinced her to come aboard his ship, the *Juana Maria*, and sail back to the mainland with him. Though nervous, she accompanied him to the mission at Santa Barbara, which at the time had a hospice and an apostolic college. There she received food and board for as long as she wanted, although she failed to assimilate into Western culture, and preferred to sleep outdoors, and wash herself with rainwater. She eventually proved too much to handle for the friars, and Nidever returned a few days later and brought her back to his own house in Santa Barbara. Weeks later, after daily English lessons, she began telling him about her experiences on the island. Apparently she had no idea how she got there, but she had vague recollections of her parents who disappeared long before she could remember. "Everybody die," she said in her best pidgin. "No more people."

## What Really Happened:

The girl's story struck a familiar chord with the friars at the mission. Twenty years earlier, San Nicholas Island was the site of a bloody massacre, and many of the victims ended up in their care. It all started apparently, in the late 1700s, when Indians began colonizing the islands for their own use. But in 1811, a group of Kodiak Indians, hired by an American sea captain, were

Mission Santa Barbara

Hubert A. Lowman

asked to go to the island and evacuate the tribe there so that an American/Russian trading company could move in and set up its own hunting operations. The Kodiaks were a viscious bunch however, and ended up raping the women and slaughtering the men.

Some Indians remained however, and they survived for the next twenty years until another sea captain tried to evacuate the island once again. That was in 1835, when the captain of the *Peor es Nada* used recruits from American forces to corral the natives onto his ship.[8] During the evacuation, a young mother who had been dragged to the ship despite protests, began screaming that her baby girl had been left behind. No one paid her any mind however, until she jumped overboard in an effort to swim back, and drowned. As a result, little Juana Maria, as she was later dubbed, was forced to learn methods of survival all alone at the age of two, or perhaps three, years old.

Many people knew about the girl, including the captain of the *Peor es Nada*, who promised that he'd return one day and look for her, but no

one managed to make the trek themselves. Finally Father Gonzales of the mission of Santa Barbara paid Captain Thomas Jeffries two hundred dollars to find her, but Jeffries merely pocketed the money and disappeared. Nidever on the other hand, took a keen interest in the girl and made good on Jeffries's promise.

One could also argue that Nidever's rescue was more of a curse in disguise, however, because as soon as Juana Maria stepped foot on the mainland, she became a minor celebrity with curious Californians, with dozens of reporters, promoters, and lookie-loos hounding her daily. That proved to be too much for the girl, and Nidever could do little to protect her. Yet the ultimate irony came on October 18, 1853, when she took a spill from Nidever's porch and she broke her back. She was already sick from dysentery at the time, and the complications resulted in her death a short time later—a mere two months after arriving on the mainland. She was buried without a grave marker somewhere on the grounds of the Santa Barbara mission, possibly where the garden is today.

# THE MYTH:

## A Little History:

When dealing with the subject of giants, it is often hard to separate fact from folklore. Genesis tells us that there was a group of titans called the Zamzummins that lived in the land of Ammon centuries ago, and Indian folklore tells us that there were similar creatures living throughout North America as recently as the sixteenth century.

## The Evidence:

In 1833, some Indian laborers found an unmarked grave in Rancho Lompoc. They were digging a gun powder pit at the time, and at first they thought it was the grave of a pauper, but as they continued to dig, they found unspeakable horrors inside. Amid strange jewelry, shells, and unidentified blocks covered with an alphabet no one had ever seen before, they uncovered a skeleton that was over twelve-feet-tall, with an oversized head and *double rows of pointed teeth* on its upper and lower jaws. Many believed that the deceased was a great figure, ruler, or deity of some kind or even a cohort of the devil himself.

Worried that they may have invoked a curse, the Indian workers convinced the land owners to rebury the remains in a secret tomb miles away, somewhere where it wouldn't be disturbed again. And according to lore, that's where it still rests today.

## The Context:

Such skeletons are not without precedent. In ancient times, Ctesias described a man-beast in India called a Martichora that had double rows of teeth and was "as large and rough as a lion, but its ears and face are like those of a man." Centuries later, Jacob Lemaire found several graves at Port Desire that contained skeletons of men measuring between ten and eleven feet with "sharklike teeth." And in 1925, a team of amateur archeologists dug up some of the Indian burial grounds at the Chatfield Mounds in Minnesota and discovered eight skeletons ranging from eight to ten feet tall.

## The Bottom Line:

Is that proof that giants once roamed California? *Of course it is!*

# THE LEGEND:

There once was a great land just off the coast of California called the Lost Continent of Lemuria where civilization began.

## What People Are Saying:

It's a well known fact that the planet was a very different place 200,000 years ago, although we've never been able to paint an accurate picture of what it was like. Studies of rock formations, shifting plates, and weather patterns suggest that the Earth was divided into two main continents, one to the east, which included North America, South America, Europe, Africa, and Asia, and one to the west, which encompassed Hawaii, and a good portion of the South Pacific. While little is known about the latter, many seem to believe that it was the mythical land of Lemuria (or Mu), which was said to contain a race of people that lived around 100,000 years ago.[9] Colonel James Chruchward, who was one of the first to allegedly find proof of this ancient land, claims that these people had their own schools and physicians, bathed in community swimming pools, and cooked food with "sun powered ovens." Moreover, says Churchward, they also had highly sophisticated machines including steam engines, flashlights, motorized boats, and airships which were supposedly powered by the "energy radiating from a single stone."

In 1931, Wishar S. Cerve released his own findings on Lemuria, based in part on Churchward's writings, and concluded that the Lemurians did in fact exist, and according to him, they dressed in long, flowing robes and sandals, and stood approximately six feet tall with slight features, long arms, spindly legs, and fair skin. Their most distinguishing characteristic however, was a walnut-sized protrusion in the center of their foreheads. These bumps, which were said to be covered in a soft, malleable skin much like the skin under our own eyes, concealed a functioning organ that gave the Lemurians the ability to communicate telepathically. As Cerve explains, they could literally send mental thoughts to each other several hundred yards away simply by focusing their minds.

This great race apparently met its Waterloo some 80,000 years ago when cataclysmic shifts accompanied by erupting volcanoes, great earthquakes, and epic floods wreaked havoc on the land. (Two California paleontologists recently confirmed that massive tsunamis struck the West Coast at that time.) According to Cerve, the Lemurian people were then forced to colonize the farthest reaches of the continent.[10] Many eventually took up along what is now the California coast, Mexico, Yucatan, and South America. Others meanwhile, moved to what is now China, the Red Sea, and India. The prime settlement however, at least according to Cerve, was in Mt. Shasta near the California border.

## The Truth:

The belief that a "Garden of Eden" existed off the California coast inhabited by a perfect race, has its obvious psychological and ideological implications. Yet there has never been a shred of credible evidence to prove the theory one way or another. The only reported debunking came shortly after Cerve's book was published in the 1930s. Edgar Lucien Larkin, the head of Mt. Lowe's Observatory in Los Angeles, allegedly trained his telescope on Mt. Shasta and claimed to see gold-covered buildings near the mountain's peak, and what looked like human activity. That

Courtesy of Red Herring

Lemurs are people, too

prompted a reporter from the *Los Angeles Times* to do some investigating of his own, and weeks later he returned saying that there was no way of knowing one way or another. Nonetheless, he refused to dismiss the idea out of hand. "It is not, therefore, incredible that the last sons of lost Lemuria are nestled at the foot of Mt. Shasta's volcano," he wrote. "The real incredible thing is that these staunch descendents of that vanished race have succeeded in secluding themselves in the midst of our teeming state."

## The Legacy:

Despite the failure to find hard evidence, there have been hundreds of firsthand experiences with what many believe to be Lemurian spirits— especially in San José, Carmel, Santa Barbara, and Mt. Shasta—the four main Lemurian "colonization areas" in California. The residents living around Mt. Shasta in particular, have seen a high level of strange occurrences which they attribute to Lemurian activity. In fact many still believe that there are Lemurians living *inside* the mountain in a vast underground city. Local lore is rife with tales of little men, midgets and dwarves, scurrying about the hillsides; strange lights hovering high in the sky just above the peak; and figures materializing out of vapors right before a visitor's eyes.[11]

# THE RUMOR:

Mt. Baldy is a holy mountain that possesses spiritual energy.

## What People Are Saying:

According to Rosemary Ellen Guiley, author of *Atlas of the Mysterious*, there are approximately a dozen holy mountains in California. They include the Marble Mountains, Mt. Lassen, Mt. Ritter, the San Bernadino Mountain, San Rafael Mountain, Sierra Madre, Birch Mountain, and Mt. Shasta. Guiley does not count Mt. Baldy as one of them, however. Courtney Milne, author of *Sacred Places of North America*, on the other hand, suggests that the mountain actually has a *negative* energy, which occasionally manifests itself in an "angry force of extraordinary power."[12]

## Where It Comes From:

Nonetheless, there are a number of people that believe otherwise. Members of the Aetherious Society for instance, a half-century old, Los Angeles–based organization dedicated to spiritual enlightenment, claim that their leader, George King, climbed to the top of the mountain in the 1950s—as per instructions from cosmic intelligence—and summoned a massive, interstellar ray out of the heavens. That ray, according to King, a former taxi-driver-cum-spiritual leader who allegedly had the power to levitate and raise the dead, then passed through his body and into the core of the mountain.

As Reverend Charles Abrahamson, author of the book, *The Holy Mountains*, explains: "Mount Baldy is just one such mountain. A similar procedure was done to eighteen similar repositories—or spiritual batteries—all over the world. And the reason that was done was to offset all the negative Karma in the world and give people a place to go where they can tap into that positive energy when they need it most."

Whether one wants to believe Abrahamson or not, there have been reports of strange phenomena around Mt. Baldy, including lights floating just above the peak, sometimes in broad daylight, disembodied, humanlike wails, and various ghost sightings.

## The Context:

Mt. Baldy is not the only mountain range in Southern California with strange powers or mysterious, floating lights. In 1892, prospector Charles Knowles reported seeing "balls of fire" shooting out the top of Borrego Mountain approximately "the size of a bushel basket." According to his description, they rose about a hundred feet above the mountain and "sprouted outwards like an artesian well" before cascading to the ground. "It was as pretty as any firework that I ever saw," he was reported to say.

The coastal town of Avila Beach, about sixty miles north of Santa Barbara has its own mystery range, too. They're called the Santa Lucia Mountains, and that's where you'll find a group of spirits called the Dark Watchers lurking just below the peak. These are said to be giant, humanlike phantoms that can only be seen around twilight, eerily prowling along the upper ridge. No one knows who they are, or what they are doing, but they have been immortalized by a number of artists ranging from Chumash Indian cave painters to the Nobel Prize–winning author, John Steinbeck.

Meanwhile, the San Jacinto mountain range near Palm Springs has its own mysterious spirit. It's called Tahquitz, and it's said to be nothing less than evil incarnate; a vicious cannibal that lives in a glass cave near the peak of the mountain. According to a Cahuilla Indian legend, the beast spies on its prey during the day, and attacks at night, eating his victims alive and keeping their souls for eternity.

Yet the scariest mountain range of all would have to be Superstition Mountain just north of El Centro. That's where people have been hearing loud, humanlike wails, screams, and cries for centuries without any discernible source. According to Indian lore, those sounds may be the victims of Wah-din-din, a terrifying, vindictive spirit bent on killing anyone that it comes into contact with. Standing a mere four-feet tall and looking like an old man, Wah-din-din is said to wander the hills looking for human souls to possess; and once he catches sight of his prey, however briefly, he will stop at nothing to track

it down—even if it takes years.

Charlie Arizona, the legendary prospector of the 1920s, can attest to another strange creature that haunts the Superstitions. According to him, there's an eight-foot-tall skeleton that glows a phosphorescent blue around the peak. He saw it with his own eyes one night after setting up camp. And apparently he's not alone. Philip Bailey, author of *Golden Mirages*, claims that such sightings are so common that the skeleton is almost a mascot to local miners. "It's generally accepted that the skeleton may belong to the man that first discovered the Phantom Mine," writes Bailey. "The Phantom Mine is known to exist somewhere in the Superstitions, but everyone that tries to look for it either gets lost or disappears . . . The skeleton may just be trying to find it again."

## ...strange phenomena around Mt. Baldy, including lights floating just above the peak, sometimes in broad daylight, disembodied, humanlike wails, and various ghost sightings.

Paul Young

Mt. Baldy

# THE RUMOR:

There's a phantom ship that sails through the Mojave on a regular basis.

"El Senor," Courtesy of Reece/Chac Mol Gallery Los Angeles

**Ghost ships in the desert?**

## What People Are Saying:

No one knew what to make of it really. Most thought it was a mirage of some sort, one of those mind tricks that occurs after weeks of starvation and blistering heat. But the two German prospectors that spent the previous two months searching for silver in the Borrego Bad Lands, thought otherwise. As they told a San Francisco reporter in 1846, they had set up camp approximately 120 miles northwest of Yuma, and forty miles directly east of Indio, when all of a sudden, just after sundown, a giant, spectral, sailing ship appeared before their eyes. "She wasn't more than a hundred yards away," said one of them. "We all saw her, too. Every one of us. She floated there like a cloud, floating right past us until she disappeared into the sunset."

It was an amazing story to say the least, and it eventually caught the interest of another reporter for the *San Francisco Examiner* who traveled to the exact same area to see for himself. And sure enough, after sixteen days of camping, he saw the very same vessel. "The craft was moving rapidly on its course with all sails set," he wrote. "It was about 80' in length, 18' breadth of beam and about forty tons of burden . . . Every portion of her was clearly defined. Yet a haze or a peculiar indescribable light was cast upon the scene . . . As strange and startling as was the weird scene, I was more than astonished at the sounds I heard: The creaking, straining noise of a sailing vessel running before a stiff breeze was plainly heard, while the distant notes of a sailor's song fell upon my ear."

## Where It Comes From:

Many historians seem to believe that the ship could have been the ghost of an expedition led by Captain Alvarez de Cordone in the seventeenth century. King Phillip III of Spain had ordered Cordone to lead a fleet into the Pacific after hearing that there were precious jewels to be found. Cordone commissioned three ships to be built in Acapulco, and set sail two years later, in 1612, with Captain Juan de Iturbe taking charge of the second ship and Captain Pedro de Rosales in charge of the third.

PHANTOM

The mission was star-crossed from the beginning, however. While the team apparently found plenty of pearls off the coast of Mexico, Rosales's ship sunk after hitting a reef near the Isla Angel de Guardia and Cordone was nearly murdered by a hostile tribe of Indians and forced to turn back. That left Iturbe to carry out the mission alone.

Iturbe's luck seemed to take a turn for the better when he came upon a narrow passageway near the terminus of what is now the Gulf of California. Believing that he had found what many called the Straight of Anian, a mythical passageway said to connect the Pacific with the Atlantic, he sailed inland until he came upon "a large Inland Sea" as he noted in his logs, nearly twice the size of San Francisco's Bay Area.[13] What happened after that, however, is still unknown. Some claim that a landslide choked the narrow passageway to the inlet and his ship was beached on a sandbar. Others claim that Indian marauders ambushed the vessel and killed everybody on board. In any case, most believe that Iturbe's ship remained there, untouched, for hundreds of years.

## The Context:

Iturbe was not the first or the last to sail a ship into the area, however. There are records of sixteenth and seventeenth-century Spanish reconnaissance missions passing through the area under direct orders of the king of Spain, and that's to say nothing of the pirate ships, pioneer explorers, and wayward fortune hunters that made the adventure on their own.

As bizarre as this all sounds, relics have in fact been found in the lower desert regions, not only in the Borrego Bad Lands, but in Laguna Salada and other former waterways leading all the way to the gulf. "Butcherknife" Ike, for example, an early 1900s prospector, once claimed that he found a fossil ship buried in a sand dune in what is now Borrego Springs. Nels Jacobson, a local farmer, reportedly found the remains of a Spanish galleon in the area of El Centro in the 1920s; and Myrtle and Louis Botts of Julian claimed that they uncovered what looked like a Viking ship around the area of the Agua Caliente Country Park in 1933.

## The Bottom Line:

Reports of phantom ships have diminished since the days of the prospectors, and it's possible that the apparitions are nothing more than mirages caused by light distortion and heat waves. But the tales of hidden relics persist, and according to a number of experts, there's a good chance that there are still a few out there.

**The ship could have been the ghost of an expedition led by Captain Alvarez de Cordone in the seventeenth century.**

SHIP

# THE RUMOR:

## The Truth:

Evidently this is true. On November 11, 1962, the *Los Angeles Times* reported that a twenty-year-old student named Don Beasly witnessed a downpour of solid rocks in Big Bear. As he told a reporter, "It wasn't hail, because it wasn't made of ice. These were real stones. I thought at first maybe kids were throwing rocks but then I saw that that wasn't possible. The stones were coming straight down from the sky. They almost 'floated' down."

Like Beasly, police assumed that somebody was using a catapult to launch the rocks from a nearby canyon, but after a month-long investigation, they couldn't find any suspects, or catapaults to speak of. What was even more curious however, was that they fell from a cloudless sky, and were unlike any other rocks typically found in the region.

*What was even more curious however, was that they fell from a cloudless sky, and were unlike any other rocks typically found in the region.*

## The Context:

Strange objects falling from the sky are not unusual in California. As a report in the *Chico Record* stated, hundreds of small fish fell from a cloudless sky on August 20, 1878, so many in fact, that they covered the roof of a store in Chico, a small town fifty miles north of Sacramento. Then, twelve years later, an identical situation occurred in Montgomery, California when thousands of small fish of an unknown origin, fell from a cloudless sky and covered buildings, broke windows and caused at least one injury.

Chico was also the sight of an incident much like Big Bear when, on March 12, 1922, it "rained stones for an entire week" as the *New York Times* reported, "causing widespread damage." Most thought that incident to be the work of pranksters, too, at least until investigators looked more carefully at the evidence and found that the rocks were uncommon for the area as well. Then on August 18, 1961, thousands of birds fell from the sky over Capitola, a small coastal town in California, pelting buildings, breaking car windows and downing power lines. Tons of carcasses littered the streets by morning, some of which were as large as sixteen inches, with wingspans of three feet or more. To this day, they remain the most mysterious events in Capitola's history.

John Toland reported an even more curious event after flying a U.S. Navy dirigible over the Santa Catalina channel in 1957. Apparently, during the flight he heard a loud *thud* near one of the overhead ballast bags. And when he went to investigate, he found a two-foot alligator wedged in the midsection of the craft. "It was the damnedest thing that I ever saw," he later told a reporter. "This thing just fell right out of the sky and right into my ship."

A similar episode happened to Mr. and Mrs. Tucker as they were relaxing in the living room of their Long Beach home in 1960. During an episode of *Bonanza* they heard a loud *thump* in their backyard, followed by a grunting noise. When they looked outside they saw a five-foot alligator laying in the yard with a stunned look on its face.

Mary Fuller of San Diego could top that story, however. While she was sitting in her parked car one morning with her eight-month-old son, *a human body* crashed through her windshield. Though she didn't know it at the time, a small plane had collided with a Pacific Southwest airliner overhead, and the body had been ejected from the wreckage.

But the town of Los Nietos Township in California takes the prize for weird things falling from the heavens. On August 9, 1869, the *San Francisco Bulletin* reported that flesh and blood fell from the sky for about three minutes. According to the report, there was little or no breeze, the sun was shining, and there wasn't a cloud in the sky. Nevertheless, residents reported a "hail" of fleshy particles filling the air for several acres. One gathered up a handful of muscu-lar fiber and "strips of hairy flesh" up to six inches in length and took it to an editor at the *Los Angeles Times*. The editor, with *Times*-like acumen, concluded that, "meat fell, we cannot doubt. But where it came from, we cannot even conjecture."

## The Bottom Line:

The famed ichthyologist E.W. Gudger has claimed that rains of fish and other objects are much more common than people realize. He cites dozens of credible cases all over the world—including spiders falling on Hungary, ducks on Baton Rouge, and live snakes on Memphis—and claims that they may be the result of waterspouts or twisters. Fundamentalists on the other hand, claim that such creatures, whether metaphoric or real, are simply falling from the "aerial waters above the firmaments" as described in the Bible.

It's a bird, it's a plane, it's human flesh!

# THE LEGEND:

Before L.A. had aqueducts, city officials hired `rainmakers` to bring water to Southern California.

Working magic: Charles Hatfield

The San Diego Historical Society Photograph Collection

## The Context:

As any arid land, Southern California has a long tradition of rainmaking lore that dates back centuries.[14] There are stories for example, of a legendary rainmaker named Hopodno that lived around the Fort Tejon area in the nineteenth century. Apparently he was so successful at bringing rain that he was revered as a god himself, and Indian tribes would travel for months to request his services. Nearby Mexico meanwhile, has its own pantheon of rainmaking heroes, including the great Montezuma, who was said to cause floods and widespread damage when crossed. And more recently, contemporary neo-pagan groups such as Wiccans have claimed that they can bring rain by knotting a cord imbued with magical properties, facing north and spitting several times.

## The Story:

Perhaps the greatest rainmaker in southern California was Charles Mallory Hatfield. In his day he was said to have completed 503 triumphant rainmaking missions that ranged from light sprinkles in Oceanside in 1902, to a world record in Sand Canyon exactly twenty years later. As he once explained his practice:

> It's all very scientific. The problem involved in the production of rain by artificial means resolves itself into the matter of localizing the ever-present air-borne moisture and condensing it to the point of precipitation. To accomplish this I use certain chemicals, the character of which must naturally remain my secret. The fumes of the chemicals are mixed with the surrounding air, which results in an overturning of the atmosphere. This first produces cirrus clouds, the forerunners of rain clouds. In a short time these cirrus clouds develop into a nimbus, or rain cloud. It's quite simple. My system is not one of bombarding the heavens.

Hatfield's technique was so successful that farmers throughout the Imperial Valley, Inyo County, Los Angeles County, and the San

Fernando Valley relied on his talents each year to bring nourishment to their crops. That's why the leaders of San Diego sent him an urgent telegram in January 1916, beseeching him to bring his talents south. "We will pay you $10,000 to fill our new reservoir [at Morena Dam]," said the note, "if you can bring us ten inches of rain." Hatfield accepted the challenge and set up four large wooden towers, approximately thirty-five feet high, at the top of Mt. Laguna. Each was topped by a three-foot-wide ten-inch-deep galvanized iron tub that Hatfield filled with a mixture of secret chemicals. And within days, the sky darkened and light sprinkles began to fall on San Diego. A week later, on January 16, the Morena Dam registered a full five inches of rain.

"You done fine, Mr. Hatfield," said the keeper of the dam. "That's mighty impressive."

Hatfield was discouraged however, and within moments he was mixing another batch of chemicals. "Yeah," he sneered, "well just wait and see what I'm *going* to do."

The following day, an even larger front moved in and dumped an unprecedented amount of rainfall, so much so, that roads and bridges were washed out, phone lines downed and rail lines immobilized. One property owner who was rescued in a rowboat, wiped the raindrops from his brow and cried, "Let's pay Hatfield ten thousand dollars to quit!"

Meanwhile, Hatfield, who had no idea what was going on, remained nestled in the back of Mt. Laguna, with his eye trained on the Morena Dam. He waited patiently for the water to reach the rim, and once it did, he threw a neutralizer in and waited for the storm to break. Four days later, after his car failed to make it through the washed-out roads, he walked into San Diego to collect his money. But by then the town had already fallen into a state of hysteria, with hundreds of people left without homes, food, or transportation. The mayor, meanwhile, who had the backing of the chief of police and members of the city council,

> **"We will pay you $10,000 to fill our new reservoir [at Morena Dam]," said the note, "If you can bring us 10 inches of rain."**

wanted to blame the entire mess on Hatfield, arguing that it would be a cold day in hell before he paid him a dime for destroying their fine city.

Amidst the commotion, Hatfield remained calm, and reminded everyone that he had been hired to fill the reservoir and that's exactly what he did. He also reminded them that they owed him $10,000. "You expect us to pay you for ruining our city?" roared the mayor. "Not unless you take full responsibility for what you have done!"

An angry mob of rednecks began forming in the background and Hatfield soon realized that if he didn't get out of there soon, he could end up swinging from a tree. "Fine," he said. "You'll be hearing from my lawyer." Yet rather than return to Los Angeles, Hatfield went right back to his towers and mixed another batch of chemicals. Then he packed up his things and disappeared.[15] Two days later, a new storm front moved in and dumped several more inches of rain. At approximately six A.M. the next morning, a portion of the Sweetwater Dam collapsed causing widespread damage. Then, at six P.M., the main wall of the Lower Otay Dam burst sending a forty-foot wall of water raging through the valley. Twenty people died in the disaster, along with the complete destruction of livestock, homes, and property.

## The Legacy:

The catastrophe did nothing to dampen Hatfield's reputation. He continued to bring rain to municipalities all over the world including towns in Wyoming, Oregon, Washington, Montana, Texas, Canada, Honduras, and Italy. He came close to selling his formula to the U.S. government in the 1940s, long after he retired, but decided that it was too powerful and would undoubtedly be misused for nefarious purposes.[16] It remains a secret to this day.

# THE RUMOR:

The `Santa Ana winds` are named after Saint Anne, the mother of the Virgin Mary.

## What People Are Saying:

Many have accredited Don Gaspar de Portola, leader of the first reconnaissance mission through California, with the naming of the Santa Ana winds even if it was indirectly. According to records, he was the one that named the Santa Ana River in 1769, (Saint Anne's river), which in turn led to the naming of *Santiago de Santa Ana Ranchero,* now the city of Santa Ana, the Santa Ana Mountains, and the Santa Ana Canyon.[17] There are no records of him naming the winds themselves, but since they're known to pass through the Santa Ana Canyon many have assumed that they were named after Saint Anne as well. But are they?

## Where It Comes From:

Like most indigenous cultures in arid lands, the first Indian settlers in the San Fernando Valley believed that the hot, powerful winds that came off the desert each fall—winds that dried out their crops and fueled massive fires—were the very incarnation of evil spirits. The Cahuilla Indians for instance, believe that they emanated from the center of the Earth, bellowing from a giant cave somewhere in the Mojave that led directly to the lair of the Devil himself. In fact, they were the first to dub them the Devil's winds.

Apparently the name existed for generations before the first Spanish settlers arrived in California in the eighteenth century. Translating the Indian phrase to Spanish, the pioneers eventually began referring to them as *Vientos de Sanatanas,* or Satan's winds. Naturally the white, mostly Protestant settlers that moved into Southern California a short time later, were uncomfortable with that name, and made an effort to think of another. California at the time, was in the throes of a great promotional campaign to sell the West Coast as a paradise on Earth—a land of sunshine and health. And what God-fearing American would want to buy a home that sat directly in the path of Satan's winds?

Meanwhile, some enterprising Anglos began referring to the Sanatanas as the "Santa Anas" (Saint Anne's) to at least hint at a benevolent nature. In fact, members of the chamber of commerce felt so strongly about the name change that they produced a press release in the early 1900s officiating the correct spelling. "In the interest of community," said the release, "please refer to the winds as 'The Santa Ana Winds' in any and all subsequent publications."

L.A. EXPOSED

170

SANTA ANA

# THE MYTH:

The rate of murder goes up when the Santa Ana winds arrive.

## What People Are Saying:

Since the Indians began calling them the Devil's winds centuries ago, it has been generally accepted that the Santa Anas possess a kind of nefarious power. When they blow, people say, violence inevitably follows. That's when "meek little wives feel the edge of their carving knife" wrote Raymond Chandler in *Red Wind*, "and study their husband's necks."

## The Truth:

Despite widespread belief, records provided by the Office of Vital Statistics show that the Santa Ana winds have absolutely *no* effect on the homicide rate in Los Angeles. In fact, from 1978 to 1998—a period that showed a significant increase in homicides from year to year—the homicide rate actually went *down* during the months of peak Santa Ana activity (October through February). Furthermore, the records also show that during the wet winter seasons of 1982–83, 1992–93, 1997–98, when the winds were virtually absent (thanks to El Niño conditions), the homicide rate actually went up. In fact it went *way* up. In 1992 for example, the city saw 2,116 homicides, the worst in L.A.'s recorded history. "I guess that proves one thing," says a representative of the National Weather Service. "If there's one thing that makes people crazy in L.A., it's rain."

## Where It Comes From:

That doesn't mean that the winds are entirely benign, however. There seems to be a growing body of evidence to support the idea that the winds can—and do—effect mood and behavior. Apparently, the phenomenon has some-thing to do with ions, miniscule, electrically charged molecules that permeate membranes of the nervous system twenty-four hours a day. As the Santa Ana winds pick up, electrons are torn loose from their host molecules through air friction, and adopted by others. Those that lose an electron are called "positive ions, or cations" while those that gain an electron are called "negative ions or anions."

Dr. Felix Sulman, head of the Applied Pharmacology Department at Hebrew University discovered that the Sharav winds (dry hot winds similar to the Santa Anas) are particularly rife with positive ions. He also noticed his patients showed a marked increase in serotonin levels, when the Sharav winds began to blow, as well as increased irritability, depression, anxiety, headaches, migraines, exhaustion, and bronchial problems. The condition is also known as SIS, or Serotonin Irritation Syndrome, a condition that has been verified by a number of credible clinics around the world. Physicians A. J. Giannini and D. A. Malone, for example, have written extensively about the condition, and they describe it as being "an anxiety state occurring in the presence of elevated levels of atmospheric or ambient cations, and is associated with elevated central and peripheral serotonin levels."

## The Bottom Line:

Sulman eventually concluded that only 25 percent of the population can be considered weather sensitive (excluding those on Prozac or other reoptic inhibitors). That means that 75 percent of the city could be drowning in a pool of positive ions and never know the difference. Yet that 25 percent could make life pretty miserable for their friends and loved ones.

WINDS

# THE LEGEND:

There's a sea monster that lives somewhere off the coast of Newport Beach.

## What People Are Saying:

On February 9, 1901, at approximately five A.M., Al Dixon maneuvered his skiff to the one-hundred-fathom curve along the coast of Newport Beach, and dropped anchor. It was a calm morning, slightly overcast with no swell to speak of. As per routine, he started digging out his fishing gear, when all at once, a high-pitched whistle nearly scared him "out of his boots," as he later claimed. He then spun around to see a giant, snakelike beast slithering along the surface of the water. According to Dixon, it had a face like a bulldog, two large, protruding, canine teeth, and two devillike horns sticking out the top of its head. "It was hard to tell but I'd say it was about one hundred feet long," he later told a reporter. "And it looked kind of like an eel. Real long and snakelike."

## What It All Means:

In ancient times, such sightings would have been seen as an evil omen. The Greeks believed that the appearance of such beasts presaged great cultural changes, disasters, and war. Folklorists, on the other hand, believe that such stories reflect unhappiness with the modern world and a desire to return to the past. Psychologists, meanwhile, have suggested that sea monsters are the work of the subconscious, representing repressed bestial and/or sexual urges struggling to break into consciousness.

## The Context:

In any case, Dixon wasn't alone in his sighting. Another monster with a dog or humanlike face, surfaced again in 1934 near Monterey. It was seen so often in fact, that the locals referred to it

William Leo Smith

Fish story: San Diego Marines catch a big one

**Psychologists meanwhile, have suggested that sea monsters are the work of the subconscious, representing repressed bestial and/or sexual urges struggling to break into consciousness.**

as "the old man of the sea." (Depending on who's telling the story it was anywhere from 45 to 150 feet long.) After that came even more sightings. A similar creature was seen at least a dozen times around the Salinas River mouth, Moss Landing's Elkhorn Slough, and Cape San Martin throughout the 1940s. Another was spotted around San Clemente in the 1950s, and another still in the Santa Monica bay in the early 1960s. Around the same time, a deep-sea diver named Forrest Adrian came face-to-face with a giant, fifteen-foot, snakelike monster as he was working on the supports of an offshore oil rig near Santa Barbara. That, too, was said to be long and ribbonlike, with a round face, small mouth, flat nose, and bug eyes.

## The Truth:

According to marine biologists the creature is not a mythical beast at all, but an oarfish, otherwise known as *Regalecus glefness*. "Oarfish are a form of fish that live pretty far below," says Paul Gregory of the Department of Fish and Game. "They're in the *regalcidae* family, which range from the coast of Chile to the Ventura area. As far as I know, very few of them are ever caught because, even with their size, they have very small mouths. Plus they're generally deep-water fish. If they come to the surface it's because they're distressed."

As it turns out, several *have* been caught. In 1901, another Newport fisherman, Joe Baracca, pulled a thirty-foot, eight-hundred-pound oarfish out of the surf not far from where Dixon claimed to see his monster; and since then, at least a half dozen similar creatures have washed up on shore at places like Venice Beach (1934), Oceanside (1946), and San Diego (1950).

# THE MYTH:

There used to be a secret island off the coast of San Diego called Taluga where gambling and prostitution were perfectly legal. But after an earthquake rocked the area, it mysteriously sank into the ocean.

## Where It Comes From:

While there is no such thing as a secret island off San Diego, there was a time when some investors tried to *build* one. In the 1970s, Joe Kirkwood, Jr., a B-movie actor famous for such 1950s epics as *Counter Punch*, *Fighting Mad*, and *The Champ* (always as Joe Palooka), heard about a shallow reef off the coast of San Diego called the Cortes Bank. At twelve miles wide and thirty-five miles long, it was larger than Catalina Island, and just a few feet under water. The news kick started his entrepreneurial engine, and pretty soon he was dreaming of a man-made island full of white sand beaches, wafting palms, and luxurious gambling casinos. "Albonia," he told friends. "That's what I'm going to call it, the island of Albonia."

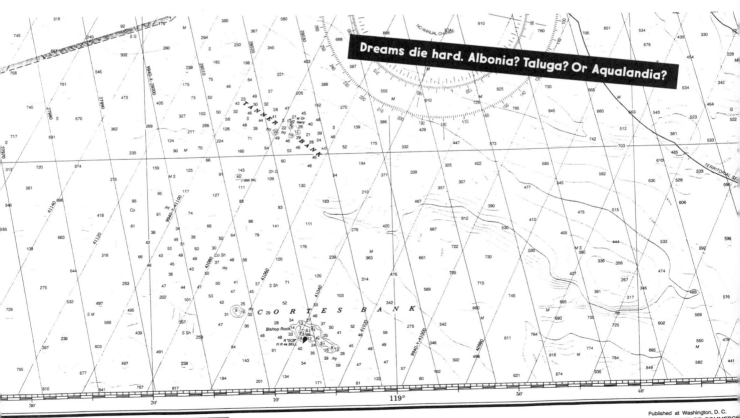

Dreams die hard. Albonia? Taluga? Or Aqualandia?

Kirkwood didn't have the resources to finance such a dream, however, and he failed to convince investors to back his idea. So with a nominal investment of his own, he purchased a giant cement-hulled freighter called the *Jalisco*, and sunk it on the southwest corner of the reef. It wasn't going to turn the reef into an island, but it would at least provide a foundation for a decent sized casino. His plans were stalled when he realized that he didn't have the money to fill the barge with anything heavy enough to provide a solid base. Cement was too expensive, and hiring a dredging device to fill it with sand was equally costly. So then he decided to fill it with *garbage*.

He convinced the City of Los Angeles to sell him L.A. garbage for a mere $1.25 per ton, and made plans to ship it off to the Cortes Bank in a freighter. But when the politicos of San Diego heard that some "Hollywood actor" wanted to dump city refuse in their front yard, they immediately put in a call to Washington to see what they could do about it. Days later, an injunction was obtained and the U.S. Coast Guard moved in to personally escort Kirkwood and his junk heap off the reef once and for all.

To complicate matters, Jack England, a Seattle attorney who had read about the controversy in the *L.A. Times*, came forward to say that *he* had plans for the Cortes bank too, plans that proved that he was the rightful owner. As he saw it, the island was going to be a West Coast version of Paradise Island in the Bahamas—a totally independent country with its own monetary sys-

**At twelve miles wide and thirty-five miles long, it was larger than Catalina Island, and just a few feet under water.**

tem and nondemocratic political system. "It's going to be called Taluga and *not* Albonia," he sneered.

But as England tried to wrestle the reef away from Kirkwood, another investor suddenly appeared claiming that *he* already laid claim to the reef years before both of them. His name was Mike Austin of Los Angeles, and he produced documents showing that the reef was put in his name several years before. He, too, wanted to turn it into a tropical paradise, only he wanted to call it Aqualandia.

## The Truth:

The Department of Justice thought the whole thing was utterly ridiculous. While the reef was technically in international waters, much farther away than Cuba is from Florida, for example, it belonged to the United States under the 1899 Rivers and Harbors Act. Therefore it was unlawful to build anything on the reef without permission from the U.S. Army; and the only thing that the U.S. Army wanted on the Cortes Bank was fish.

## The Legacy:

The entire incident eventually blew over and everybody forgot about it. But every once in a while a fisherman will recount the story of the lost continent of Taluga that sank off the coast of San Diego many years ago.

# THE MYTH:

## The Context:

If one can measure the importance of an object by the number of times it appears in legend form, then Southern California seems to have a fairly ambivalent attitude toward its most ubiquitous plant—the palm tree. In fact, compared to other plants in the area, the palm has a relatively paltry folkloric history.[18] Sycamore trees on the other hand, have spawned numerous legends and lore. There's a group of sycamores off Old Creek Road in Ojai, for example that seem to have extraordinary supernatural powers. According to D. W. Mott's 1929 book *Legends and Lore of Long Ago*, Indian sages used to gather at the foot of the trees, whenever they had an important question that had to be answered. And after several hours of meditation, they would eventually hear a response through the rustling of the leaves. "In a hollow in one of these old monarchs," writes Mott, "a crude figure like a doll made of asphaltum, had been placed; and this was supposed to represent some minor deity in communication with the Great Spirit . . . Since then, shamans have been making pilgrimages to the site for centuries to converse with the heavens."

Another sycamore along the Cahuenga Pass has earned a much more notorious reputation. It is known as the Cahuenga hanging tree, and is said to have been the killing place of dozens of nineteenth-century outlaws. As Laurie Jacobson and Marc Wanamaker point out in their book, *Hollywood Haunted*, residents in the area have noticed a distinctly negative energy surrounding the tree, and they believe that the numerous ghost sightings and suicides in its vicinity are related. Meanwhile Long Beach has its own

Smells like Clorox: A carob tree in West L.A.

Paul Young

hanging tree. It stands near what is now the Shell Oil refinery, and it too has been the source of bad vibes in the area. Apparently it was used by the sheriff's department in the nineteenth century to execute criminals, and when the conditions are just right, people have reported seeing the silhouette of a figure swinging in the wind, with the attendant rope squeaks. Another hanging tree sits at the top of Fort Hill, near present day Chinatown between Caesar Chavez and Temple, which was apparently a favorite for vigilante committees in the 1850s and 1860s. No less than twenty-two men were lynched at the tree in 1854 alone—often to the cheers of bloodthirsty crowds. Now, on certain moonless nights, it is said that the deceased can still be seen dangling from the lower branches, glowing softly like ghoulish Chinese lanterns.

## The Story:

But the most mysterious trees of all would have to be the so-called "semen trees." In the early 1980s, columnist Cecil Adams of the *LA Reader* started receiving letters from residents around Silverlake stating that they could clearly smell semen in the air during the months of October and November. While Adams joked that the smell was probably due to overactive male libidos rather than a plant, he eventually found out that there was some truth to the rumor. Apparently the offending tree is a carob tree, or *Ceratonia siliqua*, which is known to grow in Mediterranean climates. In October and November the carob tree, a large thirty-foot specimen with bluish leaves, produces a hairlike pollen-tipped fuzz that yields a kind of scent that is surprisingly similar to a man's ejaculation.

# THE MYTH:

A mysterious weeping woman, also known as La Llorana, wanders the beaches of Southern California looking for the remains of her dead children.

The original femme fatale

## The Legend:

Many years ago, there was a young mother living in a remote valley in the foothills of Southern California. Her husband left her many months before, and she did all that she could to provide for her three children. Times were hard, however, and she eventually lost her will to go on. Soon she took to locking herself in her bedroom for days on end, refusing to come out for anyone, including her children.

Then one night, after days of going without food, her youngest began wailing uncontrollably. That prompted the eldest child, who was about to turn six, to pound on his mother's door, pleading for her to come out. Instead she ordered him away, screaming, "Leave me alone! I want to be alone!" He didn't listen, however, and all three began to shriek and wail. Finally, hours later, the woman ripped open the door in a sudden burst of anger, screaming, "I said shut up! Shut up! Shut up!" Seeing the fury in her eyes, the eldest tried to escape out the back door, but got caught in the latch. That gave his mother the chance to grab him by the hair, yank his neck back, and in a moment of pure, unbridled rage, with a large kitchen knife slit his throat from ear to ear. "You see what happens to naughty little boys?" she screamed at the other two. Then she attacked them in the same way, chopping and hacking away at both of them until they were decimated.

Hours later, after she had poured their remains into a large gunnysack, she carried the entire bloody mess down to the water's edge in a wheelbarrow. Some say that she waded out into the water as far as she could go, while others say that she climbed into a small boat. In any case, she dumped the remains into the sea and waited for every last piece to disappear.

No one saw the woman again after that. Apparently she locked herself in her room for weeks while trying to convince herself that it was all a bad, horrific dream. Then one day, after regaining her courage, she decided to go into the kitchen and make herself something to eat. And that's when she realized that she hadn't been dreaming at all. Because there, across the walls and ceiling, across the tables and chairs, and across the windows and floor, were large puddles of blood in bold, explosive marks.

Horrified, she ran outside and down the road. She ran as far and as fast as she could in no particular direction, with tears flooding her eyes and choking her throat. Finally, after several miles, she collapsed to the ground out of sheer exhaustion. By chance she stumbled upon a knife that happened to be lying in the grass. Still hysterical, she picked it up, squeezed her eyes shut, clenched her teeth and, with a single, sweeping gesture, plunged the blade into her chest.

All at once, she came face-to-face with God. "Please, Father," she begged. "If you bring my children back, I promise to give them all the love that they deserve. I will never forgive myself for how I mistreated them and I will accept your gravest punishment."

God eventually agreed to let her return to

## All at once, she came face-to-face with God.

the living, provided that she find all the pieces of her children within a nine year period. If unsuccessful, however she would have to take the lives of three children, but only when they reached the age of her eldest son. Otherwise she'd remain in purgatory forever.

From that day on she began haunting the beaches, lakes, and riverbeds for miles around, always in a long, flowing black gown, and always near the water's edge, where she hoped to find pieces of her children. Locals began referring to her as La Llorona, or the Weeping Lady, and many believed that she was the very incarnation of evil.

Sadly, she never found her children even after years of searching. So when she happened to come across a young family with three young children of their own, she believed that her fortune had taken a turn for the better.

She returned to the family's home the following day, and impressed upon the young parents the importance of showering love upon their beautiful children. "For one never knows when God will decide to take them away," she said tearfully before spinning a tragic tale about the loss of her own children. The young parents felt sorry for her and offered her a room in their guesthouse. "We've been looking for a nanny for months," the mother confessed. "Perhaps you could take care of the children, too." The woman thanked them profusely, and promised that she would take care of their children. "As if they were my own," she said.

All went well for the first couple of months. The children liked their new nanny, and she treated them with genuine affection. So when it came time to celebrate the eldest child's sixth birthday, no one seemed to notice as she carried the sleeping child right past his bedroom and up the stairs to the attic over the barn. About an hour later, after everyone had fallen asleep, she caressed the boy's forehead softly while whispering "I'm sorry" over and over. Then she placed a blade to his neck and slit his throat.

The woman struck again the following

year, killing the middle child in the exact same way, and then once again two years later on the youngest child's birthday. She failed on her third attempt however, because unbeknownst to her, the family had placed scouts throughout the house, and one of them spotted her carrying the child to the attic. Acting quickly, several guards jumped her before she could get to the child. They couldn't wrestle the knife away from her however, and during the struggle, she freed herself momentarily, and plunged the knife into her chest.

Just as before, she came face-to-face with God and pleaded for his forgiveness. But this time God laughed. He laughed long and hard. Then he peeled off a mask to reveal that he wasn't God after all, but the Devil. "Three children," he chuckled. "Ages 6, 6, and 6 . . . Welcome to Hell, my dear."

## Where It Comes From:

According to Mexican writer Gonzales Obregon, the legend of La Llorona may go back to the mid-sixteenth century, when it was popular with Mexican families. (The above version was found in a chapbook printed in Los Angeles in the 1940s.) Folklorists on the other hand, say that she may be based on La Malinche, an Indian maiden who was allegedly involved with Hernan Cortes, the Spaniard who led the conquest of the Aztecs. Others say that she could also be the descendent of the Yurok Siren, a beautiful young Indian woman whose fascinations were said to be fatal, or the sister of Toybipet, a Gabrielino Indian spirit that haunts Pomona, La Verne, and Claremont. In any case, the story has remained surprisingly elastic. Since it debuted decades ago, it has taken innumerable forms all over the world. Today for example, the woman tends to be portrayed as a femme fatale rather than a bad mother, and instead of killing children she tends to target unsuspecting men, often by luring them into fatal car crashes.

## What It All Means:

The tale has many purposes. According to folklorists, it may have been designed to scare little *niños* into behaving. At the same time, the narrative has a patriarchal subtext as well, suggesting that a woman must embrace the responsibility of motherhood rather than rejecting it; and if perchance she denies—or kills—those childlike aspects of herself, she will become the embodiment of her anima—the destructive, evil side of her feminine nature—and live in purgatory (the subconscious) forever.

> "I have high hopes of smashing my name into history so violently that it will take a legendary form—even if all the books are destroyed. That goal is the real goal as far as I'm concerned."
>
> —Scientology founder L. Ron Hubbard

# THE JOY OF SECTS

*Ever since the fifteenth-century novelist Garcia Ordonez de Montalo described an imaginary paradise in the middle of the Pacific called "California," the West Coast has seen more than its share of ideologues. The nineteenth century in particular witnessed a virtual tidal wave of self-run communes—more than any other place in the world, in fact—ranging from Katherine Tingley's Theosophical Society at Point Loma, to Marxist communes such as Llano, Kaweah, Altruria, Icaria, and Speranza in the Central Valley. These were, for the most part, true social experiments with genuine, munificent intentions, yet rarely, if ever, seen as such. Harrison Otis of the Los Angeles Times, for example, often referred to them as "spookeries" or "fairy farms," and did everything in his power to undermine their success. Ironically, it wasn't until after Otis died in 1917 that his descriptions began to ring true. Consider the following:*

L.A. EXPOSED

★ **LUCIS TRUST, 1919 (STILL ACTIVE):**
On June 30, 1895, a mysterious figure dressed in a turban entered the home of fifteen-year-old Alice Bailey and prophesied that she would work for "higher powers" some day. And sure enough, after a brief stint at Helena Blavatsky's Theosophical Society in Hollywood fifteen years later, she began receiving psychic communiqués from Master KH (Koot Hoom), an "ascended master," and published them under her own name. Her popularity eventually led to two occult organizations, the Lucifer Trust and the Arcane School, which were devoted to bringing about a "New World Order" comprised of one religion and one government.

★ **LOVE CULTS, 1925–1950:** Fifty years before the hippies made "free love" an international phenomenon, love cults flourished all over Southern California. In 1934, for example, there was a "nest of love" at 1028 Santee Street where women were forced to "speak in tongues," perform "devil dances," and engage in "soul mating" with "spiritual husbands." Five years later, the High Priestess Regina Kuhl caught the attention of the authorities when she was caught "indoctrinating" male students at L.A. City College into her "Temple of Thelma," or Purple Cult. (Apparently she had set up a temple in the basement of one of the dorms where she'd don robes, chant a few highly suggestive passages from Aleistar Crowley's *Book of Law*, i.e.

"embrace the power of the lifted lance," and engage in sexual intercourse with multiple partners.) Seven years later, Henry "King Daddy" Newson was arrested for running his own sex camp in Whittier called Ten Oaks. According to newspaper reports, he molested sixteen underage girls—mostly runaways— over the course of two years, while teaching them the "beauty" of sexual intercourse. (Several girls claimed that he "controlled" their minds through hypnosis.)

★ **DIVINE ORDER OF THE ROYAL ARMS OF THE GREAT ELEVEN, 1925–1930:**
In 1929, a pair of police officers made a gruesome discovery at the home of Mr. and Mrs. Rhoads at 330 Vermont Ave.: Underneath the floor of their bedroom was a specially built, refrigerated, "sleeping chamber" that contained the corpse of their sixteen-year-old daughter, Willa. The girl's body was found wrapped in spices and salt, and surrounded by seven dead dogs. The Rhoads later confessed that they had placed their daughter in the tomb fourteen months earlier at the suggestion of May Otis Blackburn, the leader of the Great Eleven cult in the Santa Susana Hills. (Apparently they were convinced that she would be brought back to life upon Saint Gabriel's return to Earth.) The good news was that the girl died naturally from a childhood illness. The bad news was that the Cult of the Great Eleven turned out to be as weird and frightening as anyone had ever suspected. Not only did they practice animal sacrifice, they also bilked investors out of fortunes and forced members into prostitution.

★ **I AM, 1934 (STILL ACTIVE):** While climbing Mount Shasta one day, Guy Ballard came face-to-face with the spectral vision of St. Germain, a "majestic figure" clad in a "white jeweled robe" with "light and love sparkling in his eyes." According to Ballard, the spirit handed him a cup full of "electronic essence" and a wafer of "concentrated energy." Pretty soon he was flying through space and time toward uncharted lands. That experience encouraged Ballard to start the "I Am" church, a secular denomination devoted to the worship of St. Germain. And by the end of the 1930s, he had convinced thousands of Angelenos that he could help them overcome anxiety, financial losses, and the Great Depression by chanting daily "I Am" affirmations written by St. Germain himself. He also taught that one could achieve extraordinary results by focusing the mind on the "Mighty I Am Presence," a kind of divine power hovering over each individual like a guardian angel. And to prove that it worked, he "dissolved" three Japanese subs off the coast of Panama in the early 1940s by "thinking really hard."

★ **MANKIND UNITED, 1934–1939:** Arthur Bell, a fairly well-known sci-fi writer of his day, came to the conclusion that there were two warring factions of "invisible" aliens living on Earth—good ones and bad ones. Bell, of course, had the ability to "see" such aliens and spent much of his time running around telling the good aliens where the bad ones were so that they could use their "particle beam weapons" on them. Consequently, the Mankind United Church became the first Alien Busters of the twentieth century. But before anyone could join and set off on a life of alien deposal, he or she had to donate all his material possessions—cars, homes, clothes, everything—to the church as an act of faith.

★ **CENTRAL SPIRITUAL RESURRECTION, 1934–1935:** Located at 430 N. Bunker Hill in downtown L.A., the headquarters of the Central Spiritual Resurrection—also known as the House of Skulls—was the home of "seven invisible doctors," a group of spectral beings available for consultation on a variety of subjects. (Africano No Blass, for example, covered affairs of the heart, while P. Villaverde was concerned with casting evil spells.) Visitors were encouraged to sit in a private room with one of these invisible beings and discuss his or her ailments at length. Then, at the end of the session, the "doctor" would respond with a veiled message—usually a set of tones—would be interpreted by the Center's director, R.A. Miranda, later. (Miranda, of course, was listening from another room and playing the tones on a homemade instrument.)

- **SWAMI AT DHARA, 1940:** When officers arrested Swami At Dhara (Marion Vincent Goddard) on May 24, 1940, at his home at 5757 Franklin Avenue, they found hundreds of stolen items, including furs, gems, and valuables. Apparently, At Dhara had convinced a bevy of young women—including his wife and mistress—to pilfer the merchandise at his request. So great was his power over his subjects, that one later testified that she tried to kill herself by driving her car off a cliff just so that At Dhara, whom she described as being "as beautiful as a golden-haired Greek god," would get her insurance money. As she told a reporter, "He said that was the ultimate act of compassion, and that I would come back as a beautiful soul."

- **WKFL FOUNDATION OF THE WORLD, 1948–1958:** One of the most famous cults in Southern California, Krishna Venta's WKFL (for Knowledge, Faith and Love) began as a quiet monastery in Box Canyon in 1948. It was there that Venta taught his followers to set up food services for the poor, offer free room and board to the wayward, and help firefighters and emergency relief groups in times of need. He taught them that smoking was healthy, human beings evolved from space aliens, and that he was none other than Jesus Christ himself. (To prove it, he liked to show his detractors that he was born without a belly button.) His views on casual sex bothered some, however, including two of his followers, Brother Kamenoff and Brother Muller, who placed twenty sticks of dynamite under his compound in 1958 and blew him to smithereens after they discovered that he had seduced their wives.

- **UNARIOUS SOCIETY, 1954 (STILL ACTIVE):** Founded in 1954 by Dr. Ernest and Ruth Norman in El Cajon, CA, the Unarious Society uses a lot of scientific mumbo jumbo (metaphysics, fourth dimension theory, harmonic convergence) to teach students some very nonscientific ideas ("infinite eye," inter-dimensional channeling, reincarnation). The group's main goal, however, is to "promote better communication" between earthlings and the 4,000 beings said to be living on nearby planets. By doing so they are hoping to persuade the "Intergalactic Federation" that the Earth is ready to become the thirty-third member of the "Restored Brotherhood of Terrestrial Planets Located Within the Milky Way."

★ **SCIENTOLOGY, 1954 (STILL ACTIVE):** Like Arthur Bell, L. Ron Hubbard was a successful sci-fi writer before starting his own church in 1954. (It wasn't officially recognized as a religion until the early 1990s.) He, too, professed to be in contact with "higher beings" and supposedly based a number of his writings on "transmissions from the heavens." Nonetheless, the church portends to be a "scientific" enterprise that attempts to return people back to their "pure" states—otherwise known as Operating Theatans (OTs). Through such "scientific" practices as TR drills, engram recognition, and the exorcising of psychological implants, members ultimately learn how to blame all their problems on mysterious, outside forces (namely the head of the galactic federation, Xenu). They also learn that every aspect of their lives—including those around them—can be tightly manipulated and controlled. With that in mind, it's not surprising that the organization has been known to go after detractors with vicious, unrelenting attacks, FBI-inspired snooping, massive law suits, and outright physical violence.

★ **THE PROCESS CHURCH OF THE FINAL JUDGEMENT, 1963 (POSSIBLY STILL ACTIVE):** Started by an ex-Scientologist named Robert Moore in 1963, the Process Church was based on the worship of four co-equal deities: Christ, Jehovah, Lucifer, and Satan. The purpose, according to Moore, was that one must love completely and without prejudice—good and evil—to fully embrace the power of the heavens. Nonetheless, Moore, who changed his name to DeGrimston, seemed to have a greater predilection for the darker side. He wore black robes exclusively, practiced occult animal sacrifices, and employed a swastika as his primary insignia. (Rumors of his church practicing human sacrifices, Hitler worship, and murder have been greatly exaggerated, however.)

★ **FOUR P MOVEMENT, 1967–1972:** Being an offshoot of the Process Church, the members of the Four P Movement were fascinated with the occult. But according to reports, the group took things a lot further than the Process Church ever dreamed of. Led by a mysterious figure known as the Grand Chingon, members not only sacrificed animals—particularly Dobermans—but humans, too. (They allegedly used a six-bladed dagger to remove a victim's heart and then pass it around as an appetizer.) When cult member Stanley Dean Baker was arrested in 1970 for a moving violation, officers found a human finger in his pocket. Baker claimed that the digit had belonged to a human sacrifice victim and then took the officers to a burial site where he claimed to have buried a number of people for his church. What's more, it was also revealed that Charlie Manson was a Four P member after his stint as a Scientologist, as was David Berkowitz a.k.a. the Son of Sam killer.

★ ***THE CULT OF HITERNIA, 1990–91:*** In the late 1980s Barry Briskman came to Earth to gather up a few young earthlings and take back to the planet Cablell, a distant celestial body governed by a beautiful queen named Hiternia. And for the next year and a half the fifty-three-year-old erstwhile drifter found nearly a dozen female candidates—mostly teenage runaways—and convinced them that they had been "chosen" to accompany him back to his planet. But first he had to put each girl through a series of tests, break down their "sub-cons" (Subconscious Intelligence Barriers), and double their IQs. One thirteen-year-old later claimed that she had sex with Briskman because he needed to "inject her" with "IRFs," or "special immunities" that would ward off space diseases during her travels. (Apparently this went on for several weeks, and after each sexual encounter, Briskman contacted "Andy," the super Andrak 4000 computer based on planet Cablell, and input the results). Briskman was eventually arrested in 1995 and sentenced to twenty years in prison for child molestation.

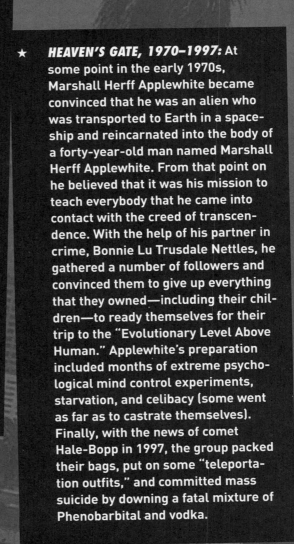

★ ***HEAVEN'S GATE, 1970–1997:*** At some point in the early 1970s, Marshall Herff Applewhite became convinced that he was an alien who was transported to Earth in a spaceship and reincarnated into the body of a forty-year-old man named Marshall Herff Applewhite. From that point on he believed that it was his mission to teach everybody that he came into contact with the creed of transcendence. With the help of his partner in crime, Bonnie Lu Trusdale Nettles, he gathered a number of followers and convinced them to give up everything that they owned—including their children—to ready themselves for their trip to the "Evolutionary Level Above Human." Applewhite's preparation included months of extreme psychological mind control experiments, starvation, and celibacy (some went as far as to castrate themselves). Finally, with the news of comet Hale-Bopp in 1997, the group packed their bags, put on some "teleportation outfits," and committed mass suicide by downing a fatal mixture of Phenobarbital and vodka.

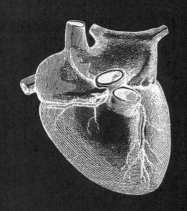

Roosevelt called this
the century of the
Common Man. Balls!
It's the century of
the Communist
cutthroat, the fag,
and the whore!

—WALT DISNEY

# DESIGNING

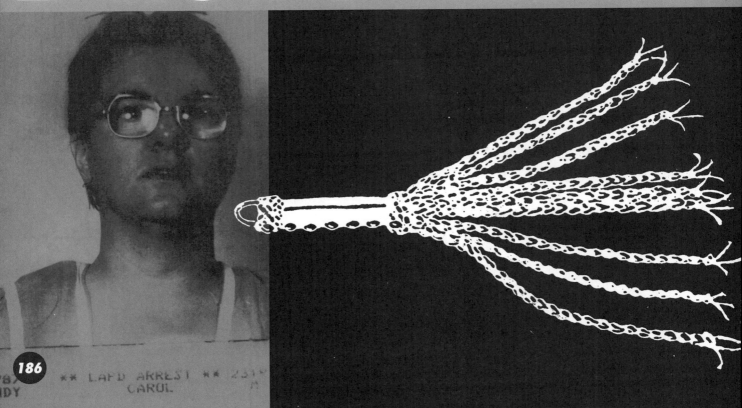

# DYSTOPIA

## CRIMELORE IN THE CITY OF ANGELS

# THE RUMOR:

## A woman killed the Black Dahlia.

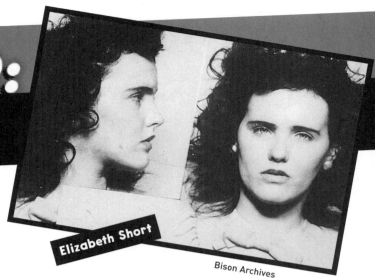

**Elizabeth Short**

Bison Archives

## What Happened:

At approximately 10:30 A.M., on January 15, 1947, two LAPD officers found the mutilated remains of Elizabeth Short, a twenty-two-year-old brunette from Medford, Massachusetts, lying in an empty lot near the corner of Thirty-ninth and Norton Avenue. Her body had been cut in half, just above the pelvic bone, and placed face-up, as if to resemble a sex doll, with arms and legs splayed. Rope burns were found on her wrists and ankles, suggesting that she had been hog-tied for hours; one of her nipples had been removed with a sharp knife, and there were dozens of incisions across her chest and pubic area, apparently made while she was still alive.[1] What's more, there was a deep chunk of flesh cut out of her left leg just above the knee, severe bruises and abrasions around her neck and head, and a large gash running from ear to ear, across her mouth, giving her a gruesome, clownlike grimace. Yet what was even more baffling, at least for homicide detectives, was that someone had drained her corpse of its vital fluids and scrubbed it clean with a brush—inside and out.

## A Little History:

No other crime in L.A.'s long and sordid history has captured the imaginations of Angelenos as much as Elizabeth Short's murder. That has to do with the utter brutality of the crime itself, as well as numerous unanswered questions that still haunt the case. In fact, no one really knows what happened to her in the days preceding her death nor will they ever. All that is really known is that Short, who jokingly referred to herself as the Black Dahlia after her favorite movie, *The Blue Dahlia*, had moved to San Diego a couple of weeks before she was found, apparently to stay with a friend. On January 9 she asked a new acquaintance, Robert "Red" Manley, a traveling salesman who was in San Diego on business, to give her a ride back to L.A. to meet her sister. Manley agreed and took her to the Biltmore Hotel later that evening, and together they waited for half an hour before she assured him that he could go on without her. "Don't worry about me," she said. "I'll be all right."

That was the last time that Manley or anyone else saw Elizabeth Short, at least until her body was discovered in South Central L.A. five days later. "I think that she met a man during those five days," explains veteran crime writer James Ellroy. "A man who had never killed anybody before, and never killed anyone after. Nobody saw the two of them together. He left no physical evidence on the body or at the crime scene; and he had no discernable connection to her. How are all the cops in the world going to solve it? It's impossible."

## Where It Comes From:

Since then, a virtual army of writers, investigators, and crime aficionados have tried to solve the case on their own. The theory that the killer was a woman was first suggested in 1948 after a reporter found a copy of the coroner's report suggesting that Short had an abnormally small vagina. That led to the belief that she couldn't have sex with a man, which in turn led to the theory that she might have been a lesbian. Ben Hecht, screenwriter of *Notorious* and *Scarface*, picked up on that idea and wrote a fairly convincing article for the *Los Angeles Times* saying, "There's no denying the fact that this is a sex crime first and foremost . . . And in nearly all torture cases and mutilation after death, homosexuality is the basic motive."

## The Truth:

The idea fails to make sense when you consider the nature of the crimes committed, however. While it wasn't made public at the time, the coroner later claimed that there was a four-inch

cut in her abdomen, just above her pubic hair, that was used for sexual intercourse. There was also a ball of pubic hair that had been hand-plucked and stuffed into her vagina, and a piece of skin—rumored to be with decorated with a rose tattoo—found deep inside her rectum. While it's possible that a female killer could have committed such perverse acts, few detectives took much stock in the theory.

## What Probably Happened:

Since no forensic evidence had been found, detectives were forced to rely on speculation, hearsay, and circumstantial evidence. Over fifty people confessed to the crime after reading about it in the newspaper, yet detectives failed to take any of them seriously. Apparently they concentrated on five to ten individuals whom they considered to be the most viable suspects, one of

Remains of the day: Short's mutilated corpse

Delmar Watson Photography

which was Short's father who showed a curious lack of remorse after the news of her death. Another was a serial killer dubbed the Cleveland Butcher, who was known to dissect his victims and drain them of their blood much like Short's killer. Apparently he operated entirely in Ohio (from 1935 to 1938) and detectives had no way of linking him to the crime. Another still was Dr. Walter Alonzo Bayley, a mentally unstable physician who owned an office six blocks from the Biltmore Hotel and a house near Thirty-ninth and Norton. At the time there were rumors of a "mad abortionist" working in Hollywood, an abortionist that not only performed illegal abortions, but molested and perhaps killed his patients. Short may have been under the impression that she was pregnant at the time, which may or may not explain why she was so secretive about her return to L.A.[2]

More recently Mary Pacios, a former friend of Short, has come up with the most outlandish theory of all: that film director Orson Welles was the killer. Pacios, who claims that she spent twelve years investigating the murder, cites a number of coincidences, including the fact that Welles had a history of mental instability and violence; had an obsession with "sawing women in half" during magic acts; and designed a set for *The Lady From Shanghai* that featured mutilated corpses almost identical to Short's disfigured body—just three weeks before Short was found.

Yet perhaps the most interesting was a slippery character named Al Morrison. During the investigation, an informant told an undercover cop that Morrison bragged about giving Short a ride home one night after spotting her walking home from the Hollywood Canteen. Morrison allegedly took her to an uninhabited house on East Twenty-first street by San Pedro and Trinity

and attacked her after she refused to have sex with him. In recounting his story, Morrison supposedly went into great detail about how he used the bathtub to cut her body in half, and used two cement sacks to carry her remains to Thirty-ninth and Norton.[3] It was that kind of detail that convinced author John Gilmore and lead investigator John St. John to believe that Morrison was the real killer. But as Gilmore points out in his book, *Severed,* Morrison was probably an alias for Arnold Smith, the original informant. And to make matters even more confusing, Smith was probably an alias for Jack Anderson Wilson, a drifter, thief, and one-time murder suspect in the 1944 killing of twenty-year-old Georgette Bauerdorf who was also killed in a bathtub.

Unfortunately the LAPD could never investigate Wilson/Smith/Morrison. A few days after the police received the tip, he passed out in his room at the Seventh Street Hotel downtown, dropped a cigarette, and burned to death in a hotel fire.

## The Bottom Line:

While Gilmore and St. John were convinced that Wilson was the real assassin, the theory is hardly perfect. In fact veteran reporter Will Fowler, who was the first reporter to see her body at Thirty-ninth and Norton in 1947, calls Gilmore's theory "fiction." In any case, the fascination will undoubtedly continue for years to come. Not only because it remains unanswered, but because of its latent symbolism: the loss of innocence, the evil nature of Hollywood, the death of the anima, and the suggestion of magico-religious sacrifice.

# THE LEGEND:

In the 1920s, some of the Chinese merchants in Chinatown sold a potent alcoholic drink that contained opium.

## A Little History:

Opium has been called the Victorians' aspirin. It was prescribed for just about everything from infant teething problems to diarrhea, and could be purchased for less than a penny at the local chemist. It could also be found in scores of over-the-counter products including Mrs. Winslow's Soothing Cough Syrup, Ayer's Cherry Pectoral, Dover's Powder, Darby's Carminative, and McMunn's Elixir.

That changed with the dawn of the twentieth century, however. While companies such as Fook Hing of Hong Kong continued to import as much as 100,000 pounds of opium into California every year, California authorities began increasing the tax on such imports until it simply became too expensive to ship in. Then came the Pure Food and Drug Act of 1906, which curtailed the use of opiates in consumer products; the Opium Exclusion Act of 1909, which curtailed importation; and finally the Harrison Narcotics Act of 1914, which basically outlawed the drug for consumer use once and for all.

Addicts still found ways to score, however. As Bruce Henstell points out in *Sunshine and Wealth,* users continued to purchase sixty-dollar-tins (a half-pound of pure opium) at the corner of Los Angeles and Commercial streets (equal to $987.60 in current dollars), while Hollywood drug parties endured right through the 1920s.[4]

## Where It Comes From:

For the better part of the twentieth century, there has been a persistent rumor of an opium-laced cocktail that was supposedly served at select taverns in Chinatown well into the 1930s and 1940s. It was no secret, after all, that there were more opium dens than saloons in Chinatown, and that most of them were strictly off limits to Anglo customers. "If [Anglos] used them at all," wrote *California Illustrated Magazine* in 1892, "they did so in secret."

Meanwhile, such cocktails were already known in other parts of the world. As Martin Booth notes in *Opium: A History,* Europe had its laudanum, for example, a well-known opium libation made from a mixture of red wine, sugar, and poppy juice. The Middle East had its Black Drop, another particularly popular concoction made with fermented crab apple juice, nutmeg, saffron, yeast, and opium; and England had its Godfrey's Cordial, a slightly bitter mixture that combined opium, molasses, and sassafras.

## The Truth:

The only record of an opium-laced cocktail found in historical records, is a cocktail called Cal-orine, a fictional libation invented by humorist Rob Wagner in the 1920s. Cal-orine was Wagner's attempt to spoof California's health consicousness. According to a fake ad that he ran in a local paper, it was supposed to "help all persons suffering from hardening of the heart, bad debts, tired oversouls, underfeeding of the romance glands, fiscal failure, prolapses of the intellect, ingrowing principle, anxiety neurosis, spiritual shellshock, repressed desires, lost key-to-the-scriptures, dementia dieteticus, and pure cussedness." According to Wagner, the ingredients included fruit juice, cocaine (or *cinemopolis favoritus*), "Hollywood alcohol," marijuana and, of course, opium.

# CAL-ORINE

The Fountain of Perpetual Youth! For ages men have sought it—Jason in the Argo; Marco Polo in his wanderings; Ponce de Leon *thought* (!) he had found it in Florida, but it was not until Cabrillo sailed his galleons into San Diego harbor, that the age-old search was rewarded! Here in CALIFORNIA men first bathed in The Magic Fountain and were made young. Here they came to partake of The Lotus, never caring to return Elsewhere.

Since that time the sons of Adam have poured into CALIFORNIA—somnambulists, scenario writers, neurotics, ne'er-do-wells, morons, extra people, sad-eyed Susans and weary Williams—all the inframen of Elsewhere—and after one bath in the glorious sun and moonshine, have come out beautiful in body and spirit (see cut to left)

## THE SUPERMEN OF THE NEW CIVILIZATION—

## CALIFORNIANS!

It was for the great hordes of unfortunates unable to come to the GARDEN OF THE GODS that Dr. Wagner, The Great Humanitarian, after 607 experiments, at last evolved his marvelous

### CAL-ORINE

which is nothing more nor less than

*Dr. Wagner*

## Concentrated Calories of California Climate

| FORMULA | |
|---|---|
| FORMULA | lots |
| Fruit juices—orange, prune, and grape | some |
| Opium — *Papaver Matillaja* | much |
| Cocaine—*Cinemopolis favoritus* | full content |
| Hollywood-alcohol | saturate |
| Marihuana-Coo-Coo Mexicana | trace |
| H₂O | |

*This marvelous mixture (which can be made by any chemist) is entirely impotent unless fermented and cured in the peculiar actinic rays of CALIFORNIA sunshine, which alone gives it its pep and purity and renders it free from bunkoids and the deadly baccalaureate.*

CAL-ORINE is recommended to all persons suffering from hardening of the heart, bad debts, tired oversouls, underfeeding of the romance glands, fiscal failure, prolapsus of the intellect, ingrowing Principle, anxiety neurosis, spiritual shellshock, repressed desires, lost Key-to-the-Scriptures, dementia dieteticus and pure cussedness

For sale by all Elsewhere druggists (except in Florida where the word California is forbidden by law). $1 per bot

Dr. Wagner's CAL ORINE

Bottled by THE CALIFORNIA CLIMATE CO. LOS ANGELES

*If you can't come to CAL. — Use CAL-ORINE*

...*prescribed for just about everything from infant teething problems to diarrhea, and could be purchased for less than a penny at the local chemist.*

# THE RUMOR:

Los Angeles has more female serial killers than anywhere else in the world.

Los Angeles Examiner/USC Special Collections

**Louise Peete**

## What People Are Saying:

When Aileen Carol Wuornos was arrested in Florida in 1990 and charged with the slayings of at least seven men, the press claimed that she was America's first female serial killer. Yet according to Michael Kelleher, author of *Murder Most Rare: The Female Serial Killer,* there have been at least one hundred cases of killer-ladies since 1900, and many were far more violent than Wuornos. But for some unknown reason, modern culture has remained relatively ambivalent toward bloodthirsty women (unlike ancient societies, which have a great pantheon of murderous women). Few cases seem to get reported in the media, and when they do, they are generally underplayed or forgotten.

According to Kelleher, the reason for Wuornos's popularity may be because she was one of the first to kill *like a man* (i.e., acting to gratify sexual urges alone). "History is replete with dozens of female serial killers," writes Kelleher, "who were far more lethal and often more successful in their determination to kill than their male counterparts. Whereas the male serial killer is most often driven to repetitive acts of sexual homicide, the typical female serial killer is a much more complex criminal whose motivations are often wide-ranging and anything but simple. She is a quiet killer who is often painstakingly methodical and eminently lethal in her actions."

## The Evidence:

L.A.'s first "official" female serial killer was Louise Peete, an attractive, well-poised, bespectacled,

schoolteacher type that was allegedly responsible for nearly a half-dozen killings. She moved to L.A. in 1920 and managed to hoodwink Jacob Denton, an entrepreneur with mining interests, into giving her an apartment in the Miracle Mile district. Months later, after she weaseled her way into his affairs, she eventually gained control of his business and began writing checks on his account. (She actually tried to tell the bank that Denton had been in an accident and lost his arm—his *check-writing* arm.) When she tried to put his entire estate into her name, however, probate officers called the LAPD, who in turn, sent a detective to investigate. Days later, Mr. Denton's body was discovered in the basement of her apartment building at 675 South Catalina Street, stuffed under a stairwell with a .32-caliber bullet hole in the back of his neck.

That was not the first or last time that Peete exacted her deadly charms. She was also linked to the murder of a bank clerk in Dallas in 1913

Designing Dystopia

**193**

(also shot in the neck) and many have speculated that she killed all three of her husbands. In any case, after serving twenty years in state prison for the murder of Denton, the former call girl from Denver went to work for Mr. and Mrs. Logan, a wealthy, elderly couple living in Pacific Palisades. The Logans, like many who followed Peete's case in the papers, believed in her innocence—so much so that they gave her seventy-five dollars a month to take care of the ailing Mr. Logan. And not before long, Peete began weaving her web of deceit. First she filed a petition with the Superior Court to have Mr. Logan declared "mentally ill, dangerous, and insane" which led to his incarceration at the Patton State Mental Hospital. That empowered Peete to act as his executor in the event that Mrs. Logan happened to have an accident. And sure enough, Mrs. Logan disappeared a short time later, allegedly after her husband returned home late one night and beat her in a drunken rage. According to Peete, she "ran away to a resort somewhere" to convalesce. Yet in truth, Peete had shot her in the neck while she was talking on the phone one evening, and buried her body

*...most seem to enjoy killing with partners rather than doing it alone.*

beneath an avocado tree in the backyard. Seven months later, the LAPD found the remains of Mrs. Logan at 713 Hampden Place and Peete was hauled away once again, this time for life.

Since then, the number of female serial killers has been rising steadily in Southern California. But according to Kelleher, most seem to enjoy killing with partners rather than doing it alone. The most famous female death-squad was Susan "Sadie Mae" Atkins, Patricia "Katie" Krenwinkle, Leslie "Lulu" Van Houten, Mary Brunner, and Linda Kesabian—collectively known as the Manson Family. In 1969 they were charged in the brutal slayings of nine people found at the Tate and LaBianca houses. But according to some of sources, they may have killed as many as twenty to thirty between the years 1967 to 1969.

Yet the most *twisted* female serial killer in California history was probably Carol Mary Bundy. She was eventually caught and tried for the murder of seven prostitutes, yet there are many that believe that she and her accomplice, Douglas Clark, killed as many as fifty. Generally their killing spree followed the same pattern: Using an unregistered car, they'd cruise Sunset Boulevard looking for hookers, usually with Clark in the driver's seat and Bundy in the back. When they'd find a woman that they liked, they'd don the role of husband and wife with Bundy asking if she could buy her hubby "something special" for his birthday. Then, with the woman securely in the passenger seat, they'd drive to a remote area to consummate the act. Meanwhile, as Clark unzipped and the woman went down on him, Bundy would fish out Clark's gun and slip it to him moments before he orgasmed. The idea, which they apparently succeeded in doing on numerous occasions, was to blow the woman's head off at the moment of ejaculation. And if that wasn't sick enough, they once decapitated a woman and keep her head as a trophy and sex toy.[5]

1986 was something of a landmark year for female serial killers in California. That was when

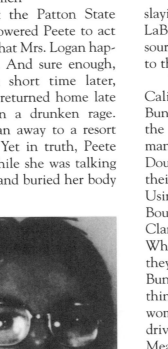

Carol Mary Bundy

Dorthea Puente, a sedate fifty-seven-year-old caretaker, began methodically poisoning her clients at her boarding house in Sacramento. Apparently this went on for several months until people began noticing thousands of rats and vermin infesting the area—not to mention a nauseating stench that could be noticed five blocks away. Finally, on November 14, 1988, the authorities came by to investigate and eventually discovered seven bodies buried in her backyard, all of which had been patients in her care.[6] Puente was finally tracked down and captured in Los Angeles a month later.

1986 was also the year that two lesbian nurses, Gwendolyn Graham and Catherine Wood, decided to kill someone *while* they were having sex with each other. Their first idea was to kill six people whose consecutive names would spell out the word *murder*. Instead they simply suffocated ten elderly patients chosen at random, and each time that they did, they gratified themselves sexually.

More recently Dana Sue Gray, a forty-year-old ex-party girl, went on a brief but horrific killing spree in Riverside County in the mid-1990s. Like Graham and Wood, she also targeted retirees. Her first was a sixty-six-year-old woman named June Roberts, a so-called friend of hers who pissed her off one day. Gray tied her to a chair, strangled her with a telephone cord, and beat her to death with a wine bottle. And within minutes of the murder, she was on a shopping spree with Roberts's credit cards. A couple of days later she did the same to fifty-seven-year-old Dorinda Hawkins—who miraculously survived—and then to eighty-seven-year-old Dora Bebe who gave up the ghost a short time later. Gray was finally arrested and sent to death row in 1998.

## The Bottom Line:

As Kelleher suggests, these women are just the beginning. Since the 1960s the number of killer ladies has been multiplying exponentially. Perhaps it has something to do with more women in positions of power, or perhaps it suggests a subtle shift in the patriarchal paradigm. Nonetheless, Southern California, or even the U.S., is *not* the female serial capital of the world. That distinction goes to Germany—at least for now.

# THE RUMOR:

Gangs in South Central L.A. have an initiation rite where prospective members are forced to rape a white woman, castrate a child, or murder a cop.

## A Little Background:

Few rumors in urban city life seem to evoke the kind of outright trepidation as the rumor of gang initiation rites. In the late 1990s, for example, there was a small panic over an alleged initiation rite that supposedly targeted unsuspecting drivers through South Central L.A. According to the rumor, which was subsequently reenacted in dozens of TV shows and movies, gang pledges were asked to drive around at night with their headlights off, waiting for good Samaritans to "flash" them with their own headlights. Once that occurred, the initiate would then be forced to turn around, chase after the car, and murder the driver in cold blood.

Designing Dystopia

## The Truth About Flashing:

Despite the rumor's extraordinary popularity the LAPD insists that there has never been a single case of "headlight flashing" in the entire history of the department. In fact, even gang members themselves seem to be confused over the rumor. As one veteran says, "I've never heard of anything like that ever happening. If people are going around saying that, it's just because they want to spread more lies about gangs."

Like many urban tales, the rumor may have some factual elements to it. After all, it's not uncommon for gang members to turn out their headlights before drive-by shootings, if only to conceal themselves. But that also means that rival gang-bangers may shoot *at* an approaching car without its lights on. As veteran gang member, Sanyika "Monster Kody" Shakur says, "When you roll down the street without your lights on, people automatically going to take you as an enemy coming in to dump [open fire]. So if you see that, sometimes you want to dump first. It's just a self-defense tactic."

## Where It Comes From:

If the rumor has achieved a level of acceptance with the general public it may be because gang initiation rites are known to involve extreme forms of violence. Asian gang pledges, for example, are said to endure knife wounds and burns. Neo-Nazis are said to receive brutal beatings and cuts and African-American and Latino gang initiates—like their Mafia predecessors—are said to receive the greatest respect for committing the most egregious crimes. "There's no question that they're asked to kill somebody as an initiation rite," says a representative of the DA's office. "They either have to go out and jack somebody, beat the shit out of somebody, or kill somebody. There's no question about it. It's a fact." Yet according to gang expert Al Valdez the widespread fear that street gangs are targeting citizens is somewhat misplaced. "They target other gang members," he says. "That's their first priority."[7]

## The Context:

It should also be noted that such fears are hardly new. Folklorist Richard M. Dorson recounted a horrific story in his (1981) book, *Land of the Mallrats*, that allegedly took place in the 1960s. According to Dorson, it started at a local Kmart when a young white woman decided to take her son shopping. At one point the boy asked his mother if he could go to the bathroom—alone. The mother agreed and escorted him to the men's room where she waited by the door. Apparently she waited for nearly twenty minutes before she had the store manager check on him. According to Dorson, they found the little boy laying in a pool of blood with his penis cut off. The police were then called, but before they could arrive they found three black boys trying to sneak out the back, one of which had the white boy's bloody penis in his pocket. "We had to do it," explained one of them. "Or they wouldn't let us in [to the gang]."

## What It All Means:

Oliver Pilat was one of the first to pick up on the obvious racism of the rumor. In a 1965 issue of the *Realist*, he suggested that the tale—which had been retold in numerous variations throughout New York City—was not only a blatant fabrication, but deliberate political and racist propaganda. According to him it was devised to "simulate the so-called white backlash in the cities."

The rumor of gang members randomly targeting white, middle-class Angelenos is not entirely different. If it has political and/or psychological functions, it helps vilify African Americans and/or ethnic groups, and undermines their chances for economic and social equality. Robert H. Knapp of the Boston Rumor Clinic once described such rumors as "wedge-drivers" for their ability to polarize groups. Such rumors tend to increase during transitional or crisis periods, and often belie deep-seated racist attitudes and xenophobia. In fact, of the 1,089 rumors that Knapp's clinic examined, a whopping sixty-six percent were of this sort, making them by far the most common rumors of all.

# THE RUMOR:

The LAPD has an elite, under-cover "assassination squad" that dresses like gang members and commits drive-by shootings.

Jean Pierre Gorin

Mob rule

## What People Are Saying:

When playwright Anna Deavere Smith interviewed a number of residents in South Central for her 1993 play, *Twilight*, she discovered that the rumor of an assassination squad was rampant within the African-American community. A typical story was told to her by Theresa Allison, founder of Mothers Reclaiming Our Children: "When they killed [my son] Tiny—when I say *they* I mean the police—they shot at him forty-three times. Five bullets went into Tiny. No bullets went in nobody else. I think what they do is, they want it to look like a drive-by shooting . . . When they killed Tiny, they were in unmarked cars. When they shot my nephew they were dressed like gang members—duck walkin', with hard beanies, jackets, no badges or anything—all over the project. This was going to be listed as a drive-by shooting and then they were gonna put it on another project. This is what they do all the time."

## The Truth:

Allison was not alone. Residents of South Central have been whispering about an elite LAPD "death squad" since the 1960s. Yet according to crime experts, the rumor is completely unfounded. "Think about it," says Myra Thomas of the DA's office. "For a cop to dress like a gang-banger and go into the hood to shoot somebody would be the same thing as going on a suicide mission. They would be *asking* to get shot. And cops don't do that. I don't care how crazy they are."

## Where It Comes From:

While the LAPD may not have an assassination squad, it has been known to use extra–legal methods to exterminate gang members. Sanyika "Monster Kody" Shakur, for example, a notorious street thug in his own right, has claimed that the LAPD has guided his gang into battle with rivals on occasion, and then allowed the shooting to commence without interference from other officers. "Our [hunting] missions [for rival gang members] were successful largely because we had logistical help from LAPD CRASH units," wrote Shakur in his autobiography, *Monster*. "For four nights in a row, we had been getting helpful hints from 'our friends' in blue—as they liked to call themselves . . . [They would] tell us exactly where to go, [and they'd say], if you get your crew and go now I'll make sure you are clear. But you only get fifteen minutes [to kill whoever you want]."

Such stories are hardly uncommon either. As the recent LAPD debacle involving the Rampart Division revealed, there was an entire subculture operating within the LAPD throughout the late 1980s and early 1990s devoted to gang extermination. As the *Los Angeles Times* reported, "This secret fraternity of antigang officers and supervisors committed crimes and celebrated shootings by awarding plaques to officers who wounded or killed people." What's more, the officers apparently had their own initiation rites and internal slogans, and repeatedly practiced drug-dealing, thievery, witness intimidation, extortion, perjury, frame-ups, and cover-ups—often with the blessing of their superiors. And, as if that wasn't disturbing enough, reports revealed that many of the officers were working under the approval of the FBI, which levied significant pressure on the LAPD and the INS to use "any means necessary" to "curb the activities of the Eighteenth Street Gang" through illegal arrests and deportations.

## A Little History:

As shocking as the news about the Rampart Division was, it pales in comparison to the malfeasance of the past. In the years 1953 to 1973 for example, the LAPD worked closely with the FBI to mount several Counter Intelligence Programs (COINTELPRO) specifically to "disrupt, destabilize, cripple, destroy, or otherwise neutralize dissident individuals and political groups throughout Southern California." Under the guidance of J. Edgar Hoover and his L.A. affiliate, these programs were designed to foment mistrust among black militant groups, and often used the press to do so. As Ward Churchill suggests in *The COINTELPRO Papers,* the bureau often used fake editorials, political cartoons, and graffiti to incite wars between rival groups. (Planting stories about one gang declaring "war"

on another gang for example.)

The stakes rose significantly with the Watts riots of 1965, however, because that's when the CIA stepped in to augment the FBI's proactive policing policy. As Churchill notes, scores of infiltrators, paid informants, and provocateurs were placed within various black militant groups specifically to incite members into performing acts of violence *against the public*. That way the LAPD could rush in with their guns blazing and "subdue" the radicals without fear of retribution.

There's some convincing evidence, for example, that the agency hired some provocateurs to instigate a full-scale riot at the 1972 Republican convention, which at the time was scheduled for San Diego. The purpose, of course, was to give law enforcement an excuse to round up and arrest all known insurgents throughout the state.

Meanwhile the FBI also poured money into at least three different militant left-wing organizations in Southern California including the Secret Army Organization (SAO), Ron Karenga's United Slaves (US), and the Guardians of the Oglala Nations (GOONS). All of which were paid to "disrupt, neutralize, and destroy" rival groups such as the Black Panthers and the American Indian Movement; and all received weapons, guerrilla training, and explosives from bureau-backed sources.

As Churchill notes, these tactics bore their first malignant fruit when members of Karenga's United Slaves assassinated Panther leaders "Bunchy" Carter and John Higgins in a classroom at UCLA's Campbell Hall on January 17, 1969. A short time later "Geronimo" Pratt, a highly decorated officer in the Vietnam War and the newly appointed leader of the Panthers after Carter, narrowly missed being shot to death when his house was raided by the LAPD, FBI and CCS (Criminal Conspiracy Section) officers.[8] Then came the execution of Panther leader George Jackson inside San Quentin, the disappearance of Panther Fred Bennett (his body was never found), the murder of Sandra "Red"

Pratt (Geronimo's wife), whose body was found in a sleeping bag on the side of the road. By the end of the 1970s at least thirty-four "insurgents" suffered the same fate and the Black Panther party was effectively wiped out.

In a 1969 memo from the FBI in Los Angeles to J. Edgar Hoover in Washington, the L.A. office took credit for the shootings, beatings, and "high degree of unrest" in the black neighborhoods of South Central, yet failed to acknowledge the vile consequences as a result.

# THE RUMOR:

West Hollywood once had a famous whorehouse where all the hookers were made to resemble famous Hollywood actresses.

## What People Are Saying:

This idea has been going around L.A. for the better part of the last century, and is widely believed by both police officers and hookers alike. In recent years, two books have compounded the veracity of the story: James Ellroy's 1990 roman noir, *LA Confidential*, and Charles Higham's 1993 biography, *Merchant of Dreams: Louis B. Mayer, MGM and the Secret Hollywood*.

In the former, Ellroy, who's known for peppering his stories with factual elements drawn from L.A.'s lurid past, includes a subplot about an exclusive call service catering to men desiring to bed imitation stars like Rita Hayworth, Ava Gardner, and Veronica Lake. As Ellroy describes the operation, "Pierce [Patchett] finds girls with middling resemblances to movie stars, [Dr. Terry] Lux performs plastic surgery for exact resemblances. Call them Pierce's concubines. They sleep with Pierce and selected clients—men who can help him put together movie deals."[9]

In *Merchant of Dreams*, Higham claims that MGM financed a similar whorehouse in West Hollywood in the 1930s, which he claims was

USC Special Collections

L.A.'s notorious Lee Francis

quite well-known within the industry. As he writes, "Visiting exhibitors and overseas representatives were always accommodated by the madam, the beautiful Billie Bennett, whose girls were always the exact doubles of the stars . . . Irving Thalberg would always stop by to watch the girls in action or to sit and play the piano in the lobby."

Designing Dystopia

Paul Young

## The Truth:

The name Billie Bennett has gone virtually unrecorded in the annals of L.A.'s crime history, and Higham seems to be the only one that has ever found any evidence that she had a celebrity house of skin.[10] "Whorehouses were pretty common back then," says a representative of the Police Historical Museum. "And just because there isn't record of a Billie Bennett doesn't mean that she didn't exist. Vice was pretty secretive back then, and the department was known to be pretty corrupt. So even if she did have a place like that, you probably wouldn't find much documentation of it."

## Where It Comes From:

While one could point to numerous reasons as to why such a rumor would surface—from the psychological to the folkloric—there are a number of historical antecedents to consider. During the Victorian period for example, the term "actress" was often synonymous with the term "prostitute," primarily because European theaters were often located near, or adjacent to, brothels. Meanwhile, as the movie industry picked up steam on the West Coast in the early 1900s, it was relatively common for pornographers to use look-alikes for the stars, which in turn led to rumors of legitimate movie stars working as sex performers on the side. More recently, alleged "star brothels" have appeared in the news on occasion, though rarely authentic. In the mid-1990s for example, the LAPD raided a prostitu-

tion ring in the Hollywood Hills which reportedly operated out of a house belonging to Connie Stevens. While the hookers weren't starlets, the connection to Stevens, who later claimed to be "just the landlord" and had no idea of any such activities, rekindled the celebrity-brothel rumor once again. "People simply want to sleep with movie stars," explains Ted McIlvenna of the Institute for the Advanced Study of Human Sexuality. "And the stronger the desire, the stronger the fantasy."

Nonetheless, the original rumor may go back to Lee Francis, the most famous madam of the 1930s. In her day, Francis had at least four houses under her dominion, each with its own swimming pool, tennis court, full-service restaurant, fully stocked bar, and of course, dozens of sporting girls to choose from. According to Serge Wolsey's 1941 exposé, *Call House Madam*, these brothels were not only used for sexual purposes, but they provided men with a place to conduct business meetings, play cards, or simply go for an afternoon swim. Movie stars were common, of course, including *female* stars. According to Lee Francis's 1965 autobiography, *Ladies on Call*, superstar Jean Harlow, for example, would come by late at night to steal a male customer for her own. Or, when she was feeling particularly daring, she'd hire a female prostitute and use one of the rooms on the premises.[11] "I had several well known women who would come by my house," wrote Francis. "They would come in, hire the services of my girls, and take them upstairs with the same candor and obvious purpose as any man. One must not confuse the average society woman who takes on one of my girls with (lesbians). She is merely sex hungry and either afraid to risk entertaining a man because of the possible consequences, or squeamish at the thought of sleeping with any other male than her husband. So in the strict sense of the word, she's not a woman-lover."[12]

## The Bottom Line:

With all the *real* stars at the House of Francis, it's certainly possible that people assumed that they were on Francis's payroll, which in turn, may have led to the rumor.[13]

# THE RUMOR:

For every trick that a `hooker` makes, twenty-five cents goes to the police department.

## What People Are Saying:

While this may sound a little bit like the infamous "pizza payoff" rumor that went around New York in the 1960s (for every slice of pizza eaten, seven cents goes to the Mafia), there may be more to it than anyone would care to admit. In truth the LAPD has had a long and fruitful relationship with ladies of the night, one that is as old as the department itself.

## A Little History:

In 1906 members of the Good Government League and Deputy DA Thomas Woolwine, attacked L.A.'s mayor Arthur C. Harper for conspiring with the city's chief of police and a notorious gangster to gain a monopoly on prostitution and illegal liquor in the city. That in turn led to an investigation by Woolwine, who later discovered that Harper, a well-known habitué of saloons and brothels, had repeatedly sold phony stocks to madams and illegal distributors as an excuse to hide monthly payments, bribes, and extortion fees. The news caused a sensation at the time, yet it failed to raise as much as an eyebrow within the department. After all, it was no secret that the LAPD had helped to set up the city's first red-light district not far from downtown twenty years earlier specifically to cater to visiting investors, politicians, and industrialists.[14]

Misha "Sugar" Levine

Tricks of the trade: A Hollywood street-walker conducting business

In any case, the news was scandalous enough to ruin Harper's career and force him out of office. The LAPD, meanwhile, went right on collaborating with prostitutes. In the 1920s, for example, Guy McAfee, the head of the LAPD's vice division, worked out an arrangement with Albert Marco (a.k.a. Marco Albori), one of the first Mafia bosses in the city. As historian Bruce Henstell has revealed, McAfee helped provide police protection for all of Marco's sixty-five bordellos in Southern California, and in return he received a good portion of the profits.[15]

A few years later, one of McAfee's associates, Charlie Crawford, another key player inside city hall and a major mob racketeer, followed a similar route when he set up a bordello at the corner of Fourth and Virgil. According to Lee Francis, who was installed as the madam, the house was set up specifically to cater to Mayor George Cryer and his cronies, and had the full protection of the LAPD. "I had to pay $150 to one [official], $50 to another, and twenty-five percent of the net to another," Francis remarked. "It was all very dramatic. Even to my leaving the money in a tin can in the backyard so that a city hall messenger could pick it up."

Around the same time, John P. Mills, a highly respected real estate developer and crony of the city's DA, Buron Fitts, came under attack for procuring underage girls from a local madam. Leslie White, a police investigator, was the first to expose the prostitution ring, and after questioning the madam he learned that Mills forced her to deliver a fresh virgin to his door each week. And apparently he wasn't alone either. As the madam later testified, there were at least a dozen men inside city hall that used her services, and an equal number in Hollywood. That led to a widespread investigation which ultimately

> **...Mills forced her to deliver a fresh virgin to his door each week.**

netted the DA himself, Buron Fitts, after he admittedly accepted a piece of real estate to drop rape charges against Mills.

Brenda Allen, arguably the most infamous madam of all time, came to power in 1940 after snitching on another well-known madam of the day, Almadel "Anne" Forrester, otherwise known as the Black Widow. Like her predecessor, Allen made arrangements with the boys downtown, too. In fact, her partner was none other than Sergeant E. V. Jackson, the head of administrative vice. Together they ruled L.A.'s sex world for eight years until a nosy cop accidentally stumbled upon their illicit affair in early 1948 and tried to put a stop to it. That in turn led to one of the most embarrassing episodes in department history, with dozens of cops, administrators, and the mayor himself indicted on conspiracy charges. (Apparently Allen paid Jackson $5,000 per week—plus all the hookers that he wanted—while Allen herself made $9,000 *per day*.)

## The Evidence:

While brothels are generally believed to be a thing of the past, there's little question that madams are still working closely with the LAPD today. As former policewoman Norma Jean Almodovar reveals in *Cop to Call Girl*, Anna Fischer and her partner Jill O'Conner, two of the most successful madams of the 1980s, provided girls to police officers anytime that they wanted—for free. In fact, they *paid* their girls to sleep with cops as a quid pro quo for police protection.

Apparently Madam Alex (Elizabeth Adams), the notorious Beverly Hills madam who was in operation around the same time, had a similar arrangement. In fact, she not only supplied the

LAPD and the sheriff's department with her best girls, she also told them which stars were doing drugs, which gangsters were in town, which dealers were expecting drug shipments, and more. As she later boasted, "That's why I've never spent a day in jail."

Heidi Fleiss on the other hand, Alex's most famous protégé, refused to let the LAPD get freebees and that may be why she was arrested on pandering charges in 1993. As she told reporters, "[I was arrested] because I wouldn't make girls sleep with [the cops] for free like Alex did. So they decided to make an example of me."[16]

More recently Jody Gibson, a.k.a. "Sasha of the Valley," a.k.a. Babydoll, the fledgling disco queen, told reporters that she had an affair with a detective in the Beverly Hills Police Department for several years. In a lengthy testimony, Gibson, a forty-one-year-old former model who sent hookers on $3,000 dates with movie stars, pro athletes, and big-time executives, claimed that this officer was "in bed" with the same Mafia associates that financed her call-girl service, and that he often "shielded her" from LAPD investigations. What's more, she also said that she had numerous sexual romps with the officer "all over" the Beverly Hills police station, including in the holding cell, hallways, and stairwell.

## The Bottom Line:

Prostitutes—especially high-class prostitutes—have always been important to the LAPD. Not only are they great informants, but they're also easy to extort and manipulate. Yet it would be overstating the fact to say that the LAPD works with every hooker in the city. Prostitutes can number in the tens of thousands at any given moment, and most have to deal with harassment, threats, and flat-out police brutality on a daily basis.

# THE RUMOR:

L.A. had its very own Bluebeard in the early days of Hollywood.

Deadly charms: L.A.'s first serial killer

33755
JAMES P. WATSON
MURDER I DEG. — AGE 42
LOS ANGELES LIFE
NAT. ARK.
MAY-18-1920

## The Truth:

It's true. There was a Bluebeard running around L.A. in the early part of the century—in fact there were several. Perhaps the most notorious, however, was a character by the name of James P. Watson, and his story goes something like this:

## The Legend:

In 1919, Kathryn Wombacher, a dressmaker in Spokane, Washington, decided to look in the personal ads for some male company. After selecting a notice, she made a date with a man named Walter Andrew, a federal agent that had recently moved to Spokane on a special case. While Andrew wasn't exactly the most handsome man in the world, he was smart enough, and apparently financially secure enough, to make a decent husband. So she was ecstatic when, after a brief courting period, he produced a ring and proposed.

The honeymoon didn't last long, however. They fought often, mostly over Wombacher's need to wear the pants in the family. As a result, Andrew disappeared on extended leaves without telling her of his whereabouts—other than the fact that he was "working on a case" and was "sworn to secrecy." Naturally Wombacher became suspicious and assumed that he was seeing another woman. So when he announced that he was going to Los Angeles for an undetermined amount of time, she put her foot down, demanding he take her with her. "I can't do that," he argued. "It's against bureau policy!"

That didn't stop her from finding his name on a registry and showing up on his doorstep days later with a suitcase in hand. "You're my husband," she argued. "I want to be with you." Andrew was livid, of course, but eventually demurred, finding her a small apartment in Hollywood. Then he announced that he was going on yet *another* assignment, this time to Washington where he was tracking an international jewel thief. Frustrated and angry, Wombacher found the Nick Harris Detective Agency in downtown L.A. and gave them a call. "I want you to follow my husband," she demanded. "I think he's seeing another woman."

Detective J. B. Armstrong eventually discovered that Wombacher's suspicions were correct. Andrew was seeing another women, a woman who lived less than a mile away. But that was only part of the bad news. Evidently this other woman was also his *wife*. She married him in a civil ceremony two weeks earlier.

The news was shocking to say the least, but that was nothing compared to what she was about to find out. Because after Armstrong uncovered a trunk that Andrew had kept hidden in a private locker—a trunk filled with marriage licenses, bankbooks, wedding rings, and photographs—he concluded that Andrew had been married to no less than twenty-two women in the previous ten years, women that he had met through personal ads. And as if that wasn't bad enough, most of them were either missing, dead, or murdered.

When the LAPD finally found Andrew, whose real name was James P. Watson, a known psychopath sought in the connection of at least four different homicides in three different states, he was at a local café romancing yet another woman. He was then taken into custody and thrown into a high-security cell where he was beaten repeatedly until he confessed to his crimes. At first he claimed that he had only killed his first wife. Then he admitted to killing three more until finally he swore that he had killed seven. But it wasn't until he took a small squad of officers to a plot of land in El Centro that anyone really understood the scope of his crimes. Because there, buried in a shallow marsh, were the acid-burned remains of twelve women that had been beaten, knifed, drowned, and chopped to death in the previous three years.

## The Bottom Line:

Investigators eventually found proof that he had killed sixteen women, yet most believed that he slaughtered many more; and to this day he ranks as one of the deadliest killers in California history. But what is even more baffling than his blood lust is how he managed to espouse so many women despite the fact that he was physically deformed. As the police report confirmed, he had a one inch penis *and* an undeveloped vagina!

*When the LAPD finally found Watson, he was at a local café romancing yet another woman.*

# THE RUMOR:

There is an elaborate kidnapping ring that steals infants from amusement parks and sells them on the black market.

**Rewards of $50,000 OKd in Child Kidnaping Cases**

## What People Are Saying:

It has been said that just about every theme park in Southern California has been infiltrated with an organized kidnapping ring based in Eastern Europe or South America. According to the rumor, these groups have their own elaborate codes and diversionary tactics, which enable them to snag babies out of carriages and scoot them out of the park before the parents have a chance to react. And once they have them in their clutches, they sell them to various adoption businesses or occult groups worldwide.

**Female Abductors**

**Babynapers: Deep Needs, Desperation**

## The Truth:

Fortunately, the rumor appears to be false. Disneyland, for example, has only had *one* reported kidnapping in its entire history, and even that was committed outside the park. (The victim was a sixteen-year-old boy who was forced into a car at gunpoint by some rival gang members in the 1980s, driven approximately ten miles, and dumped on a side street unharmed.) Nonetheless, Disney officials are still besieged with calls from concerned parents. "They always want to know about the alleged 200 kidnappings a year," explains a park representative. "How anyone could actually believe that figure is a mystery to me. When someone is kidnapped, it's all over the news. It becomes a national crisis. But when was the last time that you heard about

someone being kidnapped? Not in years, right? So how could it be possible that there are 200 infants being kidnapped from Disneyland each year? It just doesn't make sense."

## What It All Means:

As a number of folklorists have pointed out, such rumors gain popularity because parents subconsciously believe that such large, impersonal entertainment complexes, such as Disneyland, are trying to capitalize on their own inability to provide their children with meaningful entertainment at home.

Meanwhile, they also reflect the xenophobic fears of middle-class families who see foreigners—whether it's Middle Easterners, Russians, or Latin Americans—as mistrustful or dangerous. "The story has been retold in numerous variations for centuries," writes folklorist Jan Harold Brunvand. "And in each case the central idea is a racist or otherwise prejudiced one: Certain people—members of a feared minority—are out to get 'our' children."

## Where It Comes From:

Nonetheless, according to some law enforcement officials, there *are* organized crime syndicates secretly working at some of the parks in Southern California. They're not out for infants however, but wallets. "Pickpocket rings are more common than people realize," says Sean Collinsworth of the L.A. County Sheriff's Department. "Especially in the summer months when the parks are operating at full capacity. And some of these rings are highly sophisticated and well trained. I've been told that they even have schools in Colombia—some of which are run by women—that are just like regular academies with grading systems, tests, homework, everything. So when they finally arrive here they know *exactly* what they're doing."

# THE RUMOR:

There's a male madam that runs a brothel in West Hollywood catering exclusively to homosexual clients.

## The Truth:

While male prostitution has been flourishing in the City of Angels at least since World War II, most vice detectives scoff at the idea of a male brothel. After all, male prostitutes, or hustitutes, are generally more independent, transient, and capricious than their female counterparts, and rarely, if ever, need the kind of protection that a madam generally provides. "Most of the male hustlers that I've seen are pretty tough and can handle themselves," says Sergeant Robert Harms of the sheriff's vice division. "So it doesn't make sense that they would give someone half of their money for protection that they don't need."

## The Evidence:

While the rumor could be construed as little more than a homoerotic fantasy, police records show that there have been a number of male brothels over the years catering to both bisexual and gay customers. Sergeant Charles F. Stoker wrote about such a place in *Thicker 'n Thieves*, and according to his account, it was run by a "male madam" known as Little Brother. "The place was heavily draped and thickly carpeted," writes Stoker. "Drinks were placed on low tables on the floor. The room abounded with pillows. People lay in corners of the room, in which smoke from marijuana resembled the Los Angeles atmosphere on a smoggy day. Little Brother and his 'waiters' were clad in costumes which reminded one of a scene from *The Arabian Nights*—baggy silk pants, embroidered blouses, and turbans wound around their heads."

Author John Rechy, who earned notoriety for his semi-autobiographical novels *City of Night* and *The Sexual Outlaw,* described a similar place in David Ehrenstein's 1998 book, *Open Secret.* Apparently it was located in the hills of Los Feliz and existed through the 1950s. "There were two people on the road kind of spotting things, who would check you out," he explained. "Then you went up and there was this house that had been converted into a dance hall. I remember that they served soft drinks. No liquor. Men danced

Flying the colors

Misha "Sugar" Levine

with men, women with women. They had a system of flashing lights that warned when the police were on their way. And that was the signal for lesbians to team up with gay men."

Around the same time a male madam, known as Scotti to his associates, ran a similar operation out of a gas station at Hollywood and Fairfax. There customers could get a little more from the station attendants than a mere lube job. "Scotti was smarter then some of his competitors," claims a veteran of L.A.'s gay scene. "Because he refused to accept money from his boys or his clients. He'd only accept gifts: gold watches, silver trinkets, stocks, bonds, you name it. Some of his regular clients, who greatly appreciated his services, even went so far as to give him pieces of property. So when he finally retired in the 1970s, he not only had a clean record, but a healthy portfolio."

Robert Bolton, a towering African-American that worked out of a massage parlor on Santa Monica Boulevard in the 1960s and 1970s, eventually achieved infamy for peddling male flesh, too. In fact, according to some sources, he supplied trade to producers, actors, directors, politicians, and visiting luminaries from all over the world. Rather than work in a house, however, he preferred to have his clients dial a private number and make their requests with code numbers. The number eight for example, meant "the works."

Yet the most infamous male madam would have to be Billy Bryars, the wealthy son of an oil magnate, and a part-time producer of gay porn. Bryars was said to have a stellar group of customers using his "brothel" at the summit of Laurel Canyon. In fact, some have claimed that none other than J. Edgar Hoover, the founder and chief executive officer of the FBI, was one of his best clients.[17]

According to Anthony Summers's book, *Official and Confidential: The Secret Life of J. Edgar Hoover,* Hoover spent most of his summers at the Del Charro Hotel in La Jolla with his assistant director and lover, Clyde Tolson. That's where Bryars would send his boys, generally in personal limousines, and have them meet Hoover and Tolson for a little afternoon fun.

And from there, they'd drive into the nearby foothills for sexual romps, apparently under the protective gaze of fellow FBI agents.

No one has been able to unearth hard proof of such rendezvous, of course, but when Bryars fell under police scrutiny in 1973, allegedly for trafficking in child pornography, officers obtained a number of confessions from some of his hustlers, and some of them identified Hoover and Tolson as "Mother John and Uncle Mike," and claimed that they had serviced them on numerous occasions.

## The Bottom Line:

Why male madams have failed to achieve the kind of mythical stature as some of their female counterparts has perplexed folklorists and criminologists for years. Perhaps it has something to do with the fact that male prostitutes seem less transgressive, or heroic, than their female counterparts. Or perhaps it has to do with the general, closeted nature of homosexuality itself, which has always avoided mainstream exposure. In any case, male madams are undoubtedly real and continue to flourish to this day.

# THE LEGEND:

The LAPD secretly sold snuff movies made by Charlie Manson and his family members.

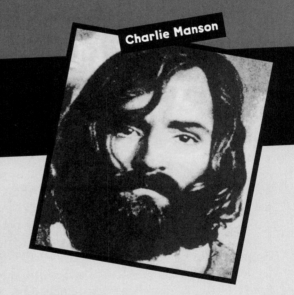

Charlie Manson

## What People Are Saying:

Perhaps no other criminal has spawned more rumors and tall tales than Charlie Manson. He, of course, is the diminutive psychopath that orchestrated the slaughter of actress Sharon Tate and her friends on August 8, 1969, and may have been responsible for as many as thirty-three homicides throughout Southern California. But since the 1970s, there has been a persistent rumor he was also involved in a pornography/snuff ring that operated out of Los Angeles.

## Where It Comes From:

Apparently the rumor surfaced during Manson's trial in 1970, when a number of witnesses claimed that they had seen him making movies at the Spahn Ranch in Chatsworth—itself a former movie set—which he had commandeered and transformed into his home. According to testimony, these movies allegedly depicted sex orgies, "devirginizing ceremonies," LSD sessions, occult sacrifices involving animals and human beings, and numerous murders. What's more, it's well known that Manson and his group had the equipment necessary for making such movies. Family member Bobby Beausoleil, who once acted in the movie *Mondo Hollywood*, supposedly stole a car and some camera equipment from filmmaker Kenneth Anger in 1967 after performing in his cult classic *Lucifer Rising*. Then, the following year, Manson allegedly broke into an NBC station wagon in Malibu and stole thousands of dollars' worth of equipment including a

# Girl, 10, Claims Father Filmed Murders of 3 Children

camera and lights. And a short time later, Beausoleil was charged with breaking into producer Jack Gerald's offices on Sunset Boulevard, and taking all of his video equipment.[18]

Ed Sanders, the author of the *The Family*, claims that an anonymous porn producer contacted him in 1970, and offered to sell him seven hours of Manson snuff/porn that had been pilfered from the LAPD's evidence locker. While Sanders never saw the footage, he was convinced the offer was genuine.

Coincidentally, there was also another rumor going around at the same time suggesting that actress Sharon Tate, the wife of filmmaker Roman Polanski, was involved in a pornography ring of her own. Beausoleil helped start the rumor when he claimed that Tate and her friends were known to cruise the Sunset Strip looking for young kids to star in their filmed-sex parties. Actor Dennis Hopper allegedly made a similar claim years later, saying that "they were shooting all kinds of porno up there." Another witness also alleged that he knew of a certain well-known actress that went to the Tate house on the day of the murders to perform in a porno shot by Voytek Frykowski—a film that was supposedly found by homicide detectives—and that she tried to return the following day to get it back.

Were people confusing Tate's alleged pornos with Manson's alleged snuff ring? Or were the rumors an urban legend concocted in the shadow of a sensational trial?

## The Truth:

Prosecutor Vincent Bugliosi was well versed in the rumors about Manson and Tate's alleged porno/snuff operations, and he took them very seriously. Yet he never found a shred of evidence to prove that the claims were true. In fact, he obtained a copy of an alleged Tate porno from Jeffrey "Pic" Pickett, a one-time suspect in the murders and discovered that it was little more than a home movie of Frykowski sitting around

with a group of friends smoking pot and getting into a "domestic argument." In fact, the only "porno" that was confiscated by the LAPD, was a video cassette discovered in Tate's closet shortly after the murders that apparently showed her making love to her husband, Roman Polanski, in private. That, of course, may have started the rumor in the first place. But as far as Manson's movie career, there seems to be credible evidence suggesting that he acted out the role of the movie director, which apparently he did often, yet little proof that he actually distributed films of any kind. In fact, there are records that he fenced most of the stolen film equipment nearly as quickly as he obtained it.

## The Context:

Since then, the subject of snuff movies—the deliberate killing of a human being for a sexual stimulus—has continued to haunt investigators and law enforcement officials around the world. (Some have dubbed them the Bigfoot of crime.) The media has reported a number of cases allegedly involving snuff, but rarely, if ever, mention that any film was ever found. In 1982, the *Los Angeles Times* reported that Arthur Dill was using his ten-year-old daughter as a sex slave in the basement of his house in Northern California. Quoting sheriff's detective Sergeant Robert Humphrey, the *Times* claimed that the girl was forced to submit to the father's friends and associates, who paid anywhere from fifty-five dollars to eighty-five dollars, and forced to participate in numerous ritual killings where a video or movie camera was utilized to document the events. The story was sensational, of course, yet the *Times* failed to report that the daughter suffered from Munchausen syndrome and that the investigators failed to find any evidence to prove that any movies were actually made.

A few years later, the *Los Angeles Times* reported that Fred B. Douglas, a furniture upholsterer in Garden Grove, was operating a snuff

Fred Douglas

ring operation out of a small shack in the Mojave Desert.[19] Douglas, who was later tried and convicted on first-degree murder charges, allegedly lured women under the pretense of shooting test shots of the girls, and then slaughtered them on camera. Again the *Times* didn't report that officers failed to find evidence that any film had been shot, traced, or recovered.

More recently, the *London Times* reported that there were dozens of Mexican immigrants being murdered to satisfy the insatiable demands of the porno industry in the San Fernando Valley. "One man is running the operation from his home in Southern California," said the 1990 article. "Officers believe that he may be responsible for the murder of twenty-five women."

Despite the charges, no one has found any proof of a snuff film industry in Southern California.[20] Yet the idea cannot be discounted so easily. As Sergeant Richard Valdemar of the L.A. County Sheriff's Department, Special Investigations, explains, "You have to remember, these things are *very* expensive. People that are into extreme fetishes will pay a fortune for these kinds of things. If you wanted to buy one you'd probably have to put up at least $10,000 up front. Then *maybe* you'd get your video. But only after they've thoroughly checked you out— which is another reason why no one in the mainstream media has been able to track one down. And I'd venture to say that if these things exist, they're probably made on commission. Because it's highly unlikely that people are going around killing people saying, 'Gee, I wonder if we could sell this thing?' If they're made at all, they're made for one person, and one person only. So if you ask me, they're real. But they're *extremely* rare."

## The Bottom Line:

In the late 1990s, Israeli journalist Yaron Svaray set out on a two-year journey to find an actual snuff movie. That journey took him to nearly a dozen countries, and in each case, law enforcement officials told him that his undertaking was futile. As an FBI agent remarked, "As far as anyone in the bureau knows, there has never been a legitimate snuff movie ever found." Nonetheless, Svaray, who posed as a wealthy buyer, came across a dozen films that he saw with his own eyes. In Berlin, he came across a movie depicting a young girl being raped and stabbed to death by neo-Nazis. In New York he attended a group screening arranged by Russian Mafiosi where men paid $1,500 per person to see a woman get raped and slaughtered. In Paris he arranged for a snuff movie to be shown to actor Robert De Niro who was said to be working on a screenplay about the snuff trade. And in Belgrade he was shown a "sample reel" containing dozens of snuff murders at the hands of organized crime members. As Svaray remarks in his book *Gods of Death*, "If I learned one thing from [this experience] it's that the degradation of the individual was only a small part of a much larger problem, and that is blood sells."

> "...the degradation of the individual was only a small part of a much larger problem, and that is blood sells."

# THE RUMOR:

There used to be a mad serial killer that liked to use rattlesnakes as a weapon.

## A Little Background:

While this rumor may be a slight exaggeration, a number of Southern California killers have shown a fondness for rattlesnakes over the years, including Charles Dederich, the notorious leader of Synanon who allegedly placed a rattler in Paul Morantz's mailbox after he threatened to expose his corrupt business practices. None however, have been quite as perverse as Robert S. James, a.k.a. Major Raymond Lisenba, a.k.a. "Rattlesnake James."

Born and raised in Alabama, James always liked to consider himself a ladies' man, and women often fell for his Southern charms. But underneath his desire to seduce women was a profound misogyny that often reared its ugly head at moments when women were least guarded —during lovemaking. That's when James usually turned to strangulation, beatings, and acts of sheer horror. Perhaps that's why so many crime writers have suggested that he may have killed as many as six of his former lovers, including Winona Wallace, his third wife, who was found facedown in her bathtub four years before James arrived in L.A.

## The Legend:

In 1936, Robert James decided to kill his fifth wife, Mary Busch, in exactly the same manner.

The prosecution demonstrates his lethal method

Los Angeles Examiner/USC Special Collections

They met in 1935, after she answered an ad for a manicurist at his barbershop at Eighth and Olive. And within days of saying "I do," James had her take out a $10,000 life insurance policy naming himself as the sole beneficiary, and began cooking up ideas on how to get rid of her.

One afternoon, while at his barbershop, a drifter by the name of Charles Hope wandered in for a chat. He claimed that he had just spent the afternoon at an amusement park in Long Beach where he had seen a rattlesnake kill a chicken in a sideshow. Trying not to act too suspicious, James quizzed him about the snake, asking him how poisonous it was and if it were for sale or not. Then he produced a crisp hundred-dollar bill and flashed it before Hope's eyes saying, "This could be yours if you can find me a real killer and bring it to me."

Meanwhile, as Hope went off to procure a rattler, Mary hit James with some unexpected news: she was pregnant. At first James laughed, saying that was the last thing that he needed. But when his wife began crying softly, mumbling something about how a baby would bring love to what had become a loveless marriage, he flew into a rage, screaming that he wouldn't allow her to have a baby under any circumstances. Mary then ran off to the bedroom with tears in her eyes, and as she did, James began plotting what would become one of the most twisted murder scenarios in L.A. history: He'd force Hope to perform an abortion on her—as if he were a doctor—and inject her with rattlesnake poison after she was tied down.

And apparently, that's just what he did. On August 4, 1935, just after midnight, he introduced his wife to her "abortionist," Dr. Hope, who appeared in a hospital gown. Mary was so intoxicated at that point, thanks to the five cocktails that James had forced down her throat, that she didn't notice Hope's bumbling. "Now just relax," he told her while strapping her down to a large table and fitting her with a blindfold. "I'm going to have to take your shoes off to administer a little anesthesia. You might feel a small sting but it's nothing to worry about."

At that point James entered the room carrying a large wooden box containing the two snakes inside and placed it at the foot of the table. He then motioned for Hope to hold her down as he dropped her foot inside. All at once, the snakes sunk their teeth into her flesh, and Mary winced in pain. Moments later, as the venom seeped into her blood, she let out a low guttural wail. "Just relax," said Hope trying to settle her down. "Once the drug kicks in you won't feel a thing."

Apparently the venom took a lot longer than they expected, however, and within thirty minutes her foot had grown to the size of a watermelon. "What's happening?" she cried over and over. "What are you doing to me?"

*All at once, the snakes sunk their teeth into her flesh, and Mary winced in pain.*

Apparently this went on for a couple of hours until finally, after both failed to come up with an alternate plan, James ordered Hope to perform an abortion on Mary just in case she survived. Hope supposedly then went back into the room, removed her panties, spread her legs and poked around with a coat hanger until he felt something "pop."

Finally, after failing to come up with any alternatives, James tried to force more alcohol down her throat thinking that it would speed up the poison. When that failed, the two men picked her up, carried her outside to a nearby fishpond, and held her head underwater until she drowned.

Though the police were suspicious of Mary's alleged "accidental" drowning, they didn't arrest James on suspicion of murder, at least not at first. They arrested him on incest charges after they found him in bed with an underage girl who just happened to be his niece. Finally, by April 1936, the DA had enough evidence to prosecute him on the murder of Mary Busch James and he became the last man in California history to be hanged to death.

# THE RUMOR:

Richard "the Night Stalker" Ramirez liked to remove the eyeballs of his victims and mail them to the cops just to taunt them.

Serial killer as rock star: Richard Ramirez

## A Little Background:

Few of Southern California's serial killers have terrified the public quite like Richard "the Night Stalker" Ramirez has. In the early 1980s, rumors of his killing practices, which included mutilation, necrophilia, Satanic blood rituals, decapitation, and cannibalism were rampant through the city. That in turn led to a city-wide increase of gun sales, with many stores running out of stock.

## Where It Comes From:

According to Philip Carlo, author of *The Night Stalker: The Life and Crimes of Richard Ramirez,* most of the rumors about the Night Stalker's killing methods were greatly exaggerated—including his practice of removing eyeballs and sending them to people. The rumor may have started after the news of his fourth victim, Maxine Zazzara, was announced in 1984. Because on that night, he committed the most heinous murder of his entire career. Apparently it began at around three A.M. when Ramirez broke into Zazzara's Whittier home and found Zazzara's husband, Vincent, passed out on the couch. Without the slightest hesitation, Ramirez placed a .22 handgun to Vincent's temple and squeezed the trigger. The bullet entered his head at a slight angle and spun around his skull at least a half dozen times, cutting his brain to ribbons.

Ramirez then walked into the kitchen to look for something to eat as he often did during his killing jags. Then he made his way to the back of the house and found Maxine sitting on the edge of the bed with a shotgun in her arms. Vincent had hidden the gun under the bed a few days earlier after a recent spate of burglaries in the area. "What do you want?" she asked. "What are you doing here?"

There was a momentary standoff until Ramirez went for his own gun. Then Maxine pulled the trigger—but nothing happened. Her husband had removed the shells earlier in the day when he found out that his grandchildren were coming over. Furious, Ramirez shot her three times in the chest. But that wasn't enough. As Carlo claims, he had to *humiliate* her. After slapping, beating, and kicking her body, he ran back into the kitchen and returned moments later with a kitchen knife. Then he tried to remove her heart. "He couldn't get through the rib cage, however, and he left a gaping inverted cross sliced into her chest," writes Carlo. "So he decided on her eyes; that would be his way of having a piece of her soul. Quickly, yet carefully, he cut away her eyelids, removed both her eyes, and put them in a little jewelry box that he found, laughing as he did so. Then he stabbed her in the stomach, throat, and pubic area." And as if that wasn't enough, he then had sex with her corpse.

## The Bottom Line:

No one, save for Ramirez, knows what happened to Maxine's eyes. Some have speculated that he may have sent them to someone as a joke, perhaps even the lead homicide detective on his case. But there are no records of him doing so. Instead he just continued finding new ways of killing people. By August 30, 1985, he had already dispatched thirteen people with live wires, machetes, crowbars, handguns, and Uzis—and had sex with nearly half of the bodies afterward. None were mutilated quite as badly as Maxine, however. In fact, she was the only victim that lost her eyes.

## The Legacy:

Ironically, Ramirez finished his murderous career with a storybook ending. After his arrest in 1985, and subsequent trial, jailers reported that he had over a dozen females vying for his affections daily, some of which tried to please him by removing their panties in front of him. By the time that he was finally sentenced for forty-six felony counts—receiving nineteen death sentences— he literally had women fighting over him. Finally, on October 3, 1996, he married twenty-five-year-old, Doreen Lioy of Burbank in a private ceremony at San Quentin. Today Lioy, who has a degree in English literature, is said to have a fairly successful career writing for teen magazines.

# THE LEGEND:

L. Ewing Scott killed his wife and buried her body in the wet cement of the 405 Freeway.

## The Context:

The idea of bodies being buried in unusual places has always been of great fascination to people throughout the world, and has been a part of folklore for centuries. New Yorkers for example, have been telling stories about corpses hidden in the Brooklyn Bridge for generations—the victims of Mafia retribution—and similar tales can be found in Chicago, Detroit, New Orleans, and elsewhere. Los Angeles on the other hand, has its own gallery of hidden bodies, but few, if any, are related to Mafia assassinations.[21]

## What It All Means:

Translating the language of the everyday to the language of psychoanalysis, hidden bodies tend to personify the "killed off" aspects of the ego buried deep within the unconscious. For folklorists, however, a body being entombed in an unnatural place tends to suggest a warning, or omen of death. It transforms an average place to one that needs to be approached with respect and/or fear. Bridges, on the other hand, generally symbolize the connection between the real world and the spirit world. In other words, tales about bodies

Disappearing act: Ewing and Evelyn in Morocco

in bridges symbolize the fear of, or the blocking of, the spiritual aspects of one's persona.

## Where It Comes From:

Ever since the 1960s, there has been a persistent rumor that a woman was buried inside the 405 Freeway.[22] The story actually began a few years earlier, in May 1955, when Mrs. Evelyn Scott, a well-known socialite in Beverly Hills, suddenly disappeared from her home without a trace. Her husband, L. Ewing Scott, claimed that she had suffered a nervous breakdown and checked herself into an asylum somewhere in Mexico. "And frankly," he told friends, "I couldn't care less."

Eventually the DA had a strong enough case to try Scott on first-degree murder charges—even without a body. Apparently there was enough circumstantial evidence to do so, including a pair of prescription glasses and dentures—her *only* pair of dentures—later discovered in Scott's incinera-

tor. What's more, Scott had brazenly given away her clothing, cancelled her subscriptions and appointments, deleted her name from their bank accounts, and tried to "escape" to Canada with a new girlfriend. That gave the prosecution enough ammunition to convict him of first-degree murder and send him to San Quentin for the rest of his life.

No one ever found Evelyn's corpse, however, and that led to the rumor that he must have thrown it into the wet cement of the 405 Freeway, which was still under construction at the time.

Scott was eighty-one years old when he was finally released, and when a reporter asked him what he was going to do with his new freedom, he mumbled something about going back to L.A. to file a dissolution of marriage.

"But how are you going to find Evelyn after all this time?" asked the reporter.

"Easy," said Scott. "I heard she had been arrested twice in Mexico for drunk driving."

Designing Dystopia

## The Truth:

Evelyn wasn't in Mexico, however. Nor was she poured into a concrete piling for the 405 Freeway either. By Scott's own admission she was resting in a shallow grave approximately six miles due east of the Sands Hotel in Las Vegas. Apparently Scott put her there in 1956 after clubbing her to death with a rubber mallet. He admitted as much to reporter Diane Wagner in 1990. "I killed her because she tried to poison me," Scott explained. "Just like she poisoned her [six] previous husbands."

## The Legacy:

L.A. has seen plenty of cement tombs since then. In the early 1990s, for example, a new home-owner decided to dig up an old patio in his back-yard and found a corpse buried inside—a corpse that turned out to be the husband of the previous owner. But that was nothing compared to what officers found in La Habra a couple of years later. That's when a resident along Willow Street found a 200-pound block of cement on his front lawn, a block that was oozing blood. Officers later discovered that it contained the remnants of a severed arm and perhaps a foot. That led to a wider investigation which eventually yielded four more concrete blocks haphazardly dumped around the neighborhood. And when officers looked in those, they found more body parts, including another foot, a hand, and parts of a leg. Finally, after looking through missing person reports, officers concluded that the victim was a twelve-year-old boy named Juan Delgado, a Salvadorian transplant who had disappeared days earlier. That in turn led to a search of the Delgado household where a massive, 1,500-pound block of cement was discovered in the back of the house. That, too, was oozing blood, and when detectives looked in that, they discovered Delgado's head and torso. Finally, after Delgado's family had been cleared, police concluded that John Samuel Ghobrial, a former butcher and an Egyptian immigrant who had been given a shed in the back of the house, was a prime suspect. Ghobrial, who had lost an arm when someone threw him in front of a train, was the boy's cousin and an alleged child molester, and police believe that he killed the boy when he tried to expose his sexual crimes. He has not been tried or convicted of any of the allegations made by the LAPD and so the matter remains open to question at the time of this writing.

Another cement tomb?

Paul Young

# THE LEGEND:

When a cop finds a pile of shit at the scene of a robbery it means that the victim is marked for death.

A fresh calling card

Paul Young

## A Little Background:

While it's rarely written about, the criminal underground has a vast array of visual codes to choose from. Male prostitutes along Santa Monica Boulevard, for example, have an entire set of nonverbal cues that they use to communicate with prospective clients. A black handkerchief worn on a hustler's body for instance, suggests that he likes to partake in S&M. A yellow handkerchief, on the other hand, means that he's into golden showers. Conversely, madams have their own sartorial signals as well. In the 1930s, it was common for a madam to wear a red dress to alert her clients that her brothel was under police stakeout. Green or white attire on the other hand, meant that the coast was clear.

Meanwhile, the Mafia has its own codes involving both symbolic and traditional signs. If a Mafioso wants everyone to know that his victim was a police informant, for instance, he may stuff a dead bird in his mouth; or if he wants to scare someone and make him think he's marked for death, he may send him a dead fish.[23]

Even police officers have their own visual cues that they use in secret. LAPD CRASH units in the 1990s for example, were said to issue special plaques to officers that were involved in shootings. According to special report by the *Los Angeles Times,* the plaques generally consisted of playing cards—usually a number two perforated with two bullet holes. A red heart for instance, meant that the officer shot a suspect, while a black spade meant that he killed him.

Such codes are not just for the streets, however. Lynn Franklin, a twenty-year veteran of the Beverly Hills Police Department, mentions a practice in his book *Sawed Off Justice* that is occasionally used in the criminal courts system. "It's a code word that everyone agrees on," writes Franklin. "Usually it's the name of a nonexistent witness. [But] it changes every month or so. When I first heard it, the name was Mrs. Green. How it works is the lawyer asks for a postponement, telling the judge, "Your honor, I have been unable to locate an important witness for the defense—*Mrs. Green.*" As soon as the judge hears the code word he or she knows that the attorney's client is a bum. As Franklin put it, "What the lawyer is really telling him is, 'I haven't got my money from the defendant up front yet so I want him to remain on bail another couple of weeks so he can rip off some more people until he gets enough to pay me. Then I'll be ready to go to trial.'"

## The Evidence:

One of the most ubiquitous codes in the criminal underworld—believe it or not—is the use of *feces.* "It happens a lot more than people think," says Monte Nicholson, a former detective for the L.A. County sheriff's department. "We used to find piles of shit at break-ins, robberies, even murders. It happened all the time."

When Connie Fletcher interviewed police officers for her book, *What Cops Know,* several veterans told her that the practice was most common with thieves. "A lot of cat burglars like to defecate on the floor or on the living-room rug," said one officer. "I remember there was this one that really got his *cajones* off by going into the house knowing that somebody was there, and doing something to let them know that *he* was there . . . He defecated on the bed, sometimes with the occupants still in it."

## The Context:

Albert Friedman, an editor for UCLA's folklore journal *Western Folklore,* claims that the custom is just as common in other parts of the world. But the way that the rite is practiced differs slightly from country to country. French thieves, for example, generally like to drop their "calling cards" in the owner's shoes, pockets, or hat. German burglars seem to prefer displaying their doo-doo in some eye-catching place such as on a table or windowsill. In contrast, Dutch prowlers prefer doing the filthy deed in a highly personal-ized space, such as a closet, dresser, or bed. Americans on the other hand, favor pristine surfaces such as a white kitchen, bathtub, or bed setting.

## What It All Means:

Excrement was a potent symbol for some North American Indian tribes in the seventeenth century. It was often used in healing ceremonies and/or rituals, and was often associated with birth and/or riches. But for modern man such "calling cards" have a slightly different connotation. As Professor Bob Morneau at Cal State Northridge once told crime reporter Philip Carlo, "If you go to a [crime] scene and you find a dump, most guys would say, hey look, the pig took a shit. But you must realize that by doing that, the [guy] is talking to you—telling you that sex is a part of why he's [doing what he's doing]. Remember, sex is whatever *feels* good."

# THE LEGEND:

Benjamin "Bugsy" Siegel, the most notorious mobster in L.A. history, was murdered for failing to pay back the $6 million that he borrowed to build the Flamingo Hotel in Las Vegas.

## What Happened:

On the night of June 20, 1947, Benjamin "Bugsy" Siegel, the Mafia's top crime boss on the West Coast, had a seat in the living room of Virginia Hill's mansion in Beverly Hills. It was a typical evening for the gangster. Virginia, his girlfriend, was in Paris on yet another shopping spree, Chick, his bodyguard, had a girl upstairs, and Al "the Russian" Smiley, a long-time busi-ness associate and friend, sat across from him and filled him in with recent developments. But what was typical suddenly turned horrific when four steel-jacketed slugs from an army-issue rifle suddenly exploded through a side window and hit Siegel squarely in the face. Smiley, who immediately dove into a nearby fireplace, later claimed that he saw Siegel's right eyeball sail fif-teen feet across the room shortly before five more bullets came crashing into his head, neck, and chest. By the time it was over, nine rounds had been unloaded into the gangster, closing the book on L.A.'s most infamous Mob boss.[24]

## What People Are Saying:

As a peer of Meyer Lansky, Lucky Luciano, Frank Costello, and Vito Genovese, Siegel was considered a true aristocrat of the underworld. Yet by the time of the murder, he had compromised his reputation to such a degree that he was considered a pariah within mob circles. He no longer took advice from his Mafia peers, nor did he care about their concerns, and many believe that he paid for such defiance with his life. After all, the Mob invested over $6 million into his Flamingo Hotel, the first full-service, luxury hotel-casino in Las Vegas, and no one, not even his mentor Meyer Lansky, had seen a dime in return.

## The Truth:

According to author Dean Jennings, Siegel wasn't killed for failing to pay back his $6 million debt as many have suggested. If anything, he was killed for being a lousy manager. Because even after the debacle of the hotel's construction, which went far and above the original budget, Siegel failed to understand the daily operations of a hotel. Card cheats, thieves, and corrupt floor managers drained the casino's bank by the millions, while staff operations and expenditures escalated to extraordinary highs. Realizing that they were going to lose their investment, Siegel's investors decided that they were going to need to replace Siegel with someone that knew what they were doing. Siegel eventually caught wind of the rumor however, and claimed that *no one* was going to take away his baby. Not without a fight anyway.

Fortunately, after months of reorganizing his costs and installing a tight security system to curtail thieves, Siegel managed to bring the Flamingo into the black. In fact, by May 1947, it became quite clear that Siegel was going to be able to pay off his debt ten times over.

Los Angeles Examiner/USC Special Collections

You talkin' to me? Benny Siegel circa 1940

Nonetheless, one of his mobster associates, Little Moe Sedway, who secretly coveted the casino, began a whispering campaign behind Siegel's back, saying that Bugsy was skimming money off the profits and stashing it in a Swiss bank account with the help of his girlfriend Virginia Hill. Siegel subsequently had Sedway permanently barred from the club and threatened to have him killed. Sedway refused to back down, however, and went to New York with his partner, Gus Greenbaum, and had a sit-down with Siegel's bosses. That's when it was decided that Bugsy had to be assassinated.

Edward Anhalt, meanwhile, believes that Siegel may have been killed for other reasons. While doing research on a screenplay about Siegel's life for actor Tony Curtis, he interviewed Sidney Korshack, the infamous Mob fixer who once represented Siegel in the early 1940s. And according to Korshack, a certain Mob boss back east heard through the grapevine that Siegel was abusing Virginia Hill on a daily basis. And according to Korshack, this boss had a crush on Hill, and was insanely jealous of Siegel. So when he heard Siegel had beaten her so badly one night that she had to fly to Paris to recuperate, he called Bugsy directly, and told him to back off.

Supposedly Siegel told him to go "fuck himself" and hung up the phone. "That's when they whacked him," said Korshack. "It was all because of Virginia Hill."

## The Real Truth:

And yet there's another theory that makes even more sense. In the 1930s, James Ragan ran a race wire service out of Chicago that fed bookies instantaneous results from horse races all over the country. Despite the high fee—anywhere from $100 to $1,200 per week—nearly every bookie in the country wanted a piece of the action. Not surprisingly, the Mafia saw the potential of such services, so Al Capone employed Willie Bioff to set up Trans America, a national service designed to go head to head with Ragan. Ben Siegel, who was already on the West Coast at the time, was chosen to take control of the operation and received approximately $25,000 per month in return.

Trans America flourished under Siegel's direction, yet at some point, during his financial difficulties with the Flamingo, he not only *doubled* the fee for the service, but he poured *all* of the profits back into the hotel without returning a dime to the Mob. That led to a virtual tidal wave of complaints by bookies and Mob bosses alike. Meanwhile, Capone had Ragan assassinated in Chicago, which led to an intensive police investigation far more comprehensive than he ever expected. As a result, the Mob ordered Siegel to shut down Trans America for a while, at least until things cooled off. Yet Siegel, who was struggling under the debts of his hotel, took the order personally and assumed that he had been fired, or worse, cut off. So he responded with a terse ultimatum stating that he'd shut the service down, but for no less than $2 million up front. Some say that's all the Commission needed to hear.

## The Bottom Line:

According to Chuck Giancana's *Double Cross*, it was Sam "Mooney" Giancana, the head of the Chicago family, that received the official orders to carry out Seigel's assassination. Giancana in turn hired Frankie Carbo, a well-known New York mafioso and former Siegel associate, to be the triggerman. The reason? Apparently it wasn't only because of Siegel's pilfering of race wire money. It was because of *everything*—his debts, his mismanagement of the Flamingo, his treatment of Hill, his handling of Trans America, and the fact that he was thinking of setting up a heroin operation out of Mexico without consulting Luciano. "Siegel was a fuckin' cowboy who got too big for his own good," Giancana told his brother. "We voted to get him out of the way down in Havana after he had the balls to defy Lansky and the whole goddamned Commission on top of that."

BUGSY

# THE LEGEND:

Sunset Boulevard was the site of one of the bloodiest Mafia gang wars in L.A. history, otherwise known as the "Battle of Sunset Strip."

## A Little History:

To understand what happened in the so-called Battle of the Sunset Strip of 1949 one needs to go back to the early part of the twentieth century, to when the first real Mafia presence became known in Los Angeles. Before that, gangsters such as Guy McAfee, Farmer Page, Charlie Crawford, and Tutor Sheerer ran most of the rackets in the city, often in collusion with the LAPD and Mayor Frank Shaw's administration. But once alcohol became illegal in 1919, Italian mobsters such as August Polambo, Dominic De Ciola, Antonio Torizzio, Tony Matranga, Joe Adrizzone, and Joe Bernardo moved in, transforming a relatively organized—albeit corrupt—system, into a bloody nightmare. At least thirty men were gunned down along the Italian section of Darwin "Shotgun Alley" Avenue in 1925 alone, and by the end of the decade, there was a full-scale turf war underway.

One of the masterminds behind the bloodshed was Jack Dragna, an immigrant from Sicily, and the president of the Italian Protection League. Stocky, with a blunt nose and a red hot temper, Dragna was "the unofficial mayor of the Italian ghetto" as author Judith Moore described him, settling family disputes and enforcing discipline. Thanks to Prohibition, however, he was able to muscle in on the bootleg liquor market, and eventually maneuvered himself into position as the leader of L.A.'s first Italian crime family. Together with a relatively small team of killers, he brought L.A.'s La Cosa Nostra into national prominence. In fact, to this day, he remains the only L.A. boss to be included on the national crime commission.

Dragna's power was compromised somewhat with the arrival of Benjamin Siegel in the 1930s, however. After all, Siegel had the blessing of Lansky himself, and Dragna understood that if he wanted to stay in business, he was going to have to turn over his bookmaking operations, casino interests, racetrack betting, and gambling ships to Bugsy. Thus Siegel, who made his presence known by assassinating Les Bruneman, a key member of the old-school, LAPD-backed syndicates, solidified his control of the rackets, including the extras' union, by 1937. Dragna on the other hand, who was known euphemistically as the "Al Capone of Los Angeles," still remained the godfather of the L.A. family, and continued to settle disputes, arrange hits, and oversee drug trafficking throughout the city.

That changed with Siegel's assassination in 1947, however. Because without Siegel, L.A. immediately fell into "open territory" again, free for any Mafia family to move in and set up shop. That's why Dragna went back east to organize the allocation of Bugsy's assets and ensure his place as the boss. But by then there was another gangster on the scene, one that wanted his own piece of the pie, and his name was Mickey Cohen.

## The Story:

Mickey Cohen never paid any respect to Jack Dragna, even when he had to work with him on occasion under Siegel's reign. And apparently the feelings were mutual. As Cohen remarked years later, "Dragna was of the old school where only Italians ran things, and certainly not Jews like Benny (Siegel) with his Eastern ways. But that didn't bother Benny none. 'Fuck Dragna' was his attitude, and he did." Cohen, of course, idolized Siegel and started treating Dragna in much the same way. In fact, he began building his own empire within days of Siegel's removal, with gambling casinos, prostitution rings, and extortion rackets, and never paid Dragna or the L.A. family a dime. (The Commission had agreed that Cohen would inherit Siegel's bookmaking operations but declined to give him anything else.) The power struggle also had its racial implications in that Dragna refused to admit Jews into his outfit just as his true Mafia predecessors had in the past. Therefore Cohen allied himself increasingly with East Coast Jewish mobsters while Dragna beefed up his Italian muscle. That led to a slight "lieutenant gap," with each side trying to outdo the other in recruits. Eventually, by the end of the decade, Dragna had the edge, using his winery in Rancho Cucamonga to initiate the likes of Jimmy Regace, Charlie Dippolito, and Jimmy Fratianno—guys with genuine Mafia pedigrees and serious killing power. (Royalty like Johnny Roselli, on the other hand, could still move back and forth between the two.)

But if there was a spark that set off a war between the two, it occurred the night that Cohen found Jimmy Utley, one of Dragna's top lieutenants, at Lucy's El Adobe. Apparently

> **"It's not so hard to understand. Those guys were nothin' but amateurs, that's all. I've seen ten-year-old punk kids that had more on the ball than dem guys."**

Utley had previously persuaded some of Cohen's bookies in West Hollywood to come over to his side of the fence and Cohen didn't like it one bit. After all, West Hollywood was *his* territory, and *he* paid off the sheriff.[25]

Utley refused to back off, however, and continued recruiting even more bookies on the West Side. So Cohen sent Hooky Rothman, his number one killer, to "make a visit" with some of Utley's new recruits, and the following morning three bookies were found dead in their apartments, each beaten to death with a baseball bat.

Days later, Dragna arranged for three men, Frank Bompensiero, Biaggio Bonventre, and Sam Bruno, to whack Cohen at his haberdashery at the southeast corner of Halloway and Palm. Three of Cohen's men were hit in the ambush, including Hooky Rothman who caught a shotgun blast to the face. Yet Cohen escaped without a scratch having gone to the bathroom moments before the ambush to wash his hands.

The second attack occurred in front of Sherry's Restaurant on Sunset Boulevard on July 20, 1949. Cohen was there with his entourage—including actor Dee David, Special Agent Harry Cooper, and columnist Florabel Muir—drinking and enjoying the entertainment. But at approximately four A.M., as they were leaving the club, they were met by a storm of gunfire from across the street. One shot from a 30.6 went through Cohen's shoulder, while the rest of the group took the remainder of the buckshot. There was only one fatality in the incident, however. This time it was Neddy Herbert, one of Cohen's most valued friends.

After that Cohen's attorney, Sam Rummel, made sure to alert the LAPD of Cohen's whereabouts,[26] which of course, gave him a veil of police protection. Dragna refused to back down, however, and ordered attacks on Cohen's lieutenants. Both Frank Niccoli and Dave Ogul disappeared a short time later, and their bodies were never found. Then, the following week, two assassins ambushed Sam Rummel outside of his house and placed the business end of a shotgun in his mouth and pulled the trigger.

Cohen finally got the message and made overtures of reconciliation. He never offered to relinquish any of his territories or give any money to the L.A. family, however, and that infuriated the Italians further. So around a year later, Dragna sent Sam Bruno, a seasoned killer with numerous kills to his credit, to wait outside of Cohen's house with a high-powered rifle. Cohen arrived at approximately four A.M., and Bruno unleashed a fusillade of firepower. Three minutes later, the assassin ran off to a getaway vehicle thinking he succeeded. Yet Cohen miraculously emerged from the wreckage once again without a scratch.

A similar scenario played itself out about a week later when Dragna's men climbed into the basement of Cohen's house and planted a bomb directly under his bedroom. What they failed to realize however, was that Cohen had installed a large safe directly under the bed. So when the bomb detonated, it blew *outward* rather than upward, shattering windows three doors away.

## The Bottom Line:

"It was beyond all understanding," wrote Demaris in *The Last Mafioso*. "[Mickey's luck] was beyond any odds ever dreamed up by a gambler, beyond human comprehension. There was something inhuman about it, something almost supernatural."

Cohen had a slightly better explanation, however. As he once told author Peer Nugent, "It's not so hard to understand. Those guys were nothin' but amateurs, that's all. I've seen ten-year-old punk kids that had more on the ball than dem guys."

# THE LEGEND:

In the early days of Los Angeles, racism was so rampant that the mayor used vigilante groups to suppress minorities.

## A Little History:

Racism and its inherent ideological function, has been one of L.A.'s uglier secrets, going on for the better part of the last 200 years. Even a cursory scan of early newspapers, magazines, pamphlets, and novels, shows countless references to "worthless" Indians, "duplicitous" Chinese, "thieving" Mexicans and "lazy" blacks. And that tension ultimately fueled a significant portion of L.A.'s crime rate which, not surprisingly, grew far worse than both San Francisco and New York combined. As the *Los Angeles Star* wrote in 1853, "With all our natural beauty and advantages, there is no country where human life is of so little account. Men hack one another to pieces with pistols and other cutlery, as if God's image were of no more importance than a stray dog."

## The Truth:

With so many murders, robberies, and kidnappings on hand, the courts could only process ten percent of the cases filed by police officers, leaving scores of criminals free. That in turn led to the rise of vigilance committees, which stepped in to take care of outlaws on their own, often with the complete absolution of the mayor himself.[27] Judge Lynch, for example, formed the Los Angeles Rangers in 1854 with some of the city's top judges, lawyers, and businessmen including tycoon Phineas Banning of the Banning Railroad. And there was the Los Angeles Home Guard, another bloodthirsty paramilitary organization, made up of notable citizens, and the much-feared El Monte Rangers, a group of Texas wranglers that specialized in killing Mexicans.[28]

CHS/TICOR/USC Special Collections

As one would expect, there was no regard for the victim's rights in such kangaroo courts. Victims were often dragged from their homes, jail cells, or even churches, and beaten, horse-whipped, tortured, mutilated, or castrated before being strung up on the nearest tree. (If the vigilantes were in a particularly charitable mood however, they might only cut off an ear, nose, or hand.) Twenty-two men suffered such a fate in 1854 alone, while San Francisco only saw eight by comparison.

To outsiders, such barbarism was unbelievably appalling. When J. Ross Browne came to Los Angeles from New York in 1881 for example, he was astounded at the fact so many Angelenos engaged in manhunting with such candor. "Why would you sit at the breakfast table at the Queen of Angels and hear the question of going to shoot men as commonly discussed as would be duck shooting in any other country?" he asked. "And at dinner, the question would be, 'Well, how many did they shoot today?'"

## The Legacy:

One of the worst cases of vigilante justice in California history took place in L.A.'s Chinatown in 1871. At the time the Chinese were competing with Mexicans for most of the hard labor being done in the area. Consequently, they, too, were forced to suffer the ignominy of racism and injustice. As a typical front page article in the *Los Angeles Times* remarked in 1889, "Not only do the Chinese revel in crime, but they delight to draw the detested white race down to their level." As a result, they couldn't vote, own property, or interact in civil decisions whatsoever and many were forced into narcotics, prostitution, and gambling just to make a living.

By the 1860s, two rival gangs had established themselves in Chinatown: the Hong Chows and the Nin Yungs. Both kept their activities well within Chinatown's borders, yet they still made city officials *very* nervous. In 1870, the chief of police tried a stopgap measure utilizing regular sweeps through Chinatown, but that only exacerbated the tension. Finally, in 1871 the tensions exploded into a massive, citywide insurrection.

Historians differ in opinion on how the riot started. The *Los Angeles Star*, for example, claimed that it occurred after a Los Angeles police officer, Robert Thompson, went to issue a warrant to one of the tong members working in what was then called Nigger Alley. But rather than accept the writ, the man produced a gun and shot him to death on the spot. That in turn led to a chain reaction that ended with a virtual slaughter of dozens of innocent men and women.

Yet historian Horace Bell claims that something else happened, something far more consistent with the history of the LAPD. As he suggests in *On the Old West Coast*, Thompson wasn't there to issue a warrant at all, but to steal money that was hidden away in the back of the Chinese man's shop. Thompson had seen the money days earlier after Ah Choy, a local merchant, had taken him there under the auspices of proving that he could make bail. Apparently Choy had been arrested after a rival merchant issued a complaint against him, and the chief of police failed to believe that he had the money to go free on his own recognizance. So Choy took Thompson to his shop and showed him a trunk stuffed with $7,000 in cash. Choy was subsequently let go, and given his court date while Thompson secretly conspired with a fellow officer to sneak into Choy's store later that night and take his savings.

According to Bell, Choy caught Thompson red-handed, and shot him in self-defense. Thompson's partner, meanwhile, was apprehended by some of Choy's associates, and held inside the building until Choy could figure out what to do. That's when word got out that gang members had taken hostages and killed at least one officer, and a mob began to form outside. Choy tried to allay the tension by saying that he would turn himself in, but it was no use.

Moments later a bullet crashed through a window and hit Thompson's partner in the leg. Then all hell broke loose. Choy's associates returned fire as vigilantes from all over the city, commanded by the chief of police himself, descended upon Chinatown, and attacked every Asian that they could get their hands on. By morning twenty-two men were dangling from trees.

Not surprisingly, not a single Anglo received punishment for the melee, yet several "poor Mexicans," and "one lone Irishman," as Bell writes, were given harsh sentences.

## The Bottom Line:

The Chinatown riot of 1871 may have alleviated some of the racial tension toward the Chinese at the time, but it was only temporary. In 1882 Congress passed an act that basically kicked very Chinese "visitor" out of California once and for all and prohibited any more from coming in for the next ten years. The bill was declared unconstitutional, however, and Chinese immigrants were allowed to go on with their lives. But that didn't stop the rampant racism. In 1893 there were anti-Chinese riots in the valley that resulted in numerous bloody skirmishes. Meanwhile two additional factions of tongs, the Bing Kongs and the Hop Sings, had risen out of the ashes of the riot and had taken control of the gambling and narcotics in Chinatown.

By the turn of the century, the mistrust of the Chinese had been transferred to *all* Asians. Thus Japanese and Filipino farmers—who had been *invited* to California as seasonal farm workers—became the victims of vigilante attacks by neighboring farmers as well. Asian leaders eventually went to the state capital to complain, and to their surprise the authorities were sympathetic to their pleas. To compensate for their losses, the governor granted them a munificent offering—a free, one-way ticket back to China.

VIGILANTES

# GETTING TO
# KNOW YOUR
# PENAL CODE

Are you a good citizen? Do you abide by the laws and statutes of California? Well think again. Whether you realize it or not, you may be breaking the law a lot more often than you realize. Thanks to hundreds of outdated laws that have been on the books since the nineteenth century, you can still be fined for any of the following:

★ Staging a bullfight in your backyard.
★ Shooting a rabbit from any public transportation.
★ Selling a snake on the street.
★ Flying a balloon more than five feet off the ground.
★ Washing your neighbor's car without permission.
★ Failing to put money into a parking meter that already has time on it.
★ Wearing backless shoes while driving (driving barefoot is legal however).
★ Residing in a garage or transforming it into a living space.
★ Taking a bath in a business office (in Carmel only).
★ Bathing two babies in a single bathtub at once.
★ Sitting on top of a table at an outdoor restaurant.
★ Dancing cheek to cheek (in Compton only).
★ Wiggling on the dance floor (in Stockton only).
★ Poking meat at an outdoor market.
★ Peeling an orange in a hotel room.
★ Hunting moths under a street lamp.
★ Killing a monarch butterfly.
★ Either selling or possessing a hippopotamus.

# HANKY SPANKY

Misha "Sugar" Levine

According to the good folks at The Pleasure Chest, otherwise known as the "Greatest Erotic Department Store in the World," gay prostitutes in Los Angeles have been using colored handkerchiefs to advertise the kind of sex they're into for decades. Apparently the practice began in the 1940s when lavender hankies or scarves were displayed in breast pockets to signify one's homosexuality. In time, that evolved into a left/right system to differentiate between those that "gave" and those that "received." Now male hustlers have over a hundred different colors, patterns, and fabrics to choose from, each with its own specific meaning. (The right/left system is still employed.) They including the following:

★ MUSTARD = Has eight inches or more.
★ APRICOT = Likes fat men.
★ GOLD = Into two-on-one.
★ MOSQUITO NETTING = Likes sex in public places.
★ BROWN LACE = Into noncircumcised men.
★ LIGHT BLUE = Blow jobs only.
★ RED = Likes fisting.
★ LIGHT GREEN (worn on the right side) = Likes to be humiliated.
★ RED WITH A WHITE STRIPE (worn on the right) = Lies to get shaved.
★ PALE YELLOW (worn on the right) = Likes to be drooled on.
★ CORAL (worn on the right) = Likes to suck toes.
★ MAROON (worn on the left) = Likes menstruating women.
★ MEDIUM BLUE (worn on the left) = Likes cops.
★ DARK PINK (worn on the right) = Enjoys nipple torture.
★ YELLOW (worn on right) = Likes to be urinated on.
★ CREAM (worn on right) = Will suck the cum back out.
★ FUR = Will do bestiality.
★ BROWN = Into feces.

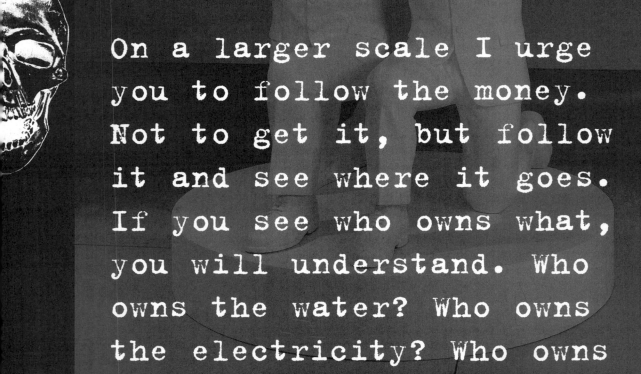

On a larger scale I urge you to follow the money. Not to get it, but follow it and see where it goes. If you see who owns what, you will understand. Who owns the water? Who owns the electricity? Who owns the country?

—OLIVER STONE

Barbara Kruger

# THE SHADOW OF DISCONTENT

## CORRUPTION AND CONSPIRACY IN THE LAND OF SUNSHINE AND HEALTH

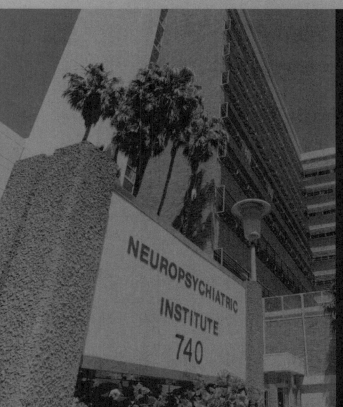

NEUROPSYCHIATRIC INSTITUTE 740

# THE ALLEGATION:

The CIA is shipping heroin and cocaine into the impoverished areas of L.A. to insure that the death rate among African Americans remains high.

Robbie Conal and Deborah Ross/photo by Alan Shaffer

## A Little History:

Despite the CIA's continual denial of covert drug dealing, there's a great deal of evidence suggesting that the agency has been facilitating major drug traffickers for the better part of the last fifty years. But as researcher Alfred W. McKoy suggests in his book, *The Politics of Heroin: CIA Complicity in the Global Drug Trade*, the reasons may have less to do with making money and spreading addiction, than they do with the CIA's obsession with Cold War politics. As McCoy clearly demonstrates, the agency is far more interested in fighting the war against Communism than the war on drugs, and to win that war it

believes that it must align itself with anti-Communist regimes in territories threatened by Communist take-over—even if those same regimes traffic in drug running, war crimes, and Mafia activities. As McKoy writes, "Nothing will stand in the way of what the [CIA] sees as an almost biblical mission: which is to save Western freedom from Communist darkness."

The CIA's direct collaboration with drug manufacturers has never been so cut and dry, however. According to McKoy, the practice began in the 1940s when French intelligence agents moved into the mountainous region of Indochina to support the anti-Communist Hmong tribes at war with Maoist regimes. At the time, the Hmong tribesmen had a rudimentary, yet successful, heroin production which gave them enough money and political clout to survive. To win the war, however, they needed far more money, weapons, and political prowess than they had, which is why the French, who had little money or resources of their own, began nourishing their production of illegal narcotics. That eventually led to "Operation X," a secret collusion between French intelligence agents, drug dealers, and weapons manufacturers.

Not surprisingly, when the CIA moved into Indochina in 1950 to alleviate French troops, they began a cozy relationship with the Hmongs, too. Yet according to McKoy, the agency never profited from heroin production as the French had. After all, the CIA had a healthy budget of its own and didn't need to look for creative ways to fund their guerrilla activities. But by the end of the 1960s, when funds for covert activities began to hemorrhage thanks to the escalation of the Vietnam War, the agency suddenly realized that they, too, had to lean on the Hmong's heroin trade for guns and cash as well. In fact, by 1968, the CIA had financed the construction of nearly a dozen heroin refineries, placed numerous key figures in government positions to help clear shipments though international borders, set up distribution networks with the Mafia, and arranged money-laundering schemes through CIA-controlled banks all over the world.

According to Alexander Cockburn and Jeffery St. Clair, a similar practice occurred once again in Afghanistan in 1979 when U.S. forces were sent in to ostensibly checkmate the advancing Soviet army there, and again in 1980 when the U.S. moved into Nicaragua to combat Cuban-based Sandanista rebels.[1] *Covert Action Quarterly* recently reported that the activity continued right through the 1990s, with drug dealing in both Haiti and Kosovo in 1999.

## Where It Comes From:

In 1996 Gary Webb, a reporter for the *San Jose Mercury News,* discovered that two major drug lords in California, Oscar Danilo Blandon and Norvin Menses, were bringing cocaine into Los Angeles and selling it through a street dealer named "Freeway" Ricky Ross. He also discovered that they were given CIA clearances at Army bases for deliveries, received access to government banks in Florida to launder their money, and given freedom to purchase and transport weapons for the contras *and* street gangs throughout Los Angeles.

Webb couldn't provide any solid evidence of a CIA collusion in the actual drug trafficking, however. Despite numerous testimonials, eyewitness accounts, and public records suggesting as much, he never found a smoking gun to prove that the CIA had initiated the practice. As a result, the mainstream press attacked him with a barrage of recriminations. In 1996, the *Washington Post* ran a story with the headline, *The CIA and Crack: Evidence is Lacking of an*

*Alleged Plot* which debunked certain details in Webb's report—namely the number of tons that Blandon allegedly imported to the U.S. and his allegations that crack was invented in Southern California. Meanwhile the *Los Angeles Times* and the *New York Post* printed their own equally dismissive reports. The former claimed, "There is no evidence that any significant drug profits from the Nicaraguan ring were pumping back to the contras;" while the latter claimed that "the CIA had no record of Mr. Blandon before he appeared as a central figure in the series in the *Mercury News.*"

## The Evidence:

Eventually Webb *did* find evidence to support his theory, however. In fact, he found a lot of evidence. As he wrote in the *LA Weekly* in 1998, "[A CIA report] shows that by 1987 the U.S. government was sitting on six years' worth of cables and reports from field agents, station chiefs, informants, assets, private citizens, and some of the contras themselves all indicating that Ronald Reagan's freedom fighters were shipping planeloads of cocaine and marijuana into the U.S. CIA and Justice Department files bulged with evidence of contra drug running, including eyewitness testimony from inside informants. The CIA had even prepared a detailed briefing on the subject, complete with names and dates for Vice President George Bush."

Moreover, Webb also found documents clearly showing that the CIA deliberately misled U.S. customs agents by supplying false information about Blandon and others. He found a written agreement between Attorney General William French Smith and the head of the CIA William Casey that basically exempts [the CIA] from having to report dealings with drug traffickers at all. And, as if that wasn't enough, he also found evidence to prove that the CIA had its own domestic propaganda operations such as MHCHAOS which was specifically designed to combat news agencies, reporters, and journalists from exposing the operation.[2]

## The Bottom Line:

Despite the overwhelming proof that guys like Blandon were selling tons of illegal drugs, "exotic" weapons, and military communication gear to crack dealers in South Central L.A.—with complete CIA approval—Webb was never able to prove that the CIA were trying to kill off African Americans in the inner city. As he told an audience at Santa Monica's Midnight Special Books in 1998, "I never believed—or wrote—that the CIA had a conspiracy to target South Central L.A. and the African-American community. The CIA doesn't give a damn where these drugs go. The only reason that [the drugs] ended up there was because Blandon heard that the cops in L.A. couldn't care less about South Central, and wouldn't interfere with his operations. It was simply the path of least resistance."[3] (McKoy makes a similar claim in his book, *The Politics of Heroin*, where he claims that there was little evidence to support the idea that the agency ever "directed" the drug specifically into any American city in the 1960s either.)

## The Legacy:

It should be noted that the domestic consumption of cocaine went from eighty-one tons in 1981 to 600 tons in 1991. That, of course, led to a crime rate unparalleled in California history. In fact, the *New York Times* claimed that Los Angeles was the most violent city in the country in 1992, with more homicides per capita than any other metropolitan area in the free world. Meanwhile, L.A. has since become one of the top four bulk cocaine distribution centers in the country according to a recent federal intelligence report, and has shown little, if any, progress in changing that fact.

# THE LEGEND:

The Mafia had Senator Robert Kennedy assassinated at the Ambassador Hotel.

## What Happened:

On June 5, 1968, shortly after giving an acceptance speech for the Democratic nomination for president, Senator Robert Kennedy was ushered through the back entrance of the Ambassador Hotel's Embassy Room, and into the now-infamous pantry. As he made his way through a small crowd of well-wishers he came face to face with Sirhan Bishara Sirhan, a twenty-four-year-old student of Arabic decent, who immediately began squeezing off rounds from a .22-caliber Iver-Johnson cadet revolver. Kennedy fell back into the arms of Thane Eugene Cesar, one of his security guards, as four slugs slammed into his body. Then all hell broke loose. Everybody started screaming and running toward the exits as Sirhan squeezed off more shots and six bodyguards threw themselves on both Sirhan and Kennedy. Finally, after police were summoned, Kennedy slipped into unconsciousness and died a short time later.

## What People Are Saying:

There has never been any question of Sirhan Sirhan's guilt. Dozens of witnesses saw him firing the gun, detectives found a notebook filled with anti-Kennedy scribbles in his apartment, and the LAPD secured a confession while they had him in custody. Yet despite all of the evidence, no one has ever been able to explain *why* he did it.

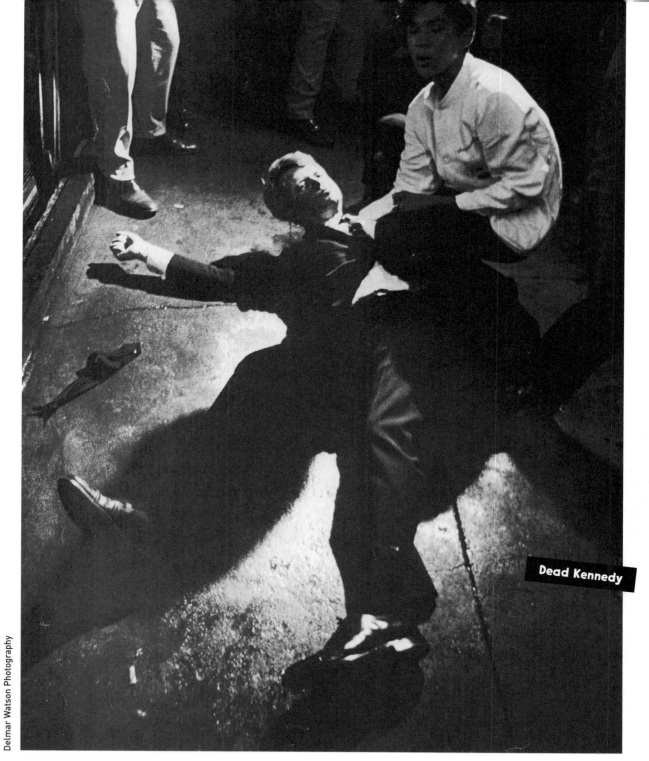

Delmar Watson Photography

Dead Kennedy

In fact, it wasn't until 1969, a full year after the event, and after hundreds of hours of psychotherapy, that he finally admitted his motive. As he allegedly told his psychotherapist, he killed Kennedy because he was a "supporter of the newly formed state of Israel." Yet that only confused the issue further. After all, why choose Kennedy when there were dozens of politicians with far greater impact on Middle Eastern policy than he had?

## A Little History:

Sirhan suffered a minor concussion in 1967 after falling from a horse, which left him with blurred vision and headaches.[4] (He had been training to become a jockey—his lifelong dream.) Some conspiracy theorists allege that through a friend at the track, he was introduced to Dr. William Joseph Bryan, Jr., the president of the American Institute of Hypnosis, who put him into an intensive hypnotherapy program to help him refocus his mind. As a result, he became reclusive, refused to talk to anyone, and went through a complete personality change, as his friends later testified.

A number of researchers have noted that Bryan was no stranger to secret brainwashing experiments either. In the 1950s, he allegedly worked on the CIA's infamous MKULTRA program, the first attempt to create a "remote control assassin" through LSD immersion and hypnosis. He also boasted about being an advisor on *The Manchurian Candidate*, the first movie to address the idea of "programmed assassins."

## The Truth:

In any case, there's a tremendous amount of evidence to suggest that Sirhan never fired the gun that killed Kennedy in the first place. Coroner Thomas Noguchi, who performed one of the most meticulous and professional autopsies of his career, stated unequivocally that the bullet that killed Kennedy was fired from *behind* his head at point-blank range. In fact, all four of the bullets that hit him—one in his lower neck, one in his back, and one that went through his shoulder pad—came from *behind* Kennedy and traveled in an upward angle toward the ceiling. "There is no way that Sirhan's gun could have fired the fatal shot," said Noguchi. "Unless bullets could travel in circles."

Even more confusing were the number of shots fired. Using sound recordings, crime scene photographs, and actual bullets found at the Ambassador Hotel, investigators have determined that ten to thirteen bullets were fired at the scene. Three landed in Kennedy, five in innocent bystanders, three in overhead tiles, and two more in the doorjamb near the entrance. Yet Sirhan's gun could only hold a maximum of *eight* bullets.[5]

Obviously there was another shooter in the room, and in all likelihood, it was either Thane Cesar, the security guard that stood directly behind Kennedy during the melee, or an associate of his. Dozens of witnesses saw Cesar with a gun in his hand, and one later claimed that he saw him "returning fire." That witness later retracted his statement after he received death threats. Moreover there are also records of Cesar purchasing a .22-caliber revolver— exactly like Sirhan's—a couple of months before the assassination.

If Sirhan was under hypnosis at the time of the shooting, as a number of credible psychiatrists have alleged, then Bryan or one of his associates would have had to been at the Ambassador moments before the shooting. And apparently several witnesses saw him in the company of a young woman described as being twentyish, with a shapely figure, peculiar nose, and polka dot dress minutes before the assassination, and according to their testimony she was guiding him around the hotel hours earlier. What's more, that same woman—who was last seen boarding a CIA-owned aircraft the following day—was spotted running through a stairwell with a man in a gold sweater, shortly after the assassination, screaming, "We shot him, we shot him!" And when one witness asked her, "Who'd you shoot?" She gleefully replied, "Senator Kennedy!"

## The Bottom Line:

Who killed Robert Kennedy? It was well known that the Mob despised Kennedy, and researchers have found numerous links to connect different mafiosi to the murder,[6] including Sam Giancana of the Chicago outfit. Still the complexity of the operation and the extraordinary cover-up by the LAPD afterward has led a number of theorists to conclude that the CIA and the FBI were also in on it from the start. After all, Kennedy was not only trying to break up organized crime in

America, he was also trying to break up the CIA and replace J. Edgar Hoover of the FBI, agencies that have a long history of working with the Mafia on assassination plots.

Yet that may only be the tip of the iceberg. As the recent investigation into the assassination of Martin Luther King in Tennessee suggests, a consortium of war-industry manufacturers may have been involved with the killing as well.[7] In a controversial case, King's defendants successfully argued that King's antiwar effort posed a direct threat to corporations such as Hughes, Boeing, and Grumman—corporations making a fortune off military contracts in Vietnam—and that he had to be silenced. And if that's true, then it raises interesting questions about Kennedy's assassination, since he, too, opposed further U.S. intervention in Southeast Asia. (Unlike then-president Lyndon B. Johnson who actively increased the war effort partly to appease those very same companies.)

# THE RUMOR:

Dr. Timothy Leary was a secret agent for the CIA.

The politics of ecstasy: Dr. Timothy Leary makes a point

## What People Are Saying:

In the late 1960s, *The Challenge*, the official organ of the Progressive Labor Party, printed an editorial claiming that Dr. Timothy Leary had a secret, right-wing agenda. "Though he claims to be a rebel and against the system," wrote *The Challenge*, "Leary does his very best to help the vicious rulers of this country by advising people, especially young people, to 'detach yourself from involvement in secular external social gains.' In Leary's mind, 'social gains' include protests—protests against corrupt school administrations, the freedom struggle, the anti–Vietnam War fight."

And as if that wasn't damning enough, *The Challenge* also claimed that Leary, who built his career on promoting LSD to the masses, had been working with government agents to help secure the arrests of key counterculture figures, some of which were close friends of his.

The Shadow of Discontent

235

To understand how his friends and colleagues could have arrived at such a conclusion, it's important to go back a few years, to the moment that Leary took magic mushrooms for the first time in Cuernavaca, Mexico in the early 1960s. Because that was the moment that he shed his previous persona of the slightly nerdy—and sober—behavioral psychologist at Harvard University, and became the most vocal proponent of hallucinogenics in the world. As he described the experience later: "It was above all and without question the deepest religious experience of my life. I discovered that beauty, revelation, sensuality, the cellular history of the past, God, the devil—all lie inside my body, outside my mind."

Upon returning to the university, he initiated the Psilocybin Research Project with some of his associates, primarily to monitor the effects of psychedelics on the subconscious. And by the following year he had a veritable parade of hipsters beating a path to his door, including Thelonius Monk, John Coltrane, Jack Kerouac, and William Burroughs. His most important guest, however, was a character named Michael Hollingshead, an employee of the British Cultural Exchange who showed up with a dose of Sandoz LSD-25, a highly potent synthetic hallucinogen manufactured in Switzerland. At the time Leary was still a virgin when it came to acid, but after he finally came down several hours later, he gave up psilocybin once and for all, and began using LSD exclusively.

Meanwhile, unbeknownst to Leary, the CIA had its own LSD research program in the works, one that involved numerous high-level, top-secret experiments dating back to the 1940s, and the agency was less than happy about Leary's constant proselytizing in public.[8] Yet despite warnings, ultimatums, and flat-out threats, the gangly doctor continued to hawk the drug's virtues in magazines, newspapers, and television shows across the country. Finally, after scores of complaints, police harassment, and public ridicule, Leary and his associate, Richard Alpert, were summarily dismissed from their teaching duties at Harvard and forced to go into private practice.

Such disgrace had its upside, however, as Leary's private LSD practice became more popular than ever, so much so that he found himself the subject of constant, invidious attacks by the DA's office. Finally, he packed his bags and moved to a commune in Laguna Beach called the Brotherhood of Eternal Love in 1968, the same year that Congress passed legislation making the sale of LSD a felony. The commune was in all respects, a truly munificent enterprise. Members grew their own food, ran their own market, organized yoga and meditation centers, taught Eastern philosophies, and preached peace, love, and understanding. Unbeknownst to the general public, however, they were also the largest distributor of illegal LSD in the world. The commune purportedly earned $200,000,000 per year by distributing Orange Sunshine, an extraordinarily strong dose of LSD formulated by the infamous San Francisco acid king, Augustus Owsley III.

Things took a turn for the worse when two Laguna Beach police officers found Leary smoking a joint in his car and he was subsequently booked on possession charges and sent to prison for an astounding ten years. Meanwhile the commune itself suffered its own series of setbacks, including the fatal overdose of Farmer John, the original founder of the commune, the arrest of Owsley in Berkeley, and the accidental drowning of a young girl on the Brotherhood's property.

Things were looking pretty bleak when, out of the blue, a character named Ronald Hadley Stark stepped into the picture and took control of the commune. Looking like a swarthy Alfred Hitchcock, Stark was less than popular with the staff, yet within days he had reworked the group's financial structure, hired new LSD chemists in Belgium, and worked out a plan to make the commune richer than ever before.

In fact, most were astounded at the amount of acid that Stark brought in with his very first shipment: twenty kilos, enough for fifty million acid trips.

And this is where things get really weird. In 1970, a short time after his incarceration, Leary managed to escape from prison with the help of a radical left-wing faction called the Weather Underground. From there he went to Europe where he met up with Eldridge Cleaver, the leader of the Black Panthers. And according to Leary, the idea was to talk to him about the violence that the Panthers were fomenting throughout the U.S. But the meeting went poorly— apparently after Leary tried to foist some acid on Cleaver—and he was forced to leave in a hurry. From there he went to Switzerland where he was finally apprehended by American agents in 1971 and extradited to California to face conspiracy charges.

In 1972, thirteen government agencies descended upon the Brotherhood's commune in Laguna Beach and arrested everybody in sight. Stark, however, was nowhere to be found. Curiously, he escaped at the last minute, flying to Sicily where he eventually took over narcotics operations for the Mafia.[9]

### The Truth:

Did Leary secretly work for the CIA? Researchers like to point out a number of curious coincidences that seem to suggest that he was. After all, Leary had been associating with CIA agents since the 1950s, both socially and professionally. In fact, his original partner in the Psilocybin Research Center, Frank Barron, was alleged to be a CIA affiliate, and some have argued that Leary was in the company of secret agents at the time that he was apprehended in Switzerland, and that means that he may have found Cleaver under the auspices of the CIA. Moreover, when Stark was finally apprehended in 1975 with 4,600 kilos of heroin and cocaine, an Italian judge stated that

there was "scrupulously enumerated proof" that he had been a CIA agent since 1960. Additionally, it is also known that the money used to finance the Brotherhood's operation in Laguna was channeled through Castle Bank in the Bahamas, a known CIA proprietary. And there's also evidence that the CIA ordered 100 million LSD tablets to send to enemy troops in Vietnam, possibly through the Brotherhood's distribution network essentially to render them incapacitated. "If you look back, many things that we thought were accidents turned out were not accidents," said Leary in a 1978 issue of *High Times*. "The entire LSD movement itself was sponsored originally by the CIA, to whom I give great credit. I would not be here today if it had not been for the foresight and prestige of the CIA psychologists. So give the CIA credit for being truly an intelligence agency."

Nonetheless, according to recently released FBI files, the extent of Leary's involvement with the agency may be less extensive than some have suggested. Apparently the only time that he truly worked with the CIA was shortly after his arrest in 1971 and his subsequent deportation back to the U.S. on conspiracy charges. That's when Leary was threatened with multiple life sentences and forced to turn state's evidence to save his hide. That may have been less than noble, yet according to a number of sources, he never disclosed any truly damaging information. In fact, some of the members of the Weather Underground who were ratted out by Leary, in 1970 after helping him escape, later claimed that they understood his actions. In other words, he wasn't a secret agent, but a snitch.

> "The entire LSD movement itself was sponsored originally by the CIA, to whom I give great credit. I would not be here today if it had not been for the foresight and prestige of the CIA psychologists."

# THE RUMOR:

Lockheed Martin sells fighter jets to rogue nations behind the back of the U.S. government.

Paul Young

mental in helping Nabusuke Kishi succeed to prime minister earlier in the decade.

Apparently Kodama accepted Lockheed's proposal, and was given a base salary of $138,000, plus a $4 million bonus for each and every "package sale" that he made (meaning three planes or more). And over the course of the next twenty years he proved his weight in gold. Not only did he convince key figures within Japan's military complex to purchase Lockheed fighter jets, he also managed to sway Japan's commercial airline industry to buy Lockheed's new wide-bodied passenger jet, the Tri-Star L1011—all through extortion, grafts, influence peddling, and sheer intimidation.

## Where It Comes From:

This rumor is basically true. Shortly after the close of World War II, Lockheed actively arranged and implemented a number of covert deals to peddle their firepower to foreign leaders. In 1956 for example, a senior sales executive for Lockheed secretly approached Yoshio Kodama, a notorious figure among Japan's power brokers, and asked him to "persuade" certain military leaders to buy some of their jets. As David Kaplan and Alec Dubro note in their book, *Yakuza*, Kodama had extensive ties to Japan's most powerful crime family, and was well versed in strong-arm tactics, extortion, gun running, drug trafficking, and murder. Yet he was also one of the most powerful political figures in the country, with a sphere of influence that could literally place politicians in office. In fact, he was instru-

## The Context:

Japan was not the only country that Lockheed went after, however. Similar operations were mounted in Italy, Indonesia, Saudi Arabia, Turkey, Spain, Brazil, and the Philippines. In war-torn Germany, for example, Lockheed officials apparently went after Franz Joseph Strauss, Germany's minister of defense, and made substantial donations to his fledgling political party, the Christian Socialist Union, an extreme right-wing group that many considered to be an extension of the Nazi party.

Finally, in 1975, the entire operation was exposed when Northrop, one of Lockheed's main competitors, admitted to a Senate subcommittee that *they* had secretly made arrangements with a number of overseas "consultants" to help them sell weapons, too, just as Lockheed had done in

L.A. EXPOSED

Japan. The subcommittee responded by initiating a comprehensive investigation of all weapons manufacturers in the U.S., including Boeing, McDonnell Douglas and Grumman. That in turn led to one of the most embarrassing scandals of the Cold War era, with dozens of indictments levied against top aerospace executives and public officials alike, including Treasurer Robert Waters who committed suicide shortly after being subpoenaed.

## President Indicates Help for Lockheed
### Also Will Seek Federal Projects for West to Ease Unemployment

In fact, as Kaplan and Dubro suggest in their book, Kodama wasn't just helping to sell Lockheed planes in Japan, he also funneled millions of CIA dollars—$12.6 million to be exact—into political and gangster coffers alike. The purpose was twofold: first to promote the growth of the Liberal Democratic Party (the LDP), a staunch, ultra-nationalist, political faction that would be beholden to the U.S.;[10] and second to bring the various Yakuza families operating in Japan under their thumb.

## The Real Story:

There's much more to the story than meets the eye, however. In the case of Lockheed, for example, there's substantial evidence to prove that the CIA was involved with their operation from the start. Apparently it began with the American occupation of Japan in 1945, shortly after Japan's unconditional surrender. That's when CIA operatives began infiltrating various Japanese leftist fronts in an attempt to checkmate Communist advancement in the area. But to do that, the agency believed that it had to collaborate with the Yakuza, Japan's right-leaning organized crime group, and gain their trust—and muscle. Kodama thus became an indispensable agent for the CIA, since his influence over Yakuza leaders was without peer. In fact, it was the CIA that released Kodama from Tokyo's Sugamo Prison in 1948, where he was awaiting trial at the international military tribunal for war crimes; and it was also the CIA that sponsored many of Kodama's "black bag jobs" in China and elsewhere, which included smuggling drugs and weapons of mass destruction.

## The Legacy:

Has the practice disappeared? In 1989 the *New York Times* reported that the U.S. was catching up to Russia in arms sales to third-world countries. In that year alone, U.S. weapons manufacturers sold over $9.2 billion worth of weapons to foreign countries, and by 1996 it was said that the "big eight," which includes Lockheed, were providing thirty-five percent of all the weapons used around the world.[11] That pales in comparison to recent figures, however. Thanks to the extraordinary salesmanship of the Clinton Administration, that figure jumped to sixty-three percent by 1998. So with that in mind, it should be of no surprise that the U.S. spends just as much time *starting* wars in foreign territories as it does condemning them.

FIGHTER JETS

# THE ALLEGATION:

Mass murderer Charles Manson was secretly working for the FBI.

## What People Are Saying:

In the early 1970s, Mae Brussell, the legendary talk-show host and researcher, claimed that she found evidence that Charles Manson, the diminutive cult leader responsible for at least nine murders in California, had a cozy relationship with the FBI. In fact, she even went so far as to say that he was an assassin for the agency. As she put it, "The FBI had direct orders to break up all radical leftist groups by any means necessary. Black leaders were to be neutralized by FBI provocateurs, which included assassination when necessary . . . and Charles Manson had the ability and the desire to carry out some of those assassinations."[12]

## The Evidence:

When Paul Krassner investigated Brussell's theory for the *Realist*, he uncovered some interesting evidence of his own. A former deputy sheriff, Preston Guillory, told him that the sheriff's department had specific instructions *not* to arrest Manson despite dozens of reports of illegal activities going on at the Spahn Ranch. "My contention is this," said Guillory. "The reason Manson was left on the street was because our department thought that he was going to launch an attack on the Black Panthers. We were getting intelligence briefings that Manson was anti-black and he had supposedly killed a black leader. He was a very ready tool, apparently, because he did have some racial hatred and he wanted to vent it. But they hadn't anticipated that he might attack anyone other than the Panthers."

To back his theory, Guillory stated a number of interesting coincidences. For example, just before the Tate/LaBianca killings in 1969, Manson was arrested twice for statutory rape, yet he was released without being charged. Even more vexing, however, was that he was still on parole at the time, and no one has ever been able to figure out how a parolee could escape incarceration for committing a felony—not once, but *twice*. "I always thought he was a snitch," says Krassner. "That's the only explanation I had for why they would leave him alone. But the question was who was calling the shots? How far up the ladder did it go?"

Judging from the FBI's extensive campaign against the Black Panther party in the 1960s and 1970s, it may have gone all the way up to J. Edgar Hoover himself. After all, both Hoover and Manson had their own plans on how to escalate the bloodshed between militant African Americans in Los Angeles. The former had his COINTEL programs and the latter had his Helter Skelter. Both were involved with Vacaville Prison in California where covert LSD brainwashing experiments were being conducted by CIA operatives. Both had access to an American Indian campsite located a short distance from Manson's

> "I always thought he was a snitch."

**New Evidence Reveals...**

# CHARLES MANSON IS ILLEGITIMATE SON OF ADOLF HITLER

home base at the Spahn Ranch—a campsite initially set up by the FBI to monitor subversives. And both seemed to be after Voytek Frykowski, a long time friend of Roman Polanski's, who was later found slaughtered at Sharon Tate's house in 1969. (As the theory goes, the former wanted Frykowski for international drug trafficking and the latter wanted Frykowski because the FBI asked him to take him out.)

## What It All Means:

Such parallels may make for enticing conspiracy theories, yet the evidence is still purely speculative at this point. Nonetheless, it's not hard to understand the public's extraordinary fascination with Manson. Since his incarceration in 1970, he has taken on a folk-hero status among certain disenfranchised groups—in particular, young, insecure, fringe-following, white males. After all, Manson not only tried to build a private all-white utopia populated by young nubile women ready to do his bidding, he also attacked every mainstream ideal represented by Sharon Tate and Hollywood. For folklorists and psychiatrists alike, that makes Manson the symbol of the Lion King, the dark, sinister forces of the unconscious, which when ignored, ultimately explode in paroxysms of repressed urges. Perhaps that's why serial killers remain so popular with disenfranchised whites. Indeed, they not only embody the most vile impulses imaginable—impulses that are the very antithesis of mainstream, white authority figures—but embody their own infantile desires, oedipal wishes, and arrested ego development.

# THE RUMOR:

The staff at the McMartin preschool sexually abused their children and performed satanic rituals in secret underground tunnels.

## McMartin Case Exams Show Sex Abuse, Doctor Testifies

## Where It Comes From:

Los Angeles experienced a tremendous rumor-panic after Mrs. Judy Johnson called the Manhattan Beach Police Department in 1984 and claimed that her son had been sexually sodomized by a "Mr. Ray" at the McMartin pre-school. Mr. Ray was presumed to be Raymond Buckey, a member of the McMartin staff, and a preliminary examination of Johnson's son showed proof of sexual abuse. A short time later, dozens of children began making similar claims—suggesting that Buckey had forced them to perform in pornographic movies; engage in oral and anal sex with strangers (often in far away places); drink blood; lie in coffins; and par-ticipate in occult animal sacrifices. That led to one of the most expensive criminal trials in American history, with 300 criminal indict-ments against seven McMartin staff members and three years of sensational news coverage. In 1983, most seemed to be on the side of the par-ents, but by the end of the year, shortly after the newly appointed DA Ira Reiner stepped into the picture, all but fifty-two counts were dropped against the McMartins and public opinion shifted dramatically. Suddenly reporters claimed that there wasn't enough evidence to back up molestation charges; child psychologists claimed that the children were either coaxed or told what to say during the interviews, and Judy Johnson, the woman who initiated the panic,

was painted as a woman with severe mental problems.[13]

Debbie Nathan, an award-winning journal-ist and reporter, failed to find any credible proof of molestation and decided that the entire affair was a hoax. And 60 Minutes weighed in with their own investigation which suggested that it was the McMartins that were the real victims in the drama.

Finally, in 1991, after six years and $15 mil-lion in taxpayer dollars, a jury declared that Virginia McMartin was innocent of all counts. Raymond Buckey, on the other hand, failed to come out unscathed. While he was cleared of thirty-nine of the fifty-two counts, the jury dead-locked on the remaining thirteen. He was even-tually set free after his second trial ended in a hung jury.

## The Evidence:

Despite the media's blanket dismissal of the charges, there's some curious evidence that can-not be discounted so easily—some of which has been deliberately suppressed by law enforcement officials and the media alike. Many of the chil-dren, for example, showed signs of sexual abuse, including venereal diseases and rectal bleeding. Moreover, during one of its preliminary reports, the Los Angeles Times claimed that medical examiners "found scars, tears, enlarged body

# McMartin School Abuses Far Greater Than Indictment Indicates, D.A. Says

openings, and other evidence indicating blunt-force trauma consistent with the repeated sodomy and rape." Nonetheless, that same report was later discounted by physicians who claimed that the wounds could have been self-inflicted, or that the evidence proved nothing.

Perhaps even more vexing was the fact that many of the children claimed that the crimes were committed in underground tunnels beneath the school. Yet when District Attorney Ira Reiner took a team of surveyors to the property, he failed to find any tunnels to speak of. On the other hand, when a private investigator, Ted Gunderson, a twenty-eight-year-old veteran of the FBI, went to the same area under the auspices of concerned parents in the area, he found *several* tunnels. In fact, he found one that ran from the bathroom, hidden by a rollaway bathtub; another that led to a large nine-foot chamber hidden beneath the property; and another that ran to an apartment building next door. Nonetheless, the LAPD refused to take Gunderson's discovery seriously, despite the fact that he had credible documents of the excavation as performed by a professional archeologist, two professional geologists, and a photographer. And that's because the grounds were bulldozed a short time later.

Yet if the McMartins were molesting children at their school, the question remains, how could they have orchestrated a conspiracy of such magnitude? How could someone like Raymond Buckey sway city officials, the LAPD,

and the national, mainstream press? According to researchers such as Alex Constantine, who documented Gunderson's findings in his *Constantine Report,* the answer is obvious. The sexual molesters named by the children may have been very prominent figures, including actors, sports figures, and politicians. And no one wanted that kind of information released.[14] On the other hand, the McMartins were not found to be responsible and all charges against them were dismissed.

## What It All Means:

As some sociologists have pointed out, the panic over the McMartin case may have been compounded by the emotional instability of the times. The 1980s were, after all, a period of considerable repression, and stories of child abuse, as horrific as they may be, may have served a psychological function when played out on a grand scale as the McMartin trial was. For in times of enhanced oppression, children tend to represent a lost innocence or purity that the public yearns to protect and embrace—an innocence representing the subconscious and its submission to the ego. Yet in the case of the McMartin scandal, the battle was less about the children's innocence than it was about the "innocence" of institutions such as parenthood, the education system, and the media itself.

# FBI Probes Possible Preschool Pornography Filming

Barbara Kruger

Loves of a blonde: Barbara Kruger's homage to the Kennedy clan

## What Happened:

On August 5, 1962, at approximately 4:30 A.M., officers found the nude body of Marilyn Monroe in the bedroom of her home at 12305 Fifth Helena Drive in Westwood, California. She was still holding the receiver of a telephone in one hand and a mink coat in the other. Empty vials of prescription drugs were found strewn about the floor, a half-empty bottle of champagne sat next to her bed, and a Frank Sinatra record was still playing on a nearby turntable. Theodore J. Curphey, chief medical examiner/coroner, eventually concluded that she had died at approximately 8:30 in the evening after taking an overdose of thirteen milligrams of Nembutal and eight milligrams of chloral hydrate pills. It was ruled a suicide.

## A Little History:

Most conspiracy theories about Marilyn's death seem to go back to her alleged affair with John F. Kennedy, the thirty-fifth president of the United States. According to a number of testimonials, their affair apparently began after meeting at the national Democratic convention in downtown L.A. in 1960, where Kennedy was campaigning for the presidential nomination. From there they met again at Romanoff's restaurant in Beverly Hills during a reception there, and once again at Peter Lawford's house in Malibu, where they allegedly consummated their relationship for

## Was she murdered because she knew too much?

the first time during an after-hours party. Yet opinions vary on how many times they met after that. White House phone logs prove that they spoke on the phone on numerous occasions, yet proving that the two had physical affairs has been difficult. Adela Gregory and Milo Speriglio, the authors of *Crypt 33: The Final Word,* claim that the FBI took dozens of pictures of them having sex in various locations, including an unnamed swimming pool, an unidentified bedroom, and an anonymous hotel room somewhere.

On August 1, 1962, John's younger brother, Robert, arrived in Los Angeles to give a speech to the Bar Association. Apparently he met Marilyn later that evening at Lawford's Malibu house for an impromptu dinner. Some have speculated that Marilyn organized the dinner herself, while others claim that RFK arranged the affair, primarily to tell her to stay away from his brother. In any case, the two supposedly ended up making love that night and Marilyn allegedly fell in love once again.

On August 4, 1962, Marilyn told writer Bob Slatzer that she was going to tell the world about her relationship with Bobby and announce their plans to marry.[15] But Bobby never had plans to make her his wife, and he allegedly gave her another ultimatum. That forced Marilyn, who was already suffering from intense emotional pain, to claim that she was going to expose the contents of her diary—contents that allegedly included some pretty unsavory tidbits regarding the Kennedy's collusion with organized crime members. As the theory goes, Robert either had to have her silenced to protect himself, or Marilyn simply killed herself out of her own masochistic self-hatred.

On the other hand, there seems to be some evidence that her death may have been part of the Mafia's personal vendetta against the Kennedy administration. As Chuck Giancana suggests in *Double Cross: The Inside Story of Sam Giancana,* the Mafia had a long-standing relationship with the Kennedy family, in par-

ticular Joe Kennedy, and hoped to use that relationship to their own ends. So with the help of Sam "Momo" Giancana, the head of the Chicago family in the 1960s, and Frank Sinatra, the Mafia allegedly put their muscle behind JFK to ensure his election in 1960, and in return were given the assurance that they were going to get free reign of the underworld. But by 1962 it had become painfully obvious that the Kennedy administration had no intention of keeping their end of the bargain. In 1960, for example, a mere nineteen organized crime figures had been indicted thanks to J. Edgar Hoover's protection. But within the first year of the Kennedy administration, 121 mafiosi were indicted, and thanks to RFK's tireless efforts, the majority went to prison. That left the Mafia with one option—to get Bobby out of the way.

Some historians have suggested quite convincingly that J. Edgar Hoover was already under the Mafia's thumb after securing some private pictures of him in sexually compromising positions with his gay lover, Clyde Tolson, and there may be some truth to the idea that they tried to do the same with RFK in 1962.

## The Theory:

After Marilyn was snubbed by RFK for the last time, she checked into the Cal-Neva Lodge, a gambling casino/hotel in Nevada co-owned by Frank Sinatra. Meanwhile, a team of surveillance experts hired by the Mafia went to work at her house in Westwood, setting up cameras and recording equipment. Then the following day, Lawford set up another dinner party in Robert's honor—at Sinatra's urging—where he would play on Kennedy's soft spot for Marilyn, and convince him that he had to go over and see her just one more time. That would give the Mob plenty of opportunities to catch Kennedy with his hand in the cookie jar. The plan fell apart, however, when Kennedy realized how intoxicated

Marilyn was and decided to go home instead. Perhaps Marilyn had already taken the fatal overdose by then, or perhaps the idea was that Kennedy would be implicated in her death. In any case, she died a short time later.

## What Probably Happened:

The real key to Marilyn's mystery seems to lie in the hands of the man that gave Marilyn her drugs in the first place, Dr. Ralph Greenson. Apparently on August 5, the day of her death, Dr. Greenson gave her a fresh prescription of Nembutal. Yet when her body was found the following morning, all fifty pills were gone. Those believing that she committed suicide have suggested that she simply ate all fifty. In fact Marilyn's biographer, Barbara Leaming, claims that she downed the pills just to get revenge on Greenson. Yet Thomas Noguchi, the L.A. coroner that performed the autopsy, failed to find *any* trace of the drug in her stomach or intestinal tract. That means that Marilyn had to administer the pills, all fifty of them, *rectally*. And, indeed, there's no doubt that she could have done that on her own, but if she was trying to kill herself it certainly seems more plausible that she would have simply downed them with a glass of water. In other words, in all likelihood, someone helped her.

At least one neighbor claimed to have seen Greenson arrive at Marilyn's house in the early evening with a man looking like Robert Kennedy. And if Kennedy was there, he was there to have a showdown with the already intoxicated actress, and tell her to back off from the Kennedy family once and for all. That may have caused Marilyn to become hysterical, perhaps to the point of hurting herself. That in turn may have forced Greenson to order everyone out of the room so that he could give her a sedative. There are records that Greenson then left and met up with the rest of the group for dinner at a nearby restaurant. And there are also records of Marilyn trying to make a number of frantic phone calls to Lawford around the same time. In any case, the group apparently reconvened at Marilyn's house two hours later, and that's when they found her unconscious—maybe even dead. Whether Kennedy was there or not is still a matter of speculation.[16]

## The Bottom Line:

Did RFK order the OD? Did the Mafia pull it off? Were they working together? Or was it simply an accident?

Despite the hundreds of books written on the subject, no one has ever been able to solve the mystery conclusively. Part of the reason, of course, has to do with the cover-up done by federal agents: telephone records were erased, Marilyn's diary was destroyed, a crumpled piece of paper with Kennedy's phone number—supposedly found in Marilyn's hand—disappeared, and alibis were invented and validated. In other words, until there is a full disclosure of FBI files—including the tape-recorded surveillance of her house—no one will ever know for sure.

# THE LEGEND:

L.A. would be as dry as the Sahara if William Mulholland hadn't conspired with L.A. city leaders to "rape" the Owens Valley, and steal its water.

## What It All Means:

This is perhaps one of the most widely believed conspiracy theories in L.A. history: that William Mulholland, the former head of the Department of Water and Power engaged in deception, widespread violence, and wholesale murder to transform what was once the barren, desolate wasteland of Los Angeles into the lush paradise that it is today. The ideological function of such a story should be fairly obvious: that Los Angeles is completely artificial; that beneath its glistening, idyllic façade, is something "sinister and barren," as critic Mike Davis has suggested, "incapable of sustaining even a tiny fraction of the current multitudes on its own." What's more, the legend also suggests that L.A.'s life force (symbolized by water) is the result of a criminal act (symbolized by Mulholland), and therefore tainted, unworthy, and counterfeit.

## Where It Comes From:

Critic Morrow Mayo was one of the first reporters to bring the story of the Owens Valley to the public's attention. In an impassioned essay written in the 1930s, he painted a moving portrait of the original Owens Valley homesteaders and their plight to transform the valley into a thriving, farming community. And according to

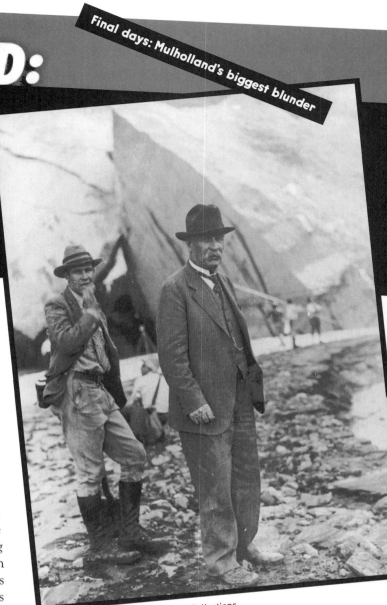

Los Angeles Examiner/USC Special Collections

him, they succeeded brilliantly. Not only did they succeed in harnessing the wealth of runoff from the nearby Sierras, but they produced bountiful crops and an almost idyllic farming cooperative. That changed with the arrival of William Mulholland, however. With papers signed by the mayor of L.A. and President Roosevelt himself, the water czar laid out his plans for what was going to be "the marvel of the modern world," a 244-mile aqueduct stretching from the Owens Valley to the heart of Los Angeles. And as compensation, he claimed, he

The land L.A. never forgot

fortune off the deal. And when the farmers tried to retaliate by sabotaging key DWP facilities along the aqueduct, Mulholland lined his waterway with armed guards and fought back with unlimited firepower. To date no one actually knows how many people died in the skirmishes, but it has been estimated to be in the hundreds.

## The Truth:

A number of historians have debunked Mayo and McWilliams's version of the Owens Valley incident, however. Historian Remi A. Nadeau, for example, claims that the actual events were much less dramatic than most people would like to believe. In his well-researched book, *The Water Seekers*, he admits that L.A.'s forefathers used "questionable political methods to kill federal development in the valley and undermine the ability for them to farm effectively." And he also admits that Mulholland's consortium, which was backed by President Roosevelt, benefited financially from the enterprise, primarily through extralegal activities and unethical business practices. Yet the farmers were not driven from their homes as many have speculated, or subjected to violent attacks, sabotage, or assassinations.

## The Legacy:

In any case, the myth lives on—and so does the war. In 1998 the valley residents were forced to file suit against California's Department of Water and Power—and this time they won. It seems that the Owens Valley—which turned into a dustbowl shortly after the aqueduct was built—was by far the largest single source of air pollution in the U.S. On windy days as much as eleven tons of dust partly tinged with arsenic and toxic metals, filled the air and sent thousands of people to the hospital every year. As a result, L.A. was ordered to return some of its water—nine percent of its intake—to irrigate some of Owens Valley again, a move that could have been avoided if Mulholland had kept his word in the first place.

was going to provide them with their own reservoir, a new and improved irrigation system, new housing developments, and a direct rail line to Los Angeles.

Mayo and others have suggested that Mulholland never actually planned to build any of the amenities that he promised. Instead he simply diverted *all* of the water to Los Angeles and left the farmers to deal the consequences, namely land devoid of irrigation. As Mayo put it, "The City of Los Angeles moved through this valley like a devastating plague. It was ruthless, stupid, cruel, and crooked."

Another critic, Carey McWilliams, added to Mayo's thesis when he published his classic *Southern California: An Island on the Land* in 1946 claiming that the entire scenario was designed by a cabal of rich power brokers—including Mulholland, L.A. civic leaders, industrialists, and politicians—who were bent on making a

# THE LEGEND:

Jack Parsons, one of the cofounders of Jet Propulsion Laboratories in Pasadena, practiced black magic with Scientology's L. Ron Hubbard while developing missiles for the U.S. War Department.

## A Little Background:

The legend of John "Jack" Whiteside Parsons began in 1936, on a moonless Halloween night in a remote valley of the San Gabriel Mountains. That's where he and a team of fellow Caltech scientists launched one of the first rockets in American aeronautical history; a rocket that eventually led to the formation of Jet Propulsion Laboratories, a big-science division of Caltech, and an essential precursor to NASA. In fact, Wernher von Braun, the genius behind Germany's military rocket research program of 1937, was so impressed with Parsons that he once called him the true father of American aerospace.

If Parsons, who was the first to perfect solid rocket fuel, failed to achieve the recognition that he deserved, it was partly because of his private life. After all, the wild-eyed, darkly handsome, maverick was known to indulge in sci-fi novels, symbolist poetry, arcane sexual practices, and all kinds of occult rituals and ceremonies. That made him somewhat less than credible in the eyes of his peers. In fact, some called him a "devil worshiper" behind his back and made fun of his bohemian lifestyle in the press.

In 1939, Parsons happened to chance upon a secret fraternal order in Pasadena called Ordo Templi Orientis (OTO). Originally based in Germany under the direction of Theodor Reuss, the OTO was devised on Masonic foundations, and devoted to the teachings of such arcane subjects as Rosicrucianism, the Illuminist movement, the Qabala, and Early Christian Gnosticism. Aleister Crowley had taken over leadership of the order from his home base in Scotland at the time that Parsons and his wife Helen joined in 1939, and under his direction the OTO shifted into slightly darker waters, with elaborate black masses and sex magic rituals.[17]

Parsons showed remarkable skill at learning the OTO's curriculum and fellow members were astonished at how easily he moved through the ranks. So when the supreme "Outer Head", Aleister Crowley, began thinking about replacing the then-leader of the lodge, Wilfred T. Smith, with someone a little more reliable, Parsons, aka *Thelma Obtentum Procedero Amoris Nuptiae*, was the natural choice.[18] If Crowley resisted at first, it was because he considered Parsons "too bohemian," as he put it; too swayed by popular culture to be a true leader of the OTO. Nonetheless, after Smith announced that he was quitting the lodge, Crowley caved to pressure and appointed Parsons the grand master of the OTO's Pasadena Agape Lodge in 1943.

## The Evidence:

In the mid-1940s, Parsons's home along Pasadena's Millionaires' Row became a popular hangout for writers, artists, and musicians— much to the dismay of his neighbors who often complained of orgies, marijuana use, and loud music. Sci-fi writers in particular enjoyed his hospitality, including Ray Bradbury, Robert Heinlein, and Jack Williamson. But it was L. Ron Hubbard, the future leader of Scientology that apparently took the greatest interest in the scene. He arrived in 1945 for one of Parsons's

The Shadow of Discontent

many parties, and enjoyed himself to such a degree that he returned a couple of months later asking for a place to stay. Parsons demurred and offered him a trailer in the backyard where Hubbard allegedly seduced Parsons's then-wife Sara a short time later.

In January 1946, after fully inculcating Hubbard in the ways of the OTO, the two men set out to conduct a series of occult experiments based on Crowley's *Book of Law* and John Dee's Enochian manuscripts. Parsons described the experiments in his notes as "relating to the invocation of an elemental being, or Goddess, or force, called Babalon." Apparently Parsons believed that the world was under the influence of an elemental spirit called Horus at the time, a terrible, destructive energy that was leading civilization toward chaos and catastrophe. As he wrote in his *Book of Babalon*, "[Horus's] manifestations may be noted in the destruction of old institutions and ideas, the discovery and liberation of new sexual energies, and the trend toward power governments, homosexuality, infantilism, and schizophrenia." By invoking Babalon, he believed, he was going to usher in a new harmonious age which would ultimately put an end to patriarchy and rapacious world destruction once and for all. But to do that he would have to impregnate this feminine spirit, or angel, which in turn would lead to the birth of what occultists call a moonchild, a pure, supernatural being.

The project officially began on January 4, 1946, at nine P.M. in the attic of Parsons's house in Pasadena. That's when he and Hubbard armed themselves with a battery of Enochian tablets, charts, and alphabets, and set forth to conduct eleven days of magical rites which included chanting in Enochian, invoking spirits, and having sex.

On January 18 at sunset, after moving the experiments to the outskirts of the Mojave, Parsons and Hubbard achieved the first stage of their goal. "The feeling of tension suddenly snapped," wrote Parsons. "I turned to [Hubbard] and said, 'It is done,' in absolute certainty that the operation was accomplished. I returned home and found a young woman answering the requirements waiting for

me. She is describable as an "air of fire" type with bronze red hair, fiery and subtle, determined and obstinate, sincere and perverse, with extraordinary personality, talent, and intelligence."

The woman's name was Marjorie Cameron, a young artist who later became an important part of the nascent Southern California art scene. Parsons felt that Cameron was the incarnation of the Scarlet Woman who had been sent to him. Her function was to provide a vessel to bring forth the moonchild and apparently she went along with the idea willingly.

The project was stalled, however, when Hubbard was forced to return to the East Coast on a business trip. They resumed activities on March 1, shortly after Hubbard's return. This time they built an altar, dressed in robes—Hubbard in white, Parsons in black—and played Hubbard's selection of Rachmaninoff's "The Isle of the Dead." Once again they commanded the obedience of planetary spirits, spoke in tongues, had visions of empyrean heights, and supposedly had repeated sexual intercourse with Cameron.

Unfortunately, Cameron didn't produce a moonchild as they hoped, but that didn't discourage Parsons. Hubbard, on the other hand, slipped away in the middle of the night—this time with Parsons's second wife, Sara "Betty"

Marjorie Cameron on the cover of the avant garde art journal, *Semina*

L.A. EXPOSED

250

# ...had visions of empyrean heights, and had repeated sexual intercourse...

Northrop, and the entire contents of Parsons's savings account.[19] Nonetheless, Parsons continued with the project on his own with an even greater resolve than before. On October 31, 1948, he began another set of rituals that lasted for seventeen days straight until, according to him, a female spirit appeared to him and instructed him to perform a rite called "the Black Pilgrimage." "[She] told me it is not certain that you will survive," wrote Parsons. "But if you survive you will attain your true will and manifest the Antichrist."

## The Legacy:

Did Parsons manifest the Antichrist? Did he bring forth Babalon? Did he introduce a moonchild into the world? No one will ever know for sure. Yet what is known is that Parsons let his passion for the occult compromise his professional life to a great degree. General Motors, for example, who had heard about his secret rituals, refused to keep him on staff when they purchased his company Aerojet in 1944. (Parsons's designs for that company eventually led to the first ballistic missiles.) From there he went to Hughes Aircraft in 1947, where he was fired once again a couple of years later when his superiors charged him with stealing sensitive documents.[20] Finally in 1950, after failing to get work anywhere else, he began working as a special effects technician for Hollywood while allegedly bootlegging high explosives from Mexico.

Hubbard, meanwhile, had problems of his own. In 1951 his wife Sara sued him for divorce claiming that she had been subjected to "systematic torture on a daily basis." According to court testimony, she swore under oath that Hubbard had tried to get her to commit suicide in 1950 if only to prevent him from being labeled a divorcee. And when she refused, he allegedly attacked her with "beatings, strangulation, and scientific torture experiments." The final straw came on February 23, 1951, when two of Hubbard's thugs kidnapped Sara and forced her to sign a statement under the threat of physical violence—a statement which, according to court records, gave Hubbard custody of their child and the promise that she wouldn't tell anyone about his *real* activities.

The following year, Parsons told a close friend that he had come up with a breakthrough that would revolutionize the field of explosives forever. A short time later, while working in his garage, he accidentally dropped a container of fulmite of mercury, a highly unstable explosive material, which in turn ignited Parsons's stockpile of tetranitromethane. According to the *Los Angeles Times*, the blast blew off his right arm, broke both legs, and ripped a gaping hole in his face. Surprisingly, Parsons survived but only temporarily. He died forty-five minutes later on June 17, 1952.[21]

## The Bottom Line:

The Church of Scientology has done all it can to deny the fact that Hubbard had anything to do with Parsons and the OTO. In 1969, after the *London Sunday Times* printed an account of Hubbard's involvement with the occult, the church responded with a dismissal claiming that Hubbard was sent to Pasadena by Naval Intelligence to *spy* on Parsons's black magic operation, and proudly boasted that they brought about his downfall. They also tried to suppress the fact that Hubbard based his own religion, Scientology, on some of Aleister Crowley's writings including specific symbols, his grading system, his use of hypnotic implants, and the concept of the OTO. Yet there are too many corroborated accounts to dismiss Parsons's version of the story, and in all likelihood, there's even more salacious material that has never been reported. In any case, the legend lives on.

# THE RUMOR:

The FBI and the LAPD have a secret assassination squad designed to target rappers.

## The Evidence:

In 1993, a year after the Los Angeles riots, eight skinheads were arrested in Los Angeles. In their possession was an itinerary outlining their plans to blow up the First AME Church, L.A.'s most popular, all-black congregation, a cache of weapons, and a "kill-list" naming all the African Americans that they were planning to murder. Apparently the list included Rodney King, Jesse Jackson, and rapper Eazy-E (Eric Wright) of the gangsta rap group, Niggas With Attitude.

As a matter of policy, federal agents warned King, Jackson, and everyone else on the list to take precautions—all except Eazy-E that is.

And Jerry Heller, Easy's business partner, believed it was deliberate. "When the federal government chooses not to inform a person who's marked for death by a serious hate group who obviously can carry out that threat," he fumed, "that's astonishing and horrifying."

A short time later, Suge Knight, the CEO of the rap label Death Row Records, was the subject of an extensive FBI probe as the result of his business relations with drug dealers and known Mafia figures.[22] Consequently, his telephone lines were tapped, agents were stationed outside of his place of business, and at least one informant was placed inside his inner circle without his knowledge. That means that on the night of September 7, 1996, when he left the Mike Tyson fight in Las Vegas with his number one rap star, Tupac Shakur, FBI agents were right there. That also means that when an assassin pulled up next to Knight's car and unleashed a fusillade of .40-caliber bullets, cutting Shakur down in his prime, FBI agents witnessed the event, yet did nothing to stop the murder or assist in the apprehension of the killer.

Meanwhile Bad Boy Records, Death Row's primary competitor, found itself under similar watchful eyes, apparently for similar reasons. So when Biggie Smalls, Bad Boy's number one rap artist, fell victim to an assassin's bullet on March 9, 1997, the FBI was right there once again, watching the entire scenario play itself out without lifting a finger to intervene.

## The Context:

For anyone that knows anything about the FBI's COINTELPRO operations in the 1960s and 1970s, there may be more to the FBI's behind-the-scenes activities than anyone would care to admit. Originally set up to infiltrate Communist party groups in the 1940s, COINTELPRO (counter intelligence programs) set out to "neutralize" antiwar demonstrators, left-wing journalists, Latino gang members, American Indians, and other insurgents at any cost. Yet COINTELPRO's most vicious attacks were reserved for the Black Panthers. According to political researcher Mae Brussell, no less than thirty-four Black Panthers were assassinated in the late 1960s—mostly by hired assassins, alleged rivals and/or provocateurs secretly backed by the FBI.

Meanwhile the Nixon administration also agreed to let the CIA instigate operation MHCHAOS, a.k.a. CHAOS specifically to combat "foreign funding" to underground newspapers in the U.S. But by the end of 1968 that program had evolved to include a domestic terrorism campaign against public figures—especially musicians. In a typical interdepartmental communiqué that was later revealed by the Senate Intelligence Committee in 1976, agents were instructed to:

Show [rock and rollers] as scurrilous and depraved. Call attention to their habits and living conditions, explore every possible embarrassment. Send in women and sex. Break up marriages. Have members arrested on marijuana charges. Investigate personal conflicts or animosities between them. Send articles to the newspapers showing their depravity. Use narcotics and free sex to entrap. Use misinformation to confuse and disrupt. Obtain specimens of their handwriting. Provoke target groups into rivalries that may result in death.

Courtesy of Robbie Conal

Shakur was a prime candidate for such an attack. In 1993—the same year that his troubles began—he donated money to Black Panther causes, financed efforts to release former Panther leader "Geronimo" Pratt from prison, performed at Panther-oriented functions, and announced plans for a new political party called the New African Panthers.[23] Meanwhile, as his popularity grew, he took every opportunity to attack the U.S. government in his music. (*2Pacalypse Now*, for example, is chock-full of overt condemnations of the FBI, CIA, and President George Bush.) In fact, then-vice president Dan Quayle was known to denounce him in public, calling him a "public enemy" who "encouraged violence, cop killing, and disrespect to women."

## More Evidence:

In the 1990s, the New York Police Department's intelligence division began a concerted effort to undermine the Black Liberation Movement in the same way that COINTELPRO attacked the Panthers twenty years earlier. In fact, according to an investigation by John Potash for a 1999 issue of *Covert Action Quarterly*, the NYPD may have used Jacques Agnant, to facilitate Shakur's arrest in 1993 and direct him to a near-fatal ambush at a recording studio a short time later.[24]

Moreover, there's some compelling evidence

to support the idea that the LAPD followed a similar pattern on the West Coast. In a controversial June 2001 *Rolling Stone* article, reporter Russell Sullivan obtained a quote from Russell Poole, a former police officer and lead investigator on the Biggie Small's assassination, claiming that several LAPD officers were aware of the Biggie Small's murder, and some may have been involved with its orchestration and subsequent cover-up. Citing an internal affairs report #96-1408, Sullivan "outed" some of the officers that had allegedly infiltrated Suge Knight's Death Row Records as part of a federal task force, and claimed that at least two of them, David Mack and Kevin Gaines, may have been involved with committing the crime. Chief Bernard Parks on the other hand, publicly denounced Poole—as did a number of mainstream publications—claiming that his charges were "unsubstantiated" and "inconsistent with the facts." That didn't surprise Poole however, who maintained that the LAPD deliberately whitewashed the entire affair to avoid any possible scandal. (David Mack eventually went to jail on bank robbery charges and Kevin Gaines died in an "accidental shooting" by a fellow police officer.) "I had become convinced that LAPD officers were involved in the conspiracy to kill Biggie Smalls," explained Poole. "And none of the brass wanted to hear that."

## The Bottom Line:

Such coincidences, as well as the alleged infighting between Death Row and Bad Boy, the railroading into jail, the excessively lengthy prison sentences, the use of gang members as triggermen, the failure of investigators to make a single arrest—even three years after the murder—and the elimination of over a dozen key witnesses certainly points to a possible conspiracy.[25] Yet as the *Washington Post* reported on May 12, 2001, the FBI has a long history of failing to provide law enforcement with essential information in criminal trials. The case of the Ku Klux Klan member, who remained free for thirty years despite the FBI's clear knowledge of his participation in the 1963 murder of four black girls in Alabama, is a prime example. But as Oklahoma Governor Frank Keating, who once served as the FBI's director claims, that does not prove anything but the FBI's sheer ineptitude. "It's just that the FBI's system is so bureaucratic and cumbersome that it's difficult to track everything down," he says. "There's no secret agenda, I can assure you that."

# THE MYTH:

All the richest men in the city get together once a year at a secret club located somewhere in the California Mountains to decide on the fate of Los Angeles, California, and the country.

## A Little History:

It should be of no surprise that rumors of clandestine cabals of the rich and powerful are rampant in Los Angeles. After all, it's no secret that Henry E. Huntington, E. H. Harriman, Harrison Gray Otis, William G. Kerckhoff, and other early industrialists made themselves very rich by gaining control of the city's resources, often through questionable or extralegal means. Nor is it any secret that every industrialist worth his salt had to be a member of the California Club, the University Club, the Jonathan Club, the Bolsa Chica Gun Club, the Freemasons, and the ultrasecret, ultraexclusive Bohemian Grove. The latter in particular was the granddaddy of secret fraternal orders, and apparently it still exists today. Located on a 3,000-acre ranch hidden in the hills of Northern California, the Grove hosts an annual, summertime event that draws the top CEOs, high-ranking officials, politicians, and movie moguls for two weeks of fun and frivolity. According to G. William Domhoff's *The Bohemian Grove and Other Retreats*, most activities are based on artistic pursuits, communing with nature, and round-table discussions. Yet there are still plenty of male bonding rituals including drinking parties, mischievous pranks, and carousing with hookers.

## Where It Comes From:

Although decidedly more laid back than the Bohemian Grove, Los Rancheros Visitadores, Southern California's answer to the Bohemian Grove, holds its own annual meeting near Santa Barbara exclusively for wealthy businessmen, politicians, and Hollywood moguls alike. John Mitchell, the club's founder, based the club on the legend of the annual cattle roundups along

Boys will be boys: members of Los Rancheros Visitadores

Herald-Examiner Collection/Los Angeles Public Library

El Camino Real in the 1800s. As he once told a reporter in the 1940s, "It's about camaraderie and all-American values; something that we can certainly use a little more of in today's world." With that in mind, he devised a week-long horseback ride through the Santa Ynez Mountains not unlike the ride once taken by the "visiting ranchers" of California's Mexican era—complete with Old West stagecoaches and chuck wagons—stopping each night for an impromptu campsite.

The ride has been cut back significantly since the 1930s, however, primarily to accommodate greenhorns. Nonetheless, it still concludes at the 10,000-acre Alisal Guest Ranch near the town of Solvang where members get to enjoy a top-notch rodeo, skeet and trap shooting, Western art galleries, and live entertainment. According to some sources, that's also where they can pick up a few sporting girls bussed in from neighboring Las Vegas.

## What People Are Saying:

The rumor, of course, is that the *real* reason that members get together is to decide national and statewide elections, devise new ways of making themselves even richer, and to come up with ploys to get rid of "undesirables." It has been reported, for example, that Grove meetings were essential in putting Woodrow Wilson in office in 1916, primarily by giving him California. And it has also been reported that the decision to put the atomic bomb on an industrial basis was originally initiated in a secret meeting in the Grove's bathhouse in 1942. Furthermore, there seems to be some evidence that Ronald Reagan not only refrained from running for the presidency in 1967 after coming to a "private understanding" with Richard Nixon that same year, but that he secretly conspired with Claude Kirk of Florida to have the president of the University of California fired for supporting antiwar demonstrations on campus. "When you put people like that together," says one Grove veteran, "you're going to get significant conversations. But no one actually goes there specifically to do that."

## The Legacy:

In recent years Allen and Co.'s week-long conference in Sun Valley, Idaho has become *the* meeting place for the richest men in the country—including most of Hollywood's upper echelon. Yet unlike the Rancheros or the Bohemian Grove, which are steeped in the symbolism of the Wild West, the camp is focused entirely on making money. *Big* money. As the *Los Angeles Times* reported in 1998, the conference has helped foster some of the biggest entertainment deals of the twentieth century including Seagram's acquisition of MCA, Sony's purchase of Columbia/TriStar, and Disney's $19 billion acquisition of Capital Cities/ABC.

## The Bottom Line:

As long as there are super-rich, super-autocratic, super-white power players in L.A., there will always be elite clubs designed to cater to their egos.

# THE RUMOR:

Nicole Simpson and Ron Goldman were murdered by the Mob.

## A Little Background:

On the night of June 12, 1994, at approximately 10:15 P.M., Nicole Brown Simpson, the former wife of former football legend, O. J. Simpson, and her friend Ron Goldman, were brutally attacked and murdered on the front steps of Nicole's house at 875 South Bundy Drive in Brentwood. Goldman wasn't supposed to be there, however. He came by to return a pair of glasses that Nicole's mother had left at his restaurant, Mezzaluna, earlier in the evening. Nicole's two children, were sleeping inside.

Meanwhile, less than a mile away, a limo driver showed up at O. J. Simpson's Rockingham estate at approximately 10:30 P.M. to take him to the airport. But Simpson wasn't there, or at least didn't appear to be there, and no one answered the bell at the gate. Frustrated, the driver walked back to his car and had a seat on the front bumper to wait for a while longer. Nearly thirty minutes later, after several more attempts at ringing the bell, he caught a glimpse of a tall man in dark clothing walk across the driveway and enter the house. Seconds later, Simpson's voice came across the intercom saying that he had just gotten out of the shower and to wait a few more

Paul Young

minutes. At 11:15, Simpson loaded his luggage into the car, and they left for the airport.

In the following days, LAPD detectives found "a mountain of evidence" against O. J. Simpson, "proving without a doubt" that he killed Nicole Brown Simpson and Ron Goldman. First there was evidence at the crime scene itself, which included footprints matching a pair of his shoes; a ski mask containing evidence of his hair; blood drops on the ground and back gate matching his; and a bloodied left-handed glove which matched a right-handed glove found on his property. Then there was all the evidence found at his Rockingham estate, including splashes of Ron's and Nicole's blood on his socks and truck; and a "murder kit" found in the back of his Bronco consisting of a body bag, a shovel, and gloves. What's more, he left Robert Kardashian's house five days later with a travel bag, money, a passport, and a disguise, obviously trying to flee the country. And that's to say nothing of his history of spousal abuse and violent behavior.[26] According to police records, he threatened Nicole so badly— even after their divorce—that she made out a will weeks before the murder. As she told a friend, "He's going to kill me."

But did he?

## What People Are Saying:

Ever since that night of June 12 the rumor mill has been buzzing with whispers of an alleged conspiracy. Author Alex Constantine, for example, has meticulously researched Simpson's connection with the drug trade and found that Simpson may have been involved with a number of drug dealers, including Casimin "Butch Casey" Sucharski, a friend of his since his days on the Buffalo Bills. In 1993, the DEA tried to set up a sting to catch both Simpson and Sucharski but Simpson slipped away before officers arrived. Sucharski, on the other hand, wasn't so lucky. He served a stint in county jail until June 26, 1994, when he was assassinated execution-style in Florida. As Constantine suggests, Nicole may have been assassinated for similar, drug-related reasons either because she knew too much, or because she was a ready pawn in a larger game.

Yet there's another side of Simpson's life that may provide more even more significant clues to

NICOLE SIMPSON

the mystery. Aside from drugs, it seems that Simpson also had an interest in sports betting. The *New York Daily News* reported that Al Cowlings, Simpson's closest friend and companion, testified before a grand jury against a major, $70-million-per-year bookmaking operation in May 1996, an operation run by the so-called Russian/Armenian Mafia. It has been suggested that Simpson was involved in the operation. If Nicole knew about that operation, and she threatened to expose it to the authorities, it certainly would have made a few people nervous. And if that's true, then it may be possible that *someone* went ahead and organized Nicole's murder, or perhaps, forced Simpson to help ensure her silence—perhaps someone with Mafia connections.

## The Other Evidence:

Donald Freed and Dr. Raymond Briggs present a compelling case in *Killing Time: The First Full Investigation* arguing that there's enough evidence to support the idea that Simpson may not have committed the murders alone—if at all. Using a number of meticulous time lines, they tracked the events of June 12 and determined that there are too many inconsistencies with the testimonies. Why, for example, was there *someone else's skin* under Nicole's fingernails—skin that didn't belong to Simpson or Ron? Why were there "control wounds" on Ron's neck—wounds caused by a knife being *held* to his throat to keep him still? Why were *two* types of knife wounds found on the victims? Why were there prints from a *second* set of shoes at the scene? Why did several witnesses say that they saw four men running from the crime scene around 10:45 that night? Why did Ron have bruised hands—obviously from fighting—yet Simpson didn't appear to have any? Why was there a substance something like EDTA—the substance that police put in blood to keep it from coagulating—found in *all* the blood discovered at Simpson's house? And why were death threats made against potential witnesses and associates during the course of the trial?

Arguably the most extraordinary twist in the story came in 1998 when a former Simpson associate, William Benson Wasz, came forward to claim that he wanted to cooperate with the DA's office in the investigation of Simpson's associate and attorney, Robert Kardashian. According to Wasz, Kardashian—who was known to share numerous financial affairs with Simpson, and who once joked that he was a member of the Armenian Mafia—hired Wasz in 1994 to follow Nicole Simpson and take pictures of her with other men. Wasz supposedly caught her on film a short time later, making out with football star Marcus Allen during a secret rendezvous. Kardashian then contacted Wasz once again a few weeks later, and allegedly offered him $15,000 to organize Nicole's murder and place the blame on one of O. J.'s girlfriends. (Wasz claims that he has proof of the transaction in the form of a diary entry which was later confiscated by police and a $7,000 down payment.) According to an extensive investigation by reporter Joe Bosco, Wasz then decided to back out of the plan after realizing that the plan failed to provide a sufficient escape route and that he'd probably take the fall himself. As a result Nicole's killers were forced to find someone else for the job.

## The Bottom Line:

Despite Bosco's intriguing allegations, there's little proof that Kardashian had anything to do with Nicole's murder. What's more, the DA's office has since investigated Wasz's claims and found them to be implausible at best. Kardashian, they claim, has never been a suspect in the case, and they consider Wasz, who was later arrested for theft, a less than credible witness. Yet it should also be noted that Kardashian may have been cooperating with the LAPD at the time of Wasz's charges, helping them to get indictments against organized crime figures involved with sports betting. Still, the idea that he worked with the LAPD to orchestrate a conspiracy of such massive proportions—involving dozens of people operating with split second timing and risking death-penalty convictions—fails to jibe with the facts.

# THE RUMOR:

LAPD intelligence officers keep wiretaps on celebrities, politicians, and the wealthy as a matter of policy.

## D.A.'s Office Admits Secret Wiretapping

## What People Are Saying:

As long as there have been celebrities in Los Angeles there have been rumors that somewhere, deep in the bowels of police headquarters, is a roomful of audio and videotape featuring some of L.A.'s biggest names engaged in a variety of illicit acts, from phone sex to drug dealing. Not surprisingly, the LAPD has repeatedly denied such claims passing the rumor off as an urban legend at best. "I've never even heard of anything like that," says Lieutenant Alba, of the LAPD. "First of all, it's illegal [to tape someone], and second of all, it just wouldn't make sense for us to do anything like that."

## A Little History:

In 1938, only three years after William "Red" Hynes and Police Chief James Davis established a domestic espionage division, the "Red Squad," Clinton J. Taft, director of the American Civil Liberties Union, slapped a $243,300 lawsuit against the mayor of the city of L.A. charging that "none of the activities of the intelligence bureau were being used for the purpose of enforcing the law." Instead, claimed the ACLU, Hynes used his Red Squad to spy on regular citizens, wealthy industrialists, politicians, reporters, critics, and people within the movie industry for no other reason than to harass, extort, and coerce private citizens.[27]

It was also revealed around the same time that Earl Kynette, the head of the LAPD's intelligence division, had not only used the Red

Squad to spy on Clifford Clinton, a reformer bent on exposing LAPD corruption, but to destroy Clinton's business, threaten his wife and children, and place bombs in his house. In fact, a car bomb nearly took the life of Harry Raymond, Clinton's chief investigator, shortly before he exposed Kynette's extralegal activities.

Such scandals eventually helped reformers attack the LAPD with greater success than ever before. Yet despite such efforts, no one has ever been able to curtail the department's obsession with spying on citizens. Chief William Parker, perhaps the greatest police reformer of all, was a staunch proponent of domestic espionage. "He called it spying Soviet style," writes Joe Domanick in *To Protect and Serve*, and he actively encouraged his men to break into homes, plant bugs, tap phone lines, and compromise the privacy of thousands of Angelenos—including the mayor, members of the commission, and the governor of California.

Mayoral hopeful Sam Yorty knew all about Parker's secret reign of terror, and he publically promised to do something about it once elected to office. Yet he, too, became another rabid proponent of domestic spying, so much so that he initiated two new intelligence units during his tenure: the Criminal Conspiracy Section (CCS) and the Public Disorder Intelligence Division, (PDID). What's more he also greatly expanded the LAPD's own intelligence division from twenty full-time officers to eighty-four.[28]

In 1978 the ACLU dropped another bombshell when it charged Yorty and Police Chief Ed

Davis with illegally spying on tens of thousands of innocent Angelenos. The case, which sent shock waves through city hall, claimed that the LAPD had used "extralegal means" to obtain over 2.5 million dossiers on over 55,000 honest citizens throughout Southern California, including members of the PTA, the National Organization of Women, the Beverly Hills Democratic Club, the Ford Foundation, the League of United Citizens to Help Addicts, the World Council of Churches, the governor's office, and dozens of movie stars.

To make amends, Mayor Tom Bradley announced that the LAPD had destroyed over 2 million of the very same files, and that domestic spying would henceforth cease. Unfortunately, the LAPD failed to make good on that promise. Four years later Jay Paul, an undercover officer working in the LAPD's elite PDID, tried to sell some dirt on a school official that had been obtained through illegal wiretaps and got caught red-handed. That caused another public outcry against the LAPD, forcing police chief Daryl Gates to denounce Paul in the press and dismiss him as a "rogue cop." Meanwhile, investigators found all 2.5 million dossiers in his garage—the same dossiers Bradley promised to destroy—and there was evidence that he was transferring them to a new, computerized database sponsored by the John Birch Society—at the request of the LAPD.

## The Evidence:

According to Mike Rothmiller and Ivan G. Goldman's 1992 book, L.A. Secret Police, Chief Daryl Gates never stopped spying on Angelenos— not even for a second. In fact, he raised it to levels that Chief William Parker would have been jealous of.[29] "The LAPD's Organized Crime Intelligence Division (OCID)," wrote Rothmiller, "maintained secret, Stalinesque dossiers on virtually every mover and shaker in Southern California, including movie stars, politicians, and city officials. [Some of which] were kept in privately rented storage units unbeknownst to both friends and enemies of the LAPD."

Apparently there's nothing to suggest that the LAPD will curtail their spying practices any time soon. In 1994 Congress authorized a half-billion dollars to be spent by Telecom in an effort to make their digital communications infrastructure easier to tap by the Feds. At the same time the LAPD significantly relaxed its requirements for undercover probes, making wiretaps infinitely easier than ever before. And in 1998 the FBI revealed that Los Angeles had earned the dubious distinction of being the wiretap capital of the U.S.[30]

# THE LEGEND:

Stafford Warren, dean of UCLA's medical program, secretly injected radioactive plutonium in unsuspecting subjects in his laboratory in the 1940s.

## The Context:

It's hard to believe now, but there was a period when radioactive material was actually considered to be good for you. In the early part of the twenti-

eth century for example, one could actually buy a small, radioactive device right over the counter, and use it to combat fatigue, sluggishness, and bad circulation. Radium Life of Los Angeles, for instance, produced a gadget called the "emanator" which sold widely with Angelenos. Looking a bit like a coffee maker, it was really nothing more than a small beaker large enough to hold a liter of water, and a ten-inch piece of radioactive, cement-covered uranium. Each night consumers were directed to fill the beaker with water, insert the "emanator" and wait until morning to enjoy a fresh glass of radioactive $H_2O$ for breakfast.

## A Little History:

In 1945 Stafford Warren was considered the top radiologist in the country. His work with X rays and radioactive treatments brought him numerous awards and honors, and his experiments were discussed widely in medical journals. But 1945 was also the year that the U.S. military needed to set safety standards for the production of the first atomic weapons. Warren, of course, was the first choice for the job, and he apparently took little convincing. After a brief meeting in his New York office, he agreed to oversee all atomic experiments for the military, including the construction of weapons and various live tests. He also was the first to record the devastation at Hiroshima and Nagasaki firsthand, which surprisingly did little to change his mind about the effects of radium to research.

## The Evidence:

Working with a top-secret clearance from the military, Warren contacted a number of hospitals around the country in an effort to find patients that would either knowingly, or unknowingly, ingest radium directly into their bodies. By the end of the following year, eighteen subjects had been injected with varying degrees of polonium, plutonium, uranium, or other radioactive elements, yet none of them were warned of the possible consequences. (Most of the subjects were being treated for other, unrelated health problems such as broken legs, head injuries, or breast cancer, and were simply informed that they were getting a new, advanced treatment. Little did they know that they were being exposed to a highly toxic substance that could lead to blood disease, cell death, tumors, and the mutation of their DNA.) In one particularly

Los Angeles Examiner/USC Special Collections

Class of Nuke 'Em High: Stafford Warren makes a point

egregious case, for instance, a four-year-old Australian boy was flown to California in 1946 with a rare form of bone cancer. Unbeknownst to him or his family, he was injected with a hefty dose of plutonium and put under surveillance for a week. He then returned to Australia a week later without any follow-up investigation or treatments, and died the following year.

Warren eventually realized the consequences of continuing such experiments on the public, however, and decided to restrict them to Veterans Administration centers around the country—in particular, the VA center in Brentwood. After that, the experiments continued under an even greater cloak of secrecy.[31]

The Shadow of Discontent

# Over 2,000 human radiation experiments

## The Bottom Line:

Over 2,000 human radiation experiments were conducted on human subjects from 1945 to 1974, mostly on pregnant women, children, prisoners, soldiers, airmen, and sailors. Yet despite the obvious ethical and moral questions involved, Warren—who founded UCLA's medical school in 1947—never questioned the practice. As he saw it, the research was vital to protect the health and safety of nuclear weapons workers who, after all, were working to ensure America's place as the world's greatest superpower.

## The Legacy:

The mainstream press has been curiously quiet about the human radiation experiments over the years. In fact, it wasn't until the early 1980s, when the *Albuquerque Tribune* released a series of articles on the subject, that any attention was paid to it. Yet even then, the story continued to remain curiously underplayed. The *Los Angeles Times*, for instance, justified the practice by stating that "one in four people develop cancer anyway," and only "small amounts of radioactive materials were used in the experiments."

And even after the board of supervisors approved a measure to suspend all medical research at the VA hospital in Brentwood, citing a six-year study that revealed gross negligence, a severe lack of adherence to policy, and the failure to disclose possible hazards to patients, the *Los Angeles Times*, applauded the action by saying, "There's no evidence that the hospital's lax oversight of research practices has harmed people or animals. Instead, the suspension is a preemptive measure."

## THE LEGEND:

UCLA's doctors, under the guidance of Dr. Louis Joylon West, have been secretly implanting electronic devices in unsuspecting victims as part of a huge "Big Brother" plot to control criminal behavior in the U.S.

Paul Young

## What People Are Saying:

Stafford Warren's story is not the only facet of UCLA's dark medical history. Another alleged mad scientist was Dr. Louis Joylon "Jolly" West, the former head of UCLA's psychiatry department and the Neuropsychiatric Institute. In many ways, Jolly's contribution to medical science is far more frightening than a few microcuries of injected plutonium. After all, according to conspiracy lore, he may have performed hundreds of secret CIA-backed LSD experiments on unsuspecting subjects; devised Orwellian behavior modification programs for the criminal justice department; and developed a procedure to implant electronic devices into the brains of unsuspecting children for CIA-anchored tracking experiments.

"I've heard all that before," says West in an interview given shortly before he passed away in 1999. "I'm supposedly the secret guy behind the CIA's mind-control program. And I've seen myself portrayed in exposés, novels, and movies. But the fact is, it's all a big exaggeration. I never did half the things people have said about me."

## Where It Comes From:

Much of the intrigue of West's career goes back to his early experiments with LSD in the 1950s. West was a young Air Force psychologist at the time with a keen interest in experimental therapies. He had previously examined returning POWs from the Korean conflict, and decided that LSD might provide a clue to the alleged brainwashing techniques used by the Chinese. Although the drug was still untested and considered possibly dangerous, West began using the pharmaceutical in his own, personal experiments, believing that it held tremendous potential in breaking down ego defense mechanisms. Meanwhile Allen Dulles, the head of the CIA, had his own interest in the drug, and immediately dispatched an agent to check on his progress. "One day an agent came down and started asking me all these questions," recalls West. "And he found out that I really didn't know beans about LSD."

And apparently West wasn't lying either. After becoming the head of psychiatry and neurology at the University of Oklahoma, he injected the equivalent of 1,000 hits of acid into an aging elephant donated by the local zoo. The purpose, he claimed, was to determine if madness—or violence—was chemically induced. Instead the animal fell over and went into severe convulsions. "It proved one thing," says West in his own defense. "That LSD could cause convulsions. No one knew that at the time."

Nonetheless, his experiments earned him a credible reputation among sociologists who were seeking to understand the root causes of violence in the human animal. So much so, that the attorney general asked West to treat Jack Ruby shortly after he killed Lee Harvey Oswald in 1963. (Although some conspiracy theorists have suggested that he murdered Ruby, who died of cancer a short time later.) In any case, shortly after moving to Los Angeles in the early 1960s, he initiated plans for the Center for the Study and Reduction of Violence at the Vacaville correctional facilities, with a secondary facility at UCLA called the Center for the Study of Violent Behavior. The purpose of these programs, which were backed by then-governor Ronald Reagan, were to create a complex behavior model that could pinpoint criminal behavior *before* it happened. In other words, West wanted to create a "techno-elite" that would have the power to ferret out likely criminals, corral them into behavior modification programs, and release them back into the world with electronic transponders for tracking purposes.

And if that wasn't draconian enough, West's ideas for "behavior modification" included psychosurgery, electronic implants, experimental drug treatments, and a host of new electronic devices designed to control the brains and bodies of offenders.

## The Legacy:

Many believe that West's theories provided the basis for some of the electronic behavior modification experiments that occurred in the late 1960s, and early 1970s. Dr. Delgado at Yale

University, for example, supposedly expanded on West's ideas when he stopped a bull from charging by pushing a button on a radio transmitter in 1964.[32] A couple of years later, Dr. Frank Ervin of UCLA is alleged to have inserted four implants covered with electrodes into the brain of Leonard Kille, a subject known to have episodes of violence. Then came more experiments by Barton L. Ingraham at Berkeley, Professor Ralph K. Schwitgebel at Harvard, and Dr. Ross Adey at UCLA.

Nonetheless, West maintains that the idea of implantation was never as feasible as he or anyone else imagined. According to him, a transmitter would require a fairly cumbersome power source and an ample antenna—neither of which could be inserted into the body without being rejected. "Implants simply do not work," he explains. "And the reason is because you cannot implant ideas. You can stimulate motor skills to a small degree, and you can influence sensations and recapture hallucination scenarios in people that have epilepsy, but that is all. There is absolutely no way to place an electronic device in a human being and manipulate his or her behavior via a transmitter. It's just impossible."

Still, there seems to be some evidence that passive biometric tracking devices—not unlike the ones that West supposedly designed for teenage runaways in the early 1960s—are more prevalent than he admits. Oceanographers have already applied the technology to track porpoises and dolphins, and the American Veterinary Association has introduced an electronic device (AVID) that can be implanted into household pets in a matter of seconds with a hypodermic needle. Furthermore, Kevin Warwick, a professor at the University of Reading, successfully

> "It's all science fiction. [The idea of implants] is just a modern version of the so-called witch's mark that caused such a stink in the seventeenth century. It's just a way for people to believe in a higher power that, frankly, does not exist."

implanted an electronic device into his left arm in 1998 to help him interact with computers in his office. And according to *Wired* magazine, the device was large enough to have its own power supply, and has remained in his body for the last two years without any side effects whatsoever.

Perhaps that's why rumors of a secret implant program allegedly operating out of UCLA's Neuropsychiatric Institute have gained some level of concern. In fact there seems to be some evidence that the center has been conducting experiments on unsuspecting kids either as a safeguard against abduction or as a way to mark those that show traits common to criminals at a young age. "These biometric tracking devices are either inserted into nasal cavities and ear canals," notes Alex Constantine in *Psychic Dictatorship*, "or they're implanted surgically, directly into the brain [and] global positioning system satellites can track these minute transponders [around the world]."

Constantine cites the case of a three-year-old girl that was discovered to have such a device in her cranium. Apparently, the girl's therapist made the discovery while she was looking at a set of the girl's X rays. After a brief investigation, the therapist deduced that the implant was inserted a few months earlier when the child was forced to undergo an obscure brain operation at Dr. West's Neuropsychiatric Institute at UCLA.

"I'm telling you it's nothing but science fiction," says West. "It's *all* science fiction. [The idea of implants] is just a modern version of the so-called witch's mark that caused such a stink in the seventeenth century. It's just a way for people to believe in a higher power that, frankly, *does not exist*."

# MISSION CONTROL

While fraternal orders and secret societies were much more common in the nineteenth century, many are still flourishing in backrooms, temples, and covens throughout Southern California—including the following:

★ **BUILDERS OF THE ADYTUM:** An authentic mystery school devoted to teaching the Sacred Tarot, the Holy Qabala, and a vast array of unusual healing methods such as the Vibratory Attunement Ritual. Located at 5101 N. Figueroa in downtown L.A.

★ **E CLAMPUS VITUS:** A spoof of the Freemasons, with silly entitlements, pseudo rituals, and riotous ceremonies. Once popular with the miners of the 1800s, there are still factions getting together in places like Kern, Tulare, Fresno, and Nevada Counties.

★ **INDEPENDENT ORDER OF ODD FELLOWS:** Formerly a secret society for the captive Israelites in Babylon, the Odd Fellows have become a staunch, right-wing faction devoted to philanthropic pursuits including visiting the sick, burying the dead, and taking care of orphans. No drinking, smoking, or drug-taking allowed.

★ **FREEMASONS:** The granddaddy of them all, with roots allegedly going back to the building of King Solomon's temple. The first L.A. lodge opened its doors in 1858 and has since attracted some of Hollywood's most important free-thinkers, anticlericals, and power mongers, including Louis B. Mayer and Ronald Reagan. Today it continues to have a distinctly Protestant, anticlerical bias, adopting the trappings of chivalric orders of centuries past.

★ **INSTITUTE OF DIVINE METAPHYSICAL RESEARCH:** Founded by Dr. Henry Clifford Kinely in 1931 (supposedly after he miraculously painted a message from the supreme creator Yahweh-Elohim on his bedspread in a trance), the DMR is basically a mix of theosophy and the occult. Popular with New Agers and artists alike.

**KU KLUX KLAN:** Infamous for its extreme racist views, the Klan grew in Southern California in the 1920s thanks to support of the LAPD, who often hired members to help round up minority criminal groups and alleged Communists. Today the right-wing organization continues to have a tenuous, if not secretive, connection with some police agencies and military forces throughout Southern California, and is currently based in Glendale.

**KNIGHTS OF COLUMBUS:** Originally created as a lodge for Catholic priests and clergymen, this order has been known to conduct some of the most elaborate and frightening initiation rituals of all. They also have the best handshake. Since then it has remained an important social order for Catholics, mafiosi, and celebrities alike, including Frank Sinatra. Its former headquarters can be found at 1441 North McCadden in Hollywood.

**LOS RANCHEROS VISITADORES:** Less of a secret society than a highly exclusive fraternal order catering to top executives, politicians, and moguls in California. The group meets once a year for a week-long ride through the Santa Ynez foothills on horseback with the attendant male-bonding rituals.

**OLD ORDER OF DUNKERS:** Much like the Amish, the Dunkers believe that all worldly possessions and frivolous entertainment—TV, dancing, movies, etc.—are works of Satan. As a result, they live in their own communes, operate their own schools, and dress strictly in nineteenth-century clothing. Based primarily in Stanislaus County.

**ORDER OF THE EASTERN STAR:** The female version of the Freemasons was originally formed as a devotion to the lives of five biblical women representing fidelity, constancy, loyalty, faith, and love. Today the order supposedly draws a number of high-level female Hollywood executives into its fold, although its greatest membership tends to be in Orange County, where it's popular with middle-class Republicans.

**ORDO TEMPLI ORIENTIS:** In Austria it was called the Oriental Templar Order (OTO), a benevolent society devoted to the study of Freemasonry, Rosicrucian ideas, Illuminist beliefs, Christian Gnosticism, and the hidden traditions of the East. Since the 1920s, however, when it became known as the Ordo Templi Orientis, it has adopted a number of occult practices including a black mass and various sex rituals. The first California lodge opened in Pasadena in the 1930s, and has since moved to the inland empire.

★ **THE ORDER OF THE THELMIC GOLDEN DAWN:** An offshoot of the OTO, yet is considerably more complex and convoluted. In fact, according to the group's treatise, the course can take several lifetimes to complete, and there are titles one can achieve after going "beyond the unknown." Today the group is primarily based in the San Fernando Valley.

★ **ROSICRUCIANISM:** There's still a great deal of confusion over the origin of this order, yet much of Europe's intelligentsia fell into its fold in the nineteenth century—primarily due to its focus on arcane mysteries as Sufism, Arabian occultism, the Qabala, and the works of Hermes Trismegistus. Today its main lodge is in San José, with chapters in L.A., Long Beach, and San Diego, and still inspires a number of artists including Kenneth Anger.

★ **SANTERIA:** Originally based in Cuba, Santeria has its roots in Catholicism and native Nigerian practices. Much of the practice has to do with the manipulation of idols representing its four gods: Eleggua, Oggun, Ochosi, and Oshu. Occasionally animal sacrifices are performed, along with incantations, dancing, music, and fortune-telling practices. Said to have 30,000 adherents in L.A. alone.

★ **SATANISM:** Less a society than a lifestyle, practitioners contend that Satanism has nothing to do with such Christian notions as heaven and hell and everything to do with gaining control of spiritual, earthly, and inner powers. In the 1940s there was a small enclave of Satanists in L.A., growing to extraordinary proportions by the 1970s. Today there are dozens of grottos and/or temples (meeting places) throughout Southern California—especially in the San Fernando Valley.

★ **WICCA:** Like Satanists, Wiccans want to harness the feminine energy of the universe and use it to influence events. They do not worship Satan, however, since Satan is a male god. In 1997 it was reported that there were over 1,500 practicing witches in Long Beach alone and another 5,000 in Orange County. But according to the *Times*, the most important place for witchcraft in Southern California is Ojai, which has been described as having the most witchcraft activity in the entire country.

The Shadow of Discontent

# NOTES

## Chapter 1

**1** The rumor is leveled at men, too, although less often. In the 1930s it was said that Paul Bern, Jean Harlow's husband, was a hermaphrodite. In 1965 it was widely rumored that James Brown wanted to get a sex change so that he could marry his bandmate, Bobby Byrd; Mark Wahlberg was born with a third nipple, Bruce Jenner tried to get a sex change once, Michael Jackson had himself castrated to keep his voice high, and actor Steven Mackintosh was the first genuine transsexual in Hollywood—all of which are false.

**2** Not all rumors are malicious, however. Former stripper-turned-disco-queen Amanda Lear actually tried to pass herself off as a transsexual in 1976 at the urging of David Bowie—despite the fact that she was having a well-publicized affair with Bryan Ferry at the time.

**3** Erben was half Jewish actually, and he was able to hide that fact from German officials who still awarded him an official Nazi party card and Aryan certificate. There have never been any records that Erben was a member of the SA, SD, or the SS, however.

**4** In fact, like Erben, Flynn tried to enlist in the OSS, and there are numerous records of him reporting to General Brett on German activities in Latin America and Mexico. In a famous episode, he contacted President Roosevelt and asked if he could work as an American agent in Ireland—where his father was a professor specializing in race studies and eugenics. Not surprisingly, Roosevelt refused to answer the request.

**5** Possibly the most bizarre case of a klismaphiliac (someone who gets off on this kind of stuff) was the twenty-year-old gay man that admitted himself to a hospital with a solid mass filling his backside. Apparently he and his boyfriend stirred up a batch of concrete mortar and poured the mixture through a funnel into his ass. Evidently he believed that once the substance hardened he could pull it out like a "dildo." Instead the mass hardened and nearly killed him. "I didn't know that it would expand," said the victim. "I thought it would be the same shape as a poop." Yet an attorney in Los Angeles may have topped that story. As the December 1996 issue of *Foaftale News* reported, the attorney checked into the trauma ward with a cell phone stuck up his butt. According to Dr. Dennis Crobe, his phone rang three times during the extraction, and he "made so many jokes about it that he just about had us rolling on the floor. By the time that we finished, we really did expect to find an answering machine in there."

**6** It has also been said that Longie Zwillman, the notorious New Jersey Mafia boss, who was known to keep a locket of Harlow's blond pubic hair, was insanely jealous of Bern. So when he found out that Bern struck her after their wedding night he put a contract out on him. In fact Zwillman once boasted of having Bern killed, but it was later revealed to be idle boasting.

**7** Chaplin was also known to rent Hearst's yacht for his own private parties, as he did in April 1925, which only exacerbated the rumor of his alleged affair with Davies.

**8** Chaplin's servant, Toriachi Kono, did in fact claim that he was on board with Chaplin that day, and that he even saw Ince's body being taken off in a stretcher. But Kono has been proven to be a less than credible source.

**9** Hopper has never admitted that he made love to a quadriplegic; only author John Gilmore has claimed to be privy to that information. He has admitted to accidentally "burning" Natalie Wood's genitals when he placed her in a bathtub of champagne. Nonetheless, Hopper's need for stimulus has led him into some dark waters. Sally Kirkland claimed that he nearly cut her finger off with a knife during the making of *Human Highway,* and around the same time actor Rip Torn alleged that he threatened him with a blade, too. Hopper has also been known to prowl his neighborhood searching for FBI agents, and he once shot up his house in Taos trying to kill imaginary intruders and phantoms. His most insane stunt, however, was when he built his own Russian Death Chair—the legendary Soviet "trick" used to fake executions. Basically Hopper laid down inside a box that was wired with six sticks of dynamite. The explosion—which was strong enough to decimate a car—never touched Hopper, since he was protected by a vacuum created by the blast.

**10** It was widely reported that Mansfield was decapitated in the crash, yet the undertaker later confirmed that her head was "definitely attached." The reason for the rumor had to do with a blond hair which was found on the hood of the car. In any case, her three children who were in the backseat, miraculously survived.

**11** Zeena LaVey also debunked his claim that he ran away and joined Clyde Beatty's circus as a child; that he served as a police photographer for the SFPD in the early 1950s; that his house, the infamous Church of Satan headquarters, was a former brothel; that he once carried on a sexual affair with Marilyn Monroe while she was a stripper at the Myan Theater; and that he was the technical advisor of Roman Polanski's *Rosemary's Baby.* All of which, according to Zeena, were sheer exaggerations. But as far as Mansfield goes, Zeena claims that her father only met her once, specifically as a publicity stunt. And writer May Mann claims that Mansfield only called LaVey while entertaining friends, and just to make fun of him.

**12** Columnist James Bacon claims that the real story—the one that *Confidential* couldn't print—had it that Mitchum walked into Charles Laughton's kitchen and grabbed a dish and a bottle of catsup. He then unzipped his pants, placed his cock on a plate, and smothered it in tomato sauce. A moment later, he returned to the party carrying the plate in front of him yelling, "Which one of you wants to eat first?" Then again, according to author James Ellroy, the *real* story was that the event occurred on the set of *Night of the Hunter.* Supposedly, during a lunchtime break, Mitchum placed his cock in a hot dog bun, covered it in catsup, and turned to director Charles Laughton—who was still very much in the closet—and his boyfriend, and said, "Which one of you fags wants to eat this?"

**13** After all, despite Mitch's penchant for apocrypha, there are plenty of stories about him that seem to be true. He did in fact spend time in a Savannah jail; he did serve time on a chain gang; and he probably got into more barroom brawls than just about any other actor in history—including one where he beat up a sergeant for calling his group of friends "Hollywood faggots." On another occasion, he decked a rowdy heckler that turned out to be none other than Camp Carson, a professional boxer with nineteen knockouts.

**14** The *New York Times* reported that one of her most famous clients was Monica Lewinsky *before and during* her illicit affair with President Clinton.

**15** Payton, who eventually ran a whorehouse in Mexico in the 1960s, was a genuine stag film regular in the 1950s. In fact, some claim that there's a well-known sex loop circulating among stag aficionados featuring Payton having sex with actor Tom Neal on the floor of the Olympic Auditorium's boxing ring. Meanwhile Dennis Hopper, the mad rebel of *Easy Rider,* can be seen in L. M. Carson's documentary *American Dreamer* having sex with a woman in a bathtub.

**16** The popular myth that the most notorious "home movies" of the late sixties to early seventies were allegedly made by Rock Hudson, Richard Chamberlain, Jayne Kennedy, and Shirley MacLaine may well be specious. Meanwhile publisher Hugh Hefner of *Playboy* was known to have a bodyguard named "Scooby" who recorded the sex acts of the stars during his many parties at the mansion. Hef would then screen the scenes in his bedroom.

**17** There have been bigger Hollywood names in XXX fare, however, including Farley Granger, Cameron Mitchell, Aldo Ray, Jan Sterling, and Malcolm McDowell, although they were only in movies where the sex scenes were added later, without their knowledge. However, one could argue that the countless "home movies" made by stars in the privacy of their own homes could count as pure hardcore fare, including the infamous home tapings allegedly made by Rob Lowe, Arsenio Hall, Pamela Anderson with Tommy Lee, Dennis Rodman with Carmen Electra, Jennifer Lopez, and producer Don Simpson. Simpson in particular, was known to shoot hardcore S&M movies in his home, including scenes of him urinating into a toilet and forcing a woman to lick it clean. Meanwhile, there's a rich vein of rock-and-roll home porn allegedly made by the likes of Rod Stewart, Axl Rose, Mark McGrath, Kid Rock, and many more.

**18** Barresi later retracted his story, stating flatly that he had never engaged in "homosexual activity" with Travolta. As the *New York Times* reported in April 2001, Barresi claimed that his life had been turned "upside down" by the sensational press revolving around the case, and he simply wanted it to stop. But it should also be pointed out that this is the same man who reportedly convinced three well-known transsexuals to reverse their claims of sexual congress with Eddie Murphy in the early 1990s by offering them nearly a quarter of a million dollars in bribes.

# Chapter 2

**1** Originally the sign was on the outside of the building. But it was brought inside after some vandals attacked it in the early sixties.

**2** The internationally renowned artist Ed Keinholz memorialized Barney's Beanery in his classic work *The Beanery* in 1965, now permanently displayed at the Royal Dutch Museum.

**3** It should be noted that there was another L.A. landmark filled with celebrity names that will never be uncovered. In the 1940s there was a fast-food joint at the corner of Vine and Melrose called "Hollywood's Famous Door." As the name suggests, it featured a front door that was literally covered in hundreds of star autographs.

**4** Apparently the legend is based on a Hopi tale of a widespread holocaust that allegedly occurred in 3000 B.C. Hopi forefathers believe that their ancestors constructed thirteen great underground cities throughout the Pacific Coast with a special "chemical" that could melt rock. Supposedly the one under what is now L.A. included a subsurface maze built some 5,000 years ago and extended from what is now the central library to Dodger Stadium. The tenants were not "lizard people" per se, but the tunnels themselves were said to be in the shape of a lizard, which gave them their name—the lizard people. In 1934 G. Warren Shufelt, a mining engineer, claimed that he found evidence of such tunnels with his special "radio X-ray" machine. He drilled a 350-foot hole under what is now Fort Moore Hill and supposedly found a large treasure room. But after an accidental cave-in, it was sealed forever.

**5** Similar, albeit less extensive, underground facilities are also said to be under Lockheed's Helendale radar facility (also used for stealth technologies), TRW's Capistrano test site near Camp Pendleton (used for "Star Wars" research and chemical laser testing), and Phillips Laboratory at Edwards Air Force Base (used for research in energy weapons). The most mysterious of all, however, is the alleged underground, multi-operational military base on the Cabazon Indian reservation in Palm Springs. According to lore, the base is the headquarters for all kinds of government malfeasance including arms smuggling, drug trafficking, secret weapons manufacturing—including biological weapons—and international spying.

**6** The rumor may also have gotten a boost when, in 1929, city workers discovered a long-buried underground pathway to the Pelanconi House in the Plaza. The tunnel, it seems, was originally part of the main water channel, La Zanja, that brought water from the Los Angeles River to the original pueblo. La Zanja may in fact be the original source for the alleged underground tunnels.

**7** Designer Roy Halston Frowick once held a similar contest inside Studio 54's bathroom in the 1970s. Yet rather than staying power, Halston allegedly gave the top prize to the guy who could ejaculate the farthest. And more recently, producer Jon Peters allegedly hired girls from madam Heidi Fleiss's stable and ordered them to dress in French maid outfits and be "available" to any of his guests at *his* parties.

**8** Not to be confused with the in-house masseuse named Doc who doubled as a call girl.

**9** She also lived at 1616 North Curson in 1936, but didn't stay there long.

**10** Officials point out, however, that stringent regulations for waste disposal only went into effect in the 1960s. Before that, hospitals used the drainage system just like everybody else—much of which poured directly into the ocean. In other words, it's entirely possible that in the early part of the century, fetuses *were* being washed down the sewers on a fairly regular basis.

**11** Washington actively attacked movies that were suspected of being pro-German. *Spirit of '76*, for example, was seized under Title XI of the espionage act, and its producer, Robert Goldstein, a German Jew, received a ten-year prison sentence. Moreover, German spies were

not uncommon in Hollywood during World War I. As Kevin Brownlow has pointed out, Captain Horst von der Goltz was a German intelligence agent who performed in a number of Hollywood epics, including *The Prussian Cur* in 1918. In fact, British and American agents intercepted German plans to establish a Moving Picture Bureau in Hollywood as early as 1915. That would have allowed the Germans to produce propaganda under the Hollywood name. Meanwhile, the notorious bandit Caryl Chessman notes in his autobiography, *Cell 2455, Death Row*, that he once got his hands on some very incriminating material apparently stolen out of a Beverly Hills wall safe by another cat burglar. As he put it, "This important Hollywoodian was apparently actively engaged in a sly plot to use the movie industry for propaganda purposes on behalf of Der Fuhrer and Company." Some believe the star in question was Errol Flynn.

**12** In the 1990s Congress approved a $1 billion budget to be used exclusively for antidrug advertising on prime-time TV. The networks agreed to the deal, even though it required that they get two slots for the price of one. By the late 1990s, however, many of the networks had failed to fulfill their end of the bargain, and complained about having to give Barry R. McCaffrey's office of the national drug control policy a "second" spot for free. Eventually a compromise was struck where Washington would "forget about" the second spots if producers incorporated antidrug themes in their prime-time shows. Not surprisingly, nearly every major prime-time show, including *ER*, *90210*, *Chicago Hope*, *The Practice*, *The Smart Guy*, *The Wayans Brothers*, and *7th Heaven*, produced an episode that was overtly antidrug—but only after the scripts were "approved" by Washington. As a result, the networks were able to turn around and resell those empty slots to other clients. As *Salon* magazine reported in January 2000, producers made millions off the deal—despite the fact that it was clearly illegal. After all, as payola laws clearly state, any and all sponsors must be disclosed to the public. Nonetheless, the *LA Times* reported a scant four months later that McCaffrey's office had worked out a similar deal with Hollywood producers to inject similar messages into Hollywood movies.

**13** The *New York Times* reported in 1977 that the CIA's annual operating budget for propaganda between the years 1950 and 1975 was nearly $300 million, and included as many as 2,000 full-time employees. Some of that was, of course, directed toward domestic operations. After all, it is a matter of public record that hundreds of newspapers, news services, radio stations, and magazines have been either subsidized or owned by American intelligence organizations. CBS, for example, was considered to be one of the CIA's greatest assets in the 1950s, and James S. Copley, editor of the *Copley News Service* in San Diego, once admitted that his service was nothing more than a CIA front, giving spooks the ability to work "legitimately" for the likes of the *San Diego Union* and the *Evening News*.

**14** There's plenty of evidence that some of the material is made for the domestic market as well—primarily to "control" such scandalous affairs as the Kennedy assassination, human radiation experiments, the Iran/Contra affair, and other political matters. What's more, there's also evidence that the CIA had its own multimillion-dollar research program to develop subliminal messages for motion pictures. According to Martin A. Lee, author of *Acid Dreams: The Complete Social History of LSD*, that program led to numerous tests in American movie theaters in the 1950s, mostly on unsuspecting subjects.

**15** It should be noted that the 124 midgets hired to perform in *The Wizard of Oz* in 1938 stayed at the Culver Hotel and the Adams Hotel in Culver City. Since then there have been a number of rumors about the antics of the group. In the early 1960s, one of the diminutive actresses went on the *Jack Paar Show* visibly drunk. She then went on to say that all the midgets were drunk during the production, and that they had innumerable parties, both on and off the set. But her claims have since been discounted by historians.

**16** It should be noted that there were genuine Japanese terrorists working in Southern California. The mysterious Black Dragons, for example, tried to blow up a handful of key military installations. Meanwhile, there are also documents proving that Fifth Columnists in Mexico, working for the Nazi party, built airfields near the California border to prepare for an all-out attack against bases and ports in Southern California.

**17** Baron Long is an important figure in the history of L.A.'s social life. Not only did he open the first all-night club in 1912, the Vernon Country Club—where he hired, and fired, Rudolph Valentino as a male dancer—but he was also responsible for such landmarks as the famous Ship Café in Venice, the Sunset in Santa Monica, the Nat Goodwin Café on the Goodwin pier, and the most important of all, the Biltmore Hotel.

**18** Stone amulets or statues known as *hei tikis* are often placed near ancient ceremonial grounds to protect them from trespassers. As anthropologists discovered in the 1920s, these *tikis* are said to be very much alive, and they're often highly vindictive. If anyone tries to trespass on the grounds, or worse—steal one of the statues—the angry spirits will send *tupapaaus* or ghosts after them to inflict them with bad luck.

**19** The only questionable thing that Lipps ever did was the time that he allegedly stole the Del Tahquitz Hotel in Palm Springs from his own client, the iconoclastic silent film star Fritzi Ridgeway. Apparently Lipps was her attorney, and soon realized that she was an incompetent manager. Apparently, she'd shoot at trespassers with a shotgun. Yet, rather than encourage her to find a partner, he simply had her sign a piece of paper which, unbeknownst to her, gave him the right to take control of the hotel. That was his first entry into the world of resorts. Two Bunch Palms was his next.

**20** It should also be mentioned that there was another Chicago Mafia associate in nearby San Diego called William Lippin, and it's certainly possible that someone simply confused Billie Lipps with Billy Lippin.

# Chapter 3

**1** This detail came from Cooley's version of the events during his trial. Some, however, believe that it was Cooley that administered the cigarette burns.

**2** There's some discrepancy over where the gas came from, however. Some reports claim that there was a can still filled with a third of a gallon of gasoline lying on the floorboards. Others claim that it was outside the car, in the bushes.

**3** When Fuller's uncle told the detective that he thought the owners of PJ's had something to do with the murder, they told him, "Whoa, stop right there. You don't want to get involved with this, old man, it's bigger than you think."

**4** Some have suggested that Larry Nunes, a financial investor in Keane's Stereo-Fi Corporation and the owner of a company called Record Service, was a mob "associate." And it should also be mentioned that Nunes was very tight with Melody. In fact, he ended up marrying her best friend.

**5** Apparently the song contained lyrics that joke about Geffen killing rock and roll, killing "punk and soul," and selling America "one big lie."

**6** Supposedly the weapon was an oversized hammer that was used as a prop for a Mr. Clean commercial. The killer apparently found it at the scene and attacked him while Ivers was *sitting* on his bed.

**7** Taylor's partner, the shadow ex-convict Mzee Shambulia, was erroneously rumored to be behind the hit. And it was also rumored that Shambulia was a member of the FBI-backed U.S. Organization responsible for assassinating members of the Black Panthers. Not surprisingly, Shambulia was never even questioned in the case.

**8** Former fling Linda Ashcroft apparently had similar experiences. In her autobiography she refers to him as "Rear Admiral Morrison."

**9** In reality, someone threw a chicken on stage at his show in Toronto, and Cooper playfully threw it back into the crowd. Then *they* tore it to shreds.

**10** It was widely rumored at the time that he forced rap producer Easy-E of Ruthless Records to release his most popular artists (Dr. Dre, Above the Law, DOC, and Michel'le) by locking him in a room with four armed thugs, handing him a contract, and saying, "We know where your mother lives. Sign the papers." Knight allegedly pulled the same stunt again in 1996, when he forced Steve Cantrock of the prestigious accounting firm Coopers and Lybrand to sign a "confession" admitting that he stole $4.5 million from Death Row Records. Nonetheless, Cantrock has testified that he never took a dime.

**11** There was a lot of speculation over where Anderson got his money. He was known to flash wads of cash around and buy expensive toys despite no visible means of support. Meanwhile, he changed his testimony against Knight in court, saying that Knight actually tried to stop the fight. Many believed that Knight paid him off. Unfortunately, no one will ever know. Anderson was gunned down by a fellow Crip outside of a Foot Locker in South Central in May 1998. Witnesses said that Anderson shot first. Yet the Las Vegas police, the Compton police, and the DA have all dismissed the idea that he was Shakur's killer. Despite the L.A. *Times*'s attempt to paint him as a gangster, he was in fact a good kid who shied away from drugs, did well in school, and was simply at the wrong place at the wrong time.

**12** The rumor has been retold numerous times since then, always with a different star that we love to hate including Elton John, David Bowie, Prince, Marc Almond, and David Gahan.

**13** Supposedly the "somebody" was Carter's son, Chip.

# Chapter 4

**1** The monster may or may not have been related to the Navajo legend of the "skinwalker," a mythical werewolflike beast that was said to be about three feet tall, covered in shiny fur, and have a kangaroolike appearance. There was a similar beast seen at a construction site near the town of San Luis in Mexico in 1967. As *El Sol de San Luis* reported, a nightwatchman, José Padron, was guarding a construction site one night when he heard some noise that sounded like vandals. When he went out to look, he saw a creature that was "half man and half bird" bounding through the site. Investigators later found giant footprints that suggested that the creature weighed as much as 600 pounds. Then on the following night a group of American tourists saw the bird again, this time by San Luis's famous Cactus Inn. Another, similar beast was seen in Texas, near Brownsville, on January 3, 1976. Apparently two police officers, Arturo Padilla and Herman Galavan, made the report, saying that it looked like a giant bat buzzing their squad car. It had glowing eyes, a twelve-foot wingspan, a bat's face, and a beak. Both officers believed that the beast had been responsible for a wave of animal mutilations in the area.

**2** Similar Bigfoot sightings have also occurred in Lytle Creek, Fontana, the San Gorgonio Mountains, and Quartz Hill.

**3** An even more elaborate hoax occurred in the 1970s when a 7'4" Bigfoot "carcass" was found in a remote area of Burbank. The remains turned out to be the work of John Chambers, a Hollywood makeup artist known for his ape cos-tumes used in *The Planet of the Apes*. Recently John Landis, who worked with Chambers on *Beneath the Planet of the Apes*, revealed that it was well known within the industry that Chambers constructed the costume for the so-called "Patterson Bigfoot Film." Apparently that film—shot on October 20, 1967, near Mt. Shasta by two amateur hunters, Robert Patterson and Bob Gimlin—shows a black, fur-covered beast with large, pendulous breasts walking on two legs near a creek. Since then, the film has been studied extensively by cryptozoologists and debunkers alike, and most have admitted that the stride and muscle movement would be impossible to achieve in a costume. In fact many believe that it is the best evidence of a sasquatch in the world. According to Landis, however, Chambers *loved* the fact that no one seemed to notice that the film was shot at a place called *Bluff Creek*.

**4** Sounding curiously similar to L. Ron Hubbard's sci-fi claims, Van Tassel's idea was that there were "fallen sons and daughters" on earth that were members of a race called "the Builders." These people were the source of all evil, corruption, and hatred in the world, and they used the planet as their own personal playground of mass destruction. They also worked in concert to keep humankind in the dark about the true nature of things, and made sure to silence anybody—like Van Tassel—who sought to enlighten. In any case, because of his connection with Hughes and his work with the feds, many conspiracy theorists believe that Van Tassel may have been a disinformation agent, helping to confuse the public over "real" UFO encounters.

**5** Lucy Jones has heard of this and just about every amateur earthquake prediction theory under the sun. In fact, she has a filing cabinet of letters from people like Cole, Hurley, and King in her office in Caltech in Pasadena. "These guys send out hundreds of predictions a month," she explains. "Cole sent a letter predicting the Northridge quake a week before it happened. But he also sent the same letter to someone else months before. You have to remember that earthquakes occur every day. That means that some of these people are going to be right at least *some* of the time."

**6** She also believes that a spontaneous, mass murder in the world, where someone kills their family or others. When that happens, it means that there will be an earthquake in either Chile, Bolivia, or Argentina.

**7** The rumor sounds suspiciously similar to the legend of Ubar, the fabled city otherwise known as Atlantis of the Sands, said to be buried somewhere under the Sahara. A number of archeologists have sought to find Ubar, including Lawrence of Arabia, but it has never been found.

**8** Some say the massacre took place in 1829, others claim that it was in 1835.

**9** In *Lost Lemuria*, W. Scott-Elliot claims that the first race, called the First Root Race, was astral in origin, meaning that it came from outer space and left no fossil remains. The second, or the Second Root Race, was said to be Etheric. The third race was supposedly Lemurian, the fourth was Atlantean, and the fifth Aryan.

**10** The name Lemuria didn't come about until the 1900s after scientists concluded that lemurs from Asia made their way to South America via a land bridge.

**11** One woman claimed that she was sitting at home one night in 1979 with a friend when some "vapors" started pouring through the space beneath the door. Approximately fifteen minutes later, the vapors formed into four beings, each eight feet tall with high, conical foreheads. They didn't move or say anything until the woman grabbed a Ouija board. Then they carried on a conversation. The beings claimed that they had come from inside Mt. Shasta and were originally from Lemuria. Then they asked for the woman's seven-year-old daughter, claiming that they had to talk to her because she was a former high priestess in Lemuria in a past life. The daughter came out and they began communicating through telepathy. The daughter became upset, however, and the Lemurians disappeared. Years later, the daughter claimed that she just wasn't ready to talk to them at the time.

**12** Coincidentally, the Gabrielino Indians call the mountain *Joat* which means "fierce warrior."

**13** Thirty-four degrees latitude is approximately where Palm Springs is today. And it should be noted that the Salton Sea, also known as Lake Cahuilla or Blake's Lake, was considerably larger—and higher—than it is now. In fact, most of what is now the Imperial Valley was underwater at that point, and many believe that it actually connected with the Pacific Ocean through the San Gorgonio Pass and Los Angeles. Sixteenth-century maps, in fact, show a massive lake, nearly as large as Lake Superior, that was in the same area, but it was generally referred to as "the Great Lake of Thoago." Indian legends, meanwhile, tell of a great lake, sometimes called Lake Copalla, that was said to be fourteen days beyond the Colorado. It was believed to be full of great riches, and ruled by a giantess named Cinacacohola.

**14** Rainmaking practices are common all over the world, especially in dry lands. In Morocco, for example, some tribes have been known to encourage their women to remove their clothing and frolic *in the nude* on mountaintops because they believed that the gods were so prudish, that they would make it rain just to force them to cover themselves up.

**15** This plot twist may be an invention by creative historians. In all probability, he returned to the city after the most extreme damage had already occurred.

**16** There are many people that believe Hatfield's paranoid dreams have come true. There seems to be a growing community of conspiracy theorists that believe that the U.S. can control the weather, and the government is using Hatfield and Wilhelm Reich's inventions to create floodlike situations in foreign lands. The reason, according to conspiracy buffs, is to create an emergency situation that would force that country to rely on millions of dollars in foreign aid from the U.S.

**17** Actually, he named it *El Rio del Dulcisimo Nombre de Jesus*. But since it was St. Anne's Day, July 26, his men began referring to the river as Saint Anne's River instead. And apparently the name stuck. No one knows if the locals began calling the winds after St. Anne, however, yet many have noted that St. Anne, the mother of the Virgin Mary, was buried in Jehosophat, a place known for its dry hot winds. Nonetheless, there are no records of Portola naming the winds. And since he was in Southern California in the early summer, it's unlikely that there were any winds to speak of. He may have experienced them on his return trip in January 1770, however, yet there are no records that he did. In any case, the other theory that the winds were named after the Mexican dictator General Santa Anna—the man that led the charge on the Alamo and who was known to ride with the wind at his back—is even less credible. He never came within a hundred miles of Southern California.

**18** That may have something to do with the fact that the palm tree is *not* indigenous to California. Just about every single one—with the exception of the palms in Riverside and Imperial Counties—has been imported.

# Chapter 5

**1** According to the coroner's report, the killer made tiny incisions across her chest and abdomen, including X's and O's. Other, more gruesome tortures have been greatly exaggerated, however. She was not subjected to days of S&M torture, for example. Nor did she have a breast removed, or a tatoo cut from her leg.

**2** It should be noted that one of the investigators on the case later claimed that the rumor of the crazed gynecologist was *manufactured* by the police department itself to throw reporters off the trail of her *real* doctor, who knew the secret of her undersized vagina.

**3** Morrison supposedly chose the spot because it was the only area on the map that "resembled a woman's pussy."

**4** There was a significant clampdown in the late teens, however, thanks to tighter security at the port of San Pedro. But it wasn't enough to curtail the use entirely. An early issue of *Vanity Fair*, for example, described a typical Tinsel Town affair where, "In one corner of the living room there was a miniature 'drugstore' where Otto Evanhard kept company in a roar as he dispensed little packages of cocaine, morphine, and heroin. The guests at their departure, received exquisite hypodermic needles in vanity boxes which have caused many heart burnings among those invited."

**5** Supposedly Bundy kept a decapitated head in her refrigerator for a while, and encouraged Clark to use it as a sex toy on at least one occasion. Apparently she even took a picture of him in the shower, fucking the woman's head in the mouth.

**6** It was believed that she may have killed as many as twenty-five.

**7** There are exceptions, of course. Most robberies, car jackings, burglaries, and rapes are conducted against innocent victims rather than rival gang members—though not always for gang initiation rites. Moreover, there's some evidence that some gangs give the highest credit to the initiate that kills a police officer. In 1998 Daniel Banuelos of the South Side Ontario gang was charged with the attempted murder of Officer Paul Berdnik. During his trial, Banuelos admitted that his gang would have promoted him to the highest level—that of a Black Angel—if he killed a cop.

**8** Pratt was later convicted for a murder that he did not commit and railroaded into prison.

**9** Ellroy has never claimed that he based his house of celebrity skin on a real whorehouse. As he says, "I just made all that shit up. Because in Hollywood, if you have sex, sadism, and commerce, chances are it'll be true."

**10** For the record, the only hooker named Bennett in police files is a *Betty* Bennett. She was arrested in 1934 after vice officers broke into the home of pimp Jim Robinson at 1336 Berendo Street. There is no evidence that she started a brothel after that, however. And there was also a Beverly Bennett who was arrested on July 15, 1949, for shooting her boyfriend when he refused to give her some money. On the other hand, some may be confusing her with Barrie Benson, a well-known madam that had a thirteen-room Moorish castle on Schuyler Road, just north of the Sunset Strip. Chief William Parker shut her down in the early 1950s when it was discovered that she was in cahoots with Mickey Cohen. There's no evidence that she made her girls up like movie stars however, but she did admit that female customers came by on occasion, including a starlet now and then.

**11** Francis cites one instance where Harlow tied a shy, nonaggressive man to the bed and proceeded to tease him with a burning match while whispering, "Fear is more powerful than passion."

**12** Francis also claims that many of her female celebrity clients used their chauffeurs as sex partners, and brought them to her house for trysts.

**13** It should also be noted that madams have always received requests for "movie star" girls. Madam Alex, for example, used to have a regular foreign client in the 1980s who would offer as much as $10,000 for an hour with an American soap opera star. Alex would give him a look-alike instead. Fifty years earlier, there was a story going around that involved Harry Brand, the head of publicity at Fox. As columnist James Bacon remembers it: "Brand had a friend who was the senior editor at *Life* magazine. This was in the 1930s when *Life* was the most popular magazine in the country. Anyway, this editor calls Harry and says that he's coming out to Hollywood and he'd like him to fix him up with a starlet for the weekend. Harry says, 'Yeah, sure, no problem.' But after he hangs up he realizes that the editor just wants to get laid; and Harry isn't about to impose on any of the actresses that he knows. So

he hires a hooker for a couple of hundred dollars, gives her a phony studio biography, a list of credits, and arranges for her to get special treatment at certain places. So the editor comes out, meets the girl, and they have a terrific time. He really believes that he's dating a famous starlet. Monday comes around and he returns to New York and writes Harry a note: 'Thanks for introducing me to that bombshell, Harry. I had a great time with her. And I bet if I would have stayed out in L.A. a bit longer and played my cards right, I could have slept with her!' "

**14** While there were brothels on Temple, in the heart of downtown, it is widely believed that the first "official" red-light district—outside Chinatown that is—was in the area that is now Sycamore Grove in Highland Park. And according to author Remi A. Nadeau, they all had to pay a portion of their proceeds to the LAPD, and any madam that tried to open a house of her own was either shut down, or asked to move to Sycamore Grove where she would then have to pay off the boys in blue.

**15** McAfee was originally thrown off the force when he was discovered to be running crap games inside the police department itself. He was reinstated a few years later, however, and that's when he weaseled his way into vice. His partnership with Marco came to an end when Marco was arrested for shooting a rival inside Ship's Restaurant in Venice and sent to prison. Years later, McAfee was thrown off the force once again, only to reemerge as a notorious underworld crime boss in his own right.

**16** Her incarceration was undoubtedly more complex than that, possibly involving her failure to reveal information about Mafia members, and her attempt to take over Madam Alex's business by stealing her "black book."

**17** The irony, of course, is that America's greatest cop spent much of his career—not to mention taxpayer dollars—trying to dig up dirt on just about every major American figure of the twentieth century. Meanwhile, he was secretly attending ultra-exclusive gay parties in New

York and L.A.. In fact Susan Rosenstiel, a wealthy New York socialite, once claimed that she went to a party at New York's Plaza Hotel with her husband and saw Hoover—who was dressed as a woman at the time—getting serviced by two boys—one of which wore rubber gloves.

**18** Gerald plays an important part in the rumor. After all, Gerald often hired hippies—including Beausoleil—for porn movies and softcore fare. And it's certainly possible that people simply confused the notion of Beausoleil acting in some pornos with the idea that Manson was shooting snuff movies. In any case, investigating officers believe that Beausoleil and Manson sold most of the equipment shortly after stealing it to purchase drugs and/or supplies.

**19** The *Times* claimed Douglas had been arrested and tried in 1977 for trying to lure young women to appear in a snuff movie. Five years later, after Douglas had been released, he found two teenage girls in Anaheim and offered them $500 to pose nude for some pictures. According to the *Times*, he took them to a shack in the Mojave, tied them up, and killed them on camera. "Investigators found evidence of camera equipment at the scene," said the report. "Yet no film was ever found."

**20** With the exception of the tapes made by Leonard Lake and Charles Ng, that is, which have been shown at police stations around the country. In the 1980s, police officers raided their home in Calaveras County and found a number of videotapes showing Lake and Ng sexually molesting women. The tapes were found alongside a pile of bones and at least one corpse hidden in a sleeping bag. It was later revealed that the duo had been responsible for the murders of at least twelve people. Police believe that they used the videotapes for sexual stimulation and some of them did in fact include scenes of murder. Nonetheless, there is little evidence to support the idea that Lake and Ng made them to be sold on the black market.

**21** The only exception being the one of Jimmy Hoffa, the legendary head of the Teamsters, supposedly being buried in the foundation of the El Dorado Restaurant and Poker Club in Gardena. That rumor began shortly after it was revealed that Hoffa was in negotiations with the club's owner George Anthony in 1975. A short time later Hoffa disappeared, possibly after a visit to the West Coast. Ten years later, while Anthony was walking through the club with an associate, he stopped at a cement piling, gave it a pat, and said, "Hi, Jimmy." Nonetheless, the rumor is false. Hoffa—who was on his way to a lunch meeting with two Teamsters at a Detroit restaurant in 1975—was actually strangled by Mafia hitman Salvatore Briguglio inside a restaurant's back room. His body was then taken to a fender factory in Detroit, dismembered, and dumped in a vat of boiling zinc.

**22** This is actually the *second* most famous case. The body that is supposedly buried in the Colorado Street Bridge in Pasadena is actually more famous. According to locals, the bridge is haunted by a Mexican mason worker that supposedly fell from the top of the span into a vat of wet cement during the bridge's construction in 1918. Now, when one of the overhead lamps burns blue, it means that the ghost is wandering the span, looking for a victim to lure to his or her death.

**23** Not every code is universal, however. In one famous case in 1952, for example, Hal Sherry, a small-time hood in L.A., tried to muscle in on Frank Bompensiero's jukebox biz in San Diego. One night three men showed up at Sherry's door and beat him unconscious. When he finally came to about an hour later, he felt a sharp pain in his backside. He then drove to Pasadena to meet his physician, who later discovered that he had a five-inch cucumber stuffed deep inside his rectum. The message was obvious and Sherry went on to earn the moniker, the Cucumber Kid.

**24** Siegel evidently knew it was coming. According to Chick Hill, as soon as he walked into the door after having dinner at Jack's at the Beach, he said, "Chick, I smell flowers in here. Who sent flowers?" As Chick later told a reporter, there hadn't been flowers in the house for months. Nonetheless, Siegel insisted that he smelled flowers and tore through the house looking for the alleged bouquet. For Italians, the incident was significant. Because according to an old Sicilian wives' tale, if someone smells flowers where there aren't any, it means that they're going to die shortly thereafter.

**25** Supposdely the sheriff told Utley that if he killed Cohen he could control the juice money in West Hollywood which allegedly amounted to $80,000 per week.

**26** Cohen was also working as an informer—often snitching on activities of the L.A. family. Nonetheless, there seems to be some evidence that many of the attempts on Cohen's life were orchestrated by the LAPD. In fact, Sergeant Stoker of the LAPD claimed in 1980 that Cohen was threatening to expose LAPD corroboration in everything from illegal payoffs to gambling operations, and that he needed to be silenced once and for all.

**27** In fact, Stephen C. Foster, mayor of Los Angeles, resigned from office just so that he could lead a committee to hang the notorious killer Dave Brown. According to Foster, he was furious over the fact that Brown was going to get off on a legal technicality, and he wanted to issue out the "proper" form of justice.

**28** After a particularly brutal murder reported in 1857, for example, the El Monte boys charged into the home of Diego Navarro, who was rumored to have been associated with the suspects, and yanked his son out into the yard. They then threatened to burn Navarro's house down if he didn't come out. When he still refused, they grabbed his son and hanged him from a nearby tree. When Navarro finally came running out, they shot him to death, strung up his body, and left him to rot. As the Los Angeles *Star* reported, "The El Monte Rangers were behaving like voracious lions lusting in upon unfortunate victims with a frenzied appetite and hanged three (family men) without the slightest bit of evidence." They, of course, were never charged with any crimes of their own.

# Chapter 6

**1** The Sandanistas understood that President Anastasio Samoza was a U.S. puppet and that he was put in power purely to facilitate American control of Nicaraguan resources. In 1979 the Sandanistas overthrew Samoza's regime. But the following year the CIA installed its own guerrilla army, the Contras, or Reagan's "Freedom Fighters," to battle the Sandanistas and "fight communism." As Dr. Peter Dale Scott documents in *Cocaine Politics*, a large portion of the funding for weapons and training came from the sale of narcotics through South American drug cartels. How long or how extensive the practice remained in force has never been fully disclosed, however. Operation Watch Tower, for example, was known to include at least three special missions lasting thirty days each. Apparently, each mission ran at least forty cargo planes into Panama and the U.S. loaded with cocaine.

**2** As researcher David G. Guyatt revealed in 1998 in an issue of *Nexus*, there are sworn affidavits on file confirming Operation George Orwell, for example, that were designed to monitor U.S. politicians, judicial figures, law enforcement, and religious groups. The purpose was a) to provide the CIA with advance warning in case the operation was exposed, and b) provide them with leverage to force such whistleblowers into silence.

**3** There is a great deal of evidence supporting the fact that there were a number of drug dealers that specifically targeted black GIs during the Vietnam War. As McKoy notes, it was primarily a by-product of the increased opium production in the area—thanks to the CIA. It's unlikely that the dealers were acting on instructions given by the CIA, however. Most were rogue capitalists that played on GI drug habits. These dealers were mostly Vietnamese, but some were military officers. William Henry Jackson, for example, was a black GI that managed a bar in Bangkok. He sold the drug exclusively to GIs, using his military friendships to help transport it to the U.S. He was not acting for the CIA, however.

Nonetheless, such activities helped foster the rumor that the CIA was targeting blacks.

**4** Sirhan was working at the Santa Anita Racetrack as a groomer shortly before the assassination. During his apprenticeship, he met Frank Donneroumas, a small-time hood from the East Coast. Apparently Donneroumas helped him get another job at a ranch in Corona a short time later—a ranch belonging to actor Desi Arnaz who also allegedly had Mafia connections.

**5** The LAPD fired some bullets through Sirhan's gun shortly after the murder to see what kind of ballistic print they made. Ballistic experts discovered that *none* of the bullets found in Kennedy had the same print as the bullets fired with Sirhan's gun. The LAPD took care of that problem, however. They disposed of Sirhan's gun seven months *before* the trial and replaced it with a similar model. Moreover, Sirhan's defense attorney, Russell E. Parsons, who was known to work with Mickey Cohen's gang, was never able to admit evidence of the extra bullets either, because LAPD officers removed the overhead tiles and the doorjambs from the scene and had them destroyed.

**6** Thane Eugene Cesar not only had a connection to Robert Maheu, the man that hired Mafia killers to assassinate Fidel Castro for the CIA in the early 1960s, but he was placed on duty on the night of the assassination by Ace Security, which had direct links to John Alessco, the head of the Mafia's operations in San Diego. Moreover Mickey Cohen, L.A.'s gambling king after Bugsy Siegel, became the target of RFK's Mafia-clean-up campaign, and Cohen was less than happy about it. In fact he vowed revenge quite openly, saying that Kennedy had to be stopped. And it should be noted that Cohen not only ran a Mafia-controlled casino at the Ambassador Hotel, but that he had control of the Santa Anita racetrack as well, the place where Sirhan may have been "cast" in the role as assassin.

**7** A U.S. circuit court in Memphis, Tennessee, came to a similar conclusion about the assassination of Martin Luther King on December 8, 1999. In a shocking verdict, the jury ruled in favor of the prosecution which charged that a Mr. Loyd Jowers, a local restaurateur, had worked with local Mafia characters to pull off the hit. Yet according to the prosecution, Jowers and his associates were mere foot soldiers in a grander scheme that included the military industrial complex, the CIA, and the Mafia. As attorney Dr. William Pepper argued, King was killed by a "broad conspiracy that went beyond Memphis and reached into the higher levels of the government of the U.S., and some of its agents and officials." After weeks of testimony, Pepper convinced the jury that King had become an enemy of the state by his virulent antiwar efforts, and his extraordinary ability to sway the public. In other words, "He was challenging the weapons industry, the hardware, the armament industries, all that would lose as the result of the end of the war," as Pepper stated. "It had to do with money. It had to do with huge amounts of money that the war was generating to large multinational corporations that were based in the United States." Nonetheless, the Department of Justice and the mainstream press later dismissed Pepper's argument outright, saying it was "outrageous" and "far-fetched."

**8** The agency couldn't control Sandoz Laboratories, however, who made the drug available to the medical community for years. L.A.'s Dr. Oscar Janiger, for example, a psychiatrist in the 1960s and 1970s, began using it to treat compulsive disorders in some of his celebrity patients which included Cary Grant, Anais Nin, Aldous Huxley, André Previn, Jack Nicholson, and James Coburn.

**9** Stark's pattern of narrow escapes continued throughout his career. He disappeared right before agents descended upon his warehouse in Sicily, and after that he was seen infiltrating terrorist groups in Lebanon that controlled heroin traffic. And it should also be noted that his attorney was a business associate of Meyer Lansky and a key player in CIA money-laundering schemes.

**10** Kodama apparently received Lockheed's $12 million—in cash—through Deak & Company's Los Angeles and Hong Kong offices. Deak & Company was the CIA's favorite money-laundering firm at the time.

**11** None of this should be a surprise to anyone familiar with the economics of World War II, however. After all, it has since been revealed that the Ford Motor Company built trucks for Nazi commander Erwin Rommel, Standard Oil supplied fuel for German U-boats, and ITT built rockets that were used to bomb London. Daimler-Benz, meanwhile, supported Hitler's rise to power, made engines for German war planes, and more recently sent military vehicles and weapons to Iraq.

**12** Brussell also believes that Manson's "experiments" were funded by TRW and commissioned by the Defense Department and the CIA, and that he may have been brainwashed by CIA operatives while in prison. Coincidentally, Manson also shared prison facilities with Dr. Timothy Leary once.

**13** She also claimed that her son was attacked by an elephant and sodomized by her husband.

**14** Supposedly one child identified one of the city attorneys as his molester, as well as a well-known action star.

**15** Slatzer, who has been widely dismissed as a credible source, also claimed that she was pregnant with Kennedy's baby.

**16** Robert allegedly went home after that, but he was never able to document his whereabouts conclusively on the night of Marilyn's death.

**17** Crowley was obsessed with the writings of Elizabethan occultist Dr. John Dee at the time, and began incorporating many of Dee's writings into the OTO's curriculum. Dee's Enochian treatise in particular was essential to the rituals performed by the OTO. Through chanting, manipulating symbols, and reciting invocations, Dee believed that one could contact various elemental spirits—or angels—living in the universe and bring them into the physical plane. By doing so, the practitioner could exact extraordinary physical changes in the world—from healing sickness to ushering in the Apocalypse. These practices were also highly controversial, particularly because they involved sexual activity. Apparently, he believed that at the moment of complete surrender—the moment of orgasm— the mind suddenly "opened up." And once that door was open, the practitioner could literally see angels, communicate with the gods, and travel the heavens.

**18** Smith's primary duty was to guide members through a succession of ten grades designed by Aleister Crowley from his home base in Scotland. (Crowley never set foot inside the Agape Lodge himself.) But Smith was also known to pay special attention to female members, however, and was known to seduce them quite openly—including Parsons's then-wife Helen. In fact, Smith ran off with Helen shortly after leaving the lodge.

**19** Evidently Hubbard began having an affair with Sara Northrop within days of moving into Parsons's house, and they were eventually married on August 10, 1946, despite the fact that Hubbard was already married to another woman, Margaret Grubb, at the time.

**20** He had been contacted by a representative from the newly created state of Israel and asked if he would consider drawing up plans for a munitions plant. He was merely considering the proposition when his secretary found out and reported him. The case nearly went to trial until it was determined that a trial would place too many sensitive documents in the hands of the public.

**21** The official ruling on Parsons's death was as an accident, yet there's some compelling evidence to suggest otherwise. It was known, for example, that he was working with the Mexican government on plans to build a bomb factory in Mexico at the time of his death. Yet despite warnings by Naval Intelligence officers, he refused to rescind his activities. Furthermore, as many of his friends have argued, the idea that he would accidentally drop an explosive is absurd at best. After all, this was a man that spent his entire life working with highly unstable chemical mixtures. In fact, no one knew how to handle explosives better than he did. Meanwhile, others have suggested that he was murdered by Lieutenant Earl Kynette, the corrupt police official who ordered the car-bombing of a private detective in 1938. Parsons had testified against Kynette, which ensured his incarceration, and many believe that Kynette exacted revenge as soon as he was paroled in 1952. In any case, Parson's mother, Ruth, took his death badly. She swallowed a fatal dose of Nenbutal a few hours later. And according to author John Carter, police officers found a number of unsavory, homemade movies at the Parsons's household, including movies of him having sex with his mom.

**22** As the *Los Angeles Times* disclosed in 1999, Michael Harris, "Freeway" Ricky Ross's protégé, and a major drug dealer in his own right, originally set up Death Row Records as a money-laundering operation. Knight eventually took over the company, keeping Dave Kenner—Harris's lawyer—as his own, and supposedly continued to work with organized crime figures.

**23** His mother, Afeni Shakur, for example—an admitted member of the Black Panthers—was arrested in 1969 and charged with thirty counts of "planning to destroy elements of society." His surrogate father, Mutulu Shakur—also a Panther—became one of the FBI's ten most wanted in 1980 after robbing a Brinks armored truck and going into hiding. Other family associates affiliated with the Panthers included Assata Shakur, who was convicted of the execution-style killings of two New Jersey state troopers and was charged with committing numerous acts of domestic terrorism, and Elmer "Geronimo" Pratt, Tupac's godfather, who was nearly assassinated in an FBI ambush on December 8, 1969, and later railroaded into jail for a murder that he did not commit.

**24** There were a number of reports stating that there was a police car sitting outside the studio *during* the shooting. Furthermore, the first cops on the scene were the same cops that arrested Shakur for rape earlier.

**25** To date there have been *thirteen* retaliation killings following Shakur's death alone. The first was Yafeu Fula, the only person who said that he could identify Shakur's shooter, and the last was Orlando Anderson, the one many claimed to be his assassin.

**26** When officers responded to a 911 call in 1989, they found Nicole lying on the ground covered in mud. Her face was covered with bruises, her lip was cut, and she had a hand imprint around her neck. When she saw the officers she cried out, "Please help me . . . he's going to kill me." Private Investigator Don Crutchfield claimed that the beating occurred after Nicole suggested that they both get AIDS tests. If Simpson overreacted it was because his father, an admitted homosexual, died of AIDS in 1986.

**27** As General Order 107-B of the California Public Utilities Commission states, your private phone calls can only be monitored if you agree to be recorded, if you hear a beep or warning tone every fifteen seconds, or if law enforcement officials get special permission.

**28** It should be noted that then-governor Ronald Reagan signed Executive Order 1233 which expanded the range of activities that LAPD intelligence agencies could legally engage in surveillance of citizens. Meanwhile there are numerous records of wiretapping operations directed at the general public. Operation MINARET, for example, specifically involved the illegal monitoring of telephone lines ranging from members of radical political groups to celebrities.

**29** During Jerry Brown's gubernatorial campaign, for example, Gates apparently asked his OCID officers to find proof that Brown was a homosexual, either to ruin his chances at election or control him once he was in office. Gates's men never found that kind of evidence, however, but they did uncover a rumor that Brown once painted his bedroom black. That was apparently enough to prove that he was into S&M. Similarly, years later, when Gates began feuding with Mayor Tom Bradley, it is interesting to note that certain unsavory aspects of Bradley's past were suddenly made public, namely his shady business dealings with Michael Milken, his alleged misappropriation of $2 million from the city treasury, and his failure to disclose $200,000 in investments.

**30** More than 1,000 phone lines are being monitored by police officers on any given day, and as the public defender's office revealed in 1999, just one of those may lead to an average of 250 "handoffs"—the monitoring of *other* phones that have *not* been cleared for wiretaps. The handoff technique was first adopted by the LAPD in 1985 and by 1999 it was estimated that nearly 500 people had been incarcerated on evidence obtained illegally by officers.

**31** A short time later, the experiments were extended to prisons. Inmates at correctional facilities in Oregon and Washington, for example, were offered five dollars to have their testicles dosed with radiation, ten dollars for a biopsy, and $100 to go through the entire program. All in all, 131 inmates partook in the experiments from 1950 to 1963, and nearly all suffered from severe burning, inflammation, and bleeding of the scrotum.

**32** In justifying his experiments, he stated, "We need a program of psychosurgery for political control of our society. The purpose is physical control of the mind. Everyone who deviates from the given norm can be surgically mutilated."

# INDEX

Page numbers of illustrations and photographs appear in italics.

# D

la la land,

lotus land,

libido land,

Plastic land,

The City of Angels,

The City of Fallen Angels,

The City of Dreams,

The City of Broken Dreams,

The City of Queens,

Tinseltown,

Tattletown,

Ho Town,

Hollyweird,

Babylon,

Flake Central,

Paradise with a lobotomy.